National Continuing Care Directory

Retirement Communities with Nursing Care

SECOND EDITION

Edited by
Ann Trueblood Raper and Anne C. Kalicki
American Association of Homes for the Aging

An AARP Book
published by
American Association of Retired Persons
Washington, D.C.
Scott, Foresman and Company
Glenview, Illinois

PUBLISHER'S NOTE

Continuing Care Retirement Communities are listed in this book for information purposes only; their inclusion does not constitute endorsement or recommendation by the American Association of Homes for the Aging, the American Association of Retired Persons, or Scott, Foresman and Company.

Copyright © 1984, 1988

Scott, Foresman and Company, Glenview, Illinois
American Association of Retired Persons, Washington, D.C.
All Rights Reserved
Printed in the United States of America

1 2 3 4 5 6-RRC-93 92 91 90 89 88

Library of Congress Cataloging-in-Publication Data

National continuing care directory : retirement communities with
   nursing care / edited by Ann Trueblood Raper and Anne C. Kalicki
   (American Association of Homes for the Aging).—2nd ed.
       p.   cm.
   Includes bibliographies and indexes.
   ISBN 0-673-24885-2 (Scott, Foresman)
   1. Life care communities—United States—Directories.
   2. Retirement communities—United States—Directories. 3. Aged-
   -Care—United States. I. Raper, Ann Trueblood. II. Kalicki, Anne
   C. III. American Association of Homes for the Aging.
       [DNLM: 1. Homes for the Aged—United States—directories. 2. Long
   Term Care—United States—directories.   WT 22 AA1 N19]
   HV1454.2.U6N37 1988
   362.1'6'02573—dc19
   DNLM/DLC
   for Library of Congress   87-28831
                                                     CIP

Contents

FOREWORD

In 1900, the year I was born, an adult could expect to live to age forty-seven. Today, the average life expectancy is closer to seventy-five.

These additional years of life are a blessing, of course. Most older Americans today view their retirement years as a time of continued vitality and activity.

At the same time, seniors are confronted with a new challenge: how to meet their future housing and health care needs with the resources they have available to them in their retirement. Many are concerned, and rightly so, that increased longevity and increasing long-term care costs will conspire to destroy their independence and leave them no option but to "spend down" to poverty.

Continuing care retirement communities (CCRCs) represent one solution to this dilemma. They are designed for independent older people, in reasonably good health, who are willing to pay an entrance fee and a monthly service fee in return for a place to live, services, and access to nursing care for the duration of their lives.

Their popularity is growing, and for a good reason. A high-quality CCRC offers a self-financed insurance that will protect residents against loneliness, boredom, social and physical isolation, and inactivity. Persons in CCRCs can maintain financial independence with the assurance that dependence upon government support is less likely to be necessary. Healthy residents can enjoy a host of cultural and leisure activities knowing that, if they should become frail or ill as they grow older, all their needs will likely be met in a familiar environment.

The decision to contract for continuing care is especially serious because of the relative permanence of the arrangement. Withdrawing from a contract is possible but may involve forfeiting some of the entry fee. You should request copies of the community's most recent annual report or financial statement to determine that the community is financially sound.

Because selecting a lifecare community is such a weighty matter, I am pleased to see the publication of this updated *National Continuing Care Directory*, coproduced by the American Association of Homes for the Aging and the American Association of Retired Persons. The book is an invaluable guide to evaluating individual CCRCs and understanding the terms of continuing care contracts.

This 1988 edition expands the listings of continuing care facilities to include a wider range of choices classifiable under that term. It also features worksheets to help consumers compute current living expenses at the CCRC they are considering. A checklist of services is also included so that the consumer can make notations during site visits.

Continuing care retirement communities are an important option in elderly housing and health care, and this directory is an excellent guide to helping consumers understand them. I urge you to study it carefully.

Congressman Claude Pepper
Chairman, Subcommittee on
   Health and Long-Term Care
House Select Committee on
   Aging

Introduction

Philip and Jeanette Curtis, a married couple in their early seventies, have enjoyed being homeowners for four decades. Now they are ready to be relieved of continual housekeeping and yard maintenance chores in order to have more time and energy for other activities. With their four children scattered around the country and busy with their own work and families, the Curtises wish to remain as independent as they are now. Still, they worry about finding help—and especially nursing care—should they need it in the future. They are typical of couples choosing continuing care, an arrangement allowing them to maintain their private, independent lifestyle while providing services and assuring nursing care as it may be needed.

"Continuing care is attractive to us," the Curtises say, "because we know that we can live in our new home just as we did before, entertaining friends, working and volunteering, and having a small garden. Should the day come when one of us needs more care, it is available right here."

Edith Thompson, a librarian, has led an active life in retirement. Now she is seventy-five years old and plagued with early symptoms of arthritis. Single and without immediate family nearby, Edith wants to continue to make her own decisions and be independent despite her likely need for assistance in the future. Edith has savings and a pension but is concerned about meeting her future health care costs. By moving to a continuing care retirement community that offers a contract for lifetime care, she can preserve her independence and her resources—financial as well as physical—because the services and care she will require are close at hand and the payment plan is manageable.

"I think the great advantage of continuing care is the peace of mind that comes from knowing the right kind of care is here and that when I need that care my monthly costs won't skyrocket. No one knows what the future holds," Edith remarks, "but we *can* plan for it and direct it to a certain extent. I've always paid my own way and been responsible for myself, and I don't intend to stop now!"

These cases are illustrative of the many people who have chosen one of the several kinds of continuing care plans available at continuing care

1

retirement communities nationwide. Yet continuing care is still unknown to many who are seeking retirement homes and nursing care.

What is continuing care? How much does it cost? Where is it available? What does "refundable entry fee" mean? How can a consumer compare continuing care plans? When should one begin to consider continuing care? Questions like these are often posed by consumers considering retirement and nursing care options, as well as by those seeking additional information about continuing care. They are answered in this revised edition of the *National Continuing Care Directory.*

Continuing care will not appeal to everyone, and it is beyond the financial reach of some. But for those who are investigating various retirement-living options and planning for the future, this directory provides comparative information to help consumers make informed choices.

This directory is published as a result of the collaboration of the American Association of Homes for the Aging and the American Association of Retired Persons, which share a desire to present accurate, useful information about retirement-living choices.

The original edition of this directory, published in 1984, was supported by a grant from The Commonwealth Fund. The American Association of Homes for the Aging remains grateful to The Commonwealth Fund for its substantial assistance. This revised edition, as intended, keeps alive the impact and expands the value of The Commonwealth Fund's initial support.

For purposes of future editions, please send corrections, updates, or information about new continuing care retirement communities to

National Continuing Care Directory
American Association of Homes for the Aging
1129 20th Street N.W., Suite 400
Washington, DC 20036

Continuing Care Communities

A continuing care retirement community is distinguished from all other kinds of housing options for older people (such as rental units, assisted living facilities, or nursing homes) by its offer of a long-term contract that provides a residence, services, and nursing care—a continuum of care.

WHAT IS CONTINUING CARE?

- **Commitment by a community to a resident.** The continuing care contract is intended to remain in effect for more than one year, usually for the rest of one's lifetime, and represents the long-term commitment of the continuing care provider to the community resident.

- **Residence and nursing care in one community.** The continuing care contract provides housing, services, and nursing care—usually in one location—coordinated or directly managed by a single administrator responsible to the community's board of directors. Hospital care, medical services, and physician visits are rarely included in continuing care contracts, though the community may coordinate appointments and provide transportation.

- **Guaranteed nursing care.** The continuing care contract is secured by an entrance fee plus monthly fees that cover in advance some or all services and care, a form of insurance for one's later years. At a minimum, the contract guarantees access to nursing care services; at a maximum, it covers the full cost of nursing care.

The amount of health and nursing care included in the contract and the fees paid distinguish the three types of continuing care plans listed in this directory and defined below.

3

Three Continuing Care Plans

Long-term nursing care is the most expensive medical cost that older people bear, and Medicare does not pay for most of it. Continuing care retirement communities have developed three types of continuing care contracts that assure that assistance and long-term care will be available, affordable, and nearby when they are needed. Here are descriptions of the three plans and lists of the services that each typically offers.

All-Inclusive Plan

This type of continuing care contract provides an independent living unit, residential services, amenities normally associated with retirement communities, health-related services, and long-term nursing care in return for a price, usually paid as a lump-sum entrance fee and monthly payments.

Continuing care contracts are deemed to provide an all-inclusive health care guarantee if residents, after moving to the nursing unit, continue to pay the same fee they paid for their independent living unit or if they pay the monthly fee associated with the smallest apartment unit.

By spreading the costs among all residents, the community in effect insures any particular individual against catastrophic nursing care costs. Thus, these communities can serve people with incomes that would perhaps be marginally adequate to meet their own health and nursing care costs on a fee-for-service basis.

The following services are generally included in the basic monthly fee. Check with each community—and read its contract—to determine which services are included in the monthly fee. Other services may be available.

Residential Services
>Apartment cleaning and maintenance
>Dining room service (one, two, or three meals per day)
>Flat linens laundered
>Grounds maintenance
>Kitchen appliances
>Personal laundry facilities
>Prescribed diet prepared
>Scheduled transportation by community
>Storage (outside living unit)
>Tray service (when ordered by physician)
>Utilities

Health-related Services
>Emergency call system
>Home health care (in apartment)
>Long-term nursing care
>Recreational therapy
>Social services

Modified Plan

This type of continuing care contract includes an independent living unit, residential services, and a specified amount of health and nursing care. These contracts cover a specified number of days in nursing care (either annually or over one's lifetime), ranging from as few as 5 days to as many as 60 days, 180 days, or more. Any nursing care required beyond the days covered by the contract is available for a charge that is typically 80 percent or more of the full per diem rate (the rate paid by those admitted directly to the nursing unit from outside the community). Thus, the risk of future health care and nursing care costs is shared between the community and the consumer, or resident.

The following services are generally included in the basic monthly fee. Check with each community—and read its contract—to determine which specific services are included in the monthly fee. Other services may also be available.

Residential Services
    Apartment cleaning and maintenance
    Dining room service (one, two, or three meals per day)
    Grounds maintenance
    Kitchen appliances
    Prescribed diet prepared
    Scheduled Transportation
    Storage (outside living unit)
    Utilities

Health-related Services
    Emergency call system
    Long-term nursing care (specified amount)
    Recreational therapy
    Social services

The all-inclusive plan and, to a lesser extent, the modified plan allow residents to know in advance that their monthly payments will not increase substantially if long-term nursing care is required (unless the specified amount of nursing care covered by a modified plan is exceeded). Adjustments for inflation and increased operating costs are usually made, however, after a contract is signed.

An example. Mrs. Jones pays an entrance fee of $90,000 to a community offering the all-inclusive plan, moves into a two-bedroom apartment, and begins making a monthly payment of $1,100, which includes one meal per day and a wide range of residential services and amenities. If she requires nursing care temporarily, Mrs. Jones receives it in the nursing care facility, and her monthly payment is unchanged except for an additional charge for two more meals daily. When she recovers, she returns home to her apartment.

Several years later, perhaps as many as nine or ten, Mrs. Jones again requires nursing care, and it is eventually determined by joint agreement among her doctor, the social worker, Mrs. Jones's daughter, and herself that she can no longer live independently in her own apartment. Mrs. Jones gives up her apartment and continues to pay her regular monthly payment. Thus, her cost remains essentially the same even though she receives more care and service toward the end of her life. If Mrs. Jones were living in a community with a modified plan, her regular monthly payment would cease once she exceeded the specified amount of nursing care covered by her contract, and she would begin paying the daily, or per diem, rate for nursing care.

To illustrate the case of a couple, let's assume Mrs. Jones's husband is alive and sharing the apartment. Upon moving to the retirement community, they paid a $110,000 entrance fee—somewhat higher than but not double the fee that a single person pays—and they pay $1,400 each month. When Mrs. Jones is permanently moved to the nursing facility, Mr. Jones continues to reside in their apartment. He spends each afternoon with his wife and occasionally brings her to the apartment—a convenient and comforting arrangement for both of them. Had they not moved to the retirement community, the couple would have been separated by a greater distance and, since Mr. Jones no longer drives, would have had less time together once Mrs. Jones entered a nursing home.

What happens to their monthly fee once Mrs. Jones is permanently moved to nursing care? This varies a great deal from community to community; it is an important question that couples considering continuing care should have answered before signing a contract so that there are no surprises later. Under an all-inclusive plan, it is likely that Mr. Jones would be charged the monthly fee for one person, and Mrs. Jones would be charged a similar fee at the three-meals-per-day level. In some communities, the spouse who remains in independent living must move to a one-bedroom unit. Under modified and fee-for-service plans (explained in the next section), Mrs. Jones is charged the per diem rate for nursing care, while Mr. Jones pays the monthly fee for one person.

That is how all-inclusive and modified continuing care plans work on an individual basis. To understand how continuing care works with a group of residents, consider the following example.

Mr. Abercrombie moves into the same continuing care retirement community as Mrs. Jones and occupies a one-bedroom unit, paying an entrance fee of $70,000 and a monthly fee of $890. He lives at the community three years, is provided with three meals per day and other services, and participates in the wide variety of programs available. He also receives physical exams, treatment for acute illnesses, and physical therapy—for joints stiffened by arthritis—periodically over the three years. One day he dies in his apartment, never having required nursing care.

The continuing care retirement community assumes the financial risks for—and pays for— Mrs. Jones's and Mr. Abercrombie's health and nursing care covered by their continuing care contracts by spreading the cost over the whole group of residents, much as insurance companies do. That is, the higher cost of Mrs. Jones's care is averaged with the lower cost of Mr. Abercrombie's care and the costs incurred by all the other residents.

Continuing care retirement communities meet their insurance-like contractual obligations by applying actuarial principles to price the continuing care contract accurately. They also use financial and actuarial forecasting and management techniques to set aside sufficient reserve funds and/or adjust entrance and monthly fees to meet the community's obligations under the terms of its continuing care contract(s).

Fee-for-service Plan

This type of plan provides an independent living unit, residential services, and amenities and guarantees access to nursing care. Residents pay the full per diem rate for any and all health and nursing care they may require, except for minimal health care such as twenty-four-hour emergency care and possibly a few days of infirmary care that may be included in the basic monthly fee.

The following services are generally included in the basic monthly fee. Check with each community—and read its contract—to determine which specific services are included in the monthly fee. Other residential services, including dining room services, are usually available for a fee.

> *Residential Services*
> Apartment maintenance
> Kitchen appliances
> Personal laundry facilities
> Prescribed diet prepared
> Utilities

> *Health-related Services*
> Emergency call system
> Infirmary care
> Social services

Other health-related services are also likely to be available at the community, or easily accessible by the community's transportation. Fees are charged directly to individual residents for these other services. For example, many communities have arrangements with podiatrists; physical, occupational, and speech therapists; dentists; and pharmacists to serve their residents in a convenient and efficient manner.

Consider again Mrs. Jones and Mr. Abercrombie, this time living in a continuing care retirement community with the fee-for-service plan. Mrs. Jones pays a monthly fee of $675 for her two-bedroom apartment and residential service until she requires nursing care and moves permanently to the nursing facility, giving up her apartment. Then her regular monthly payments stop, and she begins paying the per diem rate for nursing care in a semi-private room, which is $60 per day, or $1,800 per month.

Meanwhile, Mr. Abercrombie pays a monthly fee of $485 for his one-bedroom apartment and residential services. He pays an additional charge for each meal he chooses to take in the dining room, as well as for the physical therapy treatments he requires from time to time. He continues to see his long-time family doctor for acute illnesses and pays his own health care bills, some of which are reimbursed by Medicare. Under this fee-for-service-plan, however, Mr. Abercrombie comes out ahead financially. Because of the nature of the plan, he has not paid anything in advance for nursing care, and he will not need any, since he dies without needing long-term nursing care.

The all-inclusive plan is often more expensive, but it is also the most comprehensive. Upon signing the contract, you know what you are getting and you know the future cost. A fee-for-service plan is less expensive initially, but your future costs are unpredictable and will depend upon the amount of care you will require. The modified plan is somewhere in between; the cost of living in your independent residence is predictable, but the cost of long-term nursing care will depend upon the amount you need.

EVOLUTION OF CONTINUING CARE

Despite the impression perpetuated by the media that continuing care is a new phenomenon, many continuing care retirement communities have celebrated two decades of operation, and more than a handful have served elderly people for thirty, forty, even one hundred years. Even older than these communities, a few benevolent associations that were established early in the 1800s accepted the responsibility of caring for older persons regardless of their ability to pay and thus provided continuing care in its most essential form.

The original continuing care communities evolved from the need to provide a modest but secure retirement for aged ministers, missionaries, and/or "deserving" single and widowed women. By pooling available resources (including the assets of residents, turned over when they entered the community) and raising additional funds from charitable contributors, the sponsoring organization sought to provide a continuity of care for the balance of residents' lifetimes in a community setting, usually old church campgrounds, large private homes, and outdated school and hospital buildings. The "contract" in these forerunners of modern continuing care retirement communities was likely to be a verbal or tacit agreement between the resident and the care provider.

Largely freed from financial worry about their future care, these early residents established libraries, conducted educational and entertainment programs, set up "buddy" systems, and, together with the managers, created a community that was at once stimulating, supportive, and cooperative. Gradually, the idea spread among nonprofit organizations as more retired people wanted this combination of financial security, health care, communal meal service, companionship among peers, and interdependent lifestyle. The national focus on care for the elderly in the early 1960s, during the creation of the Medicare and Medicaid programs, spurred the growth of continuing care.

Today, approximately seven hundred continuing care retirement communities market continuing care contracts to older persons, and the number is expected to grow in response to the dramatically increasing number of people living and enjoying good health beyond age seventy-five. Additional trends and developments in continuing care are discussed below.

Nonprofit/For-profit

Until recently, all but a few continuing care retirement communities were sponsored by nonprofit groups, usually religious or charitable organizations. Now, commercial for-profit corporations have "discovered" continuing care in their search for new markets; they are beginning to build retirement communities loosely based on the nonprofit continuing care model.

New Schemes

In response to increased costs of capital and development, both for-profit and nonprofit organizations building retirement communities today are devising new financing schemes, payment plans, and contract types. For example, all services once were automatically included in the monthly fee, while services now may be offered on an "á la carte," or pay-as-you-go, basis. Another example of a new development is the refundable-entrance-fee plan, which was developed to attract a segment of the market wanting or needing more flexibility—persons who may want to leave an estate to their heirs or who anticipate shortened life due to poor health.

States have been exercising fiscal control by tightly controlling the Certificates of Need required by retirement communities to build nursing care beds. This and other state bureaucratic and regulatory obstacles, as well as the complex actuarial and case-management aspects of continuing care, have caused some new retirement communities to eliminate or delay the provision of long-term nursing care.

Long-term Care Insurance

Traditional continuing care retirement communities with *all-inclusive plans* have been providing a form of long-term care insurance for years. Now, in response to a tremendous potential market of persons faced with bearing the full cost of the long-term care they are likely to need, private insurance companies and, most recently, the federal government have begun to develop and test long-term care insurance policies and programs. The experiences of facilities offering all-inclusive continuing care contracts have provided data for current research on long-term care insurance.

The advent of reliable, affordable long-term care insurance coverage will substantially reinforce the other benefits now available at all continuing care retirement communities. Some communities will purchase group policies for their residents, thereby reinsuring their liability for future costs for care guaranteed by continuing care contracts. And retirement communities with *modified* and *fee-for-service plans* will be attractive to individuals who have purchased long-term care insurance independent of a decision to move to a continuing care retirement community.

But long-term care insurance alone will not be sufficient to guarantee all nursing care needs. Currently, there are shortages of nurses and nursing beds, shortfalls that are projected to become even more acute in the years to come. Access to quality nursing care is becoming a primary concern of elderly consumers.

Continuing Care Without Housing

Some forward-thinking nonprofit groups are developing new ways to meet the current and potential demand for service-enriched, supportive environments and long-term care among those who choose to remain in their homes as long as possible. One such innovative long-term care delivery and finance plan is called the *Life Care at Home Plan*. Based on over three years of research and development by Brandeis University's Health Policy Center and several Quaker organizations with two decades of continuing care experience, the Life Care at Home Plan combines the services— including nursing care—associated with retirement community living with contracts that fully guarantee future nursing care costs. The difference is that this plan would be made available to individuals remaining in their own homes.

For example, with the Life Care at Home Plan, an eighty-year-old widow remaining in her own home can receive assistance with home maintenance and participate in group activities and meals at a central location. If she requires medical or nursing care, she can receive the benefits of home health care, home-delivered meals, adult day care, respite care (short stays by outside caregivers to relieve caregivers at home), an emergency response system, and all routine and acute medical care that can be provided within the limitations of her home. In addition, she can be assured of care in the Plan's nursing care facility whenever that care is needed.

In the next several years, the Life Care at Home Plan will be marketed and implemented in five or six locations. (See "Where to Get More Information" on page 399.)

CONTINUING CARE—THE BUSINESS SIDE

Continuing care retirement communities provide a range of services and amenities for residents that would be hard to find in many other settings. They are also businesses, though (whether for-profit or nonprofit), and must maintain sound financial policies in order to stay in business. In addition, continuing care retirement communities in many states have come under the eye of state legislatures, which have passed laws to regulate these communities. Since signing a continuing care contract is an important financial investment, being an informed consumer when evaluating a community means knowing something about the legal and financial sides of the community. In the following section you will find information on how to evaluate these aspects of a retirement community and how to find out more about them.

Sponsors, Owners, and Managers

Continuing care retirement communities that are historically and philosophically affiliated with religious organizations may or may not be owned and/or managed by the sponsoring organization. Religious affiliation usually does not mean the church—either local or national—is *financially responsible* for the continuing care retirement community, unless such a relationship is explicitly stated in the community's literature and contracts. However, members of these sponsoring organizations often serve as trustees or directors.

For-profit developers, investors, and corporations are entering the continuing care field and building and operating continuing care retirement communities in which they hold equity interest. Ownership may be syndicated (held by any number of investors) or centrally held by one corporation.

Due to the long-term commitment inherent in a continuing care contract, consumers should consider carefully the principal individuals' or sponsoring group's past business record and experience in providing this type of service. Consumers can use this information to evaluate their knowledge and understanding of continuing care as a long-term, service-oriented, case-management, and community-based business serving elderly, vulnerable persons. Developers should not view continuing care retirement communities solely as real estate business ventures, and consumers should be wary of those who do.

Many communities are managed by an administrator (or executive director) hired by and responsible to the board of directors or corporate owner. In others, the board or corporate owner contracts with a mangement corporation to operate the facility. In these situations, the experience and competence of the management firm is as important as that of the corporate owner. For additional information on evaluating these aspects of a community, read *The Continuing Care Retirement Community: A Guidebook for Consumers*, listed in "Where to Get More Information," on page 399.

Financial and Legal Considerations

Advance deposits

Most continuing care retirement communities require an advance deposit to secure a place on the waiting list for entrance to the community. Communities under construction usually require a deposit that is substantial enough to ensure that only those serious about living in a particular continuing care retirement community will reserve places on the waiting list. For example, they may require an advance payment of 10 percent of the entrance fee. To protect consumers, several states have regulations that require communities to hold these advance deposits in escrow accounts until certain conditions are satisfied or until the consumer withdraws the application and receives a refund. Many continuing care providers follow this practice whether or not they are required to do so.

Entrance requirements

Most continuing care retirement communities impose minimum financial requirements. Upon application to a community, you must show financial resources sufficient to meet the entrance fee and anticipated monthly fee increases, but complete financial disclosure is not usually necessary.

Requirements to be met by residents entering continuing care retirement communities vary depending upon the type of services and housing available, the type of contract and payment schedule selected, and the fees charged for the living accommodations chosen. In general, the application process may require a physician's assessment of the potential resident's physical health and mobility, evidence of sufficient financial resources, a minimum age (usually sixty-two or sixty-five), and, much more rarely, a maximum age.

Virtually none of the nonprofit, religiously sponsored communities imposes religious requirements.

Tax consequences

According to Internal Revenue Service ruling 76-481, residents of continuing care retirement communities can take a federal tax deduction for the portion of the entrance and monthly fees that each year goes toward medical expenses. (This ruling does not seem to apply to residents of retirement communities where no medical and nursing costs are prepaid or covered by the continuing care contract.) The annual proportion that can be allowed as prepaid medical costs is usually provided to residents by the community's administrator.

Contract terms

Continuing care providers may terminate a resident's contract under certain circumstances. They might do so if the community is unable to provide a type of care required—psychiatric care, for example; if a resident willfully transfers assets in order to avoid paying fees; if a resident refuses to cooperate or abide by the contract terms; or if a resident's behavior is disruptive to the life of the community. In practice, however, it is very unusual for continuing care contracts to be terminated by the community.

Residents may terminate their contracts and withdraw from the community at any time. The contract includes the terms and conditions for such a withdrawal. Policies and procedures that govern transfer from one living unit to another and from one level of care to another, whether temporarily or permanently, should also be addressed in the contract.

Care for life

Although entrance requirements include income and asset minimums to ensure that a resident can reasonably expect to be able to afford the fees, some residents who live a very long time may simply not be able to meet their expenses. One of the hallmarks of nonprofit continuing care is that residents are provided housing, care, and services for the rest of their lives, even if they outlive their incomes. Often this shortfall is covered by contributions to special funds from residents, memorials, bequests, churches, and other charitable sources. Residents who hold modified or fee-for-service continuing care contracts and who outlive their resources may be eligible to have the Medicaid program cover some of their health care costs if they are residing in a nursing care facility that is certified by Medicaid.

For more information about resident contracts, consult *The Continuing Care Retirement Community: A Guidebook for Consumers*, published by the American Association of Homes for the Aging. To obtain a copy, see "Where to Get More Information" on page 399.

Legislation, Regulation, and Accreditation

State law

Twenty-one states have enacted legislation to regulate continuing care retirement communities. These states are: Arizona (1978), Arkansas (1987), California (1978), Colorado (1981), Connecticut (1987), Florida (1977), Illinois (1982), Indiana (1983), Kansas (1986), Louisiana (1987), Maryland (1980),

Michigan (1977), Minnesota (1980), Missouri (1981), New Jersey (1987), New Mexico (1985), North Carolina (1987), Pennsylvania (1984), Texas (1987), Virginia (1985), and Wisconsin (1985). (The year in parentheses is the effective date of legislation.)

Early legislation focused on consumer protection and the requirement that a community disclose information about its operation, sponsors or owners, and financial arrangements. Today, the more comprehensive state laws regulate financial disclosure, contract specifications, reserve fund and escrow requirements, and advertising. There is no uniformity as to which state agency has responsibility to administer these regulations. One of the more problematic aspects of continuing care legislation has been to define continuing care and the facilities that provide it. Under current laws, a type of continuing care contract regulated in one state may not be regulated in another.

State regulations in New York still preclude traditional continuing care by prohibiting any payment more than three months in advance for health care services. However, several retirement communities with fee-for-service contracts have opened or are under construction in New York and are listed in this directory.

Federal law

Legislation regulating continuing care retirement communities or continuing care contracts has not been enacted at the federal level. However, an amendment to the 1984 tax law sought to define some entrance fees paid to continuing care retirement communities as among those transactions considered to be "below-interest loans." Under this amendment, such entrance fees would have been subject to new taxation requirements (in Section 7872 of the Tax Code) that taxed below-market-interest-rate loans at an imputed rate of interest equal to the average rate on funds borrowed by the federal government. This tax on "imputed interest" would have to be paid by the individual providing the loan or, in the case of a continuing care retirement community, an individual resident paying the refundable entrance fee.

To prevent these consequences for existing residents and communities, the 1984 Deficit Reduction Act contained an amendment specifically exempting all "loans" made to continuing care retirement communities prior to June 6, 1984, from the requirements. However, Congress failed to clarify whether all "loans" to continuing care retirement communities made *after* June 6, 1984, would be subject to the new tax and whether all entrance fees, however structured, would automatically be considered loans under the new law. If at some future time refundable entrance fees were determined to be "below-market" loans by the Internal Revenue Service, residents would have to pay income tax on the assumed interest earnings from the refundable balance of their entrance fees—even though they had not actually received interest payments from the community.

Legislation designed to clarify which fees might be subject to provisions of Section 7872 of the Tax Code was passed by Congress and signed into law (Public Law 99-121) in 1985.* Language accompanying this legislation stated that the more traditional nonrefundable and partially refundable entrance fee arrangements would not be considered loans and, thus, would not be subject to taxation.

Continuing care accreditation

In addition to legislative protections, potential residents can be protected through private accreditation of continuing care retirement communities. With the sponsorship of the American Association of Homes for the Aging, the recently established Continuing Care Accreditation Commission (CCAC) assesses and promotes high-quality continuing care retirement communities. CCAC standards are designed to assure consumers and the public that accredited communities meet criteria of excellence and disclosure with regard to governance and administration, residential life, financial operations, and provision of quality health care.

The mechanisms for self-evaluation and self-improvement set in motion during the accreditation process can strengthen the facility, its care, and its services. As a result, current residents may witness an improvement in their quality of life, and prospective residents may gain a tremendous advantage in being able to identify continuing care retirement communities that have been evaluated extensively and that conform to accepted standards of excellence. The accreditation process is fairly new, however, and most communities have not yet had an opportunity to be evaluated. (For more information about the Continuing Care Accreditation Commission, see "Where to Get More Information" on page 399.)

CONSUMER GUIDELINES

The typical person moving to a continuing care retirement community is seventy-five years old, has been a homeowner (70 percent of those over sixty-five own homes), is a single or widowed woman in fairly good health (although many couples are also attracted to continuing care), and has planned carefully for her future so that she may be as independent as

---

* This legislation provides an exemption from imputed interest rules for the first $90,000 of any "loan" paid to a "qualified" continuing care facility. In order to qualify for this exemption, the community must meet certain conditions, including requirements that residents be guaranteed lifetime residency and access to services, that residents of independent living units be provided with personal care or assisted living services designed to prolong their ability to live independently, that the community provide long-term nursing care without substantial additional cost, and that all facilities used to provide services to residents be owned or operated by the continuing care community.

possible. Studies have shown that people choose continuing care to achieve financial, physical, and psychological security for their last years.

Planning Ahead

Some continuing care retirement communities have waiting lists several years long, indicated in this directory by the statement "Long waiting list." Consumers desiring a place in any of these communities should make preliminary retirement plans early and get on a waiting list by paying an escrowed deposit. (See Advance Deposits on page 12.)

As a general rule, continuing care retirement communities want people to move in while they are still active, capable of getting around on their own, and able to contribute to and enjoy the benefits of community life. Current continuing care residents caution others considering such a move not to wait too long!

New continuing care retirement communities begin marketing before starting construction, because financial institutions making long-term loans generally require half the independent living units to be reserved before construction begins. They continue their marketing during construction and opening phases, offering consumers opportunities to choose from a wide selection of apartment locations, to purchase continuing care without a long wait, and to be among the "charter" residents in a new community. In this case, the listing for a community will indicate "Immediate availability." Many older continuing care retirement communities also have units ready for immediate entrance.

The step-by-step checklist presented below has been compiled to assist consumers in finding out more about continuing care and choosing the most appropriate continuing care retirement community.

CONSUMER CHECKLIST

Before you make any decisions concerning continuing care you should do the following:

_____ 1. Send for a full information packet—including the application for admission, the current fee schedule, and the resident contract—from each continuing care retirement community that interests you.

_____ 2. Visit as many continuing care retirement communities as possible to learn what is available and how they compare. Architectural styles and physical environments affect the way one lives and feels. Some communities are small, others are large; some are well-established, others are just beginning. Seek the best combination that suits your particular needs, preferences, activities, and lifestyle. Make copies of the Services Checklist and Cost-Comparison Worksheet on pages 19 and 20–21, to use on your visits.

_____ 3. Compare fees among communities. Take into account refundability of entrance fees, number of meals included in the basic monthly fee, and services—especially health and nursing care—that are included in the basic entrance and monthly fees. Fees will vary according to the age of the facility and other factors such as regional utility costs.

_____ 4. Assess the management's philosophy and relationship with residents and the sense of community among residents. Visit several times, dine with residents, talk with members of the staff, and read the bulletin board and resident handbook. Plan to stay a night or two in the guest accommodations, or sublet a resident's apartment for a short time to "take the pulse" of the community.

_____ 5. Determine whether the community has a waiting list. If so, find out how priority is assigned, whether a deposit (different from an entrance fee) is required, and, if so, how it is secured. Get an estimate of how long you will likely have to wait to move in.

Once you have selected the continuing care retirement community that best suits your needs:

_____ 1. Learn how the community was established. Learn who was originally responsible for building the facility, who (what corporation) owns the community, and who owns the land on which the facility is built.

_____ 2. Learn who serves on the current board of directors, how often board meetings are held, and whether there is an opportunity for board members and residents to meet and discuss concerns on a regular basis. Learn who currently manages the facility. Is there a management company under contract, or does the board hire an administrator? What is the administrator's background? What is the attitude toward residents?

_____ 3. Ask for floor plans either for all types of units that are available or for those units that interest you.

_____ 4. Review the continuing care contract carefully and have your professional advisors review it as well.

_____ 5. Find out how the decision to move a resident permanently to nursing care is made and what fees will be charged following that move.

_____ 6. Discover how residents are kept informed of the community's financial condition. Find out what the community's escrow and refund policies are, and make sure you have them in writing. Currently, if you move out, many continuing care contracts require that your unit be reoccupied before they will pay a refund.

_____ 7. Make certain there is a legitimate escrow account and that you have a receipt for any advance deposits you make, and learn the conditions under which they will be released to the community or refunded to you. If the community is not yet available for occupancy when you make a deposit, determine how these funds will be handled. Learn the time schedule for completion and estimated occupancy. If the community is being built in phases, learn how housing, health care, and services will be provided in the interim.

_____ 9. Ask to receive the resident newsletter while you are on the waiting list; if you are considering an immediate move, ask for back issues of the newsletter to learn about community events, future plans, and major policies.

_____ 10. Review the applicable state law, if any, that regulates continuing care contracts and providers in the state where you plan to live. Learn which state department or agency is responsible for enforcing regulations. (See "Where to Get More Information" on page 399).

_____ 11. Ask for the recent history of the nursing facility's licensing and inspections. Nursing facilities operated by continuing care retirement communities must be licensed and inspected to meet federal and state standards. Facilities certified for Medicare and/or Medicaid reimbursement must meet additional requirements.

SERVICES CHECKLIST

(Make copies as necessary)

Name of community: _____

Residential Services	Included in contract	Available for a fee
Apartment cleaning	_____	_____
How often? _____		
Carports/garages	_____	_____
Flat linens supplied	_____	_____
Flat linens laundered	_____	_____
How often? _____		
Grounds maintenance	_____	_____
Kitchen appliances	_____	_____
Meals in dining room	_____	_____
How many included? _____		
Cafeteria, buffet, or waiter service? ____		
Personal laundry facilities	_____	_____
Prescribed diet	_____	_____
Scheduled transportation by facility	_____	_____
Storage outside living unit	_____	_____
Telephone service	_____	_____
Tray service when ordered by physician	_____	_____
Utilities	_____	_____
Other _____	_____	_____
Other _____	_____	_____

Health-Related Services		
Alzheimer's disease treatment	_____	_____
Annual or routine physical exams	_____	_____
Dental care	_____	_____
Hospitalization in acute care hospital	_____	_____
Long-term nursing care	_____	_____
Occupational therapy	_____	_____
Personal care/assistance in apartment	_____	_____
Physical therapy	_____	_____
Physician's services	_____	_____
Podiatry	_____	_____
Prescription drugs	_____	_____
Psychiatric therapy	_____	_____
Recreational therapy	_____	_____
Social services	_____	_____
Speech therapy	_____	_____
Treatment for preexisting conditions	_____	_____
Other _____	_____	_____
Other _____	_____	_____

COST-COMPARISON WORKSHEET

When considering whether you can afford continuing care

- Check the continuing care contract to determine which services the monthly fee covers and which you must purchase if you need them.

- Review your present budget and note the expenses you will no longer have—for instance, lawn care, some food, utilities, and home maintenance.

- Determine how much health and nursing care is prepaid and included in the contract. Determine the availability and cost of medical and health care services locally.

COST-COMPARISON WORKSHEET: ESTIMATE OF MONTHLY EXPENSES

	In present housing	*At a CCRC*
Monthly fee		$ _____
Housing		
Insurance on personal belongings	_____	_____
Property insurance	_____	
Property taxes	_____	
Rent or mortgage payment	$ _____	
Utilities		
Electricity	_____	_____ *
Gas	_____	_____ *
Telephone	_____	_____ *
Water and sewer	_____	_____ *
Housecleaning and Home Maintenance		
Garbage and trash collection	_____	_____ *
Home maintenance (e.g., gutter cleaning, window washing)	_____	_____ *
Housecleaning service	_____	_____ *
Laundry service	_____	_____ *
Lawn service, snow removal	_____	_____ *
Routine and major repairs (e.g., heating and air conditioning service and repair)	_____	_____ *

	In present housing	At a CCRC
Food and Supplies		
Household supplies	_____	_____ **
Three meals per day	_____	_____ *
Security System	_____	_____ *
Medical Care/Insurance		
Care during temporary illness at home (e.g., tray service, emergency call system, housekeeping)	_____	_____ *
Dental and eye care	_____	_____ *
Health insurance premium	_____	_____ **
Long-term care insurance premium	_____	_____ *
Medical supplies	_____	_____ *
Medicare premium	_____	_____ *
Out-of-pocket expenses	_____	_____ *
Prescription drugs	_____	_____ *
Transportation		
Car (gasoline, maintenance, depreciation, and major repairs)	_____	_____ **
Public transportation	_____	_____ *
Entertainment		
Club/organization dues	_____	_____ **
Movies	_____	_____ **
Restaurant meals	_____	_____ **
Miscellaneous (e.g., exercise class, travel club)	_____	_____ **
Total Estimated Monthly Expenses	$ _____	$ _____

Note: When considering monthly expenses in relation to your income, remember to include extra interest income you may receive on the proceeds from the sale of your home, if any.

----

* May be provided at no extra charge; check the terms of the continuing care contract.

** May not be needed, or need and cost may be greatly reduced upon moving to a continuing care retirement community.

HOW TO USE THIS DIRECTORY

This directory contains one-page listings for 366 continuing care retirement communities and is organized alphabetically by state. As you begin to compare particular continuing care retirement communities that interest you, we suggest the following steps:

1. Consider location. Where do you want to live? Turn to the state(s) you prefer.

2. Note the type of continuing care plan: all-inclusive, modified, or fee-for-service. What level of security do you prefer, and which can you afford? Compare the fees, keeping in mind the type of continuing care and the refund plans offered. Refer to the Cost-Comparison Worksheet on pages 20–21.

3. Consider which services and amenities you will want to have available. In addition to those listed on the page entry for each community, study each community's amenities in the Special Features Index on page 403, and use the Services Checklist on page 19.

4. Look for building style and acreage. Do you want a countryside campus or a city location, a high-rise building or a ground-level unit, fresh air and space for a small garden or easy access to theaters and museums? Consider which aspects of your present lifestyle you want to keep and which you want to change in selecting a new place to live.

5. Once you have narrowed your choices, contact particular communities. Turn to the checklist on pages 17–18 for a description of the information you should have before signing a continuing care contract.

How to Study Each Listing

Here is a rundown of the information provided for each continuing care retirement community listed, starting at the top of the page.

Location

A state map showing the approximate location of the community is provided next to the address and telephone number.

AAHA Member

If the community is a member of the American Association of Homes for the Aging, "AAHA MEMBER" appears below the map. AAHA is a national organization representing not-for-profit housing, health-related facilities, and community services for the elderly. For-profit continuing care retirement communities are also listed in this directory.

Date Opened

The year in which the community first opened is given; new construction and/or renovation may have occurred since this date.

Style

Continuing care contracts are available in facilities and communities of all shapes and sizes in a wide range of settings. Some are single high-rise buildings containing all sizes of accommodations and levels of care as well as common-use facilities such as dining rooms, beauty salons, and activity areas. Other continuing care retirement communities are spread out in campuslike settings with garden apartments and low- to mid-rise buildings housing common areas and health care facilities. Still others are a combination of mid-rise buildings and garden apartments or cottages with multistory health centers and special purpose buildings.

Style and acreage descriptions for each community give a sense of its urban, suburban, or rural setting and the type of buildings each has. For some communities, the distance to the nearest city is given.

Population

The resident population is usually the total number of residents in independent living, assisted living and personal care, and nursing care; in some cases it may include only the residents in independent living units. Population figures for communities under construction or newly opened as this book went to press are absent or low in number.

Waiting List

The length of time one is likely to have to wait to move into the community is indicated by these four standard responses: Immediate availability, Waiting list may apply for some units (one to twelve months), Waiting list (one to five years), and Long waiting list (six years or more). (See Planning Ahead, page 16.)

Continuing Care Accreditation

The Continuing Care Accreditation Commission (CCAC), formed in 1985, accredited twenty-three communities in 1986 and expects to accredit fifty more in 1987. If the community is accredited, this is indicated. (See page 15 for more information about accreditation.)

Independent Living Units

It is generally expected that upon moving to a continuing care retirement community, a resident will occupy an independent living unit. If one were to travel among the continuing care retirement communities listed in this directory, one would find townhomes, duplexes, maisonettes, garden apartments, efficiencies with or without kitchens, cottages, penthouses, and standard high-rise apartments, to name a few. We have grouped these accommodations by size into four basic units in order to simplify the listings.

A *studio* is a unit that has less than two full rooms in addition to a bathroom. It may also include an alcove, kitchenette, or enclosed patio.

A *one-bedroom unit* has a separate bedroom and a living room. It may also include a small den or study, kitchen, Florida (sun) room, or enclosed patio.

A *two-bedroom unit* has two full-sized rooms in addition to the living room and may also include a kitchen, small den or study, Florida (sun) room, or enclosed patio.

A *larger-than-two-bedroom unit* is any accommodation that contains more than two full-sized rooms in addition to a living/dining room, regardless of what the unit may be named.

In some cases, the square footage for a unit does not appear in the listings. When visiting a community, be sure to check floor plans for specific units in which you are interested.

Entrance Fees

While most continuing care retirement communities set entrance fees (also called an accommodation or endowment fee) according to the unit's size, type, number of occupants, or location, a few communities scale the entrance fee according to one's age, ability to pay, or physical condition. It is not uncommon for several different payment plans to be offered.

Entrance Fee Refunds

To purchase continuing care, one is required to make a lump-sum payment, usually upon signing the contract or moving to the community. The continuing care contract should state clearly the circumstances, if any, under which refunds of entrance fees will be made as well as the amount or percentage to be refunded. Communities differ as to whether they make refunds to you if you leave the community voluntarily, to your estate in the event of death, or to you upon the termination of the contract.

Three refund plans are currently popular among continuing care retirement communities, and each has its merits. There is a refundable entrance fee; a declining, or amortized, entrance fee refund; and a nonrefundable entrance fee, or gift.

Refundable entrance fees are usually 35–50 percent higher than other entrance fees because the continuing care provider receives only the interest income that accumulates while the continuing care contract is valid. Typically, a large portion if not all of the entrance fee is refunded to one's estate; sometimes the refund is not made until the living unit is reoccupied.

Entrance fees that are amortized are "earned" by the community over a period of five to eight years. Thus, the longer you live in the community, the smaller the refund you or your estate would receive. After a specified number of years, no refund is made. Generally these fees are keyed to an actuarially based cost estimate of the present value of the future health care and service liability assumed by the continuing care provider under the terms of the contract.

Nonrefundable entrance fees, whether a nominal or significant amount, become assets of the community immediately upon payment. Many communities, regardless of which refund plan they offer, have a probationary period for new residents during which a substantial refund is made if the contract is terminated.

Monthly Fees

Monthly fees charged to residents vary according to the type of living unit they choose, the number of persons occupying the unit, and, often, the number of meals included daily. Monthly fees can change over time. Monthly fee increases are based on current operating costs and inflation rates. The continuing care contract should state the terms under which the fees may be adjusted and should explicitly state the kinds and amounts of services included in these fees.

Services

One of the many advantages of living in a continuing care retirement community is that the services and help one is likely to need as one gets older are usually available on the premises or are easily accessible. In addition, many attractive features and amenities are commonly included in the designs of continuing care retirement communities.

A retirement community may offer a continuing care contract that *includes* many services in the basic entrance and monthly fees, or it may offer a minimum service plan and provide additional services on an "á la carte" basis as you need or desire them. Under the latter plan you don't pay for services you don't use, while the former plan affords the security and simplicity of extensive services for one regular monthly payment.

Each listing provides information about four basic services that may be covered by the monthly fees—number of meals per day, housecleaning and

25

its frequency, scheduled transportation, and utilities. If not listed, these services are usually available for an extra charge. Inquire of each community which services are covered by entrance and monthly fees and which will entail additional expense. On page 19 you will find a Services Checklist, which can be copied and used to record and compare this information.

Food service and dining arrangements are among the top concerns of individuals considering a move to a continuing care retirement community. While virtually all communities serve three meals daily, they differ in how many meals, if any, per day or per month are included in a monthly payment. Some communities offer residents a choice of meal plans, with additional meals available for a charge. The number of meals included in the basic monthly fee is an important consideration in comparing the fees among continuing care retirement communities.

All retirement communities have a central dining room—and some have two or more—but the style of dining service varies. Some communities offer buffet or cafeteria services, and others have waiters. Assigned seating is used in some communities, while in others a hostess offers a choice of seating arrangements on either a first-come first-served or a reserved-seat basis.

Special features and amenities found in many continuing care retirement communities are listed below. Consult the Special Features Index on page 403 to see which of these are available at each retirement community listed.

Activities director	Hiking or walking trails
Bank	Library
Barber shop	Master TV antenna
Beauty salon	Pharmacy
Cable television	Private dining room/catering
Chapel	Religious service/chaplain
Coffee shop	Resident association
Crafts program	Sauna/spa/whirlpool
Exercise program	Security system
Fireplaces	Store/gift shop
Game room	Swimming pool—indoor
Greenhouse	Swimming pool—outdoor
Guest accommodations	Woodworking/metal shop

Assisted Living and Personal Care Units

These units, usually single rooms, are designed and staffed to provide more assistance with activities of daily living, such as bathing, eating, dressing, and taking medications, than is available to those in independent living units. Nursing services are not usually included. Some continuing care retirement communities provide personal care to residents who remain in their apartments but require more assistance.

In some communities a nonresident may move directly into a personal care or assisted living unit, bypassing the independent living level, either under a long-term contract or on a per diem or monthly basis. Under a long-term contract, an entrance fee may be charged if current and future health and nursing care services are covered by the contract.

Nursing Care

Older people often choose continuing care to ensure that health and nursing care services will be available if needed and that they can remain in a familiar environment when they need them. Thus, a wide array of nursing services is generally available at continuing care retirement communities. These services may include a staff physician on the premises who can provide convenient routine or emergency health care; an emergency call system connecting apartments with the switchboard operator or health care monitors who can provide immediate response to emergencies; physical, occupational, and recreational therapists on staff; on-site podiatry and pharmacy services; and a full-time social worker.

Under Nursing Care, each listing begins by showing the amount of care covered by the continuing care plan. Unlimited days of care are included in the all-inclusive plan. The modified plan covers a specific number of nursing care days and then shifts to a full per diem or discounted per diem rate for nursing care. The fee-for-service plan only guarantees *access* to care in the community. The resident must pay the per diem rate for all health services and nursing care required.

Cost per Day

Daily charges for nursing care are listed. These rates apply to residents with fee-for-service plans and to nonresidents admitted directly to nursing care, if the community accepts direct admissions based on space available. Some communities do not take direct admissions, reserving all their nursing beds for residents holding continuing care contracts. The community's policy for direct admissions is indicated at the bottom of each listing.

Certification

Nursing care beds in some communities are certified by the Medicare and Medicaid programs. Under the Medicare program nursing beds are certified at two levels—intermediate care and skilled care—or beds may be dually certified for both levels of care. In a continuing care retirement community that has not been certified by Medicare and/or Medicaid, one cannot rely on Medicare or Medicaid reimbursement for nursing care received in its nursing facility. Medicare, however, does not cover most long-term care.

Additional Helpful Features

Worksheets

Three checklists, or worksheets, have been included in the Consumer Guidelines section beginning on page 15. The Consumer Checklist suggests steps to take in comparing communities and selecting the most suitable continuing care retirement community for you. The Services Checklist can be detached and photocopied so that you can review each service package as you visit and compare communities. Finally, the Cost-Comparison Worksheet enables you to list all your current monthly costs and compare this list with what these costs would be under various continuing care plans.

Indexes

Following the listings are three separate indexes to assist you.

The Special Features Index, beginning on page 403, indicates the features and amenities each continuing care retirement community has available. This index will guide you to communities with the features you want.

The Metropolitan Area Index, on page 431, lists communities by the city in or near which each community is located, ignoring state boundaries. More than seventy-five cities are indexed.

Finally, an alphabetical index, on page 441, lists all communities in the directory.

Community Listings

Efforts have been made to identify and include every continuing care retirement community currently operating or under construction as of December 1986. This identification effort was part of the establishment of the National Continuing Care Data Base, a joint ongoing project of the American Association of Homes for the Aging and Ernst & Whinney, public accountants. The Data Base contains a wide array of detailed information about continuing care retirement communities that will be updated periodically and used to produce national reports and summaries of continuing care as well as in-depth studies of particular concern to continuing care administrators. (For information about the National Continuing Care Data Base, refer to "Where to Get More Information" on page 399.)

Are all continuing care retirement communities listed in this directory? While every reasonable effort was made to include all continuing care retirement communities,* some do not appear in this directory for the following reasons:

- Some administrators elected not to respond;

- Some administrators disqualified their facilities as not fitting the definition of continuing care, usually because they have no entrance fee or no *guarantee* of access to nursing care within the facility (though some do give priority to residents);

- Some facilities are under development but not yet under construction.

---

* Eleven hundred questionnaires were mailed to all known and potential continuing care retirement communities nationwide, followed by a reminder mailing. Four hundred of this group were subsequently disqualified for various reasons, leaving seven hundred communities listed in the National Continuing Care Data Base, of which approximately three hundred had not responded to mailed questionnaires by the time this directory was prepared for publication.

The information used to compile these listings was submitted by the chief executive officer of each continuing care retirement community to the National Continuing Care Data Base. Although great care was taken to prevent and eliminate errors in the final manuscript, the facts and fees given for each continuing care community may not be fully accurate or current. Neither AAHA nor AARP can be responsible for errors, omissions, and inadvertent inaccuracies that may exist in the listings. Use the information as a general, comparative guide, and contact communities directly for a current fee schedule, a description of their services, and a copy of their continuing care contract.

THREE BROAD CLASSIFICATIONS
OF CONTINUING CARE PLANS

All-Inclusive Plan

The basic entrance and monthly fees include housing, residential and health care services, and unlimited (any and all days) nursing care.

Modified Plan

The basic entrance and monthly fees include housing, residential and some health services, and guaranteed access to a limited amount of nursing care. Other services and additional nursing care are usually available for an extra fee.

Fee-for-service Plan

The basic entrance and monthly fees include housing, residential services, and guaranteed access to nursing and health care facilities. Additional services and nursing and health care are usually available for an extra fee.

Community Listings

KIRKWOOD BY THE RIVER
3605 Ratcliff Road, Birmingham, AL 35210
Telephone: (205) 956-2184

Opened in 1980 • Mixed single-level, low-rise, and high-rise buildings on 120 acres • Current resident population is 120 • Located ten miles from Birmingham • Immediate availability

AAHA
Member

HOUSING AND SERVICES

Living Units	No.	Square Feet	No. of Persons	Entrance Fee	Monthly Fee
Studio	19	325–380	1	$12,150–$37,700	$621–$810
One Bedroom	48	600–660	1	$25,000–$77,500	$700–$1,116
			2		$1,021–$1,437
Two Bedroom	24	800–1,000	1	$35,150–$108,970	$980–$1,600
			2		$1,301–$1,921
Larger Units	10	1,285	1	$45,025–$139,600	$1,270–$2,040
			2		$1,591–$2,361

Total   101 Units

Residents have a choice of entrance fee refund plans.

These fees include one meal per day, weekly housekeeping, scheduled transportation, and utilities. Special features of this community are presented in the Special Features Index at the back of the book. Ask about additional residential and health care services that may be available. Fees and services subject to change; verify with facility.

ASSISTED LIVING AND PERSONAL CARE

Assisted living units: 23
Personal care is covered by the continuing care contract: Yes
Residents may receive personal care in independent living units: No
Nonresidents may be admitted directly to assisted living units: Yes

NURSING CARE: Fee-for-Service Plan

Under this fee-for-service plan, guaranteed access to nursing care is covered by the continuing care contract. Once residents move permanently to the nursing unit, they pay 75–90 percent of the per diem rate for nursing care.

Intermediate beds: 80.

Skilled beds: 51. Cost per day: private $62.50, semi-private $58.00.

Nursing beds are not certified by Medicare or Medicaid. Nonresidents may be admitted directly to the nursing care facility.

WESTMINSTER VILLAGE
P.O. Box 670, Spanish Fort, AL 36527
Telephone: (205) 626-7007

Opened in 1983 • Mixed single-level and low-rise buildings on 53 acres • Current resident population is 208 • Located six miles from Mobile, AL • Immediate availability

AAHA
Member

HOUSING AND SERVICES

Living Units	No.	Square Feet	No. of Persons	Entrance Fee	Monthly Fee
Studio	0	—	—	—	—
One Bedroom	170	528–892	1	$42,900–$56,900	$617–$724
			2		$904–$1,011
Two Bedroom	122	792–1,168	1	$64,900–$79,900	$730–$864
			2		$1,017–$1,151
Larger Units	0	—	—	—	—
Total	292 Units				

Residents have a choice of entrance fee refund plans.

These fees include one meal per day, biweekly housekeeping, scheduled transportation, and utilities. Special features of this community are presented in the Special Features Index at the back of the book. Ask about additional residential and health care services that may be available. Fees and services subject to change; verify with facility.

ASSISTED LIVING AND PERSONAL CARE

Assisted living units: 14
Personal care is covered by the continuing care contract: Yes
Residents may receive personal care in independent living units: No
Nonresidents may be admitted directly to assisted living units: No

NURSING CARE: Modified Plan

Under this modified plan, 60 days or more are covered by the continuing care contract. Residents pay 50 percent of the per diem rate for the next 15 days of nursing care. They then pay the per diem rate less a monthly credit of 1/60 of their entrance fee.

Skilled beds: 60. Cost per day: private $62.00, semi-private $55.00.

Nursing beds are certified by Medicare. Nonresidents may be admitted directly to the nursing care facility.

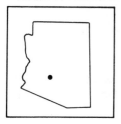

PUEBLO NORTE RETIREMENT VILLAGE
7090 East Mescal, Scottsdale, AZ 85254
Telephone: (602) 483-3999

Opened in 1985 • Mixed single-level and low-rise buildings on 20 acres • Current resident population is 96 • Immediate availability

AAHA
Member

HOUSING AND SERVICES

Living Units	No.	Square Feet	No. of Persons	Entrance Fee	Monthly Fee
Studio	4	400	1	$44,000	$570
One Bedroom	98	668–692	1	$74,900–$77,900	$666–$723
			2	$79,900–$82,900	$952–$1,009
Two Bedroom	86	875–1,336	1	$94,900–$129,900	$761–$900
			2	$99,900–$134,900	$1,047–$1,186
Larger Units	0	——	——	——	——
Total	188 Units				

Entrance fees are fully refundable.

These fees include one meal per day, weekly housekeeping, scheduled transportation, and utilities. Special features of this community are presented in the Special Features Index at the back of the book. Ask about additional residential and health care services that may be available. Fees and services subject to change; verify with facility.

ASSISTED LIVING AND PERSONAL CARE

Assisted living units: 10
Personal care is covered by the continuing care contract: Yes
Residents may receive personal care in independent living units: No
Nonresidents may be admitted directly to assisted living units: No

NURSING CARE: Modified Plan

Under this modified plan, 60 days or more are covered by the continuing care contract. Once residents move permanently to the nursing unit, they pay the full per diem rate for nursing care.

Intermediate beds: 64. Cost per day: private $85.00, semi-private $50.00.

Skilled beds: 64. Cost per day: private $90.00, semi-private $60.00.

Nursing beds are certified by both Medicare and Medicaid. Nonresidents may be admitted directly to the nursing care facility.

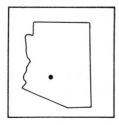

ROYAL OAKS
10015 Royal Oaks Avenue, Sun City, AZ 85351
Telephone: (602) 974-2583

Opened in 1983 • One high-rise building and garden duplexes on 32 acres • Current resident population is 480 • Waiting list

AAHA
Member

HOUSING AND SERVICES

Living Units	No.	Square Feet	No. of Persons	Entrance Fee	Monthly Fee
Studio	10	504	1	$36,000	$578
One Bedroom	119	644–916	1	$45,000–$65,700	$633–$799
			2	$49,000–$69,700	$991–$1,157
Two Bedroom	120	986–1,660	1	$67,000–$116,600	$826–$1,185
			2	$71,000–$120,600	$1,184–$1,583
Larger Units	100	——	——	——	——
Total	349 Units				

Entrance fee refunds decline over time.

These fees include one meal per day, biweekly housekeeping, scheduled transportation, and utilities. Special features of this community are presented in the Special Features Index at the back of the book. Ask about additional residential and health care services that may be available. Fees and services subject to change; verify with facility.

ASSISTED LIVING AND PERSONAL CARE

Assisted living units: 0
Personal care is covered by the continuing care contract: Yes
Residents may receive personal care in independent living units: Yes

NURSING CARE: Modified Plan

Under this modified plan, 60 days or more of care are covered by the continuing care contract. Once residents move permanently to the nursing unit, they pay the full per diem rate for nursing care.

Intermediate beds. Cost per day: private $65.00, semi-private $53.00.
Skilled beds: 100. Cost per day: private $75.00, semi-private $63.00.
Nursing beds are certified by Medicare. Nonresidents may be admitted directly to the nursing care facility.

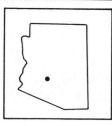

WESTMINSTER VILLAGE
9832 North Hayden Road, Scottsdale, AZ 85253
Telephone: (602) 483-2449

Opening in 1988 • Mixed single-level and low-rise buildings on 17 acres • Immediate availability

AAHA
Member

HOUSING AND SERVICES

Living Units	No.	Square Feet	No. of Persons	Entrance Fee	Monthly Fee
Studio	4	600	1	$43,500	$800
One Bedroom	71	800	1	$51,500–$62,750	$875–$1,000
Two Bedroom	175	1,250	1	$74,750–$111,250	$1,125–$1,475
Larger Units	0	——	——	——	——
Total	250 Units				

Entrance fee refunds decline over time.

These fees include one meal per day, weekly housekeeping, scheduled transportation, and utilities. Special features of this community are presented in the Special Features Index at the back of the book. Ask about additional residential and health care services that may be available. Fees and services subject to change; verify with facility.

ASSISTED LIVING AND PERSONAL CARE

Assisted living units: 0
Personal care is covered by the continuing care contract: Yes
Residents may receive personal care in independent living units: Yes

NURSING CARE: All-Inclusive Plan

Under this all-inclusive plan, unlimited nursing care is covered by the continuing care contract. When residents are in nursing care, they pay the same monthly fee they paid for their independent living unit.

Skilled beds: 60. Cost per day: not applicable.

Nursing beds are not yet certified by Medicare or Medicaid. Nonresidents may not be admitted directly to the nursing care facility.

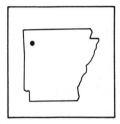

BUTTERFIELD TRAIL VILLAGE
1923 East Joyce Street, Fayetteville, AR 72703
Telephone: (501) 442-7220

Opened in 1986 • Mixed single-level and low-rise buildings on 20 acres • Current resident population is 139 • Immediate availability

AAHA
Member

HOUSING AND SERVICES

Living Units	No.	Square Feet	No. of Persons	Entrance Fee	Monthly Fee
Studio	15	405	1	$33,250	$600
One Bedroom	102	600	1	$48,000	$750
			2	$51,000	$1,150
Two Bedroom	131	843–1,162	1	$66,250–$90,250	$875–$1,050
			2	$69,250–$93,250	$1,275–$1,450
Larger Units	0	—	—	—	—
Total		248 Units			

Residents have a choice of entrance fee refund plans.

These fees include one meal per day, biweekly housekeeping, scheduled transportation, and utilities. Special features of this community are presented in the Special Features Index at the back of the book. Ask about additional residential and health care services that may be available. Fees and services subject to change; verify with facility.

ASSISTED LIVING AND PERSONAL CARE

Assisted living units: 0
Personal care is covered by the continuing care contract: No
Residents may receive personal care in independent living units: Yes

NURSING CARE: All-Inclusive Plan

Under this all-inclusive plan, unlimited nursing care is covered by the continuing care contract. When residents are in nursing care, they pay the same monthly fee they paid for their independent living unit.

Skilled beds: 40. Cost per day: not applicable.

Nursing beds are certified by Medicare. Nonresidents may not be admitted directly to the nursing care facility.

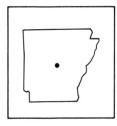

WOODLAND HEIGHTS
8700 Riley Drive, Little Rock, AR 72205
Telephone: (501) 224-4242

Opened in 1985 • Predominantly high-rise buildings on six acres • Current resident population is 60 • Immediate availability

---

HOUSING AND SERVICES

Living Units	No.	Square Feet	No. of Persons	Entrance Fee	Monthly Fee
Studio	4	413–439	1	$44,200	$420
One Bedroom	43	601–653	1	$63,200	$475
			2		$600
Two Bedroom	31	901–1,500	1	$94,900	$565
			2		$690
Larger Units	5	1,659	1	$180,000	$960
			2		$1,085
Total		83 Units			

Entrance fees are partially refundable.

These fees include one meal per day, weekly housekeeping, scheduled transportation, and utilities. Special features of this community are presented in the Special Features Index at the back of the book. Ask about additional residential and health care services that may be available. Fees and services subject to change; verify with facility.

ASSISTED LIVING AND PERSONAL CARE

Assisted living units: 0
Personal care is covered by the continuing care contract: No
Residents may receive personal care in independent living units: No

NURSING CARE: Modified Plan

Under this modified plan, 15 or fewer days are covered by the continuing care contract. Once residents move permanently to the nursing unit, they pay the full per diem rate for nursing care.

Skilled beds: 224. Cost per day: private $90.00, semi-private $60.00.

Nursing beds are not certified by Medicare or Medicaid. Nonresidents may be admitted directly to the nursing care facility.

ALDERSLY
326 Mission Avenue, San Rafael, CA 94901
Telephone: (415) 453-7425

Opened in 1921 • Predominantly single-level/garden apartments on three acres • Current resident population is 93 • Waiting list may apply for some units

AAHA
Member

HOUSING AND SERVICES

Living Units	No.	Square Feet	No. of Persons	Entrance Fee	Monthly Fee
Studio	54	180	1	$20,000–$40,000	$895
One Bedroom	31	256	1	$20,000–$40,000	$895
			2	$36,000–$65,000	$1,790
Two Bedroom	1	1,024	1, 2	$65,000	$1,790
Larger Units	0	——	——	——	——
Total		86 Units			

Entrance fee refunds decline over time.

These fees include three meals per day, biweekly housekeeping, scheduled transportation, and utilities. Special features of this community are presented in the Special Features Index at the back of the book. Ask about additional residential and health care services that may be available. Fees and services subject to change; verify with facility.

ASSISTED LIVING AND PERSONAL CARE

Assisted living units: 0
Personal care is covered by the continuing care contract: No
Residents may receive personal care in independent living units: No

NURSING CARE: Modified Plan

Under this modified plan, 15 or fewer days are covered by the continuing care contract. Once residents move permanently to the nursing unit, they pay the full per diem rate for nursing care.

Skilled beds: 13. Cost per day: private $60.00, semi-private $60.00.

Nursing beds are not certified by Medicare or Medicaid. Nonresidents may not be admitted directly to the nursing care facility.

BIXBY KNOLLS TOWERS
3737 Atlantic Avenue, Long Beach, CA 90807
Telephone: (213) 426-6123

Opened in 1966 • Predominantly high-rise buildings • Current resident population is 330 • Waiting list may apply for some units

AAHA
Member

HOUSING AND SERVICES

Living Units	No.	Square Feet	No. of Persons	Entrance Fee	Monthly Fee
Studio	39	365–465	1	$1,000	$900–$1,000
One Bedroom	76	545–615	1	$1,500	$1,190–$1,260
			2	$2,000	$1,565–$1,645
Two Bedroom	52	700–915	1	$2,000	$1,300–$1,600
			2	$2,500	$1,700–$1,985
Larger Units	0	—	—	—	—
Total	167 Units				

Residents have a choice of entrance fee refund plans.

These fees include three meals per day, weekly housekeeping, scheduled transportation, and utilites. Special features of this community are presented in the Special Features Index at the back of the book. Ask about additional residential and health care services that may be available. Fees and services subject to change; verify with facility.

ASSISTED LIVING AND PERSONAL CARE

Assisted living units: 60
Personal care is covered by the continuing care contract: No
Residents may receive personal care in independent living units: No
Nonresidents may be admitted directly to assisted living units: Yes

NURSING CARE: Fee-for-Service Plan

Under this fee-for-service plan, guaranteed access to nursing care is covered by the continuing care contract. Residents pay the full per diem rate for nursing care.

Skilled beds: 99. Cost per day: private $120.00, semi-private $61.00.

Nursing beds are certified by both Medicare and Medicaid. Nonresidents may be admitted directly to the nursing care facility.

BRETHREN HILLCREST HOMES
2705 Mountain View Drive, La Verne, CA 91750
Telephone: (714) 593-4917

Opened in 1947 • Predominantly single-level/garden apartments on 33 acres • Current resident population is 455 • Waiting list may apply for some units • Accredited by the AAHA Continuing Care Accreditation Commission.

AAHA
Member

HOUSING AND SERVICES

Living Units	No.	Square Feet	No. of Persons	Entrance Fee	Monthly Fee
Studio	148	930	1	$8,500–$29,700	$470–$1,220
One Bedroom	74	492	1	$33,600–$66,500	$355–$460
Two Bedroom	95		1	$46,600–$66,500	$460
Larger Units	2	——	——	——	——
Total	319 Units				

Entrance fee refunds decline over time.

These fees include zero, one, or three meals per day; weekly housekeeping; scheduled transportation; and utilities. Special features of this community are presented in the Special Features Index at the back of the book. Ask about additional residential and health care services that may be available. Fees and services subject to change; verify with facility.

ASSISTED LIVING AND PERSONAL CARE

Assisted living units: 74
Personal care is covered by the continuing care contract: Yes
Residents may receive personal care in independent living units: No
Nonresidents may be admitted directly to assisted living units: Yes

NURSING CARE: Fee-for-Service Plan

Under this fee-for-service plan, guaranteed access to nursing care is covered by the continuing care contract. Residents pay the full per diem rate for nursing care.

Skilled beds: 75. Cost per day: private $85.00, semi-private $73.00.

Nursing beds are certified by both Medicare and Medicaid. Nonresidents may be admitted directly to the nursing care facility.

CARMEL VALLEY MANOR
8545 Carmel Valley Road, Carmel, CA 93923
Telephone: (408) 624-1281

Opened in 1963 • Predominantly single-level/garden apartments on 25 acres • Current resident population is 244 • Located five miles from Carmel, CA • Waiting list may apply for some units

AAHA
Member

HOUSING AND SERVICES

Living Units	No.	Square Feet	No. of Persons	Entrance Fee	Monthly Fee
Studio	48	440	1	$56,300	$737
One Bedroom	72	400	1	$93,000	$835
			2	$110,600	$1,400
Two Bedroom	56	635	1	$140,700	$1,151
			2	$162,030	$1,535–$1,645
Larger Units	0	—	—	—	—
Total	176 Units				

Entrance fee refunds decline over time.

These fees include three meals per day, weekly housekeeping, scheduled transportation, and utilities. Special features of this community are presented in the Special Features Index at the back of the book. Ask about additional residential and health care services that may be available. Fees and services subject to change; verify with facility.

ASSISTED LIVING AND PERSONAL CARE

Assisted living units: 24
Personal care is covered by the continuing care contract: Yes
Residents may receive personal care in independent living units: Yes
Nonresidents may be admitted directly to assisted living units: No

NURSING CARE: All-Inclusive Plan

Under this all-inclusive plan, unlimited nursing care is covered by the continuing care contract. When residents are in nursing care, they pay the basic monthly fee for the studio (smallest) unit.

Skilled beds: 28. Cost per day: not applicable.

Nursing beds are certified by Medicare. Nonresidents may not be admitted directly to the nursing care facility.

CASA DORINDA
300 Hot Springs Road, Montecito, CA 93108
Telephone: (805) 969-8011

Opened in 1975 • Mixed single-level and low-rise buildings on 48 acres • Current resident population is 312 • Located three miles from Santa Barbara • Waiting list may apply for some units

AAHA
Member

HOUSING AND SERVICES

Living Units	No.	Square Feet	No. of Persons	Entrance Fee	Monthly Fee
Studio	110	440–560	1	$55,000	$1,251
One Bedroom	110	660–780	1	$86,000	$1,497
			2	$142,000	$2,596
Two Bedroom	41	890–1,170	1, 2	$167,000	$2,761
Larger Units	0	——	——	——	——
Total	261 Units				

Entrance fee refunds decline over time.

These fees include three meals per day, weekly housekeeping, scheduled transportation, and utilities. Special features of this community are presented in the Special Features Index at the back of the book. Ask about additional residential and health care services that may be available. Fees and services subject to change; verify with facility.

ASSISTED LIVING AND PERSONAL CARE

Assisted living units: 22
Personal care is covered by the continuing care contract: Yes
Residents may receive personal care in independent living units: No
Nonresidents may be admitted directly to assisted living units: No

NURSING CARE: All-Inclusive Plan

Under this all-inclusive plan, unlimited nursing care is covered by the continuing care contract. When residents are in nursing care, they pay the same monthly fee they paid for their independent living unit.

Skilled beds: 47. Cost per day: not applicable.

Nursing beds are certified by Medicare. Nonresidents may not be admitted directly to the nursing care facility.

CHANNING HOUSE
850 Webster Street, Palo Alto, CA 94301
Telephone: (415) 327-0950

Opened in 1964 • One high-rise building on five acres • Current resident population is 260 • Waiting list may apply for some units

AAHA
Member

HOUSING AND SERVICES

Living Units	No.	Square Feet	No. of Persons	Entrance Fee	Monthly Fee
Studio	153	350–550	1	$37,000–$64,500	$683–$865
One Bedroom	88	700–910	1	$72,500–$79,500	$975–$1,242
			2	$72,500–$79,500	$1,564–$1,844
Two Bedroom	6	1,025	1, 2	$121,400–$129,400	$1,958
Larger Units	5	——	1, 2	$143,000	$2,250
Total	252 Units				

Entrance fee refunds decline over time.

These fees include three meals per day, weekly housekeeping, and utilities. Special features of this community are presented in the Special Features Index at the back of the book. Ask about additional residential and health care services that may be available. Fees and services subject to change; verify with facility.

ASSISTED LIVING AND PERSONAL CARE

Assisted living units: 16
Personal care is covered by the continuing care contract: Yes
Residents may receive personal care in independent living units: Yes
Nonresidents may be admitted directly to assisted living units: No

NURSING CARE: All-Inclusive Plan

Under this all-inclusive plan, unlimited nursing care is covered by the continuing care contract. When residents are in nursing care, they pay the basic monthly fee for the studio (smallest) unit.

Skilled beds: 14. Cost per day: not applicable.

Nursing beds are not certified by Medicare or Medicaid. Nonresidents may not be admitted directly to the nursing care facility.

COVENANT VILLAGE
2125 North Olive Avenue, Turlock, CA 95380
Telephone: (209) 632-9976

Opened in 1977 • Predominantly single-level/garden apartments on 13 acres • Current resident population is 210 • Waiting list may apply for some units

AAHA
Member

HOUSING AND SERVICES

Living Units	No.	Square Feet	No. of Persons	Entrance Fee	Monthly Fee
Studio	56	485	1	$35,900	$591
One Bedroom	70	585	1	$47,900	$713
			2	$47,900	$1,083
Two Bedroom	21	765–1,060	1	$70,900–$72,900	$844–$918
			2	$70,900–$72,900	$1,213–$1,290
Larger Units	0	—	—	—	—
Total	147 Units				

Entrance fee refunds decline over time.

These fees include two meals per day, housekeeping, scheduled transportation, and utilities. Special features of this community are presented in the Special Features Index at the back of the book. Ask about additional residential and health care services that may be available. Fees and services subject to change; verify with facility.

ASSISTED LIVING AND PERSONAL CARE

Assisted living units: 34
Personal care is covered by the continuing care contract: Yes
Residents may receive personal care in independent living units: No
Nonresidents may be admitted directly to assisted living units: No

NURSING CARE: Modified Plan

Under this modified plan, 60 days or more are covered by the continuing care contract. Once residents move permanently to the nursing unit, they pay 90 percent of the per diem rate for nursing care.

Skilled beds: 145. Cost per day: private $75.00, semi-private $60.00.

Nursing beds are certified by both Medicare and Medicaid. Nonresidents may be admitted directly to the nursing care facility.

FRIENDS HOUSE
684 Benicia Drive, Santa Rosa, CA 95405
Telephone: (707) 538-0152

Opened in 1984 • Predominantly single-level/garden apartments on five acres • Current resident population is 59 • Waiting list

HOUSING AND SERVICES

Living Units	No.	Square Feet	No. of Persons	Entrance Fee	Monthly Fee
Studio	0	——	——	——	——
One Bedroom	42	——	1	$58,275–$67,900	$192
Two Bedroom	8	——	1, 2	$65,625	$221
Larger Units	0	——	——	——	——
Total	50 Units				

Entrance fee refunds decline over time.

These fees include weekly housekeeping, scheduled transportation, and half-payment of utilities. Special features of this community are presented in the Special Features Index at the back of the book. Ask about additional residential and health care services that may be available. Fees and services subject to change; verify with facility.

ASSISTED LIVING AND PERSONAL CARE

Assisted living units: 0
Personal care is covered by the continuing care contract: No
Residents may receive personal care in independent living units: No

NURSING CARE: Fee-for-Service Plan

Under this fee-for-service plan, guaranteed access to nursing care is covered by the continuing care contract. Residents pay the full per diem rate for nursing care.

Skilled beds: 30. Cost per day: private $89.00, semi-private $79.00.

Nursing beds are certified by both Medicare and Medicaid. Nonresidents may be admitted directly to the nursing care facility.

GRAND LAKES GARDENS
401 Santa Clara Avenue, Oakland, CA 94610
Telephone: (415) 893-8897

Opened in 1966 • One high-rise building • Current resident population is 111 • Waiting list may apply for some units

AAHA
Member

HOUSING AND SERVICES

Living Units	No.	Square Feet	No. of Persons	Entrance Fee	Monthly Fee
Studio	16	397	1	$27,300	$513
One Bedroom	68	542	1	$39,300	$667
			2	$43,230	$953
Two Bedroom	17	701	1	$51,300	$778
			2	$51,300	$1,064
Larger Units	1	1,146	1	$75,000	$905
			2	$75,000	$1,200

Total 102 Units

Entrance fee refunds decline over time.

These fees include one meal per day, monthly housekeeping, and utilities. Special features of this community are presented in the Special Features Index at the back of the book. Ask about additional residential and health care services that may be available. Fees and services subject to change; verify with facility.

ASSISTED LIVING AND PERSONAL CARE

Assisted living units: 74, at Piedmont Gardens (see page 57)
Personal care is covered by the continuing care contract: Yes
Residents may receive personal care in independent living units: No
Nonresidents may be admitted directly to assisted living units: No

NURSING CARE: Modified Plan

Under this modified plan, 15 or fewer days are covered by the continuing care contract. Once residents move permanently to the nursing unit, they pay the full per diem rate for nursing care.

Intermediate beds: 47.* Cost per day: private $70.65, semi-private $50.66.

Skilled beds: 47.* Cost per day: private $87.75, semi-private $65.33.

* at Piedmont Gardens (see page 57)

Nursing is certified by both Medicare and Medicaid. Nonresidents may not be admitted directly to the nursing care facility.

THE HERITAGE
3400 Laguna Street, San Francisco, CA 94123
Telephone: (415) 567-6900

Opened in 1925 • Mixed single-level and low-rise buildings on two acres • Current resident population is 115 • Waiting list may apply for some units

AAHA
Member

HOUSING AND SERVICES

Living Units	No.	Square Feet	No. of Persons	Entrance Fee	Monthly Fee
Studio	78	928	1	$37,500	$750
One Bedroom	7	778	1, 2	$60,000	$1,300
Two Bedroom	0	——	——	——	——
Larger Units	0	——	——	——	——
Total	85 Units				

Entrance fees are nonrefundable.

These fees include three meals per day, weekly housekeeping, scheduled transportation, and utilities. Special features of this community are presented in the Special Features Index at the back of the book. Ask about additional residential and health care services that may be available. Fees and services subject to change; verify with facility.

ASSISTED LIVING AND PERSONAL CARE

Assisted living units: 10
Personal care is covered by the continuing care contract: Yes
Residents may receive personal care in independent living units: No
Nonresidents may be admitted directly to assisted living units: No

NURSING CARE: All-Inclusive Plan

Under this all-inclusive plan, unlimited nursing care is covered by the continuing care contract. When residents are in nursing care, they pay the same monthly fee they paid for their independent living unit.

Skilled beds: 32. Cost per day: private—not applicable, semi-private $65.00.

Nursing beds are not certified by Medicare or Medicaid. Nonresidents may be admitted directly to the nursing care facility.

HOLLENBECK HOME
573 South Boyle Avenue, Los Angeles, CA 90033
Telephone: (213) 263-6195

Opened in 1895 • Mixed single-level, low-rise, and high-rise buildings on ten acres • Current resident population is 250 • Immediate availability

AAHA
Member

HOUSING AND SERVICES

Living Units	No.	Square Feet	No. of Persons	Entrance Fee	Monthly Fee
Studio	140	200–500	1	$13,000–$18,000	$780
One Bedroom	60	500–600	1	$23,000	$780
			2	$23,000	$1,560
Two Bedroom	0	——	——	——	——
Larger Units	0	——	——	——	——
Total		200 Units			

Entrance fee refunds decline over time.

These fees include three meals per day, scheduled transportation, and utilities. Special features of this community are presented in the Special Features Index at the back of the book. Ask about additional residential and health care services that may be available. Fees and services subject to change; verify with facility.

ASSISTED LIVING AND PERSONAL CARE

Assisted living units: 28
Personal care is covered by the continuing care contract: Yes
Residents may receive personal care in independent living units: No
Nonresidents may be admitted directly to assisted living units: Yes

NURSING CARE: All-Inclusive Plan

Under this all-inclusive plan, unlimited nursing care is covered by the continuing care contract. When residents are in nursing care, they pay the same monthly fee they paid for their independent living unit.

Intermediate beds: 28. Cost per day: not applicable.

Skilled beds: 84. Cost per day: not applicable.

Nursing beds are certified by both Medicare and Medicaid. Nonresidents may not be admitted directly to the nursing care facility.

INLAND CHRISTIAN HOME, INC.
1950 South Mountain Avenue, Ontario, CA 91761
Telephone: (714) 983-0084

Opened in 1979 • Predominantly single-level/garden apartments on ten acres • Current resident population is 170 • Waiting list

AAHA Member

HOUSING AND SERVICES

Living Units	No.	Square Feet	No. of Persons	Entrance Fee	Monthly Fee
Studio	0	——	——	——	——
One Bedroom	21	800	1, 2	$37,000	$60
Two Bedroom	28	1,000	1, 2	$47,000	$60
Larger Units	0	——	——	——	——
Total	49 Units				

Entrance fee refunds decline over time.

Services vary in different sections of the facility. Special features of this community are presented in the Special Features Index at the back of the book. Ask about additional residential and health care services that may be available. Fees and services subject to change; verify with facility.

ASSISTED LIVING AND PERSONAL CARE

Assisted living units: 34
Personal care is covered by the continuing care contract: No
Residents may receive personal care in independent living units: No
Nonresidents may be admitted directly to assisted living units: Yes

NURSING CARE: Fee-for-Service Plan

Under this fee-for-service plan, guaranteed access to nursing care is covered by the continuing care contract. Residents pay the full per diem rate for nursing care.

Skilled beds: 59. Cost per day: private $82.00, semi-private $62.00.

Nursing beds are certified by both Medicare and Medicaid. Nonresidents may be admitted directly to the nursing care facility.

LAKE PARK RETIREMENT RESIDENCE
1850 Alice Street, Oakland, CA 94612
Telephone: (415) 835-5511

Opened in 1965 • One high-rise building • Current resident population is 260 • Waiting list may apply for some units

AAHA
Member

HOUSING AND SERVICES

Living Units	No.	Square Feet	No. of Persons	Entrance Fee	Monthly Fee
Studio	186	392–634	1	$20,000–$29,000	$930
One Bedroom	72	742–1,044	1	$59,000–$80,000	$1,305
			2	$70,000–$91,000	$1,867
Two Bedroom	0	——	——	——	——
Larger Units	0	——	——	——	——
Total	258 Units				

Entrance fee refunds decline over time.

These fees include three meals per day, weekly housekeeping, and utilities. Special features of this community are presented in the Special Features Index at the back of the book. Ask about additional residential and health care services that may be available. Fees and services subject to change; verify with facility.

ASSISTED LIVING AND PERSONAL CARE

Assisted living units: 59
Personal care is covered by the continuing care contract: Yes
Residents may receive personal care in independent living units: No
Nonresidents may be admitted directly to assisted living units: Yes

NURSING CARE: All-Inclusive Plan

Under this all-inclusive plan, unlimited nursing care is covered by the continuing care contract. When residents are in nursing care, they pay the same monthly fee they paid for their independent living unit.

Skilled beds: 26. Cost per day: not applicable.

Nursing beds are certified by Medicare. Nonresidents may not be admitted directly to the nursing care facility.

LA SERENA RETIREMENT VILLAGE
3575 North Moorpark Road, Thousand Oaks, CA
91360
Telephone: (805) 492-2471

Opened in 1986 • Mixed single-level and low-rise
buildings on seven acres • Current resident
population is 90 • Immediate availability

AAHA
Member

HOUSING AND SERVICES

Living Units	No.	Square Feet	No. of Persons	Entrance Fee	Monthly Fee
Studio	18	529	1	$49,900–$53,900	$752
One Bedroom	70	629–706	1	$65,900–$74,500	$824–$856
			2	$65,900–$74,500	$1,174–$1,206
Two Bedroom	24	1,020	1	$102,900–$104,500	$1,043
			2	$102,900–$104,500	$1,383
Larger Units	0	—	—	—	—
Total	112 Units				

Entrance fee refunds decline over time.

These fees include one meal per day, weekly housekeeping, scheduled transportation, and utilities. Special features of this community are presented in the Special Features Index at the back of the book. Ask about additional residential and health care services that may be available. Fees and services subject to change; verify with facility.

ASSISTED LIVING AND PERSONAL CARE

Assisted living units: 38
Personal care is covered by the continuing care contract: Yes
Residents may receive personal care in independent living units: No
Nonresidents may be admitted directly to assisted living units: Yes

NURSING CARE: Modified Plan

Under this modified plan, 15 or fewer days are covered by the continuing care contract. Residents pay the full per diem rate for nursing care.

Skilled beds: 59.

Nursing beds are expected in 1988; rates not yet set. Nonresidents will be admitted directly to the nursing care facility.

LOS GATOS MEADOWS
110 Wood Road, Los Gatos, CA 95030
Telephone: (408) 354-0211

Opened in 1971 • Mixed single-level, low-rise, and high-rise buildings on 12 acres • Current resident population is 216 • Waiting list may apply for some units

AAHA
Member

HOUSING AND SERVICES

Living Units	No.	Square Feet	No. of Persons	Entrance Fee	Monthly Fee
Studio	73	352–540	1	$32,800–$42,800	$865–$906
One Bedroom	87	645–722	1	$47,100–$75,800	$990–$1,141
			2	$55,100–$95,600	$1,708–$1,859
Two Bedroom	13	1,092	1	$111,800–$133,100	$1,463
			2	$121,800–$143,100	$2,181
Larger Units	0	——	——	——	——
Total	173 Units				

Entrance fee refunds decline over time.

These fees include three meals per day, weekly housekeeping, scheduled transportation, and utilities. Special features of this community are presented in the Special Features Index at the back of the book. Ask about additional residential and health care services that may be available. Fees and services subject to change; verify with facility.

ASSISTED LIVING AND PERSONAL CARE

Assisted living units: 0
Personal care is covered by the continuing care contract: Yes
Residents may receive personal care in independent living units: Yes

NURSING CARE: All-Inclusive Plan

Under this all-inclusive plan, unlimited nursing care is covered by the continuing care contract. When residents are in nursing care, they pay the same monthly fee they paid for their independent living unit.

Skilled beds: 39. Cost per day: private $125.00, semi-private $100.00

Nursing beds are certified by Medicare. Nonresidents may be admitted directly to the nursing care facility.

MOUNT MIGUEL COVENANT VILLAGE

325 Kempton Street, Spring Valley, CA 92077
Telephone: (619) 479-4790

Opened in 1965 • Mixed single-level and low-rise buildings on 28 acres • Current resident population is 275 • Located nine miles from San Diego • Waiting list may apply for some units

AAHA
Member

HOUSING AND SERVICES

Living Units	No.	Square Feet	No. of Persons	Entrance Fee	Monthly Fee
Studio	71	456	1	$34,000	$579
One Bedroom	66	564	1	$49,900	$722
			2		$1,010
Two Bedroom	75	841–1,040	1	$83,900	$865–$980
			2		$1,135–$1,250
Larger Units	0	——	——	——	——
Total	212 Units				

Entrance fee refunds decline over time.

These fees include two meals per day, weekly housekeeping, scheduled transportation, and utilities. Special features of this community are presented in the Special Features Index at the back of the book. Ask about additional residential and health care services that may be available. Fees and services subject to change; verify with facility.

ASSISTED LIVING AND PERSONAL CARE

Assisted living units: 11
Personal care is covered by the continuing care contract: Yes
Residents may receive personal care in independent living units: Yes
Nonresidents may be admitted directly to assisted living units: No

NURSING CARE: Modified Plan

Under this modified plan, 60 days or more are covered by the continuing care contract. Once residents move permanently to the nursing unit, they pay 90 percent of the per diem rate for nursing care.

Intermediate beds: 16. Cost per day: private—not applicable, semi-private $62.00

Skilled beds: 83. Cost per day: private—not applicable, semi-private $72.00.

Nursing beds are certified by both Medicare and Medicaid. Nonresidents may be admitted directly to the nursing care facility.

MOUNT SAN ANTONIO GARDENS/ CONGREGATIONAL HOMES

900 East Harrison Avenue, Pomona, CA 91767
Telephone: (714) 624-5061

Opened in 1961 • Predominantly single-level/garden apartments on 28 acres • Current resident population is 455 • Located 30 miles from Los Angeles • Waiting list may apply for some units

AAHA Member

HOUSING AND SERVICES

Living Units	No.	Square Feet	No. of Persons	Entrance Fee	Monthly Fee
Studio	259	378	1	$28,000	$850
One Bedroom	59	747	1	$66,125	$1,275
			2	$66,125	$1,700
Two Bedroom	53	1,075	1, 2	$83,500	$1,700
Larger Units	0	——	——	——	——
Total	371 Units				

Entrance fee refunds decline over time.

These fees include three meals per day, biweekly housekeeping, and utilities. Special features of this community are presented in the Special Features Index at the back of the book. Ask about additional residential and health care services that may be available. Fees and services subject to change; verify with facility.

ASSISTED LIVING AND PERSONAL CARE

Assisted living units: 60
Personal care is covered by the continuing care contract: Yes
Residents may receive personal care in independent living units: No
Nonresidents may be admitted directly to assisted living units: No

NURSING CARE: All-Inclusive Plan

Under this all-inclusive plan, unlimited nursing care is covered by the continuing care contract. When residents are in nursing care, they pay the basic monthly fee for the studio (smallest) unit.

Skilled beds: 55. Cost per day: semi-private $75.00.

Nursing beds are certified by Medicare. Nonresidents may be admitted directly to the nursing care facility.

PIEDMONT GARDENS
110 41st Street, Oakland, CA 94611
Telephone: (415) 654-7172

Opened in 1969 • Predominantly high-rise buildings on one acre • Current resident population is 420 • Waiting list

AAHA
Member

HOUSING AND SERVICES

Living Units	No.	Square Feet	No. of Persons	Entrance Fee	Monthly Fee
Studio	89	326–380	1	$11,000–$21,600	$675
One Bedroom	105	570	1	$36,000–$43,200	$746
			2	$37,400–$49,700	$1,021
Two Bedroom	35	735	1	$51,300–$59,900	$892
			2		$1,167
Larger Units	5	1,100	1	$74,000	$978
			2		$1,253
Total	234 Units				

Entrance fee refunds decline over time.

These fees include one meal per day, monthly housekeeping, scheduled transportation, and utilities. Special features of this community are presented in the Special Features Index at the back of the book. Ask about additional residential and health care services that may be available. Fees and services subject to change; verify with facility.

ASSISTED LIVING AND PERSONAL CARE
Assisted living units: 74
Personal care is covered by the continuing care contract: Yes
Residents may receive personal care in independent living units: No
Nonresidents may be admitted directly to assisted living units: Yes

NURSING CARE: Fee-for-Service Plan

Under this fee-for-service plan, guaranteed access to nursing care is covered by the continuing care contract. Residents pay the full per diem rate for nursing care.

Intermediate beds: 47. Cost per day: private, $70.65, semi-private, $50.66.

Skilled beds: 47. Cost per day: private $87.75, semi-private $65.33.

Nursing beds are certified by both Medicare and Medicaid. Nonresidents may not be admitted directly to the nursing care facility.

PILGRIM HAVEN
373 Pine Lane, Los Altos, CA 94022
Telephone: (415) 948-8291

Opened in 1949 • Mixed single-level and low-rise
buildings on seven acres • Current resident
population is 180 • Waiting list

AAHA
Member

HOUSING AND SERVICES

Living Units	No.	Square Feet	No. of Persons	Entrance Fee	Monthly Fee
Studio	81	266	1	$9,500–$23,200	$709
One Bedroom	13	577	1	$25,400–$37,100	$824
			2	$27,940–$40,810	$1,003
Two Bedroom	4	898	1	$40,100–$51,000	——
			2	$44,110–$56,100	$927
Larger Units	2	1,519	1	$60,000–$80,000	——
			2	$66,000–$88,000	$918–$1,129
Total		100 Units			

Entrance fee refunds decline over time.

These fees include one meal per day in apartments (three in studio units), housekeeping, scheduled transportation, and utilities. Special features of this community are presented in the Special Features Index at the back of the book. Ask about additional residential and health care services that may be available. Fees and services subject to change; verify with facility.

ASSISTED LIVING AND PERSONAL CARE

Assisted living units: 16
Personal care is covered by the continuing care contract: Yes
Residents may receive personal care in independent living units: Yes
Nonresidents may be admitted directly to assisted living units: No

NURSING CARE: Modified Plan

Under this modified plan, 15 or fewer days per year are covered by the continuing care contract. Residents pay the full per diem rate for nursing care.

Skilled beds: 66. Cost per day: private $86.07, semi-private $68.12.

Nursing beds are certified by both Medicare and Medicaid. Nonresidents may be admitted directly to the nursing care facility.

CALIFORNIA

QUAKER GARDENS
12151 Dale Street, Stanton, CA 90680
Telephone: (714) 530-9100

Opened in 1965 • Mixed single-level and low-rise buildings on seven acres • Current resident population is 280 • Waiting list

AAHA
Member

HOUSING AND SERVICES

Living Units	No.	Square Feet	No. of Persons	Entrance Fee	Monthly Fee
Studio	165	375	1	$33,780	$755
One Bedroom	25	675	1	$53,160	$755
			2		$1,560
Two Bedroom	6	1,225	1	$79,500	$795
			2		$1,590
Larger Units	1	1,300	1	$85,000	$795
			2		$1,590
Total	197 Units				

Entrance fee refunds decline over time.

These fees include three meals per day (one meal for two bedroom and larger units), biweekly housekeeping, scheduled transportation, and utilities. Special features of this community are presented in the Special Features Index at the back of the book. Ask about additional residential and health care services that may be available. Fees and services subject to change; verify with facility.

ASSISTED LIVING AND PERSONAL CARE

Assisted living units: 6
Personal care is covered by the continuing care contract: Yes
Residents may receive personal care in independent living units: Yes
Nonresidents may be admitted directly to assisted living units: No

NURSING CARE: All-Inclusive Plan

Under this all-inclusive plan, unlimited nursing care is covered by the continuing care contract. When residents are in nursing care, they pay the basic monthly fee for the studio (smallest) unit.

Intermediate beds: 0.

Skilled beds: 58. Cost per day: private $95.00, semi-private $60.00.

Nursing beds are not certified by Medicare or Medicaid. Nonresidents may be admitted directly to the nursing care facility.

REDWOOD TERRACE
710 West 13th Avenue, Escondido, CA 92025
Telephone: (619) 747-4306

Opened in 1978 • Predominantly single-level/garden apartments on six acres • Current resident population is 140 • Located 30 miles from San Diego • Waiting list may apply for some units

AAHA
Member

HOUSING AND SERVICES

Living Units	No.	Square Feet	No. of Persons	Entrance Fee	Monthly Fee
Studio	10	336	1	$23,000	$440
One Bedroom	7	416	1, 2	$30,000	$512
Two Bedroom	30	1,072–1,079	1, 2	$72,500–$77,500	$670
Larger Units	0	——	——	——	——
Total	47 Units				

Entrance fee refunds decline over time.

These fees include one meal per day and utilities. Special features of this community are presented in the Special Features Index at the back of the book. Ask about additional residential and health care services that may be available. Fees and services subject to change; verify with facility.

ASSISTED LIVING AND PERSONAL CARE

Assisted living units: 25
Personal care is covered by the continuing care contract: No
Residents may receive personal care in independent living units: No
Nonresidents may be admitted directly to assisted living units: No

NURSING CARE: Modified Plan

Under this modified plan, nursing care is covered by the continuing care contract. When residents are in nursing care, they pay 60 percent of the per diem rate.

Intermediate beds: 14. Cost per day: private $82.00, semi-private, $79.00.

Skilled beds: 45. Cost per day: private $104.00, semi-private $99.00.

Nursing beds are certified by both Medicare and Medicaid. Nonresidents may be admitted directly to the nursing care facility.

ROSEWOOD RETIREMENT COMMUNITY
1301 New Stine Road, Bakersfield, CA 93309
Telephone: (805) 834-0620

Opened in 1974 • Mixed low-rise and high-rise buildings on ten acres • Current resident population is 165 • Waiting list may apply for some units

AAHA Member

HOUSING AND SERVICES

Living Units	No.	Square Feet	No. of Persons	Entrance Fee	Monthly Fee
Studio	43	332–408	1	$13,600–$20,200	$638–$667
One Bedroom	66	634–816	1	$31,900–$41,300	$752–$846
			2	$35,090–$45,430	$1,054–$1,148
Two Bedroom	30	1,150–	1	$55,900–$67,800	$895–$955
		1,665	2		$1,197–$1,257
Larger Units	0	——	——	——	——
Total	139 Units				

Entrance fee refunds decline over time.

These fees include one meal per day, weekly housekeeping, and utilities. Special features of this community are presented in the Special Features Index at the back of the book. Ask about additional residential and health care services that may be available. Fees and services subject to change; verify with facility.

ASSISTED LIVING AND PERSONAL CARE

Assisted living units: 18
Personal care is covered by the continuing care contract: No
Residents may receive personal care in independent living units: No
Nonresidents may be admitted directly to assisted living units: Yes

NURSING CARE: Modified Plan

Under this modified plan, 15 or fewer days per year are covered by the continuing care contract. When residents move permanently to the nursing unit, they pay the full per diem rate for nursing care.

Skilled beds: 79. Cost per day: private $91.00, semi-private $69.50.

Nursing beds are certified by both Medicare and Medicaid. Nonresidents may be admitted directly to the nursing care facility.

SAINT PAUL'S TOWERS
100 Bay Place, Oakland, CA 94610
Telephone: (415) 835-4700

Opened in 1966 • One high-rise building • Current resident population is 291 • Waiting list may apply for some units

AAHA
Member

HOUSING AND SERVICES

Living Units	No.	Square Feet	No. of Persons	Entrance Fee	Monthly Fee
Studio	126	——	1	$21,000–$32,375	$996
One Bedroom	120	——	1	$41,100–$67,425	$1,131–$1,289
			2	$43,300–$77,425	$1,949–$2,107
Two Bedroom	36	——	1	$94,400–$99,124	$1,368–$1,456
			2	$104,400–$109,125	$2,186–$2,274
Larger Units	4	——	1	$101,300–$101,975	$1,713
			2	$111,975	$2,313
Total	286 Units				

Entrance fee refunds decline over time.

These fees include three meals per day, weekly housekeeping, and utilities. Special features of this community are presented in the Special Features Index at the back of the book. Ask about additional residential and health care services that may be available. Fees and services subject to change; verify with facility.

ASSISTED LIVING AND PERSONAL CARE

Assisted living units: 0
Personal care is covered by the continuing care contract: Yes
Residents may receive personal care in independent living units: Yes

NURSING CARE: All-Inclusive Plan

Under this all-inclusive plan, unlimited nursing care is covered by the continuing care contract. When residents are in nursing care, they pay the same monthly fee they paid for their independent living unit.

Skilled beds: 43. Cost per day: private $106.00, semi-private $92.00.

Nursing beds are certified by Medicare. Nonresidents may be admitted directly to the nursing care facility.

SAMARKAND OF SANTA BARBARA
2550 Treasure Drive, Santa Barbara, CA 93105
Telephone: (805) 687-0701

Opened in 1956 • Mixed single-level and low-rise buildings on 17 acres • Current resident population is 293 • Waiting list may apply for some units

AAHA Member

HOUSING AND SERVICES

Living Units	No.	Square Feet	No. of Persons	Entrance Fee	Monthly Fee
Studio	95	372–400	1	$29,500–$40,000	$814
One Bedroom	59	608	1	$55,000–$78,000	$1,221
			2		$1,628
Two Bedroom	42	960–1,050	1	$105,000–$148,500	$1,424
			2		$1,628
Larger Units	0	——	——	——	——
Total		196 Units			

Entrance fee refunds decline over time.

These fees include three meals per day, weekly housekeeping, scheduled transportation, and utilities. Special features of this community are presented in the Special Features Index at the back of the book. Ask about additional residential and health care services that may be available. Fees and services subject to change; verify with facility.

ASSISTED LIVING AND PERSONAL CARE

Assisted living units: 53
Personal care is covered by the continuing care contract: Yes
Residents may receive personal care in independent living units: Yes
Nonresidents may be admitted directly to assisted living units: Yes

NURSING CARE: Modified Plan

Under this modified plan, 60 days or more are covered by the continuing care contract. Once residents move permanently to a nursing unit, they pay 90 percent of the per diem rate for nursing care.

Skilled beds: 59. Cost per day: private $104.00, semi-private $82.00.

Nursing beds are certified by Medicare and Medi-Cal. Nonresidents may be admitted directly to the nursing care facility.

SAN JOAQUIN GARDENS
5555 North Fresno Street, Fresno, CA 93710
Telephone: (209) 439-4770

Opened in 1966 • Predominantly single-level/garden apartments on 25 acres • Current resident population is 370 • Waiting list may apply for some units

AAHA
Member

HOUSING AND SERVICES

Living Units	No.	Square Feet	No. of Persons	Entrance Fee	Monthly Fee
Studio	4	477	1	$27,500	$525
One Bedroom	64	562	1	$33,000	$580
			2	$36,000	$825
Two Bedroom	32	800	1	$44,000–$54,000	$650–$665
			2	$44,000–$54,000	$895–$910
Larger Units	0	——	——	——	——
Total	100 Units				

Entrance fee refunds decline over time.

These fees include one meal per day, monthly housekeeping, scheduled transportation, and utilities. Special features of this community are presented in the Special Features Index at the back of the book. Ask about additional residential and health care services that may be available. Fees and services subject to change; verify with facility.

ASSISTED LIVING AND PERSONAL CARE

Assisted living units: 134
Personal care is covered by the continuing care contract: Yes
Residents may receive personal care in independent living units: No
Nonresidents may be admitted directly to assisted living units: No

NURSING CARE: Modified Plan

Under this modified plan, 15 or fewer days are covered by the continuing care contract. Once residents move permanently to the nursing unit, they pay the full per diem rate for nursing care.

Intermediate beds: 32. Cost per day: private $60.60, semi-private $52.00.

Skilled beds: 56. Cost per day: private $72.50, semi-private $61.00.

Nursing beds are certified by both Medicare and Medicaid. Nonresidents may not be admitted directly to the nursing care facility.

THE SCRIPPS HOME
2212 North El Molino Avenue, Altadena, CA 91001
Telephone: (818) 798-0934

Opened in 1913 • Mixed single-level and low-rise buildings on six acres • Current resident population is 140 • Located three miles from Pasadena, CA • Waiting list may apply for some units

AAHA Member

HOUSING AND SERVICES

Living Units	No.	Square Feet	No. of Persons	Entrance Fee	Monthly Fee
Studio	94	270	1	$2,500 + assets	None*
One Bedroom	6	——	1, 2	$2,500 + assets	None*
Two Bedroom	0	——	——	——	——
Total	100 Units				

*Residents receive a $75.00 monthly allowance.
Entrance fees are fully refundable within 90 days.

These fees include three meals per day, housekeeping, scheduled transportation, and utilities. Special features of this community are presented in the Special Features Index at the back of the book. Ask about additional residential and health care services that may be available. Fees and services subject to change; verify with facility.

ASSISTED LIVING AND PERSONAL CARE

Assisted living units: 21
Personal care is covered by the continuing care contract: Yes
Residents may receive personal care in independent living units: No
Nonresidents may be admitted directly to assisted living units: No

NURSING CARE: All-Inclusive Plan

Under this all-inclusive plan, unlimited nursing care is covered by the life care contract. There is no fee.

Intermediate beds: 20. Cost per day: not applicable.

Skilled beds: 25. Cost per day: not applicable.

Dual-certified beds: 4. Cost per day: not applicable.

Nursing beds are certified by Medicaid. Nonresidents may not be admitted directly to the nursing care facility.

CALIFORNIA

THE SEQUOIAS–SAN FRANCISCO
1400 Geary Boulevard, San Francisco, CA 94109
Telephone: (415) 922-9700

Opened in 1969 • One high-rise building on two acres • Current resident population is 360 • Waiting list may apply for some units

AAHA
Member

HOUSING AND SERVICES

Living Units	No.	Square Feet	No. of Persons	Entrance Fee	Monthly Fee
Studio	96	410–460	1	$33,000–$60,000	$742
One Bedroom	138	604–624	1	$69,000–$100,000	$958
			2	$80,000–$110,000	$1,530
Two Bedroom	66	929–1,064	1	$124,000–$160,000	$1,369
			2	$124,000–$160,000	$1,804
Larger Units	0	—	—	—	—
Total	300 Units				

Entrance fee refunds decline over time.

These fees include three meals per day, weekly housekeeping, scheduled transportation, and utilities. Special features of this community are presented in the Special Features Index at the back of the book. Ask about additional residential and health care services that may be available. Fees and services subject to change; verify with facility.

ASSISTED LIVING AND PERSONAL CARE

Assisted living units: 11
Personal care is covered by the continuing care contract: Yes
Residents may receive personal care in independent living units: Yes
Nonresidents may be admitted directly to assisted living units: No

NURSING CARE: All-Inclusive Plan

Under this all-inclusive plan, unlimited nursing care is covered by the continuing care contract. When residents are in nursing care, they pay the same monthly fee they paid for their independent living unit.

Intermediate beds: 0.

Skilled beds: 49. Cost per day: semi-private $70.00.

Nursing beds are certified by both Medicare and Medicaid. Nonresidents may be admitted directly to the nursing care facility.

SOLHEIM LUTHERAN HOMES
2236 Merton Avenue, Los Angeles, CA 90041
Telephone: (213) 257-7518

Opened in 1923 • Predominantly single-level/garden apartments on four acres • Current resident population is 111 • Waiting list may apply for some units

AAHA Member

HOUSING AND SERVICES

Living Units	No.	Square Feet	No. of Persons	Entrance Fee	Monthly Fee
Studio	97	——	1	$5,000–$15,000	$785
One Bedroom	0	——	——	——	——
Two Bedroom	1	——	1	$12,000	$1,000
Larger Units	0	——	——	——	——
Total	98 Units				

Entrance fee refunds decline over time.

These fees include three meals per day, biweekly housekeeping, scheduled transportation, and utilities. Special features of this community are presented in the Special Features Index at the back of the book. Ask about additional residential and health care services that may be available. Fees and services subject to change; verify with facility.

ASSISTED LIVING AND PERSONAL CARE

Assisted living units: 0
Personal care is covered by the continuing care contract: Yes
Residents may receive personal care in independent living units: Yes

NURSING CARE: Fee-for-Service Plan

Under this fee-for-service plan, guaranteed access to nursing care is covered by the continuing care contract. Residents pay the full per diem rate for nursing care.

Skilled beds: 19. Cost per day: private $75.00, semi-private $63.00.

Nursing beds are certified by Medicaid. Nonresidents may not be admitted directly to the nursing care facility.

SUNNY VIEW LUTHERAN HOME
22445 Cupertino Road, Cupertino, CA 95014
Telephone: (408) 253-4300

Opened in 1963 • Predominantly single-level/garden apartments on 13 acres • Current resident population is 75 • Waiting list

AAHA
Member

HOUSING AND SERVICES

Living Units	No.	Square Feet	No. of Persons	Entrance Fee	Monthly Fee
Studio	62	——	1	$16,000–$21,000	$660–$1,053
One Bedroom	8	——	1, 2	$26,000	$1,168
Two Bedroom	0	——	——	——	——
Larger Units	0	——	——	——	——
Total	70 Units				

Entrance fee refunds decline over time.

These fees include three meals per day, weekly housekeeping, scheduled transportation, and utilities. Special features of this community are presented in the Special Features Index at the back of the book. Ask about additional residential and health care services that may be available. Fees and services subject to change; verify with facility.

ASSISTED LIVING AND PERSONAL CARE

Assisted living units: 0
Personal care is covered by the continuing care contract: No
Residents may receive personal care in independent living units: No

NURSING CARE: Modified Plan

Under this modified plan, 15 or fewer days are covered by the continuing care contract. Once residents move permanently to the nursing unit, they pay the full per diem rate for nursing care.

Intermediate beds: 0.

Skilled beds: 45. Cost per day: private $71.00, semi-private $63.00.

Nursing beds are certified by Medicaid. Nonresidents may be admitted directly to the nursing care facility.

VALLE VERDE RETIREMENT CENTER
900 Calle De Los Amigos, Santa Barbara, CA 93105
Telephone: (805) 687-1571

New facility opened in 1987 • Predominantly single-level/garden apartments on 56 acres • Current resident population is 375 • Waiting list may apply for some units

AAHA
Member

HOUSING AND SERVICES

Living Units	No.	Square Feet	No. of Persons	Entrance Fee	Monthly Fee
Studio	32	340	1	$18,500	$810
One Bedroom	130	530–775	1	$38,000–$60,000	$810–$1,055
			2	$42,000–$64,000	$1,135–$1,380
Two Bedroom	64	900–1,200	1	$65,000–$93,000	$1,025–$1,225
			2	$69,000–$97,000	$1,350–$1,550
Larger Units	0	—	—	—	—
Total	226 Units				

Entrance fee refunds decline over time.

These fees include one meal per day (three for studios), housekeeping, scheduled transportation, and utilities. Special features of this community are presented in the Special Features Index at the back of the book. Ask about additional residential and health care services that may be available. Fees and services subject to change; verify with facility.

ASSISTED LIVING AND PERSONAL CARE

Assisted living units: 16
Personal care is covered by the continuing care contract: Yes
Residents may receive personal care in independent living units: Yes
Nonresidents may be admitted directly to assisted living units: Yes

NURSING CARE: Modified Plan

Under this modified plan, 15 or fewer days per year are covered by the continuing care contract. Once residents move permanently to the nursing unit, they pay the full per diem rate for nursing care.

Intermediate beds: 0.

Skilled beds: 54. Cost per day: private $115.00, semi-private $79.50.

Nursing beds are certified by both Medicare and Medicaid. Nonresidents may be admitted directly to the nursing care facility.

VILLA GARDENS
842 East Villa Street, Pasadena, CA 91101
Telephone: (818) 796-8162

Opened in 1987 • One high-rise building on three
acres • Immediate availability

AAHA
Member

HOUSING AND SERVICES

Living Units	No.	Square Feet	No. of Persons	Entrance Fee	Monthly Fee
Studio	36	415	1	$47,000	$675
One Bedroom	103	615	1	$68,500	$825
			2	$71,500	$1,250
Two Bedroom	32	916	1	$100,500	$975
			2	$103,500	$1,400
Larger Units	24	1,012	1	$110,750	$1,075
			2	$113,750	$1,500
Total	195 Units				

Entrance fee refunds decline over time.

These fees include one meal per day, biweekly housekeeping, scheduled transportation, and utilities. Special features of this community are presented in the Special Features Index at the back of the book. Ask about additional residential and health care services that may be available. Fees and services subject to change; verify with facility.

ASSISTED LIVING AND PERSONAL CARE

Assisted living units: 0
Personal care is covered by the continuing care contract: No
Residents may receive personal care in independent living units: No

NURSING CARE: All-Inclusive Plan

Under this all-inclusive plan, unlimited nursing care is covered by the continuing care contract. When residents are in nursing care, they pay the same monthly fee they paid for their independent living unit.

Intermediate beds: 0.

Skilled beds: 31. Cost per day: private $96.50, semi-private $73.00.

Nursing beds are certified by both Medicare and Medicaid. Nonresidents may be admitted directly to the nursing care facility.

WEBSTER HOUSE
401 Webster, Palo Alto, CA 94301
Telephone: (415) 327-4333

Opened in 1983 • One high-rise building on one acre • Current resident population is 37 • Waiting list may apply for some units

AAHA
Member

HOUSING AND SERVICES

Living Units	No.	Square Feet	No. of Persons	Entrance Fee	Monthly Fee
Studio	0	—	—	—	—
One Bedroom	16	1,000–1,040	1, 2	$255,000*	$750 $750
Two Bedroom	11	930–1,280	1, 2	$515,000*	$750
Larger Units	0	—	—	—	—
Total	27 Units				

*Equity purchase
Entrance fees are partially refundable.

These fees include weekly housekeeping, scheduled transportation, and utilities. Special features of this community are presented in the Special Features Index at the back of the book. Ask about additional residential and health care services that may be available. Fees and services subject to change; verify with facility.

ASSISTED LIVING AND PERSONAL CARE

Assisted living units: 0
Personal care is covered by the continuing care contract: No
Residents may receive personal care in independent living units: Yes

NURSING CARE: All-Inclusive Plan

Under this all-inclusive plan, unlimited nursing care is covered by the continuing care contract. When residents are in nursing care, they pay the same monthly fee they paid for their independent living unit.

Intermediate and skilled beds: Residents are provided care in a number of nearby facilities.

Nonresidents may not be admitted directly to the nursing care facility.

WHITE SANDS OF LA JOLLA
7450 Olivetas Avenue, La Jolla, CA 92037
Telephone: (619) 454-4201

Opened in 1956 • Mixed single-level, low-rise, and high-rise buildings on five acres • Current resident population is 258 • Waiting list may apply for some units

AAHA
Member

HOUSING AND SERVICES

Living Units	No.	Square Feet	No. of Persons	Entrance Fee	Monthly Fee
Studio	141	295–382	1	$31,250–$51,250	$715
One Bedroom	50	498–590	1	$63,250–$94,000	$1,255
			2	$63,250–$94,000	$1,430
Two Bedroom	9	1,007	1	$120,000–$170,000	$1,255
			2	$120,000–$170,000	$1,430
Larger Units	0	——	——	——	——
Total	200 Units				

Entrance fee refunds decline over time.

These fees include three meals per day, biweekly housekeeping, and utilities. Special features of this community are presented in the Special Features Index at the back of the book. Ask about additional residential and health care services that may be available. Fees and services subject to change; verify with facility.

ASSISTED LIVING AND PERSONAL CARE

Assisted living units: 13
Personal care is covered by the continuing care contract: No
Residents may receive personal care in independent living units: Yes
Nonresidents may be admitted directly to assisted living units: Yes

NURSING CARE: Fee-for-Service Plan

Under this fee-for-service plan, guaranteed access to nursing care is covered by the continuing care contract. Residents pay the full per diem rate for nursing care.

Intermediate beds: 0.

Skilled beds: 50. Cost per day: private $80.00, semi-private $40.00.

Nursing beds are not certified by Medicare or Medicaid. Nonresidents may be admitted directly to the nursing care facility.

WINDSOR MANOR
1230 East Windsor Road, Glendale, CA 91205
Telephone: (818) 244-7219

Opened in 1959 • Mixed single-level, low-rise, and high-rise buildings on two acres • Current resident population is 170 • Waiting list may apply for some units

AAHA Member

HOUSING AND SERVICES

Living Units	No.	Square Feet	No. of Persons	Entrance Fee	Monthly Fee
Studio	111	240–265	1	$20,500–$27,000	$650
One Bedroom	14	500–513	1	$36,000–$44,000	$1,140
			2	$36,000–$44,000	$1,300
Two Bedroom	0	——	——	——	——
Larger Units	0	——	——	——	——
Total	125 Units				

Entrance fee refunds decline over time.

These fees include three meals per day, housekeeping, and utilities. Special features of this community are presented in the Special Features Index at the back of the book. Ask about additional residential and health care services that may be available. Fees and services subject to change; verify with facility.

ASSISTED LIVING AND PERSONAL CARE

Assisted living units: 16
Personal care is covered by the continuing care contract: Yes
Residents may receive personal care in independent living units: No
Nonresidents may be admitted directly to assisted living units: Yes

---

NURSING CARE: Modified Plan

Under this modified plan, 60 days or more are covered by the continuing care contract. When residents are in nursing care, they pay 85 percent of the per diem rate.

Skilled beds: 28. Cost per day: private $95.00, semi-private $70.00.

Nursing beds are certified by Medicaid. Nonresidents may be admitted directly to the nursing care facility.

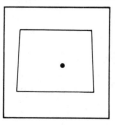

THE MEDALION
1719 East Bijou, Colorado Springs, CO 80909
Telephone: (303) 471-4800

Opened in 1969 • One high-rise building • Current resident population is 111 • Waiting list may apply for some units

AAHA
Member

HOUSING AND SERVICES

Living Units	No.	Square Feet	No. of Persons	Entrance Fee	Monthly Fee
Studio	35	516	1	$40,875–$45,100	$471
One Bedroom	32	748	1	$59,600–$61,775	$575
			2	$71,520–$74,130	$788
Two Bedroom	26	1,046	1	$76,950	$710
			2	$92,340–$94,950	$923
Larger Units	0	—	—	—	—
Total	93 Units				

Residents have a choice of entrance fee refund plans.

These fees include biweekly housekeeping, scheduled transportation, and utilities. Special features of this community are presented in the Special Features Index at the back of the book. Ask about additional residential and health care services that may be available. Fees and services subject to change; verify with facility.

ASSISTED LIVING AND PERSONAL CARE

Assisted living units: 12
Personal care is covered by the continuing care contract: Yes
Residents may receive personal care in independent living units: No
Nonresidents may be admitted directly to assisted living units: No

NURSING CARE: All-Inclusive Plan

Under this all-inclusive plan, unlimited nursing care is covered by the continuing care contract. When residents are in nursing care, they pay the basic monthly fee for the studio (smallest) unit.

Skilled beds: 32. Cost per day: private—not applicable, semi-private $51.00.
Nursing beds are certified by Medicare. Nonresidents may be admitted directly to the nursing care facility.

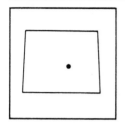

MEDALION WEST
417 East Kiowa Street, Colorado Springs, CO 80903
Telephone: (303) 471-2578

Opened in 1972 • One high-rise building on two acres • Current resident population is 129 • Waiting list may apply for some units

AAHA
Member

HOUSING AND SERVICES

Living Units	No.	Square Feet	No. of Persons	Entrance Fee	Monthly Fee
Studio	46	425	1	$35,625–$37,725	$451
One Bedroom	56	550	1	$43,325–$45,500	$511
			2	$51,990–$54,600	$734
Two Bedroom	14	788–975	1	$60,675–$73,700	$622–$712
			2	$72,810–$88,440	$845–$935
Larger Units	0	——	——	——	——
Total		116 Units			

Entrance fee refunds decline over time.

These fees include biweekly housekeeping, scheduled transportation, and utilities. Special features of this community are presented in the Special Features Index at the back of the book. Ask about additional residential and health care services that may be available. Fees and services subject to change; verify with facility.

ASSISTED LIVING AND PERSONAL CARE

Assisted living units: 12 (at The Medalion; see page 74)
Personal care is covered by the continuing care contract: Yes
Residents may receive personal care in independent living units: No
Nonresidents may be admitted directly to assisted living units: No

NURSING CARE: All-Inclusive Plan

Under this all-inclusive plan, unlimited nursing care is covered by the continuing care contract. When residents are in nursing care, they pay the basic monthly fee for the studio (smallest) unit.

Skilled beds: 32.* Cost per day: private—not applicable, semi-private $51.00.

*Medalion West residents use the medical center at The Medalion.

Nursing beds are certified by both Medicare and Medicaid. Nonresidents may be admitted directly to the nursing care facility.

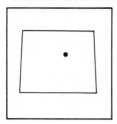

SUNNY ACRES VILLA
2501 East 104th Avenue, Denver, CO 80233
Telephone: (303) 452-4181

Opened in 1967 • Mixed single-level and low-rise buildings on 72 acres • Current resident population is 475 • Waiting list may apply for some units

AAHA
Member

HOUSING AND SERVICES

Living Units	No.	Square Feet	No. of Persons	Entrance Fee	Monthly Fee
Studio	152	380–450	1	$33,500–$40,875	$429–$464
One Bedroom	160	525–900	1	$44,400–$71,525	$534–$677
			2	$53,280–$85,830	$757–$900
Two Bedroom	70	720–1,040	1	$62,850–$76,950	$639–$743
			2	$75,420–$92,340	$862–$966
Larger Units	0	—	—	—	—
Total	382 Units				

Residents have a choice of entrance fee refund plans.

These fees include biweekly housekeeping, scheduled transportation, and utilities. Special features of this community are presented in the Special Features Index at the back of the book. Ask about additional residential and health care services that may be available. Fees and services subject to change; verify with facility.

ASSISTED LIVING AND PERSONAL CARE

Assisted living units: 0
Personal care is covered by the continuing care contract: Yes
Residents may receive personal care in independent living units: Yes

NURSING CARE: All-Inclusive Plan

Under this all-inclusive plan, unlimited nursing care is covered by the continuing care contract. When residents are in nursing care, they pay the basic monthly fee for the studio (smallest) unit.

Skilled beds: 118. Cost per day: private—not applicable, semi-private $51.00.

Nursing beds are certified by both Medicare and Medicaid. Nonresidents may be admitted directly to the nursing care facility.

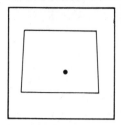

VILLA PUEBLO TOWERS
1111 Bonforte Boulevard, Pueblo, CO 81001
Telephone: (303) 545-5911

Opened in 1971 • One high-rise building on seven acres • Current resident population is 181 • Waiting list may apply for some units

AAHA
Member

HOUSING AND SERVICES

Living Units	No.	Square Feet	No. of Persons	Entrance Fee	Monthly Fee
Studio	48	478	1	$38,775–$40,875	$475
One Bedroom	87	620	1	$49,825–$52,000	$543
			2	$59,790–$62,400	$766
Two Bedroom	17	896–1,098	1	$73,700–$83,450	$673–$769
			2	$88,440–$100,140	$896–$992
Larger Units	0	—	—	—	—
Total	152 Units				

Residents have a choice of entrance fee refund plans.

These fees include biweekly housekeeping, scheduled transportation, and utilities. Special features of this community are presented in the Special Features Index at the back of the book. Ask about additional residential and health care services that may be available. Fees and services subject to change; verify with facility.

ASSISTED LIVING AND PERSONAL CARE

Assisted living units: 15
Personal care is covered by the continuing care contract: Yes
Residents may receive personal care in independent living units: No
Nonresidents may be admitted directly to assisted living units: No

NURSING CARE: All-Inclusive Plan

Under this all-inclusive plan, unlimited nursing care is covered by the continuing care contract. When residents are in nursing care, they pay the basic monthly fee for the studio (smallest) unit.

Skilled beds: 32. Cost per day: semi-private $51.00.

Nursing beds are certified by Medicare. Nonresidents may be admitted directly to the nursing care facility.

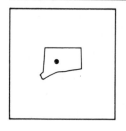

COVENANT VILLAGE AND PILGRIM MANOR

52 Missionary Road, Cromwell, CT 06416
Telephone: (203) 635-5511

Opened in 1964 • Mixed single-level, low-rise, and high-rise buildings on 25 acres • Current resident population is 360 • Located 15 miles from Hartford, CT • Waiting list may apply for some units

AAHA Member

HOUSING AND SERVICES

Living Units	No.	Square Feet	No. of Persons	Entrance Fee	Monthly Fee
Studio	36	507–552	1	$47,500	$545
One Bedroom	96	645–775	1	$62,500	$685
			2	$62,500	$895
Two Bedroom	57	910–930	1	$78,000	$820
			2	$78,000	$1,030
Larger Units	5	1,020	1	$89,500	$840
			2	$89,500	$1,050
Total		194 Units			

Entrance fee refunds decline over time.

These fees include one meal per day, biweekly housekeeping, scheduled transportation, and utilities. Special features of this community are presented in the Special Features Index at the back of the book. Ask about additional residential and health care services that may be available. Fees and services subject to change; verify with facility.

ASSISTED LIVING AND PERSONAL CARE

Assisted living units: 51
Personal care is covered by the continuing care contract: Yes
Residents may receive personal care in independent living units: No
Nonresidents may be admitted directly to assisted living units: Yes

NURSING CARE: Modified Plan

Under this modified plan, 60 days are covered by the continuing care contract. Once residents move permanently to the nursing unit, they pay 90 percent of the per diem rate for nursing care.

Intermediate beds: 30. Cost per day: private, $110.00, semi-private $73.50.
Skilled beds: 30. Cost per day: private $108.00, semi-private $87.50.
Nursing beds are certified by Medicaid. Nonresidents may be admitted directly to the nursing care facility.

CONNECTICUT

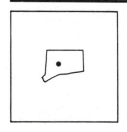

DUNCASTER
40 Loeffler Road, Bloomfield, CT 06002
Telephone: (203) 726-2000

Opened in 1984 • Mixed single-level and low-rise buildings on 72 acres • Current resident population is 250 • Waiting list may apply for some units

AAHA
Member

HOUSING AND SERVICES

Living Units	No.	Square Feet	No. of Persons	Entrance Fee	Monthly Fee
Studio	27	514	1	$54,500	$1,290
One Bedroom	109	657–822	1	$70,850–$89,900	$1,484–$1,677
			2	$78,000–$98,900	$2,129–$2,322
Two Bedroom	80	986–1,126	1	$103,000–$125,350	$1,870–$2,065
			2	$133,900–$137,900	$2,515–$2,710
Larger Units	0	—	—	—	—
Total	216 Units				

Entrance fee refunds decline over time.

These fees include one meal per day, weekly housekeeping, scheduled transportation, and utilities. Special features of this community are presented in the Special Features Index at the back of the book. Ask about additional residential and health care services that may be available. Fees and services subject to change; verify with facility.

ASSISTED LIVING AND PERSONAL CARE

Assisted living units: 0
Personal care is covered by the continuing care contract: Yes
Residents may receive personal care in independent living units: Yes

NURSING CARE: All-Inclusive Plan

Under this all-inclusive plan, unlimited nursing care is covered by the continuing care contract. When residents are in nursing care, they pay the same monthly fee they paid for their independent living unit.

Intermediate beds: 30. Cost per day: private $99.00, semi-private $85.00.
Skilled beds: 30. Cost per day: private $115.00, semi-private $106.00.
Nursing beds are certified by Medicare. Nonresidents may be admitted directly to the nursing care facility.

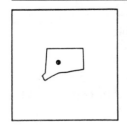

ELIM PARK BAPTIST HOME
140 Cook Hill Road, Cheshire, CT 06410
Telephone: (203) 272-3547

Opened in 1985 • Mixed single-level and low-rise buildings on 33 acres • Current resident population is 187 • Located ten miles from Meriden, CT • Waiting list may apply for some units

AAHA Member

HOUSING AND SERVICES

Living Units	No.	Square Feet	No. of Persons	Entrance Fee	Monthly Fee
Studio	0	——	——	——	——
One Bedroom	40	500–700	1	$61,900–$72,900	$469–$608
			2	$61,900–$72,900	$533–$672
Two Bedroom	0	——	——	——	——
Larger Units	0	——	——	——	——
Total	40 Units				

Entrance fees are partially refundable.

These fees include one meal per day, biweekly housekeeping, scheduled transportation, and utilities. Special features of this community are presented in the Special Features Index at the back of the book. Ask about additional residential and health care services that may be available. Fees and services subject to change; verify with facility.

ASSISTED LIVING AND PERSONAL CARE

Assisted living units: 52
Personal care is covered by the continuing care contract: Yes
Residents may receive personal care in independent living units: No
Nonresidents may be admitted directly to assisted living units: Yes

NURSING CARE: Fee-for-Service Plan

Under this fee-for-service plan, guaranteed access to nursing care is covered by the continuing care contract. Residents pay the full per diem rate for nursing care.

Intermediate beds: 30. Cost per day: private $70.00, semi-private $58.00.

Skilled beds: 60. Cost per day: private $107.80, semi-private $92.90.

Nursing beds are certified by both Medicare and Medicaid. Nonresidents may be admitted directly to the nursing care facility.

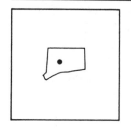

MASONIC HOME AND HOSPITAL

P.O. Box 70, Wallingford, CT 06492
Telephone: (203) 326-5931

Opened in 1984 • Mixed single-level and low-rise buildings on 215 acres • Current resident population is 678 • Located 30 miles from New Haven and Hartford, CT • Waiting list may apply for some units

AAHA
Member

HOUSING AND SERVICES

Living Units	No.	Square Feet	No. of Persons	Entrance Fee	Monthly Fee
Studio	1	300	1	$44,900	$410
One Bedroom	64	625–680	1	$57,200–$76,000	$375–$455
			2	$57,200–$76,000	$400–$605
Two Bedroom	74	810	1	$67,200–$92,700	$415–$505
			2	$67,200–$92,700	$440–$655
Larger Units	10	994	1	$104,900	$415
			2	$104,900	$440
Total	149 Units				

Entrance fee refunds decline over time.

These fees include one meal per day, biweekly housekeeping, and scheduled transportation. Special features of this community are presented in the Special Features Index at the back of the book. Ask about additional residential and health care services that may be available. Fees and services subject to change; verify with facility.

ASSISTED LIVING AND PERSONAL CARE

Assisted living units: 86
Personal care is covered by the continuing care contract: No
Residents may receive personal care in independent living units: Yes
Nonresidents may be admitted directly to assisted living units: No

NURSING CARE: Modified Plan

Under this modified plan, 15 or fewer days are covered by the continuing care contract. Once residents move permanently to the nursing unit, they pay the full per diem rate for nursing care.

Intermediate beds: 264. Cost per day: semi-private $73.50.

Skilled beds: 188. Cost per day: private $166.80, semi-private $92.61.

Nursing beds are certified by both Medicare and Medicaid. Nonresidents may be admitted directly to the nursing care facility. The nursing center is accredited by the Joint Commission on Accreditation of Hospitals.

CONNECTICUT

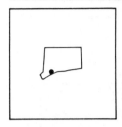

THIRTY THIRTY PARK
3030 Park Avenue, Bridgeport, CT 06604
Telephone: (203) 374-5611

Opened in 1968 • Predominantly high-rise buildings
on 14 acres • Current resident population is 475 •
Waiting list may apply for some units

AAHA
Member

HOUSING AND SERVICES

Living Units	No.	Square Feet	No. of Persons	Entrance Fee	Monthly Fee
Studio	196	318	1	$35,650	$895
One Bedroom	110	637	1	$64,425	$1,053
			2		$1,665
Two Bedroom	19	910	1	$99,900	$1,253
			2		$1,833
Larger Units	0	——	——	——	——
Total		325 Units			

Entrance fee refunds decline over time.

These fees include three meals per day, weekly housekeeping, and utilities.
Special features of this community are presented in the Special Features Index
at the back of the book. Ask about additional residential and health care services
that may be available. Fees and services subject to change; verify with facility.

ASSISTED LIVING AND PERSONAL CARE

Assisted living units: 0
Personal care is covered by the continuing care contract: No
Residents may receive personal care in independent living units: No

NURSING CARE: Fee-for-Service Plan

Under this fee-for-service plan, guaranteed access to nursing care is covered by
the continuing care contract. Residents pay the full per diem rate for nursing
care.

Intermediate beds: 72. Cost per day: private $88.00, semi-private $84.25.

Skilled beds: 28. Cost per day: private $110.25, semi-private $101.50.

Nursing beds are certified by both Medicare and Medicaid. Nonresidents may
be admitted directly to the nursing care facility.

CONNECTICUT

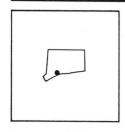

WHITNEY CENTER
200 Leeder Hill Drive, Hamden, CT 06517
Telephone: (203) 281-6745

Opened in 1979 • Mixed single-level and low-rise buildings on ten acres • Current resident population is 284 • Located five miles from New Haven, CT • Waiting list may apply for some units

AAHA
Member

HOUSING AND SERVICES

Living Units	No.	Square Feet	No. of Persons	Entrance Fee	Monthly Fee
Studio	58	296–460	1	$34,700–$49,400	$678–$763
One Bedroom	106	592–700	1	$77,000–$88,900	$849–$935
			2		$1,264–$1,350
Two Bedroom	40	839–987	1	$105,900–$123,200	$1,019–$1,106
			2		$1,434–$1,521
Larger Units	0	—	—	—	—
Total	204 Units				

Entrance fees are partially refundable.

These fees include one meal per day, biweekly housekeeping, scheduled transportation, and utilities. Special features of this community are presented in the Special Features Index at the back of the book. Ask about additional residential and health care services that may be available. Fees and services subject to change; verify with facility.

ASSISTED LIVING AND PERSONAL CARE

Assisted living units: 0
Personal care is covered by the continuing care contract: No
Residents may receive personal care in independent living units: Yes

NURSING CARE: All-Inclusive Plan

Under this all-inclusive plan, unlimited nursing care is covered by the continuing care contract. When residents are in nursing care, they pay the same monthly fee they paid for their independent living unit.

Dual-certified beds: 59. Cost per day: private $103.00, semi-private $88.00.

Nursing beds are certified by both Medicare and Medicaid. Nonresidents may be admitted directly to the nursing care facility.

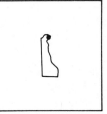

COKESBURY VILLAGE
Lancaster Pike and Loveville Road, Hockessin, DE 19707
Telephone: (302) 239-2371

Opened in 1978 • Mixed single-level, low-rise, and high-rise buildings on 52 acres • Current resident population is 375 • Located seven miles from Wilmington, DE • Waiting list may apply for some units

HOUSING AND SERVICES

Living Units	No.	Square Feet	No. of Persons	Entrance Fee	Monthly Fee
Studio	64	378–557	1	$30,000–$43,000	$1,009–$1,126
One Bedroom	52	759–782	1	$67,000–$69,000	$1,515–$1,570
			2	$67,000–$69,000	$1,901–$1,956
Two Bedroom	142	1,035–1,361	1	$82,000–$103,000	$1,871–$1,888
			2	$82,000–$103,000	$2,181–$2,274
Larger Units	0	——	——	——	——
Total	258 Units				

Entrance fee refunds decline over time.

These fees include three meals per day, weekly housekeeping, scheduled transportation, and utilities. Special features of this community are presented in the Special Features Index at the back of the book. Ask about additional residential and health care services that may be available. Fees and services subject to change; verify with facility.

ASSISTED LIVING AND PERSONAL CARE

Assisted living units: 30
Personal care is covered by the continuing care contract: Yes
Residents may receive personal care in independent living units: Yes
Nonresidents may be admitted directly to assisted living units: Yes

NURSING CARE: All-Inclusive Plan

Under this all-inclusive plan, unlimited nursing care is covered by the continuing care contract. When residents are in nursing care, they pay the basic monthly fee for the studio (smallest) unit.

Skilled beds: 55. Cost per day: private $72.00, semi-private $60.00.

Nursing beds are certified by Medicare. Nonresidents may be admitted directly to the nursing care facility.

DELAWARE

THE METHODIST COUNTRY HOUSE
4830 Kennett Pike, Wilmington, DE 19807
Telephone: (302) 654-5101

Opened in 1960 • Mixed single-level and low-rise buildings on 42 acres • Current resident population is 262 • Located seven miles from Wilmington, DE • Waiting list may apply for some units

AAHA
Member

HOUSING AND SERVICES

Living Units	No.	Square Feet	No. of Persons	Entrance Fee	Monthly Fee
Studio	148	261–430	1	$21,000–$28,000	$961–$1,435
One Bedroom	4	532	1	$42,000	$1,556
			2	$42,000	$1,921
Two Bedroom	1	724	1	$53,000	$1,677
			2	$53,000	$2,040
Larger Units	1	1,300	1	$75,000	$1,677
			2	$75,000	$2,040
Total		154 Units			

Entrance fee refunds decline over time.

These fees include three meals per day, housekeeping, and utilities. Special features of this community are presented in the Special Features Index at the back of the book. Ask about additional residential and health care services that may be available. Fees and services subject to change; verify with facility.

ASSISTED LIVING AND PERSONAL CARE

Assisted living units: 0
Personal care is covered by the continuing care contract: Yes
Residents may receive personal care in independent living units: Yes

NURSING CARE: All-Inclusive Plan

Under this all-inclusive plan, unlimited nursing care is covered by the continuing care contract. When residents are in nursing care, they pay the basic monthly fee for the studio (smallest) unit.

Skilled beds: 67. Cost per day: private $62.00, semi-private $55.00.

Nursing beds are certified by Medicare. Nonresidents may be admitted directly to the nursing care facility.

METHODIST MANOR HOUSE
1001 Middleford Road, Seaford, DE 19973
Telephone: (302) 629-4593

Opened in 1966 • Mixed single-level and low-rise buildings on 33 acres • Current resident population is 265 • Waiting list may apply for some units

HOUSING AND SERVICES

Living Units	No.	Square Feet	No. of Persons	Entrance Fee	Monthly Fee
Studio	176	144–550	1	$17,000–$34,000	$935–$1,214
One Bedroom	16	550–980	1	$32,000–$48,000	$1,214–$1,535
			2	$32,000–$48,000	$1,588–$1,842
Two Bedroom	2	836	1	$47,000	$1,279
			2	$47,000	$1,663
Larger Units	0	——	——	——	——
Total	194 Units				

Entrance fee refunds decline over time.

These fees include three meals per day, weekly housekeeping, scheduled transportation, and utilities. Special features of this community are presented in the Special Features Index at the back of the book. Ask about additional residential and health care services that may be available. Fees and services subject to change; verify with facility.

ASSISTED LIVING AND PERSONAL CARE

Assisted living units: 0
Personal care is covered by the continuing care contract: No
Residents may receive personal care in independent living units: Yes

NURSING CARE: All-Inclusive Plan

Under this all-inclusive plan, unlimited nursing care is covered by the continuing care contract. When residents are in nursing care, they pay the basic monthly fee for the studio (smallest) unit.

Skilled beds: 78. Cost per day: private $64.00, semi-private $56.00.

Nursing beds are certified by Medicare. Nonresidents may be admitted directly to the nursing care facility.

DISTRICT OF COLUMBIA

THOMAS HOUSE
1330 Massachusetts Avenue, N.W.
Washington, DC 20005
Telephone: (202) 628-3844

Opened in 1977 • One high-rise building on one acre
• Current resident population is 200 • Waiting list
may apply in some units

AAHA
Member

HOUSING AND SERVICES

Living Units	No.	Square Feet	No. of Persons	Entrance Fee	Monthly Fee
Studio	91	520	1	$21,350	$648
One Bedroom	112	700	1	$33,100	$689
			2		$1,120
Two Bedroom	0	——	——	——	——
Larger Units	0	——	——	——	——
Total	203 Units				

Entrance fee refunds decline over time.

These fees include one meal per day, biweekly housekeeping, scheduled transportation, and utilities. Special features of this community are presented in the Special Features Index at the back of the book. Ask about additional residential and health care services that may be available. Fees and services subject to change; verify with facility.

ASSISTED LIVING AND PERSONAL CARE

Assisted living units: 6
Personal care is covered by the continuing care contract: No
Residents may receive personal care in independent living units: Yes
Nonresidents may be admitted directly to assisted living units: No

NURSING CARE: Modified Plan

Under this modified plan, 15 or fewer days are covered by the continuing care contract. Once residents move permanently to the nursing unit, they pay the full per diem rate for nursing care.

Intermediate beds. Cost per day: private $84.00, semi-private $74.50.

Skilled beds: 53. Cost per day: private $100.75, semi-private $91.25.

Nursing beds are certified by Medicaid. Nonresidents may be admitted directly to the nursing care facility.

ABBEY DELRAY
2000 Lowson Boulevard, Delray Beach, FL 33445
Telephone: (305) 278-3249

Opened in 1979 • Mixed single-level and low-rise
buildings on 26 acres • Current resident population is
457 • Waiting list may apply for some units

AAHA
Member

HOUSING AND SERVICES

Living Units	No.	Square Feet	No. of Persons	Entrance Fee	Monthly Fee
Studio	31	400	1	$39,000	$551
One Bedroom	160	590	1	$55,000	$712
			2		$1,003
Two Bedroom	132	880	1	$71,300	$833
			2		$1,124
Larger Units	37	1,100	1	$88,300	$901
			2		$1,192
Total	360 Units				

Entrance fee refunds decline over time.

These fees include one meal per day, weekly housekeeping, scheduled transportation, and utilities. Special features of this community are presented in the Special Features Index at the back of the book. Ask about additional residential and health care services that may be available. Fees and services subject to change; verify with facility.

ASSISTED LIVING AND PERSONAL CARE

Assisted living units: 0
Personal care is covered by the continuing care contract: No
Residents may receive personal care in independent living units: Yes

NURSING CARE: All-Inclusive Plan

Under this all-inclusive plan, unlimited nursing care is covered by the continuing care contract. When residents are in nursing care, they pay the same monthly fee they paid for their independent living unit.

Intermediate beds: 76. Cost per day: private $85.00, semi-private $66.00.

Skilled beds: 24. Cost per day: semi-private $69.00.

Nursing beds are certified by both Medicare and Medicaid. Nonresidents may be admitted directly to the nursing care facility.

ASBURY TOWERS
1533 Fourth Avenue West, Bradenton, FL 33505
Telephone: (813) 747-1881

Opened in 1966 • One high-rise building • Current
resident population is 140 • Waiting list may apply for
some units

AAHA
Member

HOUSING AND SERVICES

Living Units	No.	Square Feet	No. of Persons	Entrance Fee	Monthly Fee
Studio	72	330–352	1	$16,500–$20,500	$569–$683
One Bedroom	32	598–660	1	$21,500–$37,000	$720–$1,023
			2	$21,500–$37,000	$1,027–$1,330
Two Bedroom	0	——	——	——	——
Larger Units	0	——	——	——	——
Total	104 Units				

Entrance fee refunds decline over time.

These fees include three meals per day, weekly housekeeping, and utilities.
Special features of this community are presented in the Special Features Index
at the back of the book. Ask about additional residential and health care services
that may be available. Fees and services subject to change; verify with facility.

ASSISTED LIVING AND PERSONAL CARE

Assisted living units: 10
Personal care is covered by the continuing care contract: Yes
Residents may receive personal care in independent living units: Yes
Nonresidents may be admitted directly to assisted living units: No

NURSING CARE: Modified Plan

Under this modified plan, 30 free days of care are covered by the continuing
care contract. Once residents move permanently to the nursing unit, they pay
the full per diem rate for nursing care.

Skilled beds: 34. Cost per day: semi-private $22.00.

Nursing beds are not certified by Medicare or Medicaid. Nonresidents may not
be admitted directly to the nursing care facility.

AZALEA TRACE
10100 Hillview Road, Pensacola, FL 32514
Telephone: (904) 474-0880

Opened in 1981 • Mixed single-level and low-rise
buildings on 56 acres • Current resident population is
332 • Waiting list may apply for some units

AAHA
Member

HOUSING AND SERVICES

Living Units	No.	Square Feet	No. of Persons	Entrance Fee	Monthly Fee
Studio	16	486	1	$38,450	$578
One Bedroom	122	867	1	$64,580	$681
			2		$944
Two Bedroom	104	1,147	1	$86,680	$857
			2		$1,120
Larger Units	0	——	——	——	——
Total	242 Units				

Residents have a choice of entrance fee refund plans.

These fees include one meal per day, weekly housekeeping, and scheduled transportation. Special features of this community are presented in the Special Features Index at the back of the book. Ask about additional residential and health care services that may be available. Fees and services subject to change; verify with facility.

ASSISTED LIVING AND PERSONAL CARE

Assisted living units: 0
Personal care is covered by the continuing care contract: No
Residents may receive personal care in independent living units: No

NURSING CARE: All-Inclusive Plan

Under this all-inclusive plan, unlimited nursing care is covered by the continuing care contract. When residents are in nursing care, they pay the same monthly fee they paid for their independent living unit.

Skilled beds: 90. Cost per day: private $96.00, semi-private $54.00.

Nursing beds are certified by Medicare. Nonresidents may be admitted directly to the nursing care facility.

FLORIDA

BAY VILLAGE OF SARASOTA
8400 Vamo Road, Sarasota, FL 33581
Telephone: (813) 966-5611

Opened in 1975 • One high-rise building on 15 acres • Current resident population is 449 • Waiting list may apply for some units

AAHA
Member

HOUSING AND SERVICES

Living Units	No.	Square Feet	No. of Persons	Entrance Fee	Monthly Fee
Studio	110	459	1	$29,900–$39,900	$430–$640
One Bedroom	133	689	1	$47,900–$69,200	$575
			2	$54,600–$75,900	$800
Two Bedroom	87	1,149	1	$79,800–$99,800	$775
			2	$86,500–$106,500	$820
Larger Units	0	—	—	—	—
Total		330 Units			

Entrance fee refunds decline over time.

These fees include one meal per day, scheduled transportation, and utilities. Special features of this community are presented in the Special Features Index at the back of the book. Ask about additional residential and health care services that may be available. Fees and services subject to change; verify with facility.

ASSISTED LIVING AND PERSONAL CARE

Assisted living units: 0
Personal care is covered by the continuing care contract: No
Residents may receive personal care in independent living units: No

NURSING CARE: All-Inclusive Plan

Under this all-inclusive plan, unlimited nursing care is covered by the continuing care contract.

Skilled beds: 107. Cost per day: private $61.00, semi-private $41.00.

Nursing beds are not certified by Medicare or Medicaid. Nonresidents may be admitted directly to the nursing care facility.

BRADENTON MANOR AND GARDEN APARTMENTS

1700 21st Avenue West, Bradenton, FL 33505
Telephone: (813) 748-4161

Opened in 1961 • Mixed single-level, low-rise, and high-rise buildings on five acres • Current resident population is 241 • Waiting list may apply for some units

AAHA
Member

HOUSING AND SERVICES

Living Units	No.	Square Feet	No. of Persons	Entrance Fee	Monthly Fee
Studio	110	300–485	1	$24,000–$34,000	$460–$635
One Bedroom	40	600–602	1	$38,000–$45,250	$690–$1,025
			2	$41,500	$790–$1,025
Two Bedroom	7	916	1	$64,600	$820
			2		$920
Larger Units	0	——	——	——	——
Total	157 Units				

Residents have a choice of entrance fee refund plans.

These fees include three meals per day, weekly housekeeping, scheduled transportation, and utilities. Special features of this community are presented in the Special Features Index at the back of the book. Ask about additional residential and health care services that may be available. Fees and services subject to change; verify with facility.

ASSISTED LIVING AND PERSONAL CARE

Assisted living units: 16
Personal care is covered by the continuing care contract: Yes
Residents may receive personal care in independent living units: No
Nonresidents may be admitted directly to assisted living units: Yes

NURSING CARE: Modified Plan

Under this modified plan, 15 or fewer days are covered by the continuing care contract. Once residents move permanently to the nursing unit, they pay about 75 percent of the per diem rate for nursing care.

Skilled beds: 59. Cost per day: semi-private $49.00.

Nursing beds are not certified by Medicare or Medicaid. Nonresidents may be admitted directly to the nursing care facility.

CANTERBURY TOWER
3501 Bayshore Boulevard, Tampa, FL 33629
Telephone: (813) 837-1083

Opened in 1977 • One high-rise building on three acres • Current resident population is 148 • Waiting list may apply for some units

AAHA
Member

HOUSING AND SERVICES

Living Units	No.	Square Feet	No. of Persons	Entrance Fee	Monthly Fee
Studio	25	505	1	$35,700	$599
One Bedroom	29	808	1	$57,645	$797
			2		$1,277
Two Bedroom	71	1,071–1,350	1	$77,700–$86,783	$993
			2		$1,473
Larger Units	0	——	——	——	——
Total		125 Units			

Entrance fee refunds decline over time.

These fees include one meal per day, weekly housekeeping, scheduled transportation, and utilities. Special features of this community are presented in the Special Features Index at the back of the book. Ask about additional residential and health care services that may be available. Fees and services subject to change; verify with facility.

ASSISTED LIVING AND PERSONAL CARE

Assisted living units: 0
Personal care is covered by the continuing care contract: No
Residents may receive personal care in independent living units: Yes

NURSING CARE: All-Inclusive Plan

Under this all-inclusive plan, unlimited nursing care is covered by the continuing care contract. When residents are in nursing care, they pay the same monthly fee they paid for their independent living unit.

Skilled beds: 40. Cost per day: private $80.00, semi-private $62.00.

Nursing beds are certified by Medicare. Nonresidents may be admitted directly to the nursing care facility.

CENTRAL PARK LODGE
9309 South Orange Blossom Trail, Highway 441
Orlando, FL 32821
Telephone: (305) 859-7990

Opened in 1980 • Mixed single-level, low-rise, and high-rise buildings on 16 acres • Current resident population is 150 • Waiting list may apply for some units

HOUSING AND SERVICES

Living Units	No.	Square Feet	No. of Persons	Entrance Fee	Monthly Fee
Studio	74	384	1	$25,000	$620
One Bedroom	54	768	1	$41,000	$880
			2	$46,000	$1,125
Two Bedroom	5	1,152	1	$57,000	$1,140
			2	$62,000	$1,385
Larger Units	0	——	——	——	——
Total	133 Units				

Residents have a choice of entrance fee refund plans.

These fees include one meal per day, weekly housekeeping, scheduled transportation, and utilities. Special features of this community are presented in the Special Features Index at the back of the book. Ask about additional residential and health care services that may be available. Fees and services subject to change; verify with facility.

ASSISTED LIVING AND PERSONAL CARE

Assisted living units: 28
Personal care is covered by the continuing care contract: No
Residents may receive personal care in independent living units: No
Nonresidents may be admitted directly to assisted living units: No

NURSING CARE: Modified Plan

Under this modified plan, 16–59 days of nursing care per year are covered by the continuing care contract. Once residents move permanently to the nursing unit, they pay the full per diem rate for nursing care.

Dual-certified beds: 120. Cost per day: private $82.50, semi-private $63.50.
Nursing beds are certified by both Medicare and Medicaid. Nonresidents may be admitted directly to the nursing care facility.

COVENANT VILLAGE OF FLORIDA
9201 West Broward Boulevard, Plantation, FL 33324
Telephone: (305) 472-2860

Opened in 1972 • Mixed single-level, low-rise, and high-rise buildings on 19 acres • Current resident population is 341 • Waiting list may apply for some units

AAHA Member

HOUSING AND SERVICES

Living Units	No.	Square Feet	No. of Persons	Entrance Fee	Monthly Fee
Studio	47	500	1	$44,000	$550
One Bedroom	146	700	1	$56,000	$660
			2	$56,000	$935
Two Bedroom	82	1,030	1	$78,000	$730
			2	$78,000	$1,030
Larger Units	0	—	—	—	—
Total	275 Units				

Entrance fee refunds decline over time.

These fees include one meal per day, biweekly housekeeping, scheduled transportation, and utilities. Special features of this community are presented in the Special Features Index at the back of the book. Ask about additional residential and health care services that may be available. Fees and services subject to change; verify with facility.

ASSISTED LIVING AND PERSONAL CARE

Assisted living units: 24
Personal care is covered by the continuing care contract: Yes
Residents may receive personal care in independent living units: No
Nonresidents may be admitted directly to assisted living units: Yes

NURSING CARE: Modified Plan

Under this modified plan, 60 days or more over a resident's lifetime are covered by the continuing care contract. Once residents move permanently to the nursing unit, they pay 90 percent of the per diem rate for nursing care.

Skilled beds: 120. Cost per day: private $80.00, semi-private $66.00.

Nursing beds are certified by both Medicare and Medicaid. Nonresidents may be admitted directly to the nursing care facility.

CROSS KEYS VILLAGE
2026 Southwest 80th Avenue, North Lauderdale, FL 33068
Telephone: (305) 945-1709

Opened in 1987 • Mixed single-level and low-rise buildings on 53 acres • Immediate availability

HOUSING AND SERVICES

Living Units	No.	Square Feet	No. of Persons	Entrance Fee	Monthly Fee
Studio	0	——	——	——	——
One Bedroom		880–977	1, 2	$14,750–$19,750	$575–$940
Two Bedroom		1,192–1,444	1, 2	$14,750–$19,750	$575–$940
Larger Units	0	——	——	——	——
Total	630 Units				

Entrance fee refunds decline over time.

These fees include one meal per day, weekly housekeeping, and scheduled transportation. Special features of this community are presented in the Special Features Index at the back of the book. Ask about additional residential and health care services that may be available. Fees and services subject to change; verify with facility.

ASSISTED LIVING AND PERSONAL CARE

Assisted living units: 0
Personal care is covered by the continuing care contract: No
Residents may receive personal care in independent living units: No

NURSING CARE: All-Inclusive Plan

Under this all-inclusive plan, unlimited nursing care is covered by the continuing care contract. When residents are in nursing care, they pay the same monthly fee they paid for their independent living unit.

Skilled beds: 120. Cost per day: rates for nonresidents not yet set.

Nursing beds are certified by both Medicare and Medicaid. Nonresidents may be admitted directly to the nursing care facility.

EAST RIDGE RETIREMENT VILLAGE
19301 Southwest 87th Avenue, Miami, FL 33157
Telephone: (305) 238-2623

Opened in 1962 • Predominantly single-level/garden apartments on 76 acres • Current resident population is 377 • Waiting list may apply for some units

AAHA
Member

HOUSING AND SERVICES

Living Units	No.	Square Feet	No. of Persons	Entrance Fee	Monthly Fee
Studio	44	325	1	$21,100	$500
One Bedroom	154	578–672	1	$27,900	$637–$642
			2	$38,500	$843–$845
Two Bedroom	91	866–1,344	1	$43,700	$774–$952
			2	$65,600	$977–$1,155
Larger Units	0	——	——	——	——
Total	289 Units				

Entrance fee refunds decline over time.

These fees include one meal per day, weekly housekeeping, and utilities. Special features of this community are presented in the Special Features Index at the back of the book. Ask about additional residential and health care services that may be available. Fees and services subject to change; verify with facility.

ASSISTED LIVING AND PERSONAL CARE

Assisted living units: 32
Personal care is covered by the continuing care contract: No
Residents may receive personal care in independent living units: No
Nonresidents may be admitted directly to assisted living units: No

NURSING CARE: All-Inclusive Plan

Under this all-inclusive plan, unlimited nursing care is covered by the continuing care contract. When residents are in nursing care, they pay the same monthly fee they paid for their independent living unit.

Skilled beds: 60. Cost per day: semi-private $65.00.

Nursing beds are certified by Medicare. Nonresidents may be admitted directly to the nursing care facility.

EDGEWATER POINTE ESTATES
23315 Blue Water Circle, Boca Raton, FL 33433
Telephone: (305) 391-6305

Opened in 1983 • Predominantly high-rise buildings on 38 acres • Current resident population is 530 • Waiting list may apply for some units

HOUSING AND SERVICES

Living Units	No.	Square Feet	No. of Persons	Entrance Fee	Monthly Fee
Studio	30	641	1	$47,500	$588
One Bedroom	91	726	1	$68,500	$632
			2		$1,074
Two Bedroom	179	1,036	1	$90,500	$716
			2		$1,217
Larger Units	60	1,346	1	$110,000	$753
			2		$1,258

Total   360 Units

Entrance fee refunds decline over time.

These fees include two meals per day, scheduled transportation, and utilities. Special features of this community are presented in the Special Features Index at the back of the book. Ask about additional residential and health care services that may be available. Fees and services subject to change; verify with facility.

ASSISTED LIVING AND PERSONAL CARE

Assisted living units: 44
Personal care is covered by the continuing care contract: Yes
Residents may receive personal care in independent living units: No
Nonresidents may be admitted directly to assisted living units: No

NURSING CARE: All-Inclusive Plan

Under this all-inclusive plan, unlimited nursing care is covered by the continuing care contract. When residents are in nursing care, they pay the same monthly fee they paid for their independent living unit.

Skilled beds: 60. Cost per day: private $91.00, semi-private $67.00.

Nursing beds are certified by Medicare. Nonresidents may be admitted directly to the nursing care facility.

FLORIDA UNITED PRESBYTERIAN HOMES
16 Lake Hunter Drive, Lakeland, FL 33803
Telephone: (813) 688-5521

Opened in 1955 • Mixed single-level and low-rise
buildings on 22 acres • Current resident population is
327 • Waiting list

AAHA
Member

HOUSING AND SERVICES

Living Units	No.	Square Feet	No. of Persons	Entrance Fee	Monthly Fee
Studio	20	335–387	1	$12,000–$16,650	$340–$365
One Bedroom	20	600–800	1	$20,000–$37,500	$115–$422
			2	$20,000–$37,500	$148–$544
Two Bedroom	50	803–1,200	1	$33,450–$71,000	$141–$487
			2	$33,450–$71,000	$172–$611
Larger Units	1	2,000	1	$85,000	$235
			2	$85,000	$253
Total	91* Units				

Entrance fee refunds decline over time.

*This section combines data on two distinct levels of care. Consult facility for specific services.

Special features of this community are presented in the Special Features Index at the back of the book. Ask about additional residential and health care services that may be available. Fees and services subject to change; verify with facility.

ASSISTED LIVING AND PERSONAL CARE

Assisted living units: 25
Personal care is covered by the continuing care contract: Yes
Residents may receive personal care in independent living units: No
Nonresidents may be admitted directly to assisted living units: Yes

NURSING CARE: Modified Plan

Under this modified plan, the continuing care contract guarantees residents access to nursing care at a discounted per diem rate.

Dual-certified beds: 150. Cost per day: private $73.20, semi-private $52.15.

Nursing beds are certified by Medicare and Medicaid. Nonresidents may be admitted directly to the nursing care facility.

FREEDOM VILLAGE
6401 21st Street, Bradenton, FL 33529
Telephone: (813) 792-7276

Opened in 1984 • Mixed single-level, low-rise, and high-rise buildings on 32 acres • Current resident population is 400 • Waiting list may apply for some units

HOUSING AND SERVICES

Living Units	No.	Square Feet	No. of Persons	Entrance Fee	Monthly Fee
Studio	39	525	1	$34,900	$650
One Bedroom	395	728–1,114	1	$46,400–$100,000	$750–$960
			2		$1,050–$1,260
Two Bedroom	115	1,256–	1	$84,700	$950
		1,425	2		$1,250–$1,360
Larger Units	0	——	——	——	——
Total	549 Units				

Entrance fees are partially refundable.

These fees include one meal per day, weekly housekeeping, scheduled transportation, and utilities. Special features of this community are presented in the Special Features Index at the back of the book. Ask about additional residential and health care services that may be available. Fees and services subject to change; verify with facility.

ASSISTED LIVING AND PERSONAL CARE

Assisted living units: 212
Personal care is covered by the continuing care contract: Yes
Residents may receive personal care in independent living units: No
Nonresidents may be admitted directly to assisted living units: Yes

NURSING CARE: Modified Plan

Under this modified plan, 22 days per quarter (88 per year) and 360 days over the resident's lifetime are covered by the continuing care contract. Once residents move permanently to the nursing unit, they pay the full per diem rate for nursing care.

Skilled beds: 180. Cost per day: private $80.00, semi-private $51.00.

Dual-certified beds: 60. Cost per day: private $105.00, semi-private $105.00.

Nursing beds are certified by both Medicare and Medicaid. Nonresidents may be admitted directly to the nursing care facility.

GULF COAST VILLAGE
1333 Santa Barbara Boulevard, Cape Coral, FL 33914
Telephone: (813) 772-1333

Opening in 1988 • One high-rise and several one-story buildings on 20 acres • Immediate availability

AAHA Member

HOUSING AND SERVICES

Living Units	No.	Square Feet	No. of Persons	Entrance Fee	Monthly Fee
Studio	11	432	1	$37,800–$56,700	$385
One Bedroom	148	575–780	1	$50,400–$102,450	$515–$700
			2	$53,400–$105,450	$815–$1,000
Two Bedroom	33	862–1,006	1	$75,600–$132,300	$770–$900
			2	$78,600–$135,300	$1,070–$1,200
Larger Units	0	—	—	—	—
Total	192 Units				

Residents have a choice of entrance fee refund plans.

These fees include one meal per day, biweekly housekeeping, scheduled transportation, and utilities. Special features of this community are presented in the Special Features Index at the back of the book. Ask about additional residential and health care services that may be available. Fees and services subject to change; verify with facility.

ASSISTED LIVING AND PERSONAL CARE

Assisted living units: 39
Personal care is covered by the continuing care contract: Yes
Residents may receive personal care in independent living units: No
Nonresidents may be admitted directly to assisted living units: Yes

NURSING CARE: Modified Plan

Under this modified plan, 15 or fewer days per year are covered by the continuing care contract. Once residents move permanently to the nursing unit, they pay the full per diem rate for nursing care.

Intermediate beds: 51. Cost per day: rates are not yet set.

Skilled beds: 48. Cost per day: rates are not yet set.

Nursing beds are certified by Medicare. Nonresidents may be admitted directly to the nursing care facility.

INDIAN RIVER ESTATES
2250 Indian Creek Boulevard West, Vero Beach, FL 32960.
Telephone: (305) 562-7400

Opened in 1986 • Mixed single-level and low-rise buildings on 100 acres • Current resident population is 239 • Immediate availability

HOUSING AND SERVICES

Living Units	No.	Square Feet	No. of Persons	Entrance Fee	Monthly Fee
Studio	30	——	1	$50,000	$588
One Bedroom	90	——	1	$72,000	$602
			2		$987
Two Bedroom	180	——	1	$95,000	$632
			2		$1,025
Larger Units	60	——	1	$119,000	$669
			2		$1,067

Total   360 Units

Entrance fee refunds decline over time.

These fees include two meals per day, scheduled transportation, and utilities. Special features of this community are presented in the Special Features Index at the back of the book. Ask about additional residential and health care services that may be available. Fees and services subject to change; verify with facility.

ASSISTED LIVING AND PERSONAL CARE

Assisted living units: 40
Personal care is covered by the continuing care contract: Yes
Residents may receive personal care in independent living units: Yes
Nonresidents may be admitted directly to assisted living units: Yes

NURSING CARE: All-Inclusive Plan

Under this all-inclusive plan, unlimited nursing care is covered by the continuing care contract. When residents are in nursing care, they pay the same monthly fee they paid for their independent living unit.

Skilled beds: 60. Cost per day: private $91.00, semi-private $68.00.

Nursing beds are certified by Medicare. Nonresidents may be admitted directly to the nursing care facility.

FLORIDA

JOHN KNOX VILLAGE OF CENTRAL FLORIDA
101 Northlake Drive, Orange City, FL 32763
Telephone: (904) 775-3840

Opened in 1978 • Predominantly single-level/garden apartments on 83 acres • Current resident population is 678 • Waiting list may apply for some units

AAHA
Member

HOUSING AND SERVICES

Living Units	No.	Square Feet	No. of Persons	Entrance Fee	Monthly Fee
Studio	82	347	1	$26,500	$522
One Bedroom	204	520	1	$51,500	$627
			2	$61,500	$958
Two Bedroom	191	640	1	$62,500	$672
			2	$72,500	$998
Larger Units	15	936	1	$70,500	$747
			2	$80,500	$1,073
Total	492 Units				

Entrance fee refunds decline over time.

These fees include one meal per day, biweekly housekeeping, scheduled transportation, and utilities. Special features of this community are presented in the Special Features Index at the back of the book. Ask about additional residential and health care services that may be available. Fees and services subject to change; verify with facility.

ASSISTED LIVING AND PERSONAL CARE

Assisted living units: 18
Personal care is covered by the continuing care contract: Yes
Residents may receive personal care in independent living units: No
Nonresidents may be admitted directly to assisted living units: No

NURSING CARE: All-Inclusive Plan

Under this all-inclusive plan, unlimited nursing care is covered by the continuing care contract. When residents are in nursing care, they pay the same monthly fee they paid for their independent living unit.

Skilled beds: 120. Cost per day: private $70.00, semi-private $63.50.

Nursing beds are certified by Medicare. Nonresidents may be admitted directly to the nursing care facility.

JOHN KNOX VILLAGE OF FLORIDA
651 Southwest Sixth Street
Pompano Beach, FL 33060
Telephone: (305) 782-1300

Opened in 1967 • Mixed single-level, low-rise, and high-rise buildings on 55 acres • Current resident population is 886 • Waiting list may apply for some units

HOUSING AND SERVICES

Living Units	No.	Square Feet	No. of Persons	Entrance Fee	Monthly Fee
Studio	121	375–562	1	$32,500–$42,000	$614
One Bedroom	257	700–790	1	$56,000–$59,500	$669
			2	$56,000–$59,500	$930
Two Bedroom	272	1,000– 1,400	1	$77,500–$86,000	$703
			2	$77,500–$86,000	$1,021
Larger Units	0	——	——	——	——
Total	650 Units				

Entrance fee refunds decline over time.

These fees include 15 meals per month, biweekly housekeeping, scheduled transportation, and utilities. Special features of this community are presented in the Special Features Index at the back of the book. Ask about additional residential and health care services that may be available. Fees and services subject to change; verify with facility.

ASSISTED LIVING AND PERSONAL CARE
Assisted living units: 28
Personal care is covered by the continuing care contract: Yes
Residents may receive personal care in independent living units: No
Nonresidents may be admitted directly to assisted living units: No

NURSING CARE: All-Inclusive Plan

Under this all-inclusive plan, unlimited nursing care is covered by the continuing care contract. When residents are in nursing care, they pay the same monthly fee they paid for their independent living unit.

Skilled beds: 120. Cost per day: not applicable.

Nursing beds are certified by both Medicare and Medicaid. Nonresidents may not be admitted directly to the nursing care facility.

LAKE POINTE WOODS
7979 South Tamiami Trail, Sarasota, FL 33581
Telephone: (813) 923-4944

Opened in 1985 • Mixed single-level and low-rise buildings on 53 acres • Current resident population is 175 • Waiting list may apply for some units

HOUSING AND SERVICES

Living Units	No.	Square Feet	No. of Persons	Entrance Fee	Monthly Fee
Studio	2	500	1	$69,900	$460
One Bedroom	120	800	1, 2	$114,900	$653
Two Bedroom	80	1,100	1, 2	$154,900	$776
Larger Units	10	1,600	1, 2	$249,800	$976
Total	212 Units				

Entrance fee refunds decline over time.

These fees include one meal per day, housekeeping, scheduled transportation, and utilities. Special features of this community are presented in the Special Features Index at the back of the book. Ask about additional residential and health care services that may be available. Fees and services subject to change; verify with facility.

ASSISTED LIVING AND PERSONAL CARE

Assisted living units: 100
Personal care is covered by the continuing care contract: No
Residents may receive personal care in independent living units: No
Nonresidents may be admitted directly to assisted living units: Yes

NURSING CARE: Modified Plan

Under this modified plan, 16-59 days are covered by the continuing care contract. Once residents move permanently to the nursing unit, they pay the full per diem rate for nursing care.

Dual-certified beds: 53. Cost per day: private $105.00, semi-private $65.00.

Nursing beds are certified by Medicare. Nonresidents may be admitted directly to the nursing care facility.

MEASE MANOR
700 Mease Plaza, Dunedin, FL 33528
Telephone: (813) 733-1161

Opened in 1964 • One high-rise building on 12 acres
• Current resident population is 400 • Immediate
availability

AAHA
Member

HOUSING AND SERVICES

Living Units	No.	Square Feet	No. of Persons	Entrance Fee	Monthly Fee
Studio	230	351	1	$6,000–$10,000	$252–$490
One Bedroom	139	715	1	$18,000	$471
			2	$26,000	$562
Two Bedroom	18	1,105	1, 2	$30,000	$615–$707
Larger Units	0	——	——	——	——
Total		387 Units			

Entrance fee refunds decline over time.

These fees include weekly housekeeping, scheduled transportation, and utilities. Special features of this community are presented in the Special Features Index at the back of the book. Ask about additional residential and health care services that may be available. Fees and services subject to change; verify with facility.

ASSISTED LIVING AND PERSONAL CARE

Assisted living units: 0
Personal care is covered by the continuing care contract: No
Residents may receive personal care in independent living units: No

NURSING CARE: Fee-for-Service Plan

Under this fee-for-service plan, emergency or temporary infirmary care is covered by the continuing care contract. Once residents move permanently to the nursing unit, they pay somewhat less than the per diem rate for nursing care.

Intermediate beds: 40.*

Skilled beds: 60.*

*A nursing care facility is expected to open in 1988. Rates not yet set.

MOORINGS PARK
120 Moorings Park Drive, Naples, FL 33942
Telephone: (813) 261-1616

Opened in 1981 • Mixed single-level, low-rise, and high-rise buildings on 53 acres • Current resident population is 420 • Waiting list may apply for some units

AAHA
Member

HOUSING AND SERVICES

Living Units	No.	Square Feet	No. of Persons	Entrance Fee	Monthly Fee
Studio	0	——	——	——	——
One Bedroom	72	780	1	$76,500	$947
			2		$1,325
Two Bedroom	166	1,452	1	$140,000	$1,325
			2		$1,703
Larger Units	46	2,006	1	$160,000	$1,452
			2		$1,830
Total		284 Units			

Entrance fee refunds decline over time.

These fees include one meal per day, housekeeping, scheduled transportation, and utilities. Special features of this community are presented in the Special Features Index at the back of the book. Ask about additional residential and health care services that may be available. Fees and services subject to change; verify with facility.

ASSISTED LIVING AND PERSONAL CARE

Assisted living units: 0
Personal care is covered by the continuing care contract: No
Residents may receive personal care in independent living units: Yes

NURSING CARE: All-Inclusive Plan

Under this all-inclusive plan, unlimited nursing care is covered by the continuing care contract. When residents are in nursing care, they pay the same monthly fee they paid for their independent living unit.

Skilled beds: 60. Cost per day: private $90.00, semi-private $73.00.

Nursing beds are certified by Medicare. Nonresidents may be admitted directly to the nursing care facility.

OAK COVE RETIREMENT AND HEALTH CENTER
210 South Osceola Avenue, Clearwater, FL 33516
Telephone: (813) 441-3763

Opened in 1975 • One high-rise building on five acres • Current resident population is 200 • Immediate availability

HOUSING AND SERVICES

Living Units	No.	Square Feet	No. of Persons	Entrance Fee	Monthly Fee
Studio	107	410	1	$33,000	$645–$945
One Bedroom	86	492	1	$55,000	$850
			2	$55,000	$1,150
Two Bedroom	39	615–820	1	$66,000	$1,000
			2	$66,000	$1,300
Larger Units	2	902	1	$88,000	$1,495
			2	$88,000	$1,795

Total   234 Units

Residents have a choice of entrance fee refund plans.

These fees include one meal per day, weekly housekeeping, scheduled transportation, and utilities. Special features of this community are presented in the Special Features Index at the back of the book. Ask about additional residential and health care services that may be available. Fees and services subject to change; verify with facility.

ASSISTED LIVING AND PERSONAL CARE

Assisted living units: 0
Personal care is covered by the continuing care contract: No
Residents may receive personal care in independent living units: Yes

NURSING CARE: Modified Plan

Under this modified plan, 60 days or more per year are covered by the continuing care contract. Once residents move permanently to the nursing unit, they pay 80 percent of the per diem rate for nursing care.

Skilled beds: 56. Cost per day: private $75.00, semi-private $65.00.

Nursing beds are certified by Medicare. Nonresidents may be admitted directly to the nursing care facility.

ORLANDO LUTHERAN TOWERS
300 East Church Street, Orlando, FL 32801
Telephone: (305) 425-1033

Opened in 1980 • One high-rise building on two acres
• Current resident population is 321 • Waiting list
may apply for some units

AAHA
Member

HOUSING AND SERVICES

Living Units	No.	Square Feet	No. of Persons	Entrance Fee	Monthly Fee
Studio	96	475	1	$33,000	$660
One Bedroom	152	600	1	$51,000	$864
			2	$58,000	——
Two Bedroom	16	1,075	1	$72,000	$1,250
			2	$79,000	——
Larger Units	0	——	——	——	——
Total	264 Units				

Entrance fee refunds decline over time.

These fees include one meal per day, weekly housekeeping, and utilities. Special features of this community are presented in the Special Features Index at the back of the book. Ask about additional residential and health care services that may be available. Fees and services subject to change; verify with facility.

ASSISTED LIVING AND PERSONAL CARE

Assisted living units: 0
Personal care is covered by the continuing care contract: Yes
Residents may receive personal care in independent living units: Yes

NURSING CARE: Modified Plan

Under this modified plan, 35 days per year are covered by the continuing care contract. Once residents move permanently to the nursing unit, they pay 73 percent of the per diem rate for nursing care.

Dual-certified beds: 60. Cost per day: private $71.00, semi-private $65.00.

Nursing beds are certified by Medicaid. Nonresidents may be admitted directly to the nursing care facility.

THE PALMS
725 South Pine Street, Sebring, FL 33870
Telephone: (813) 338-0161

Opened in 1985 • Predominantly high-rise buildings
on three acres • Current resident population is 166 •
Immediate availability

HOUSING AND SERVICES

Living Units	No.	Square Feet	No. of Persons	Entrance Fee	Monthly Fee
Studio	24	414	1	$35,000	$690
One Bedroom	78	508–650	1	$51,250	$776
			2		$1,050
Two Bedroom	12	775	1	$71,000	$890
			2	$76,000	$1,165
Larger Units	0	—	—	—	—
Total	114 Units				

Entrance fee refunds decline over time.

These fees include one meal per day, biweekly housekeeping, scheduled transportation, and utilities. Special features of this community are presented in the Special Features Index at the back of the book. Ask about additional residential and health care services that may be available. Fees and services subject to change; verify with facility.

ASSISTED LIVING AND PERSONAL CARE

Assisted living units: 26
Personal care is covered by the continuing care contract: Yes
Residents may receive personal care in independent living units: No
Nonresidents may be admitted directly to assisted living units: Yes

NURSING CARE: Modified Plan

Under this modified plan, 15 or fewer days per year are covered by the continuing care contract. Once residents move permanently to the nursing unit, they pay 80 percent of the per diem rate for nursing care.

Skilled beds: 104. Cost per day: private $70.00, semi-private $60.00.

Nursing beds are certified by both Medicare and Medicaid. Nonresidents may be admitted directly to the nursing care facility.

FLORIDA

PALM SHORES RETIREMENT CENTER
830 North Shore Drive, Saint Petersburg, FL 33701
Telephone: (813) 894-2102

Opened in 1966 • Predominantly high-rise buildings on one acre • Current resident population is 243 • Long waiting list; apply well in advance

AAHA Member

HOUSING AND SERVICES

Living Units	No.	Square Feet	No. of Persons	Entrance Fee	Monthly Fee
Studio	124	360–380	1	$16,470–$22,135	$538
One Bedroom	40	470–490	1	$21,438–$27,378	$753
			2	$23,438–$29,378	$854
Two Bedroom	14	750–1,400	1	$34,313–$93,450	$961
			2	$36,313–$95,450	$1,064
Larger Units	0	—	—	—	—
Total	178 Units				

Entrance fee refunds decline over time.

These fees include one meal per day, weekly housekeeping, and utilities. Special features of this community are presented in the Special Features Index at the back of the book. Ask about additional residential and health care services that may be available. Fees and services subject to change; verify with facility.

ASSISTED LIVING AND PERSONAL CARE

Assisted living units: 0
Personal care is covered by the continuing care contract: Yes
Residents may receive personal care in independent living units: Yes

NURSING CARE: All-Inclusive Plan

Under this all-inclusive plan, unlimited nursing care is covered by the continuing care contract. When residents are in nursing care, they pay the same monthly fee they paid for their independent living unit.

Skilled beds: 42. Cost per day: not applicable.

Nursing beds are not certified by Medicare or Medicaid. Nonresidents may not be admitted directly to the nursing care facility.

PLYMOUTH HARBOR
700 John Ringling Boulevard, Sarasota, FL 33577
Telephone: (813) 365-2600

Opened in 1966 • Predominantly high-rise buildings on 16 acres • Current resident population is 287 • Waiting list may apply for some units

AAHA
Member

HOUSING AND SERVICES

Living Units	No.	Square Feet	No. of Persons	Entrance Fee	Monthly Fee
Studio	77	525	1	$28,000–$37,000	$690–$765
One Bedroom	81	650	1	$58,000–$73,000	$780–$950
			2		$880–$1,050
Two Bedroom	70	1,400	1	$90,000–$105,000	$1,060–$1,375
			2		$1,160–$1,475
Larger Units	11	2,000	1	$144,000+	$1,850–$1,900
			2		$1,950–$2,000

Total   239 Units

Entrance fee refunds decline over time.

These fees include three meals per day (studio units only), weekly housekeeping, scheduled transportation, and utilities. Special features of this community are presented in the Special Features Index at the back of the book. Ask about additional residential and health care services that may be available. Fees and services subject to change; verify with facility.

ASSISTED LIVING AND PERSONAL CARE

Assisted living units: 0
Personal care is covered by the continuing care contract: No
Residents may receive personal care in independent living units: Yes

NURSING CARE: Modified Plan

Under this modified plan, 30 days of nursing care per year are covered by the continuing care contract.

Skilled beds: 43. Cost per day: varies according to contract classifications.

Nursing beds are not certified by Medicare or Medicaid. Nonresidents may not be admitted directly to the nursing care facility.

SAINT ANDREWS NORTH ESTATES
6152 North Verde Trail, Boca Raton, FL 33433
Telephone: (305) 487-5500

Opened in 1977 • Mixed single-level and low-rise buildings on 30 acres • Current resident population is 430 • Waiting list may apply for some units

HOUSING AND SERVICES

Living Units	No.	Square Feet	No. of Persons	Entrance Fee	Monthly Fee
Studio	31	572	1	$39,000–$42,000	$597
One Bedroom	115	750	1	$64,000–$67,000	$641
			2		$1,090
Two Bedroom	98	1,044	1	$85,000–$88,000	$727
			2		$1,235
Larger Units	43	1,255	1	$105,000–$108,000	$764
			2		$1,277–$1,791

Total   287 Units

Entrance fee refunds decline over time.

These fees include two meals per day, housekeeping, and scheduled transportation. Special features of this community are presented in the Special Features Index at the back of the book. Ask about additional residential and health care services that may be available. Fees and services subject to change; verify with facility.

ASSISTED LIVING AND PERSONAL CARE

Assisted living units: 0
Personal care is covered by the continuing care contract: No
Residents may receive personal care in independent living units: No

NURSING CARE: All-Inclusive Plan

Under this all-inclusive plan, unlimited nursing care is covered by the continuing care contract. When residents are in nursing care, they pay the same monthly fee they paid for their independent living unit.

Intermediate beds: 60. Cost per day: private $91.00, semi-private $67.00.

Skilled beds: 60. Cost per day: private $92.00, semi-private $68.00.

Nursing beds are certified by both Medicare and Medicaid. Nonresidents may be admitted directly to the nursing care facility.

SAINT ANDREWS SOUTH ESTATES
6045 South Verde Trail, Boca Raton, FL 33433
Telephone: (305) 487-6200

Opened in 1980 • Mixed single-level and low-rise
buildings on 30 acres • Current resident population is
425 • Waiting list may apply for some units

HOUSING AND SERVICES

Living Units	No.	Square Feet	No. of Persons	Entrance Fee	Monthly Fee
Studio	39	484	1	$40,000	$588
One Bedroom	107	662	1	$63,000	$632
			2	$63,000	$1,074
Two Bedroom	126	956	1	$84,000	$716
			2	$84,000	$1,217
Larger Units	48	1,255	1	$104,000	$753
			2	$104,000	$1,258
Total	320 Units				

Entrance fee refunds decline over time.

These fees include two meals per day, housekeeping, scheduled transportation, and utilities. Special features of this community are presented in the Special Features Index at the back of the book. Ask about additional residential and health care services that may be available. Fees and services subject to change; verify with facility.

ASSISTED LIVING AND PERSONAL CARE

Assisted living units: 0
Personal care is covered by the continuing care contract: No
Residents may receive personal care in independent living units: No

NURSING CARE: All-Inclusive Plan

Under this all-inclusive plan, unlimited nursing care is covered by the continuing care contract. When residents are in nursing care, they pay the same monthly fee they paid for their independent living unit.

Intermediate beds: 60.*

Skilled beds: 60.*

*Nursing units are in Saint Andrews North Estates (see page 113)

Nursing beds are certified by both Medicare and Medicaid. Nonresidents may be admitted directly to the nursing care facility.

SAINT MARK VILLAGE
2655 Nebraska Avenue, Palm Harbor, FL 33563
Telephone: (813) 785-2576

Opened in 1980 • One high-rise building on 11 acres • Current resident population is 386 • Located five miles from Clearwater, FL • Waiting list may apply for some units

HOUSING AND SERVICES

Living Units	No.	Square Feet	No. of Persons	Entrance Fee	Monthly Fee
Studio	113	450	1	$27,500	$555
One Bedroom	158	600–675	1	$39,500–$41,500	$705
			2	$39,500–$41,500	$895
Two Bedroom	53	920–1,070	1	$54,000–$66,000	$930–$1,055
			2	$54,000–$66,000	$1,120–$1,245
Larger Units	0	—	—	—	—
Total	324 Units				

Entrance fee refunds decline over time.

These fees include one meal per day, weekly housekeeping, scheduled transportation, and utilities. Special features of this community are presented in the Special Features Index at the back of the book. Ask about additional residential and health care services that may be available. Fees and services subject to change; verify with facility.

ASSISTED LIVING AND PERSONAL CARE

Assisted living units: 0
Personal care is covered by the continuing care contract: No
Residents may receive personal care in independent living units: No

NURSING CARE: Modified Plan

Under this modified plan, 30 days of nursing care per year are covered by the continuing care contract. Once residents move permanently to the nursing unit, they pay 90 percent of the per diem rate for nursing care.

Skilled beds: 60. Cost per day: private $65.00, semi-private $50.00.
Nursing beds are certified by Medicare. Nonresidents may be admitted directly to the nursing care facility.

SHELL POINT VILLAGE
Route 12, Shell Point Boulevard, Fort Myers, FL 33908
Telephone: (813) 466-1111

Opened in 1968 • Mixed single-level, low-rise, and high-rise buildings on 75 acres • Current resident population is 950 • Waiting list may apply for some units

AAHA
Member

HOUSING AND SERVICES

Living Units	No.	Square Feet	No. of Persons	Entrance Fee	Monthly Fee
Studio	65	470	1	$36,000–$45,000	$470
One Bedroom	273	470–800	1	$55,000–$76,000	$483
			2		$629
Two Bedroom	312	938–1,001	1	$68,000–$135,000	$674
			2		$826
Larger Units	8	1,825	1, 2	$225,000–$247,000	$1,016
Total	658 Units				

Entrance fee refunds decline over time.

These fees include weekly housekeeping, scheduled transportation, and utilities. Special features of this community are presented in the Special Features Index at the back of the book. Ask about additional residential and health care services that may be available. Fees and services subject to change; verify with facility.

ASSISTED LIVING AND PERSONAL CARE

Assisted living units: 120
Personal care is covered by the continuing care contract: Yes
Residents may receive personal care in independent living units: No
Nonresidents may be admitted directly to assisted living units: Yes

NURSING CARE: All-Inclusive Plan

Under this all-inclusive plan, unlimited nursing care is covered by the continuing care contract. When residents are in nursing care, they pay the same monthly fee they paid for their independent living unit.

Skilled beds: 180. Cost per day: private $118.00, semi-private $59.00.

Nursing beds are not certified by Medicare or Medicaid. Nonresidents may be admitted directly to the nursing care facility.

SOUTH PORT SQUARE
23023 Westchester Boulevard, Port Charlotte, FL
33952
Telephone: (813) 625-1100

Opened in 1987 • Mixed single-level and low-rise buildings on 39 acres • Waiting list may apply for some units

HOUSING AND SERVICES

Living Units	No.	Square Feet	No. of Persons	Entrance Fee	Monthly Fee
Studio	100	528	1	$30,500	$650
One Bedroom	260	804	1	$46,500	$750
			2	——	$1,050
Two Bedroom	120	1,256	1	$76,500	$950
			2	——	$1,250
Larger Units	0	——	——	——	——
Total	480 Units				

Entrance fees are partially refundable.

These fees include one meal per day, scheduled transportation, and utilities. Special features of this community are presented in the Special Features Index at the back of the book. Ask about additional residential and health care services that may be available. Fees and services subject to change; verify with facility.

ASSISTED LIVING AND PERSONAL CARE

Assisted living units: 74
Personal care is covered by the continuing care contract: No
Residents may receive personal care in independent living units: No
Nonresidents may be admitted directly to assisted living units: Yes

NURSING CARE: Modified Plan

Under this modified plan, 360 days are covered by the continuing care contract. Nursing care is free for 22 days in every 90 (maximum—360 free days); thereafter, residents pay the full per diem rate for nursing care.

Dual-certified beds: 120. Cost per day: private $65.00, semi-private $57.00.

Nursing beds are certified by both Medicare and Medicaid. The nursing unit is accredited by the Joint Commission on Accreditation of Hospitals. Nonresidents may be admitted directly to the nursing care facility.

FLORIDA

SOUTHWEST FLORIDA RETIREMENT CENTER
950 Tamiami Trail South, Venice, FL 33595
Telephone: (813) 484-9753

Opened in 1982 • Predominantly high-rise buildings on 15 acres • Current resident population is 315 • Waiting list may apply for some units

AAHA Member

HOUSING AND SERVICES

Living Units	No.	Square Feet	No. of Persons	Entrance Fee	Monthly Fee
Studio	35	414	1	$33,750	$673
One Bedroom	152	582–730	1	$40,950	$819
			2		$1,029
Two Bedroom	49	830–1,100	1	$49,900	$1,108
			2		$1,318
Larger Units	0	—	—	—	—
Total	236 Units				

Entrance fee refunds decline over time.

These fees include one meal per day, housekeeping, scheduled transportation, and utilities. Special features of this community are presented in the Special Features Index at the back of the book. Ask about additional residential and health care services that may be available. Fees and services subject to change; verify with facility.

ASSISTED LIVING AND PERSONAL CARE

Assisted living units: 106
Personal care is covered by the continuing care contract: Yes
Residents may receive personal care in independent living units: No
Nonresidents may be admitted directly to assisted living units: Yes

NURSING CARE: Fee-for-Service Plan

Under this fee-for-service plan, guaranteed access to nursing care is covered by the continuing care contract. Once residents move permanently to the nursing unit, they pay 90 percent of the per diem rate for nursing care.

Skilled beds: 60. Cost per day: private $87.00, semi-private $64.00.

Nursing beds are certified by both Medicare and Medicaid. Nonresidents may not be admitted directly to the nursing care facility.

VILLAGE ON THE GREEN
500 Village Place, Longwood, FL 32779
Telephone: (305) 682-0230

Opened in 1986 • Mixed single-level and low-rise buildings on 29 acres • Current resident population is 196 • Located ten miles from Orlando, FL • Immediate availability

AAHA
Member

HOUSING AND SERVICES

Living Units	No.	Square Feet	No. of Persons	Entrance Fee	Monthly Fee
Studio	0	——	——	——	——
One Bedroom	72	801–967	1	$104,000–$134,000	$825–$860
			2		$1,197–$1,232
Two Bedroom	60	1,161–1,402	1	$148,000–$181,000	$888–$911
			2		$1,260–$1,283
Larger Units	36	1,542–1,925	1	$203,000–$220,000	$932–$973
			2		$1,304–$1,345
Total	168 Units				

Entrance fees are fully refundable.

These fees include one meal per day, weekly housekeeping, scheduled transportation, and utilities. Special features of this community are presented in the Special Features Index at the back of the book. Ask about additional residential and health care services that may be available. Fees and services subject to change; verify with facility.

ASSISTED LIVING AND PERSONAL CARE

Assisted living units: 0
Personal care is covered by the continuing care contract: No
Residents may receive personal care in independent living units: Yes

NURSING CARE: All-Inclusive Plan

Under this all-inclusive plan, unlimited nursing care is covered by the continuing care contract. When residents are in nursing care, they pay the same monthly fee they paid for their independent living unit.

Skilled beds: 30. Cost per day: not applicable.

Nursing beds are not certified by Medicare or Medicaid. Nonresidents may not be admitted directly to the nursing care facility.

THE WATERFORD
601 South U.S. Highway 1
Juno Beach, FL 33408
Telephone: (305) 627-3800

Opened in 1982 • Mixed single-level, low-rise, and high-rise buildings on 16 acres • Current resident population is 379 • Located ten miles from West Palm Beach, FL • Waiting list may apply for some units

AAHA
Member

HOUSING AND SERVICES

Living Units	No.	Square Feet	No. of Persons	Entrance Fee	Monthly Fee
Studio	56	290–435	1	$38,000	$616–$698
One Bedroom	117	653	1	$70,000	$820
			2		$1,233
Two Bedroom	105	986–1,044	1	$100,500	$1,062
			2		$1,475
Larger Units	29	1,416	1	$134,833	$1,234
			2		$1,647
Total	307 Units				

Entrance fee refunds decline over time.

These fees include one meal per day, housekeeping, scheduled transportation, and utilities. Special features of this community are presented in the Special Features Index at the back of the book. Ask about additional residential and health care services that may be available. Fees and services subject to change; verify with facility.

ASSISTED LIVING AND PERSONAL CARE

Assisted living units: 0
Personal care is covered by the continuing care contract: No
Residents may receive personal care in independent living units: No

NURSING CARE: All-Inclusive Plan

Under this all-inclusive plan, unlimited nursing care is covered by the continuing care contract. When in nursing care, residents pay the same monthly fee they paid for their independent living unit.

Dual-certified beds: 60. Cost per day: private $122.00, semi-private $73.00.

Nursing beds are certified by both Medicare and Medicaid. Nonresidents may be admitted directly to the nursing care facility.

WESTMINSTER OAKS
4449 Meandering Way, Tallahassee, FL 32308
Telephone: (904) 878-1136

Opened in 1982 • One high-rise building on ten acres • Current resident population is 200 • Waiting list may apply for some units

HOUSING AND SERVICES

Living Units	No.	Square Feet	No. of Persons	Entrance Fee	Monthly Fee
Studio	39	433	1	$33,250–$37,750	$515–$675
One Bedroom	50	735	1	$56,250	$835
			2	$58,500	$945
Two Bedroom	24	1,065	1	$74,500	$1,145
			2	$74,500	$1,195
Larger Units	0	—	—	—	—
Total		113 Units			

Residents have a choice of entrance fee refund plans.

These fees include one meal per day, scheduled transportation, and utilities. Special features of this community are presented in the Special Features Index at the back of the book. Ask about additional residential and health care services that may be available. Fees and services subject to change; verify with facility.

ASSISTED LIVING AND PERSONAL CARE

Assisted living units: 28
Personal care is covered by the continuing care contract: Yes
Residents may receive personal care in independent living units: No
Nonresidents may be admitted directly to assisted living units: Yes

NURSING CARE: Modified Plan

Under this modified plan, 15 or fewer days are covered by the continuing care contract. Once residents move permanently to the nursing unit, they pay 75 percent of the per diem rate for nursing care.

Skilled beds: 60. Cost per day: semi-private $48.50.

Nursing beds are not certified by Medicare or Medicaid. Nonresidents may be admitted directly to the nursing care facility.

WESTMINSTER TOWERS
70 West Lucerne Circle, Orlando, FL 32801
Telephone: (305) 841-1310

Opened in 1975 • One high-rise building on four
acres • Current resident population is 416 • Waiting
list may apply for some units

AAHA
Member

HOUSING AND SERVICES

Living Units	No.	Square Feet	No. of Persons	Entrance Fee	Monthly Fee
Studio	170	475	1	$28,000–$34,000	$605
One Bedroom	85	718	1	$46,500	$795
			2	$52,500	$1,050
Two Bedroom	17	1,188	1	$72,000	$1,250
			2		$1,400
Larger Units	0	—	—	—	—
Total	272 Units				

Entrance fee refunds decline over time.

These fees include one meal per day, scheduled transportation, and utilities.
Special features of this community are presented in the Special Features Index
at the back of the book. Ask about additional residential and health care services
that may be available. Fees and services subject to change; verify with facility.

ASSISTED LIVING AND PERSONAL CARE

Assisted living units: 32
Personal care is covered by the continuing care contract: Yes
Residents may receive personal care in independent living units: No
Nonresidents may be admitted directly to assisted living units: Yes

NURSING CARE: Modified Plan

Under this modified plan, 15 or fewer days are covered by the continuing care
contract. Once residents move permanently to the nursing unit, they pay about
75 percent of the per diem rate for nursing care.

Skilled beds: 120. Cost per day: semi-private $49.00.

Nursing beds are certified by Medicaid. Nonresidents may be admitted
directly to the nursing care facility.

WINTER PARK TOWERS
1111 South Lakemont Avenue, Winter Park, FL 32792
Telephone: (305) 647-4083

Opened in 1965 • Mixed single-level, low-rise, and high-rise buildings on 20 acres • Current resident population is 413 • Waiting list may apply for some units

AAHA Member

HOUSING AND SERVICES

Living Units	No.	Square Feet	No. of Persons	Entrance Fee	Monthly Fee
Studio	280	295–395	1	$25,500–$28,000	$695–$725
One Bedroom	21	487	1	$48,000	$1,120
Two Bedroom	0	——	——	——	——
Larger Units	0	——	——	——	——
Total	301 Units				

Entrance fee refunds decline over time.

These fees include three meals per day, weekly housekeeping, scheduled transportation, and utilities. Special features of this community are presented in the Special Features Index at the back of the book. Ask about additional residential and health care services that may be available. Fees and services subject to change; verify with facility.

ASSISTED LIVING AND PERSONAL CARE

Assisted living units: 32
Personal care is covered by the continuing care contract: Yes
Residents may receive personal care in independent living units: No
Nonresidents may be admitted directly to assisted living units: Yes

NURSING CARE: Modified Plan

Under this modified plan, 15 or fewer days are covered by the continuing care contract. Once residents move permanently to the nursing unit, they pay 75 percent of the per diem rate for nursing care.

Skilled beds: 121. Cost per day: semi-private $49.00.

Nursing beds are not certified by Medicare or Medicaid. Nonresidents may be admitted directly to the nursing care facility.

LENBROOK SQUARE
3747 Peachtree Road, Atlanta, GA 30319
Telephone: (404) 233-3000

Opened in 1983 • One high-rise building on four acres • Current resident population is 320 • Immediate availability

AAHA
Member

HOUSING AND SERVICES

Living Units	No.	Square Feet	No. of Persons	Entrance Fee	Monthly Fee
Studio	15	344	1	$42,253	$663
One Bedroom	90	720	1	$90,063	$1,070
			2	$94,690	$1,422
Two Bedroom	165	1,013	1	$119,558	$1,277
			2	$124,213	$1,628
Larger Units	0	—	—	—	—
Total	270 Units				

Entrance fees are fully refundable.

These fees include one meal per day, weekly housekeeping, scheduled transportation, and utilities. Special features of this community are presented in the Special Features Index at the back of the book. Ask about additional residential and health care services that may be available. Fees and services subject to change; verify with facility.

ASSISTED LIVING AND PERSONAL CARE

Assisted living units: 0
Personal care is covered by the continuing care contract: No
Residents may receive personal care in independent living units: Yes

NURSING CARE: All-Inclusive Plan

Under this all-inclusive plan, unlimited nursing care is covered by the continuing care contract. When residents are in nursing care, they pay the basic monthly fee for the studio (smallest) unit.

Intermediate beds: 60. Cost per day: semi-private $50.00.

Nursing beds are not certified by Medicare or Medicaid. Nonresidents may be admitted directly to the nursing care facility.

ARCADIA RETIREMENT RESIDENCE
1434 Punahou Street, Honolulu, HI 96822
Telephone: (808) 941-0941

Opened in 1967 • One high-rise building on three acres • Current resident population is 320 • Long waiting list; make reservations in advance

HOUSING AND SERVICES

Living Units	No.	Square Feet	No. of Persons	Entrance Fee	Monthly Fee
Studio	200	399–629	1	$34,000–$52,000	$625–$732
One Bedroom	70	650–798	1	$61,000–$71,000	$838
			2	$82,000–$96,000	$1,253
Two Bedroom	0	——	——	——	——
Larger Units	0	——	——	——	——
Total	270 Units				

Entrance fee refunds decline over time.

These fees include three meals per day, biweekly housekeeping, and utilities. Special features of this community are presented in the Special Features Index at the back of the book. Ask about additional residential and health care services that may be available. Fees and services subject to change; verify with facility.

ASSISTED LIVING AND PERSONAL CARE

Assisted living units: 0
Personal care is covered by the continuing care contract: No
Residents may receive personal care in independent living units: No

NURSING CARE: Modified Plan

Under this modified plan, 15 or fewer days are covered by the continuing care contract. Once residents move permanently to the nursing unit, they pay the full per diem rate for nursing care.

Skilled beds: 58. Cost per day: semi-private $63.00.

Nursing beds are certified by Medicare. Nonresidents may not be admitted directly to the nursing care facility.

SUNNY RIDGE MANOR
2609 Sunnybrook Drive, Nampa, ID 83651
Telephone: (208) 467-7298

Opened in 1980 • Predominantly single-level/garden apartments on eight acres • Current resident population is 164 • Waiting list may apply for some units

HOUSING AND SERVICES

Living Units	No.	Square Feet	No. of Persons	Entrance Fee	Monthly Fee
Studio	117	380	1	$30,000	$490
One Bedroom	40	600	1	$45,000	$539
Two Bedroom	0	——	——	——	——
Larger Units	0	——	——	——	——
Total	157 Units				

Entrance fees are partially refundable.

These fees include three meals per day, weekly housekeeping, and utilities. Special features of this community are presented in the Special Features Index at the back of the book. Ask about additional residential and health care services that may be available. Fees and services subject to change; verify with facility.

ASSISTED LIVING AND PERSONAL CARE

Assisted living units: 0
Personal care is covered by the continuing care contract: No
Residents may receive personal care in independent living units: No

NURSING CARE: All-Inclusive Plan

Under this all-inclusive plan, unlimited nursing care is covered by the continuing care contract. When residents are in nursing care, they pay the basic monthly fee for the studio (smallest) unit plus the per diem rate.

Skilled beds: 30. Cost per day: private $25.00, semi-private $20.00.

Nursing beds are not certified by Medicare or Medicaid. Nonresidents may not be admitted directly to the nursing care facility.

APARTMENT COMMUNITY OF OUR LADY
9500 West Illinois Route 15, Belleville, IL 62223
Telephone: (618) 397-6700

Opened in 1966 • Mixed single-level and low-rise buildings on 14 acres • Current resident population is 230 • Located 20 miles from Saint Louis, MO • Waiting list may apply for some units

AAHA
Member

HOUSING AND SERVICES

Living Units	No.	Square Feet	No. of Persons	Entrance Fee	Monthly Fee
Studio	91	286–392	1	$17,000	$728
One Bedroom	66	542	1	$35,000	$929
			2		$1,414
Two Bedroom	16	784	1	$45,000	$1,184
			2		$1,590
Larger Units	0	—	—	—	—
Total		173 Units			

Entrance fee refunds decline over time.

These fees include three meals per day, weekly housekeeping, scheduled transportation, and utilities. Special features of this community are presented in the Special Features Index at the back of the book. Ask about additional residential and health care services that may be available. Fees and services subject to change; verify with facility.

ASSISTED LIVING AND PERSONAL CARE

Assisted living units: 0
Personal care is covered by the continuing care contract: No
Residents may receive personal care in independent living units: No

NURSING CARE: Modified Plan

Under this modified plan, 90 days of free care, repeatable after a 30-day period of wellness, are covered by the continuing care contract. Once residents move permanently to the nursing unit, they pay the full per diem rate for nursing care.

Intermediate beds: 16. Cost per day: private $54.00, semi-private $44.00.

Skilled beds: 37. Cost per day: private $69.00, semi-private $59.00.

Nursing beds are certified by Medicare. Nonresidents may not be admitted directly to the nursing care facility.

APOSTOLIC CHRISTIAN RESTHAVEN
2750 West Highland Avenue, Elgin, IL 60123
Telephone: (312) 741-4543

Opened in 1985 • Predominantly single-level/garden apartments on five acres • Current resident population is 65 • Waiting list may apply for some units

AAHA Member

HOUSING AND SERVICES

Living Units	No.	Square Feet	No. of Persons	Entrance Fee	Monthly Fee
Studio	0	——	——	——	——
One Bedroom	10	600	1	$42,000	$193
			2		$386
Two Bedroom	2	810	1	$55,000	$220
			2		$440
Larger Units	0	——	——	——	——
Total		12 Units			

Entrance fees are partially refundable.

These fees include utilities. Special features of this community are presented in the Special Features Index at the back of the book. Ask about additional residential and health care services that may be available. Fees and services subject to change; verify with facility.

ASSISTED LIVING AND PERSONAL CARE

Assisted living units: 0
Personal care is covered by the continuing care contract: No
Residents may receive personal care in independent living units: No

NURSING CARE: Fee-for-Service Plan

Under this fee-for-service plan, guaranteed access to nursing care is covered by the continuing care contract. Residents pay the full per diem rate for nursing care.

Intermediate beds: Cost per day: private $68.00, semi-private $56.00.

Skilled beds: 49. Cost per day: private $77.00, semi-private $65.00.

Nursing beds are not certified by Medicare or Medicaid. Nonresidents may be admitted directly to the nursing care facility.

ILLINOIS

BAPTIST RETIREMENT HOME
316 Randolph Street, Maywood, IL 60153
Telephone: (312) 344-1541

Opened in 1907 • One high-rise building on two acres • Current resident population is 155 • Located ten miles from Chicago, IL • Waiting list may apply for some units

AAHA Member

HOUSING AND SERVICES

Living Units	No.	Square Feet	No. of Persons	Entrance Fee	Monthly Fee
Studio	94	168	1	$24,500*	$780*
One Bedroom	10	576	1	$34,500*	$830*
			2	$49,000*	$1,560*
Two Bedroom	0	——	——	——	——
Larger Units	0	——	——	——	——
Total	104 Units				

*Costs vary depending on age and sex.
Entrance fees are nonrefundable.

These fees include three meals per day, weekly housekeeping, scheduled transportation, and utilities. Special features of this community are presented in the Special Features Index at the back of the book. Ask about additional residential and health care services that may be available. Fees and services subject to change; verify with facility.

ASSISTED LIVING AND PERSONAL CARE

Assisted living units: 28
Personal care is covered by the continuing care contract: Yes
Residents may receive personal care in independent living units: Yes
Nonresidents may be admitted directly to assisted living units: No

NURSING CARE: All-Inclusive Plan

Under this all-inclusive plan, unlimited nursing care is covered by the continuing care contract. When residents are in nursing care, they pay the same monthly fee they paid for their independent living unit.

Intermediate beds: 69. Cost per day: not applicable.

Nursing beds are certified by Medicaid. Nonresidents may not be admitted directly to the nursing care facility.

BEACON HILL
2400 South Finley Road, Lombard, IL 60148
Telephone: (312) 620-5850

Opened in 1984 • One high-rise building on 15 acres • Current resident population is 361 • Located 12 miles from Chicago • Waiting list may apply for some units

AAHA Member

HOUSING AND SERVICES

Living Units	No.	Square Feet	No. of Persons	Entrance Fee	Monthly Fee
Studio	48	500	1	$63,000	$780
One Bedroom	180	640–791	1	$77,000–$98,000	$850–$970
			2		$1,305–$1,425
Two Bedroom	72	931–1,100	1	$111,000–$130,000	$1,085–$1,210
			2		$1,540–$1,665
Larger Units	0	——	——	——	——
Total		300 Units			

Entrance fees are fully refundable.

These fees include one meal per day, weekly housekeeping, scheduled transportation, and utilities. Special features of this community are presented in the Special Features Index at the back of the book. Ask about additional residential and health care services that may be available. Fees and services subject to change; verify with facility.

ASSISTED LIVING AND PERSONAL CARE

Assisted living units: 0
Personal care is covered by the continuing care contract: No
Residents may receive personal care in independent living units: Yes

NURSING CARE: All-Inclusive Plan

Under this all-inclusive plan, unlimited nursing care is covered by the continuing care contract. When residents are in nursing care, they pay the same monthly fee they paid for their independent living unit.

Skilled beds: 45. Cost per day: not applicable.

Nursing beds are certified by Medicare. Nonresidents may not be admitted directly to the nursing care facility.

BETHANY METHODIST HOME
5025 North Paulina Street, Chicago, IL 60640
Telephone: (312) 271-9040

Opened in 1915 • One high-rise building • Current
resident population is 195 • Waiting list may apply for
some units

AAHA
Member

HOUSING AND SERVICES

Living Units	No.	Square Feet	No. of Persons	Entrance Fee	Monthly Fee
Studio	125	——	1	$7,000–$15,000	$665–$765
One Bedroom	68	——	1	$17,000–$25,000	$840–$965
			2		$1,230–$1,480
Two Bedroom	0	——	——	——	——
Larger Units	0	——	——	——	——
Total	193 Units				

Entrance fee refunds decline over time.

These fees include three meals per day, housekeeping, and utilities. Special
features of this community are presented in the Special Features Index at the
back of the book. Ask about additional residential and health care services that
may be available. Fees and services subject to change; verify with facility.

ASSISTED LIVING AND PERSONAL CARE

Assisted living units: 0
Personal care is covered by the continuing care contract: No
Residents may receive personal care in independent living units: No

NURSING CARE: Fee-for-Service Plan

Under this fee-for-service plan, guaranteed access to nursing care is covered by
the continuing care contract. Residents pay the full per diem rate for nursing
care.

Intermediate beds: 160. Cost per day: private $95.00, semi-private $75.00.

Skilled beds: 103. Cost per day: private $104.00, semi-private $84.00.

Nursing beds are certified by both Medicare and Medicaid. Nonresidents may
be admitted directly to the nursing care facility.

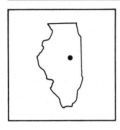

CLARK-LINDSEY VILLAGE
101 West Windsor Road, Urbana, IL 61801
Telephone: (217) 344-2144

Opened in 1979 • Mixed single-level and low-rise buildings on 30 acres • Current resident population is 290 • Waiting list may apply for some units

AAHA
Member

HOUSING AND SERVICES

Living Units	No.	Square Feet	No. of Persons	Entrance Fee	Monthly Fee
Studio	9	482	1	$24,500	$503
One Bedroom	76	536	1	$31,500	$561
			2	$33,000	$794
Two Bedroom	43	787	1	$40,500	$620
			2	$42,000	$872
Larger Units	32	875–950	1	$45,500–$50,500	$620–$872
			2	$47,000–$52,500	$620–$872

Total 160 Units

Entrance fee refunds decline over time.

These fees include one meal per day, biweekly housekeeping, and utilities. Special features of this community are presented in the Special Features Index at the back of the book. Ask about additional residential and health care services that may be available. Fees and services subject to change; verify with facility.

ASSISTED LIVING AND PERSONAL CARE

Assisted living units: 28
Personal care is covered by the continuing care contract: Yes
Residents may receive personal care in independent living units: No
Nonresidents may be admitted directly to assisted living units: Yes

NURSING CARE: Modified Plan

Under this modified plan, 15 or fewer days per year are covered by the continuing care contract. Once residents move permanently to the nursing unit, they pay 90 percent of the per diem rate for nursing care.

Intermediate beds: 12. Cost per day: private $50.00, semi-private $40.00.

Skilled beds: 40. Cost per day: private $68.00, semi-private $60.00.

Nursing beds are certified by both Medicare and Medicaid. Nonresidents may be admitted directly to the nursing care facility.

COVENANT VILLAGE OF NORTHBROOK
2625 Techny Road, Northbrook, IL 60062
Telephone: (312) 480-6380

Opened in 1964 • Mixed single-level and low-rise
buildings on 55 acres • Current resident population is
260 • Located 15 miles from Chicago, IL • Waiting
list

AAHA
Member

HOUSING AND SERVICES

Living Units	No.	Square Feet	No. of Persons	Entrance Fee	Monthly Fee
Studio	52	475	1	$40,500	$671
One Bedroom	80	550–610	1	$52,000–$57,000	$793
			2		$1,267
Two Bedroom	46	750–875	1	$70,000–$78,000	$875
			2		$1,380
Larger Units	42	1,100–1,800	1, 2	$90,000–$120,000	$700–$875
Total		220 Units			

Entrance fee refunds decline over time.

These fees include two meals per day, scheduled transportation, and utilities.
Special features of this community are presented in the Special Features Index
at the back of the book. Ask about additional residential and health care services
that may be available. Fees and services subject to change; verify with facility.

ASSISTED LIVING AND PERSONAL CARE

Assisted living units: 52
Personal care is covered by the continuing care contract: Yes
Residents may receive personal care in independent living units: No
Nonresidents may be admitted directly to assisted living units: Yes

NURSING CARE: Fee-for-Service Plan

Under this fee-for-service plan, guaranteed access to nursing care is covered by
the continuing care contract. Residents pay 90 percent of the per diem rate for
nursing care.

Skilled beds: 104. Cost per day: private $135.00, semi-private $85.00.

Nursing beds are certified by both Medicare and Medicaid. Nonresidents may
be admitted directly to the nursing care facility.

DE KALB AREA RETIREMENT CENTER
2944 Greenwood Acres Drive, De Kalb, IL 60115
Telephone: (815) 756-8461

Opened in 1980 • Mixed single-level and low-rise buildings on 17 acres • Current resident population is 151 • Waiting list may apply for some units

AAHA
Member

HOUSING AND SERVICES

Living Units	No.	Square Feet	No. of Persons	Entrance Fee	Monthly Fee
Studio	24	300	1	$13,500	$765
One Bedroom	45	500–700	1	$29,000	$1,109
			2		$1,525
Two Bedroom	3	900	1	$42,000	$1,517
			2		$2,156
Larger Units	0	——	——	——	——
Total		72 Units			

Entrance fee refunds decline over time.

These fees include three meals per day, housekeeping, and utilities. Special features of this community are presented in the Special Features Index at the back of the book. Ask about additional residential and health care services that may be available. Fees and services subject to change; verify with facility.

ASSISTED LIVING AND PERSONAL CARE

Assisted living units: 37
Personal care is covered by the continuing care contract: Yes
Residents may receive personal care in independent living units: No
Nonresidents may be admitted directly to assisted living units: No

NURSING CARE: Fee-for-Service Plan

Under this fee-for-service plan, guaranteed access to nursing care is covered by the continuing care contract. Residents pay the full per diem rate for nursing care.

Intermediate beds: 30. Cost per day: private $69.00, semi-private $56.00.

Nursing beds are not certified by Medicare or Medicaid. Nonresidents may not be admitted directly to the nursing care facility.

FAIRVIEW BAPTIST HOME
7 South 241 Fairview Avenue
Downers Grove, IL 60516
Telephone: (312) 852-4350

Opened in 1973 • Low-rise buildings on 40 acres •
Current resident population is 160 • Located 25 miles
from Chicago, IL • Immediate availability

AAHA
Member

HOUSING AND SERVICES

Living Units	No.	Square Feet	No. of Persons	Entrance Fee	Monthly Fee
Studio	86	264	1	$37,000	$881
One Bedroom	15	628	1	$74,000	$1,102
			2	$74,000	$1,750
Two Bedroom	0	——	——	——	——
Larger Units	0	——	——	——	——
Total		101 Units			

Entrance fee refunds decline over time.

These fees include three meals per day, biweekly housekeeping, and utilities. Special features of this community are presented in the Special Features Index at the back of the book. Ask about additional residential and health care services that may be available. Fees and services subject to change; verify with facility.

ASSISTED LIVING AND PERSONAL CARE

Assisted living units: 104
Personal care is covered by the continuing care contract: No
Residents may receive personal care in independent living units: No
Nonresidents may be admitted directly to assisted living units: Yes

NURSING CARE: All-Inclusive Plan

Under this all-inclusive plan, unlimited intermediate nursing care is covered by the continuing care contract. When in skilled nursing care, residents pay the same fee they paid for their independent living unit.

Intermediate beds: 65. Cost per day: private $87.78, semi-private $72.10.

Nursing beds are not certified by Medicare or Medicaid. Nonresidents may be admitted directly to the nursing care facility.

FRIENDSHIP MANOR
1209 21st Avenue, Rock Island, IL 61201
Telephone: (309) 786-9667

Opened in 1979 • Mixed single-level, low-rise, and high-rise buildings on ten acres • Current resident population is 366 • Waiting list may apply for some units

AAHA
Member

HOUSING AND SERVICES

Living Units	No.	Square Feet	No. of Persons	Entrance Fee	Monthly Fee
Studio	64	333–405	1	$27,250–$32,000	$426–$445
One Bedroom	88	610–810	1	$44,500–$72,250	$462
			2		$686
Two Bedroom	72	793–867	1	$55,250–$62,000	$499
			2	$59,250–$66,000	$749
Larger Units	0	—	—	—	—
Total	224 Units				

Entrance fee refunds decline over time.

These fees include biweekly housekeeping, scheduled transportation, and utilities. Special features of this community are presented in the Special Features Index at the back of the book. Ask about additional residential and health care services that may be available. Fees and services subject to change; verify with facility.

ASSISTED LIVING AND PERSONAL CARE

Assisted living units: 0
Personal care is covered by the continuing care contract: No
Residents may receive personal care in independent living units: Yes

NURSING CARE: All-Inclusive Plan

Under this all-inclusive plan, unlimited nursing care is covered by the continuing care contract. When in nursing care, residents pay the same monthly fee they paid for their independent living unit.

Sheltered beds: 34. Cost per day: private $50.00, semi-private—not applicable.

Skilled beds: 63. Cost per day: private—not applicable, semi-private $62.50.

Nursing beds are not certified by Medicare or Medicaid. Nonresidents may be admitted directly to the nursing care facility.

ILLINOIS

FRIENDSHIP VILLAGE
350 West Schaumburg Road, Schaumburg, IL 60194
Telephone: (312) 884-5000

Opened in 1977 • Mixed single-level and low-rise buildings on 44 acres • Current resident population is 720 • Waiting list may apply for some units • Accredited by the AAHA Continuing Care Accreditation Commission

AAHA
Member

HOUSING AND SERVICES

Living Units	No.	Square Feet	No. of Persons	Entrance Fee	Monthly Fee
Studio	310	268–418	1	$38,658	$658
One Bedroom	224	538–559	1	$61,450	$784
			2	$71,450	$1,137
Two Bedroom	98	759	1	$75,250	$877
			2	$85,250	$1,230
Larger Units	0	—	—	—	—
Total	632 Units				

Entrance fee refunds decline over time.

These fees include one meal per day, biweekly housekeeping, scheduled transportation, and utilities. Special features of this community are presented in the Special Features Index at the back of the book. Ask about additional residential and health care services that may be available. Fees and services subject to change; verify with facility.

ASSISTED LIVING AND PERSONAL CARE

Assisted living units: 0
Personal care is covered by the continuing care contract: No
Residents may receive personal care in independent living units: No

NURSING CARE: All-Inclusive Plan

Under this all-inclusive plan, unlimited nursing care is covered by the continuing care contract. When residents are in nursing care, they pay the basic monthly fee for the studio (smallest) unit if their independent living unit was a studio; they pay the next highest rate if they lived in a larger unit.

Dual-certified beds: 180. Cost per day: private $86.00–$96.00, semi-private $66.00–$76.00.

Nursing beds are certified by both Medicare and Medicaid. Nonresidents may be admitted directly to the nursing care facility.

THE GEORGIAN HOME
422 Davis Street, Evanston, IL 60201
Telephone: (312) 475-4100

Opened in 1963 • One high-rise building on one acre • Current resident population is 174 • Waiting list

AAHA Member

HOUSING AND SERVICES

Living Units	No.	Square Feet	No. of Persons	Entrance Fee	Monthly Fee
Studio	35	198	1	$18,000–$20,000	$904–$972
One Bedroom	52	366	1	$32,000–$38,000	$1,055–$1,338
			2	$38,400–$45,600	$1,744–$2,028
Two Bedroom	39	601–625	1	$45,000–$48,000	$1,379–$1,526
			2	$54,000–$57,600	$2,068–$2,216
Larger Units	6	—	1	$48,000	$1,526
			2	$57,600	$2,216
Total	132 Units				

Entrance fee refunds decline over time.

These fees include three meals per day, weekly housekeeping, and utilities. Special features of this community are presented in the Special Features Index at the back of the book. Ask about additional residential and health care services that may be available. Fees and services subject to change; verify with facility.

ASSISTED LIVING AND PERSONAL CARE

Assisted living units: 16
Personal care is covered by the continuing care contract: Yes
Residents may receive personal care in independent living units: No
Nonresidents may be admitted directly to assisted living units: No

NURSING CARE: All-Inclusive Plan

Under this all-inclusive plan, unlimited nursing care is covered by the continuing care contract. When residents are in nursing care, they pay the same monthly fee they paid for their independent living unit.

Skilled beds: 23. Cost per day: not applicable.

Nursing beds are not certified by Medicare or Medicaid. Nonresidents may not be admitted directly to the nursing care facility.

THE HOLMSTAD
Fabyan Parkway and Route 31, Batavia, IL 60510
Telephone: (312) 879-4000

Opened in 1976 • Mixed single-level and low-rise buildings on 38 acres • Current resident population is 613 • Waiting list may apply for some units

AAHA
Member

HOUSING AND SERVICES

Living Units	No.	Square Feet	No. of Persons	Entrance Fee	Monthly Fee
Studio	87	450	1	$44,500	$617
One Bedroom	163	610	1	$60,000	$719
			2		$1,101
Two Bedroom	79	875	1	$82,000	$901
			2		$1,283
Larger Units	44	825–1,100	1	$72,000–$90,000	$698–$895
			2		$922–$1,119

Total   373 Units

Entrance fee refunds decline over time.

These fees include one meal per day, biweekly housekeeping, scheduled transportation, and utilities. Special features of this community are presented in the Special Features Index at the back of the book. Ask about additional residential and health care services that may be available. Fees and services subject to change; verify with facility.

ASSISTED LIVING AND PERSONAL CARE

Assisted living units: 28
Personal care is covered by the continuing care contract: Yes
Residents may receive personal care in independent living units: No
Nonresidents may be admitted directly to assisted living units: No

NURSING CARE: All-Inclusive Plan

Under this all-inclusive plan, unlimited nursing care is covered by the continuing care contract. When residents are in nursing care, they pay the same monthly fee they paid for their independent living unit.

Intermediate beds. Cost per day: private $132.00, semi-private $78.00.

Skilled beds: 128. Cost per day: private $143.00, semi-private $84.00.

Nursing beds are certified by both Medicare and Medicaid. Nonresidents may be admitted directly to the nursing care facility.

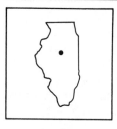

MAPLE LAWN HOMES
700 North Main, Eureka, IL 61530
Telephone: (309) 467-2337

Opened in 1955 • Mixed single-level and low-rise buildings on 40 acres • Current resident population is 200 • Waiting list may apply for some units

AAHA
Member

HOUSING AND SERVICES

Living Units	No.	Square Feet	No. of Persons	Entrance Fee	Monthly Fee
Studio	0	——	——	——	——
One Bedroom	22	480–894	1, 2	$10,000	$165–$245
Two Bedroom	44	600–1,184	1, 2	$10,000	$165–$245
Larger Units	0	——	——	——	——
Total	66 Units				

Entrance fee refunds decline over time.

These fees include scheduled transportation and utilities. Special features of this community are presented in the Special Features Index at the back of the book. Ask about additional residential and health care services that may be available. Fees and services subject to change; verify with facility.

ASSISTED LIVING AND PERSONAL CARE

Assisted living units: 0
Personal care is covered by the continuing care contract: No
Residents may receive personal care in independent living units: No

NURSING CARE: Modified Plan

Under this modified plan, 15 or fewer days per year are covered by the continuing care contract. Once residents move permanently to the nursing unit, they pay the full per diem rate for nursing care.

Intermediate beds: 18. Cost per day: private $33.00, semi-private $29.00.

Skilled beds: 62. Cost per day: private $43.50–$51.00, semi-private $39.50–$47.00.

Nursing beds are certified by both Medicare and Medicaid. Nonresidents may be admitted directly to the nursing care facility.

MEADOW CREST OF THE BENSENVILLE HOME SOCIETY

331 South York Road, Bensenville, IL 60106
Telephone: (312) 766-5800

Opened in 1978 • Predominantly single-level/garden apartments on 32 acres • Current resident population is 18 • Waiting list

AAHA Member

HOUSING AND SERVICES

Living Units	No.	Square Feet	No. of Persons	Entrance Fee	Monthly Fee
Studio	0	——	——	——	——
One Bedroom	6	900	1	$41,000	$255
			2	$41,000	$275
Two Bedroom	6	1,100	1	$53,000	$340
			2	$53,000	$355
Larger Units	1	2,200	1, 2	$90,000	$575
Total		13 Units			

Entrance fee refunds decline over time.

Special features of this community are presented in the Special Features Index at the back of the book. Ask about additional residential and health care services that may be available. Fees and services subject to change; verify with facility.

ASSISTED LIVING AND PERSONAL CARE

Assisted living units: 0
Personal care is covered by the continuing care contract: No
Residents may receive personal care in independent living units: No

NURSING CARE: Fee-for-Service

Under this fee-for-service plan, guaranteed access to nursing care is covered by the continuing care contract. Residents pay the full per diem rate for nursing care.

Intermediate beds: 145. Cost per day: private $78.00, semi-private $66.00.

Skilled beds: 89. Cost per day: private $96.50, semi-private $89.75.

Nursing beds are certified by Medicare. The nursing center is accredited by the Joint Commission on Accreditation of Hospitals. Nonresidents may be admitted directly to the nursing care facility.

ILLINOIS

THE PRESBYTERIAN HOME
3200 Grant Street, Evanston, IL 60201
Telephone: (312) 492-2900

Opened in 1914 • Mixed single-level, low-rise, and high-rise buildings on 40 acres • Current resident population is 445 • Located ten miles from Chicago, IL • Waiting list

AAHA
Member

HOUSING AND SERVICES

Living Units	No.	Square Feet	No. of Persons	Entrance Fee	Monthly Fee
Studio	28	384	1	$39,900–$41,500	$1,445
One Bedroom	60	653	1	$62,000–$65,000	$1,695
			2		$2,615
Two Bedroom	14	993	1	$83,500–$87,500	$1,870
			2		$2,790
Larger Units	18	1,950	1	$92,500–$122,000	$2,065
			2		$2,985

Total 120 Units

Entrance fee refunds decline over time.

These fees include three meals per day, housekeeping, scheduled transportation, and utilities. Special features of this community are presented in the Special Features Index at the back of the book. Ask about additional residential and health care services that may be available. Fees and services subject to change; verify with facility.

ASSISTED LIVING AND PERSONAL CARE

Assisted living units: 0
Personal care is covered by the continuing care contract: No
Residents may receive personal care in independent living units: No

NURSING CARE: All-Inclusive Plan

Under this all-inclusive plan, unlimited nursing care is covered by the continuing care contract. When in nursing care, residents pay the same monthly fee they paid for their independent living unit.

Intermediate beds: 81, sheltered beds: 51. Cost per day: private $95.00–$113.00, semi-private $85.00.

Skilled beds: 111. Cost per day: private $124.00, semi-private $108.00

Nursing beds are certified by Medicare. Nonresidents may be admitted directly to the nursing care facility.

PROCTOR HOME
2724 West Reservoir, Peoria, IL 61615
Telephone: (309) 685-6580

Opened in 1976 • Predominantly high-rise buildings on seven acres • Current resident population is 223 • Waiting list

HOUSING AND SERVICES

Living Units	No.	Square Feet	No. of Persons	Entrance Fee	Monthly Fee
Studio	140	427	1	*	**
One Bedroom	21	680	1, 2	*	**
Two Bedroom	11	776	1, 2	*	**
Larger Units	0	—	—	—	—
Total	172 Units				

*Assignment of assets.
**Not applicable.
Entrance fees are nonrefundable.

These fees include three meals per day, weekly housekeeping, scheduled transportation, and utilities. Special features of this community are presented in the Special Features Index at the back of the book. Ask about additional residential and health care services that may be available. Fees and services subject to change; verify with facility.

ASSISTED LIVING AND PERSONAL CARE

Assisted living units: 0
Personal care is covered by the continuing care contract: No
Residents may receive personal care in independent living units: No

NURSING CARE: All-Inclusive Plan

Under this all-inclusive plan, unlimited nursing care is covered by the continuing care contract.

Skilled beds: 59. Cost per day: not applicable.

Nursing beds are not certified by Medicare or Medicaid. Nonresidents may not be admitted directly to the nursing care facility.

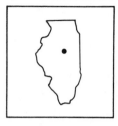

WESTMINSTER VILLAGE
2025 East Lincoln Street, Bloomington, IL 61701
Telephone: (309) 663-6474

Opened in 1979 • Mixed single-level and low-rise
buildings on 48 acres • Current resident population is
248 • Immediate availability

HOUSING AND SERVICES

Living Units	No.	Square Feet	No. of Persons	Entrance Fee	Monthly Fee
Studio	9	439	1	$24,000	$566
One Bedroom	125	523	1	$28,200	$587
			2	$30,200	$846
Two Bedroom	72	765	1	$40,300	$630
			2	$42,300	$900
Larger Units	38	860–1,046	1	$45,000–$54,300	$650–$677
			2	$47,000–$56,300	$932–$965
Total		244 Units			

Entrance fee refunds decline over time.

These fees include one meal per day, biweekly housekeeping, and utilities.
Special features of this community are presented in the Special Features Index
at the back of the book. Ask about additional residential and health care services
that may be available. Fees and services subject to change; verify with facility.

ASSISTED LIVING AND PERSONAL CARE

Assisted living units: 0
Personal care is covered by the continuing care contract: No
Residents may receive personal care in independent living units: No

NURSING CARE: Fee-for-Service Plan

Under this fee-for-service plan, guaranteed access to nursing care is covered by
the continuing care contract. Once residents move permanently to the nursing
unit, they pay 90 percent of the per diem rate for nursing care.

Intermediate beds: 39. Cost per day: private $102.00, semi-private $56.75.

Skilled beds: 39. Cost per day: private $125.00, semi-private $69.50.

Nursing beds are certified by Medicare. Nonresidents may be admitted
directly to the nursing care facility.

APOSTOLIC CHRISTIAN RETIREMENT HOME
(PARKVIEW HAVEN)
P.O. Box 797, Francesville, IN 47946
Telephone: (219) 567-9149

Opened in 1978 • Predominantly single-level/garden apartments on 19 acres • Current resident population is 61 • Immediate availability

AAHA Member

HOUSING AND SERVICES

Living Units	No.	Square Feet	No. of Persons	Entrance Fee	Monthly Fee
Studio	16	285	1	$12,000	$480
One Bedroom	8	315	1	$18,500	$670
			2	$18,500	$910
Two Bedroom	0	——	——	——	——
Larger Units	0	——	——	——	——
Total		24 Units			

Entrance fees are partially refundable.

These fees include three meals per day, weekly housekeeping, scheduled transportation, and utilities. Special features of this community are presented in the Special Features Index at the back of the book. Ask about additional residential and health care services that may be available. Fees and services subject to change; verify with facility.

ASSISTED LIVING AND PERSONAL CARE

Assisted living units: 0
Personal care is covered by the continuing care contract: No
Residents may receive personal care in independent living units: No

NURSING CARE: Modified Plan

Under this modified plan, 15 or fewer days per year are covered by the continuing care contract. Once residents move permanently to the nursing unit, they pay the full per diem rate for nursing care.

Intermediate beds: 39. Cost per day: semi-private $45.00.

Nursing beds are not certified by Medicare or Medicaid. Nonresidents may be admitted directly to the nursing care facility.

INDIANA

THE BRETHREN'S HOME OF INDIANA
Route 2, Box 97, Flora, IN 46929
Telephone: (219) 967-4571

Opened in 1968 • Mixed single-level and low-rise buildings on 100 acres • Current resident population is 109 • Waiting list may apply for some units

HOUSING AND SERVICES

Living Units	No.	Square Feet	No. of Persons	Entrance Fee	Monthly Fee
Studio	0	—	—	—	—
One Bedroom	22	520–540	1	$10,000	$385
			2	$10,000	$405
Two Bedroom	3	970–1,080	1	$15,000	$485
			2	$15,000	$505
Larger Units	0	—	—	—	—
Total	25 Units				

Entrance fees are fully refundable.

These fees include scheduled transportation and utilities. Special features of this community are presented in the Special Features Index at the back of the book. Ask about additional residential and health care services that may be available. Fees and services subject to change; verify with facility.

ASSISTED LIVING AND PERSONAL CARE

Assisted living units: 25
Personal care is covered by the continuing care contract: No
Residents may receive personal care in independent living units: Yes
Nonresidents may be admitted directly to assisted living units: Yes

NURSING CARE: Modified Plan

Under this modified plan, 15 or fewer days are covered by the continuing care contract. Thereafter, residents pay the full per diem rate for nursing care.

Intermediate beds: 86. Cost per day: private $60.00, semi-private $40.00.
Nursing beds are certified by Medicaid. Nonresidents may be admitted directly to the nursing care facility.

GREENCROFT

1310 Greencroft Drive, Goshen, IN 46526
Telephone: (219) 534-1546

Opened in 1967 • Predominantly single-level/garden apartments on 150 acres • Current resident population is 850 • Waiting list

AAHA Member

HOUSING AND SERVICES

Living Units	No.	Square Feet	No. of Persons	Entrance Fee	Monthly Fee
Studio	93	350–450	1	$500	$340
One Bedroom	354	550–800	1, 2	$1,000	$470
Two Bedroom	122	850–1,200	1, 2	$1,500	$610
Larger Units	0	——	——	——	——
Total	569 Units				

Entrance fees are partially refundable.

These fees include utilities. Special features of this community are presented in the Special Features Index at the back of the book. Ask about additional residential and health care services that may be available. Fees and services subject to change; verify with facility.

ASSISTED LIVING AND PERSONAL CARE

Assisted living units: 55
Personal care is covered by the continuing care contract: No
Residents may receive personal care in independent living units: Yes
Nonresidents may be admitted directly to assisted living units: No

---

NURSING CARE: Fee-for-Service Plan

Under this fee-for-service plan, guaranteed access to nursing care is covered by the continuing care contract. Residents pay the full per diem rate for nursing care.

Intermediate beds: 130. Cost per day: private $77.00, semi-private $56.00.

Skilled beds: 50. Cost per day: private $92.00, semi-private $66.00.

Nursing beds are certified by both Medicare and Medicaid. Nonresidents may be admitted directly to the nursing care facility.

GREENWOOD VILLAGE SOUTH
295 Village Lane, Greenwood, IN 46142
Telephone: (317) 881-2591

Opened in 1962 • Mixed single-level and low-rise buildings on 58 acres • Current resident population is 405 • Located 15 miles from Indianapolis • Waiting list may apply in some units

AAHA Member

HOUSING AND SERVICES

Living Units	No.	Square Feet	No. of Persons	Entrance Fee	Monthly Fee
Studio	87	325–402	1	$20,067	$700–$1,020
One Bedroom	86	486–734	1	$34,800–$38,000	$744–$760
			2	$37,400–$40,000	$1,202–$1,219
Two Bedroom	8	811	1	$45,200	$816
			2	$47,800	$1,305
Larger Units	52	1,300–2,000	1, 2	$50,000–$70,000	$350–$450
Total		233 Units			

Entrance fee refunds decline over time.

These fees include three meals per day, biweekly housekeeping, and utilities. Special features of this community are presented in the Special Features Index at the back of the book. Ask about additional residential and health care services that may be available. Fees and services subject to change; verify with facility.

ASSISTED LIVING AND PERSONAL CARE

Assisted living units: 60
Personal care is covered by the continuing care contract: Yes
Residents may receive personal care in independent living units: Yes
Nonresidents may be admitted directly to assisted living units: Yes

NURSING CARE: Modified Plan

Under this modified plan, guaranteed access to nursing care is covered by the continuing care contract. Residents pay 90 percent of the per diem rate for nursing care.

Intermediate beds: 48. Cost per day: semi-private $58.00.

Skilled beds: 43. Cost per day: private $81.00, semi-private $65.00.

Nursing beds are certified by both Medicare and Medicaid. Nonresidents may be admitted directly to the nursing care facility.

INDIANA ASBURY TOWERS/UNITED METHODIST HOME

102 West Poplar Street, Greencastle, IN 46135
Telephone: (317) 653-5148

Opened in 1964 • Mixed single-level and low-rise buildings on one acre • Current resident population is 68 • Immediate availability

HOUSING AND SERVICES

Living Units	No.	Square Feet	No. of Persons	Entrance Fee	Monthly Fee
Studio	26	350–375	1	$14,000–$16,000	$665
One Bedroom	28	450–550	1	$24,000–$26,000	$890
			2		$1,330
Two Bedroom	1	625	1, 2	$33,000	$1,000
Larger Units	0	——	——	——	——
Total	55 Units				

Entrance fee refunds decline over time.

These fees include three meals per day, biweekly housekeeping, and utilities. Special features of this community are presented in the Special Features Index at the back of the book. Ask about additional residential and health care services that may be available. Fees and services subject to change; verify with facility.

ASSISTED LIVING AND PERSONAL CARE

Assisted living units: 0
Personal care is covered by the continuing care contract: Yes
Residents may receive personal care in independent living units: Yes

NURSING CARE: Fee-for-Service Plan

Under this fee-for-service plan, guaranteed access to nursing care is covered by the continuing care contract. Residents pay the full per diem rate for nursing care.

Intermediate beds: 21. Cost per day: private—not applicable, semi-private $42.75.

Nursing beds are not certified by Medicare or Medicaid. Nonresidents may not be admitted directly to the nursing care facility.

INDIANA MASONIC HOMES
690 State Street, Franklin, IN 46131
Telephone: (317) 736-6141

Opened in 1916 • Mixed single-level and low-rise buildings on 440 acres • Current resident population is 564 • Waiting list

AAHA
Member

HOUSING AND SERVICES

Living Units	No.	Square Feet	No. of Persons	Entrance Fee	Monthly Fee
Studio	250	184	1	$7,500–$10,000	$150
One Bedroom	31	265	1, 2	$15,000–$27,500	$150
Two Bedroom	35	385–906	1, 2	$42,500–$59,000	$150
Larger Units	0	——	——	——	——
Total	316 Units				

Entrance fees are nonrefundable.

These fees include weekly housekeeping and scheduled transportation. Special features of this community are presented in the Special Features Index at the back of the book. Ask about additional residential and health care services that may be available. Fees and services subject to change; verify with facility.

ASSISTED LIVING AND PERSONAL CARE

Assisted living units: 0
Personal care is covered by the continuing care contract: Yes
Residents may receive personal care in independent living units: Yes

NURSING CARE: Fee-for-Service Plan

Under this fee-for-service plan, guaranteed access to nursing care is covered by the continuing care contract. Residents pay the full per diem rate for nursing care.

Skilled beds: 268. Cost per day: private $67.00, semi-private $57.00.

Nursing beds are not certified by Medicare or Medicaid. Nonresidents may not be admitted directly to the nursing care facility.

LUTHERAN HOMES
6701 South Anthony Boulevard, Fort Wayne, IN 46816
Telephone: (219) 447-1591

Opened in 1965 • Mixed single-level and low-rise buildings on 49 acres • Current resident population is 530 • Waiting list

AAHA
Member

HOUSING AND SERVICES

Living Units	No.	Square Feet	No. of Persons	Entrance Fee	Monthly Fee
Studio	57	335	1	$15,000	$295
One Bedroom	32	665–790	1, 2	$40,000	$410
Two Bedroom	8	950–1,425	1, 2	$48,000	$455
Larger Units	0	——	——	——	——
Total		97 Units			

Entrance fees are fully refundable.

These fees include utilities. Special features of this community are presented in the Special Features Index at the back of the book. Ask about additional residential and health care services that may be available. Fees and services subject to change; verify with facility.

ASSISTED LIVING AND PERSONAL CARE

Assisted living units: 88
Personal care is covered by the continuing care contract: Yes
Residents may receive personal care in independent living units: No
Nonresidents may be admitted directly to assisted living units: Yes

NURSING CARE: Fee-for-Service Plan

Under this fee-for-service plan, guaranteed access to nursing care is covered by the continuing care contract. Residents pay the full per diem rate for nursing care.

Intermediate beds: 276. Cost per day: private $48.75, semi-private $44.75.

Nursing beds are certified by Medicaid. Nonresidents may be admitted directly to the nursing care facility.

MARQUETTE MANOR
8140 Township Line Road, Indianapolis, IN 46260
Telephone: (317) 875-9700

Opened in 1981 • Mixed single-level, low-rise, and high-rise buildings on 46 acres • Current resident population is 375 • Immediate availability

AAHA
Member

HOUSING AND SERVICES

Living Units	No.	Square Feet	No. of Persons	Entrance Fee	Monthly Fee
Studio	7	418	1	$31,080	$536
One Bedroom	109	535	1	$40,320	$552
			2		$853
Two Bedroom	133	805	1	$63,420	$605
			2		$906
Larger Units	0	——	——	——	——
Total	249 Units				

Entrance fee refunds decline over time.

These fees include one meal per day, biweekly housekeeping, and utilities. Special features of this community are presented in the Special Features Index at the back of the book. Ask about additional residential and health care services that may be available. Fees and services subject to change; verify with facility.

ASSISTED LIVING AND PERSONAL CARE

Assisted living units: 0
Personal care is covered by the continuing care contract: No
Residents may receive personal care in independent living units: No

NURSING CARE: Fee-for-Service Plan

Under this fee-for-service plan, guaranteed access to nursing care is covered by the continuing care contract. Residents pay the full per diem rate for nursing care.

Skilled beds: 78. Cost per day: private $116.00, semi-private $58.00.

Nursing beds are certified by Medicare. Nonresidents may be admitted directly to the nursing care facility.

INDIANA

PEABODY RETIREMENT COMMUNITY
400 West Seventh Street, North Manchester, IN 46962
Telephone: (219) 982-8616

Opened in 1931 • Mixed single-level and low-rise buildings on 25 acres • Current resident population is 257 • Waiting list may apply for some units • Accredited by the AAHA Continuing Care Accreditation Commission

AAHA Member

HOUSING AND SERVICES

Living Units	No.	Square Feet	No. of Persons	Entrance Fee	Monthly Fee
Studio	0	——	——	——	——
One Bedroom	0	——	——	——	——
Two Bedroom	8	1,000	1, 2	$77,000	$100
Larger Units	0	——	——	——	——
Total		8 Units			

Entrance fee refunds decline over time.

These fees include weekly housekeeping and utilities. Special features of this community are presented in the Special Features Index at the back of the book. Ask about additional residential and health care services that may be available. Fees and services subject to change; verify with facility.

ASSISTED LIVING AND PERSONAL CARE

Assisted living units: 117
Personal care is covered by the continuing care contract: Yes
Residents may receive personal care in independent living units: No
Nonresidents may be admitted directly to assisted living units: Yes

NURSING CARE: Fee-for-Service Plan

Under this fee-for-service plan, emergency or temporary infirmary care is covered by the continuing care contract. Residents pay the full per diem rate for nursing care.

Intermediate beds: 150. Cost per day: private $59.60, semi-private $45.60.

Nursing beds are certified by Medicaid. Nonresidents may be admitted directly to the nursing care facility.

PINES VILLAGE
3303 Pines Village Circle, Valparaiso, IN 46383
Telephone: (219) 465-1591

Opened in 1983 • One low-rise building on seven acres • Current resident population is 105 • Immediate availability

AAHA
Member

HOUSING AND SERVICES

Living Units	No.	Square Feet	No. of Persons	Entrance Fee*	Monthly Fee*
Studio	18	440	1	$33,250	$494
One Bedroom	63	527–680	1	$43,000–$46,000	$517–$533
			2	$43,000–$46,000	$717–$733
Two Bedroom	30	796–946	1	$58,350–$63,000	$593–$617
			2	$58,350–$63,000	$793–$817
Larger Units	0	—	—	—	—
Total		111 Units			

*These are standard rates; entrance fees are lower and monthly fees higher for those over the age of 80.

Residents have a choice of entrance fee refund plans.

These fees include one meal per day, bimonthly housekeeping, scheduled transportation, and utilities. Special features of this community are presented in the Special Features Index at the back of the book. Ask about additional residential and health care services that may be available. Fees and services subject to change; verify with facility.

ASSISTED LIVING AND PERSONAL CARE

Assisted living units: 0
Personal care is covered by the continuing care contract: No
Residents may receive personal care in independent living units: Yes

NURSING CARE: Modified Plan

Under this modified plan, guaranteed access to nursing care is covered by the continuing care contract. Residents pay a discounted per diem rate for nursing care.

Intermediate beds: 145.** Cost per day: private $56.00, semi-private $52.00.
Skilled beds: 39.** Cost per day: semi-private $56.00.

**The nursing facility is Whispering Pines Health Care Center, 3301 North Calumet, Valparaiso, IN 46383.

Nursing beds are certified by both Medicare and Medicaid. Nonresidents may be admitted directly to the nursing care facility.

TIMBERCREST—CHURCH OF THE BRETHREN HOME
Box 501, North Manchester, IN 46962
Telephone: (219) 982–2118

Opened in 1968 • Predominantly single-level/garden apartments on 66 acres • Current resident population is 215 • Long waiting list; make reservations in advance

 AAHA Member

HOUSING AND SERVICES

Living Units	No.	Square Feet	No. of Persons	Entrance Fee	Monthly Fee
Studio	0	——	——	——	——
One Bedroom	6	564	1, 2	$45,750	$128
Two Bedroom	22	864	1, 2	$69,050	$128
Larger Units	4	1,008	1, 2	$80,500	$128
Total	32 Units				

Entrance fees are partially refundable.

These fees include weekly housekeeping, scheduled transportation, and utilities. Special features of this community are presented in the Special Features Index at the back of the book. Ask about additional residential and health care services that may be available. Fees and services subject to change; verify with facility.

ASSISTED LIVING AND PERSONAL CARE

Assisted living units: 103
Personal care is covered by the continuing care contract: Yes
Residents may receive personal care in independent living units: No
Nonresidents may be admitted directly to assisted living units: Yes

NURSING CARE: Modified Plan

Under this modified plan, 15 or fewer days are covered by the continuing care contract. Once residents move permanently to the nursing unit, they pay the full per diem rate for nursing care.

Intermediate beds: 46. Cost per day: private—not applicable, semi-private $37.00–$44.50.

Nursing beds are certified by Medicaid. Nonresidents may be admitted directly to the nursing care facility.

INDIANA

UNITED METHODIST MEMORIAL HOME
P.O. Box 326, Warren, IN 46792
Telephone: (219) 375-2201

Opened in 1910 • Mixed single-level, low-rise, and high-rise buildings on 700 acres • Current resident population is 410 • Waiting list may apply for some units

AAHA
Member

HOUSING AND SERVICES

Living Units	No.	Square Feet	No. of Persons	Entrance Fee	Monthly Fee
Studio	238	——	1	$18,000	$780
One Bedroom	45	——	1, 2	$35,000	$1,205
Two Bedroom	0	——	——	——	——
Larger Units	0	——	——	——	——
Total	283 Units				

Entrance fees are nonrefundable.

These fees include three meals per day, biweekly housekeeping, scheduled transportation, and utilities. Special features of this community are presented in the Special Features Index at the back of the book. Ask about additional residential and health care services that may be available. Fees and services subject to change; verify with facility.

ASSISTED LIVING AND PERSONAL CARE

Assisted living units: 0
Personal care is covered by the continuing care contract: No
Residents may receive personal care in independent living units: No

NURSING CARE: All-Inclusive Plan

Under this all-inclusive plan, unlimited nursing care is covered by the continuing care contract. When in nursing care, residents pay the same monthly fee they paid for their independent living unit.

Skilled beds: 213. Cost per day: semi-private $40.00.

Nursing beds are not certified by Medicare or Medicaid. Nonresidents may be admitted directly to the nursing care facility.

WESLEY MANOR
1555 North Main Street, Frankfort, IN 46041
Telephone: (317) 659-1811

Opened in 1961 • Mixed single-level and low-rise buildings on 52 acres • Current resident population is 331 • Immediate availability

HOUSING AND SERVICES

Living Units	No.	Square Feet	No. of Persons	Entrance Fee	Monthly Fee
Studio	117	256–418	1	$19,500–$27,500	$815–$1,410
One Bedroom	60	363–940	1	$35,000–$45,000	$1,040
			2		$1,635
Two Bedroom	10	630–992	1	$55,000	$1,265
			2		$1,860
Larger Units	0	——	——	——	——
Total	187 Units				

Entrance fee refunds decline over time.

These fees include three meals per day, housekeeping, and utilities. Special features of this community are presented in the Special Features Index at the back of the book. Ask about additional residential and health care services that may be available. Fees and services subject to change; verify with facility.

ASSISTED LIVING AND PERSONAL CARE

Assisted living units: 36
Personal care is covered by the continuing care contract: Yes
Residents may receive personal care in independent living units: Yes
Nonresidents may be admitted directly to assisted living units: Yes

NURSING CARE: Modified Plan

Under this modified plan, guaranteed access to nursing care is covered by the continuing care contract. Residents pay a discounted per diem rate for nursing care.

Intermediate beds: 85. Cost per day: semi-private $61.50

Nursing beds are not certified by Medicare or Medicaid. Nonresidents may be admitted directly to the nursing care facility.

INDIANA

WESTMINSTER VILLAGE KENTUCKIANA
2200 Greentree North, Clarksville, IN 47130
Telephone: (812) 282-9691

Opened in 1978 • Predominantly tri-level/garden apartments on 35 acres • Current resident population is 220 • Immediate availability

HOUSING AND SERVICES

Living Units	No.	Square Feet	No. of Persons	Entrance Fee	Monthly Fee
Studio	8	420	1	$32,250	$506
One Bedroom	112	672	1	$43,550	$528
			2		$775
Two Bedroom	100	903	1	$54,250	$572
			2		$819
Larger Units	0	——	——	——	——
Total		220 Units			

Entrance fee refunds decline over time.

These fees include one meal per day, biweekly housekeeping, scheduled transportation, and utilities. Special features of this community are presented in the Special Features Index at the back of the book. Ask about additional residential and health care services that may be available. Fees and services subject to change; verify with facility.

ASSISTED LIVING AND PERSONAL CARE

Assisted living units: 25
Personal care is covered by the continuing care contract: No
Residents may receive personal care in independent living units: No
Nonresidents may be admitted directly to assisted living units: Yes

NURSING CARE: Modified Plan

Under this modified plan, 60 days or more over a resident's lifetime are covered by the continuing care contract. When in nursing care, residents pay a fee that is discounted on the basis of the entrance fee they paid.

Intermediate beds: 47. Cost per day: private $58.00, semi-private $50.00.
Skilled beds: 47. Cost per day: private $65.00, semi-private $57.00.
Nursing beds are certified by Medicare and Medicaid. Nonresidents may be admitted directly to the nursing care facility.

WESTMINSTER VILLAGE NORTH

11050 Presbyterian Drive, Indianapolis, IN 46236
Telephone: (317) 823-6841

Opened in 1972 • Mixed single-level and low-rise buildings on 57 acres • Current resident population is 141 • Waiting list may apply for some units

AAHA
Member

HOUSING AND SERVICES

Living Units	No.	Square Feet	No. of Persons	Entrance Fee	Monthly Fee
Studio	—	300–350	1	$23,400–$28,600	$1,176–$1,231
One Bedroom	—	449–550	1	$30,550–$37,700	$1,355–$1,537
			2	$33,150–$40,300	$1,782–$1,982
Two Bedroom	—	550–825	1	$52,600	$1,853
			2	$55,200	$2,299
Larger Units	0	—	—	—	—
Total	104 Units				

Entrance fee refunds decline over time.

These fees include three meals per day, biweekly housekeeping, scheduled transportation, and utilities. Special features of this community are presented in the Special Features Index at the back of the book. Ask about additional residential and health care services that may be available. Fees and services subject to change; verify with facility.

ASSISTED LIVING AND PERSONAL CARE

Assisted living units: 28
Personal care is covered by the continuing care contract: Yes
Residents may receive personal care in independent living units: Yes
Nonresidents may be admitted directly to assisted living units: Yes

NURSING CARE: Modified Plan

Under this modified plan, 15 or fewer days are covered by the continuing care contract. Once residents move permanently to the nursing unit, they pay the full per diem rate for nursing care.

Intermediate beds: 38. Cost per day: private $86.00, semi-private $64.00.

Skilled beds: 39. Cost per day: private $86.00, semi-private $68.00.

Nursing beds are certified by Medicare and Medicaid. Nonresidents may be admitted directly to the nursing care facility.

WESTMINSTER VILLAGE TERRE HAUTE
1120 Davis Avenue, Terre Haute, IN 47802
Telephone: (812) 232-7533

Opened in 1981 • Predominantly high-rise buildings on 51 acres • Current resident population is 293 • Immediate availability

AAHA
Member

HOUSING AND SERVICES

Living Units	No.	Square Feet	No. of Persons	Entrance Fee	Monthly Fee
Studio	20	508	1	$25,000–$35,000	$421
One Bedroom	114	528	1	$30,000–$44,000	$454
			2	$30,000–$44,000	$670
Two Bedroom	30	792	1	$45,000–$63,000	$491
			2	$45,000–$63,000	$707
Larger Units	52	917	1	$50,000–$72,000	$524
			2	$50,000–$72,000	$740
Total	216 Units				

Residents have a choice of entrance fee refund plans.

These fees include one meal per day, biweekly housekeeping, scheduled transportation, and utilities. Special features of this community are presented in the Special Features Index at the back of the book. Ask about additional residential and health care services that may be available. Fees and services subject to change; verify with facility.

ASSISTED LIVING AND PERSONAL CARE
Assisted living units: 39
Personal care is covered by the continuing care contract: Yes
Residents may receive personal care in independent living units: No
Nonresidents may be admitted directly to assisted living units: Yes

NURSING CARE: Modified Plan

Under this modified plan, 15 or fewer days per year are covered by the continuing care contract. Once residents move permanently to the nursing unit, they pay the full per diem rate for nursing care.

Intermediate beds: 39. Cost per day: private $75.75, semi-private $58.75.

Skilled beds: 39. Cost per day: private $81.25, semi-private $64.75.

Nursing beds are certified by Medicare and Medicaid. Nonresidents may be admitted directly to the nursing care facility.

INDIANA

WESTMINSTER VILLAGE WEST LAFAYETTE
2741 North Salisbury Street, West Lafayette, IN 47906
Telephone: (317) 463-7546

Opened in 1976 • Mixed single-level and low-rise buildings on 34 acres • Current resident population is 290 • Waiting list may apply for some units

AAHA Member

HOUSING AND SERVICES

Living Units	No.	Square Feet	No. of Persons	Entrance Fee	Monthly Fee
Studio	8	445	1	$26,650	$508
One Bedroom	145	496	1	$35,100	$531
			2	$35,100	$784
Two Bedroom	70	716–992	1	$42,900–$58,000	$575–$618
			2	$42,900–$58,000	$828–$953
Larger Units	0	—	—	—	—
Total	223 Units				

Entrance fee refunds decline over time.

These fees include one meal per day, biweekly housekeeping, and utilities. Special features of this community are presented in the Special Features Index at the back of the book. Ask about additional residential and health care services that may be available. Fees and services subject to change; verify with facility.

ASSISTED LIVING AND PERSONAL CARE

Assisted living units: 0
Personal care is covered by the continuing care contract: No
Residents may receive personal care in independent living units: Yes

NURSING CARE: Fee-for-Service Plan

Under this fee-for-service plan, guaranteed access to nursing care is covered by the continuing care contract. Residents pay the full per diem rate for nursing care.

Skilled beds: 38. Cost per day: private $78.30, semi-private $61.80.

Nursing beds are certified by Medicare. Nonresidents may be admitted directly to the nursing care facility.

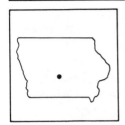

BISHOP DRUMM RETIREMENT CENTER
5837 Winwood Drive, Johnston, IA 50131
Telephone: (515) 270-1100

Opened in 1980 • One high-rise building on ten acres • Current resident population is 225 • Waiting list

AAHA
Member

HOUSING AND SERVICES

Living Units	No.	Square Feet	No. of Persons	Entrance Fee	Monthly Fee
Studio	31	377–442	1	$14,000	$485
One Bedroom	51	552–754	1	$22,000	$665
			2	$24,000	$910
Two Bedroom	6	929–961	1	$32,000	$895
			2	$35,000	$1,035
Larger Units	0	——	——	——	——
Total		88 Units			

Entrance fee refunds decline over time.

These fees include one meal per day, biweekly housekeeping, and utilities. Special features of this community are presented in the Special Features Index at the back of the book. Ask about additional residential and health care services that may be available. Fees and services subject to change; verify with facility.

ASSISTED LIVING AND PERSONAL CARE

Assisted living units: 0
Personal care is covered by the continuing care contract: No
Residents may receive personal care in independent living units: No

NURSING CARE: Modified Plan

Under this modified plan, 15 or fewer days per year are covered by the continuing care contract. Once residents move permanently to the nursing unit, they pay the full per diem rate for nursing care.

Intermediate beds: 120. Cost per day: private $61.00, semi-private $55.00.

Nursing beds are certified by Medicaid. Nonresidents may be admitted directly to the nursing care facility.

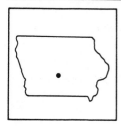

CALVIN MANOR
4210 Hickman Road, Des Moines, IA 50310
Telephone: (515) 277-6141

Opened in 1965 • One high-rise building on five acres • Current resident population is 145 • Waiting list

AAHA
Member

HOUSING AND SERVICES

Living Units	No.	Square Feet	No. of Persons	Entrance Fee	Monthly Fee
Studio	121	281–485	1	$12,500	$613
One Bedroom	16	470–680	1	$24,000	$913
			2	$24,000	$1,208
Two Bedroom	0	——	——	——	——
Larger Units	0	——	——	——	——
Total	137 Units				

Entrance fee refunds decline over time.

These fees include three meals per day, weekly housekeeping, scheduled transportation, and utilities. Special features of this community are presented in the Special Features Index at the back of the book. Ask about additional residential and health care services that may be available. Fees and services subject to change; verify with facility.

ASSISTED LIVING AND PERSONAL CARE

Assisted living units: 0
Personal care is covered by the continuing care contract: No
Residents may receive personal care in independent living units: Yes

NURSING CARE: Fee-for-Service Plan

Under this fee-for-service plan, guaranteed access to nursing care is covered by the continuing care contract. Residents pay the full per diem rate for nursing care.

Intermediate beds: 59. Cost per day: private—not applicable, semi-private $49.00.

Nursing beds are certified by Medicaid. Nonresidents may be admitted directly to the nursing care facility.

FRIENDSHIP HAVEN
South Kenyon Road, Fort Dodge, IA 50501
Telephone: (515) 573-2121

Opened in 1951 • Mixed single-level, low-rise, and high-rise buildings on 38 acres • Current resident population is 568 • Immediate availability

AAHA
Member

HOUSING AND SERVICES

Living Units	No.	Square Feet	No. of Persons	Entrance Fee	Monthly Fee
Studio	202	194	1	$7,500–$10,000	$420
One Bedroom	103	387	1	$15,000–$20,000	$420
			2		$840
Two Bedroom	5	481	1	$30,000	$420
			2		$840
Larger Units	42	1,257	1	$31,000–$48,000	$250–$300
			2		$340–$390

Total   352 Units

Entrance fees are nonrefundable.

These fees include three meals per day, housekeeping, scheduled transportation, and utilities. Special features of this community are presented in the Special Features Index at the back of the book. Ask about additional residential and health care services that may be available. Fees and services subject to change; verify with facility.

ASSISTED LIVING AND PERSONAL CARE

Assisted living units: 6
Personal care is covered by the continuing care contract: Yes
Residents may receive personal care in independent living units: Yes
Nonresidents may be admitted directly to assisted living units: No

NURSING CARE: Fee-for-Service Plan

Under this fee-for-service plan, guaranteed access to nursing care is covered by the continuing care contract. Residents pay the full per diem rate for nursing care.

Intermediate beds: 208. Cost per day: private $45.00, semi-private $42.00.
Nursing beds are certified by Medicaid. Nonresidents may be admitted directly to the nursing care facility.

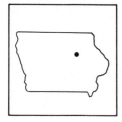

FRIENDSHIP VILLAGE
600 Park Lane, Waterloo, IA 50702
Telephone: (319) 291-8100

Opened in 1968 • Mixed single-level, low-rise, and high-rise buildings on 30 acres • Current resident population is 330 • Waiting list may apply for some units

AAHA
Member

HOUSING AND SERVICES

Living Units	No.	Square Feet	No. of Persons	Entrance Fee	Monthly Fee
Studio	116	300–450	1	$20,500–$32,500	$660–$1,050
One Bedroom	97	600–625	1, 2	$43,000	$725–$1,085
Two Bedroom	41	735–1,500	1, 2	$53,500–$58,500	$740–$1,120
Larger Units	0	—	—	—	—
Total	254 Units				

Entrance fees are nonrefundable.

These fees include one, two, or three meals per day; housekeeping; scheduled transportation; and utilities. Special features of this community are presented in the Special Features Index at the back of the book. Ask about additional residential and health care services that may be available. Fees and services subject to change; verify with facility.

ASSISTED LIVING AND PERSONAL CARE

Assisted living units: 0
Personal care is covered by the continuing care contract: No
Residents may receive personal care in independent living units: Yes

NURSING CARE: All-Inclusive Plan

Under this all-inclusive plan, unlimited nursing care is covered by the continuing care contract. When residents are in nursing care, they pay the same monthly fee they paid for their independent living unit.

Intermediate beds: 33.

Skilled beds: 17. Cost per day: private $50.00, semi-private $45.00.

Nursing beds are certified by both Medicare and Medicaid. Nonresidents may be admitted directly to the nursing care facility.

HALCYON HOUSE
1015 South Iowa Avenue, Washington, IA 52353
Telephone: (319) 653-7264

Opened in 1959 • Mixed single-level and low-rise buildings on eight acres • Current resident population is 153 • Waiting list

AAHA
Member

HOUSING AND SERVICES

Living Units	No.	Square Feet	No. of Persons	Entrance Fee	Monthly Fee
Studio	18	400	1	$11,000–$12,500	$240
One Bedroom	24	600–800	1	$20,000–$23,000	$265–$275
			2		$300
Two Bedroom	42	800	1	$20,000–$23,000	$275
			2		$300
Larger Units	6	1,200	1, 2	$35,500	$500
Total	90 Units				

Entrance fees are nonrefundable.

These fees include utilities. Special features of this community are presented in the Special Features Index at the back of the book. Ask about additional residential and health care services that may be available. Fees and services subject to change; verify with facility.

ASSISTED LIVING AND PERSONAL CARE

Assisted living units: 15
Personal care is covered by the continuing care contract: Yes
Residents may receive personal care in independent living units: No
Nonresidents may be admitted directly to assisted living units: Yes

NURSING CARE: Modified Plan

Under this modified plan, 15 or fewer days per year are covered by the continuing care contract. Once residents move permanently to a nursing unit, they pay the full per diem rate for nursing care.

Intermediate beds: 29. Cost per day: private $47.00, semi-private $42.00.
Skilled beds: 0.
Nursing beds are certified by Medicaid. Nonresidents may be admitted directly to the nursing care facility.

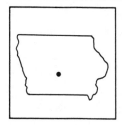

HEATHER MANOR
600 East Fifth Street, Des Moines, IA 50316
Telephone: (515) 243-6195

Opened in 1970 • One high-rise building on four acres • Current resident population is 130 • Waiting list may apply in some units

AAHA
Member

HOUSING AND SERVICES

Living Units	No.	Square Feet	No. of Persons	Entrance Fee	Monthly Fee
Studio	32	330–515	1	$21,950–$27,950	$459–492
One Bedroom	87	515–1,030	1	$39,950–$51,950	$546–$568
			2		$795–$817
Two Bedroom	0	—	—	—	—
Larger Units	1	1,410	1	$80,950	$835
			2		$1,085
Total	120 Units				

Entrance fees are nonrefundable.

These fees include biweekly housekeeping, scheduled transportation, and utilities. Special features of this community are presented in the Special Features Index at the back of the book. Ask about additional residential and health care services that may be available. Fees and services subject to change; verify with facility.

ASSISTED LIVING AND PERSONAL CARE

Assisted living units: 31
Personal care is covered by the continuing care contract: Yes
Residents may receive personal care in independent living units: No
Nonresidents may be admitted directly to assisted living units: No

NURSING CARE: All-Inclusive Plan

Under this all-inclusive plan, unlimited nursing care is covered by the continuing care contract. When residents are in nursing care, they pay the same monthly fee they paid for their independent living unit.

Intermediate beds: 31. Cost per day: not applicable.

Nursing beds are not certified by Medicare or Medicaid. Nonresidents may not be admitted directly to the nursing care facility.

HERITAGE HOUSE

1200 Brookridge Circle, Atlantic, IA 50022
Telephone: (712) 243-1850

Opened in 1963 • Predominantly high-rise buildings on 15 acres • Current resident population is 143 • Located 63 miles from Council Bluffs, IA • Waiting list may apply for some units

AAHA Member

HOUSING AND SERVICES

Living Units	No.	Square Feet	No. of Persons	Entrance Fee	Monthly Fee
Studio	51	268–343	1	$14,000–$25,900	$600
One Bedroom	12	535–818	1	$27,000	$250–$521
			2	$27,000	$316–$553
Two Bedroom	19	935–946	1	$32,500	$270
			2	$32,500	$290
Larger Units	0	——	——	——	——
Total	82 Units				

Entrance fees are nonrefundable.

These fees include scheduled transportation and utilities. Special features of this community are presented in the Special Features Index at the back of the book. Ask about additional residential and health care services that may be available. Fees and services subject to change; verify with facility.

ASSISTED LIVING AND PERSONAL CARE

Assisted living units: 12
Personal care is covered by the continuing care contract: Yes
Residents may receive personal care in independent living units: Yes
Nonresidents may be admitted directly to assisted living units: Yes

NURSING CARE: Modified Plan

Under this modified plan, 15 or fewer days per year are covered by the continuing care contract. Once residents move permanently to the nursing unit, they pay a discounted per diem rate for nursing care.

Intermediate beds: 46. Cost per day: private—not applicable, semi-private $18.80–$38.75.
Nursing beds are certified by Medicaid. Nonresidents may be admitted directly to the nursing care facility.

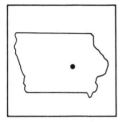

MAYFLOWER HOMES
616 Broad Street, Grinnell, IA 50112
Telephone: (515) 236-6151

Opened in 1953 • Mixed single-level and low-rise buildings on nine acres • Current resident population is 180 • Waiting list

AAHA Member

HOUSING AND SERVICES

Living Units	No.	Square Feet	No. of Persons	Entrance Fee	Monthly Fee
Studio	48	340–550	1	$20,000–$27,000	$148–$182
One Bedroom	41	600–720	1	$30,000–$38,000	$206–$229
			2		$309–$343
Two Bedroom	21	780–900	1	$39,000–$54,000	$244–$299
			2		$366–$448
Larger Units	0	——	——	——	——
Total	110 Units				

Entrance fees are nonrefundable.

These fees include scheduled transportation and utilities. Special features of this community are presented in the Special Features Index at the back of the book. Ask about additional residential and health care services that may be available. Fees and services subject to change; verify with facility.

ASSISTED LIVING AND PERSONAL CARE

Assisted living units: 34
Personal care is covered by the continuing care contract: No
Residents may receive personal care in independent living units: Yes
Nonresidents may be admitted directly to assisted living units: No

NURSING CARE: Fee-for-Service Plan

Under this fee-for-service plan, guaranteed access to nursing care is covered by the continuing care contract. Residents pay the full per diem rate for nursing care.

Intermediate beds: 26. Cost per day: private $48.00, semi-private $40.00.

Nursing beds are certified by Medicaid. Nonresidents may be admitted directly to the nursing care facility.

METH-WICK MANOR
1224 13th Street N.W., Cedar Rapids, IA 52405
Telephone: (319) 365-9171

Opened in 1961 • One high-rise building on 24 acres • Current resident population is 188 • Waiting list may apply for some units

AAHA
Member

HOUSING AND SERVICES

Living Units	No.	Square Feet	No. of Persons	Entrance Fee	Monthly Fee
Studio	129	300–345	1	$20,000	$675
One Bedroom	18	600	1	$40,000	$1,150
			2		$1,320
Two Bedroom	0	——	——	——	——
Larger Units	0	——	——	——	——
Total	147 Units				

Entrance fees are nonrefundable.

These fees include three meals per day, weekly housekeeping, scheduled transportation, and utilities. Special features of this community are presented in the Special Features Index at the back of the book. Ask about additional residential and health care services that may be available. Fees and services subject to change; verify with facility.

ASSISTED LIVING AND PERSONAL CARE

Assisted living units: 8
Personal care is covered by the continuing care contract: Yes
Residents may receive personal care in independent living units: No
Nonresidents may be admitted directly to assisted living units: No

NURSING CARE: Fee-for-Service Plan

Under this fee-for-service plan, guaranteed access to nursing care is covered by the continuing care contract. Residents pay the full per diem rate for nursing care.

Intermediate beds: 49. Cost per day: private $53.50, semi-private $48.00.

Nursing beds are certified by Medicaid. Nonresidents may not be admitted directly to the nursing care facility.

OAKNOLL RETIREMENT RESIDENCE
701 Oaknoll Drive, Iowa City, IA 52240
Telephone: (319) 351-1720

Opened in 1966 • Mixed single-level and low-rise buildings on three acres • Current resident population is 170 • Immediate availability

AAHA
Member

HOUSING AND SERVICES

Living Units	No.	Square Feet	No. of Persons	Entrance Fee	Monthly Fee
Studio	0	—	—	—	—
One Bedroom	84	379–559	1	$32,340–$39,830	$455–$503
			2	$34,870–$43,560	$790–$837
Two Bedroom	43	669–1,004	1	$55,990–$89,500	$594–$777
			2	$59,730–$89,500	$928–$1,111
Larger Units	3	1,200	1	$99,500	$868
			2		$1,203
Total	130 Units				

Entrance fee refunds decline over time.

These fees include biweekly housekeeping, scheduled transportation, and utilities. Special features of this community are presented in the Special Features Index at the back of the book. Ask about additional residential and health care services that may be available. Fees and services subject to change; verify with facility.

ASSISTED LIVING AND PERSONAL CARE

Assisted living units: 0
Personal care is covered by the continuing care contract: No
Residents may receive personal care in independent living units: No

NURSING CARE: All-Inclusive Plan

Under this all-inclusive plan, unlimited nursing care is covered by the continuing care contract. When in nursing care, residents pay the same monthly fee they paid for their independent living unit.

Intermediate beds: 16. Cost per day: private $77.00, semi-private $77.00.

Skilled beds: 32. Cost per day: private $77.00, semi-private $77.00.

Nursing beds are certified by both Medicare and Medicaid. Nonresidents may be admitted directly to the nursing care facility.

RIDGECREST RETIREMENT VILLAGE
4130 Northwest Boulevard, Davenport, IA 52806
Telephone: (319) 391-3430

Opened in 1966 • Mixed single-level, low-rise, and high-rise buildings on 23 acres • Current resident population is 417 • Immediate availability

AAHA
Member

HOUSING AND SERVICES

Living Units	No.	Square Feet	No. of Persons	Entrance Fee	Monthly Fee
Studio	97	434	1	$30,757	$644
One Bedroom	93	740	1	$58,424	$761
			2	$58,424	$1,066
Two Bedroom	38	966	1	$69,820	$872
			2		$1,229
Larger Units	0	—	—	—	—
Total	228 Units				

Entrance fee refunds decline over time.

These fees include one meal per day, biweekly housekeeping, scheduled transportation, and utilities. Special features of this community are presented in the Special Features Index at the back of the book. Ask about additional residential and health care services that may be available. Fees and services subject to change; verify with facility.

ASSISTED LIVING AND PERSONAL CARE
Assisted living units: 9
Personal care is covered by the continuing care contract: No
Residents may receive personal care in independent living units: Yes
Nonresidents may be admitted directly to assisted living units: No

NURSING CARE: All-Inclusive Plan

Under this all-inclusive plan, unlimited nursing care is covered by the continuing care contract. When in nursing care, residents pay the same monthly fee they paid for their independent living unit.

Intermediate beds: 108. Cost per day: private $76.35, semi-private $58.25.

Skilled beds: 20. Cost per day: private $100.25, semi-private $83.40.

Nursing beds are certified by both Medicare and Medicaid. Nonresidents may be admitted directly to the nursing care facility.

UNITED PRESBYTERIAN HOME
1203 East Washington Street, Washington, IA 52353
Telephone: (319) 653-5473

Opened in 1947 • Mixed single-level and low-rise buildings on 25 acres • Current resident population is 190 • Waiting list

AAHA
Member

HOUSING AND SERVICES

Living Units	No.	Square Feet	No. of Persons	Entrance Fee	Monthly Fee
Studio	37	175–360	1	$1,400–$15,000	$207–$548
One Bedroom	15	350–835	1	$10,000–$35,000	$207
			2		$270
Two Bedroom Cottages	61	720–1,200	1, 2	$15,000–$40,000	Utilities
Larger Units	0	——	——	——	——
Total	113 Units				

Entrance fees are nonrefundable.

These fees, except in cottages, include monthly housekeeping and utilities. Special features of this community are presented in the Special Features Index at the back of the book. Ask about additional residential and health care services that may be available. Fees and services subject to change; verify with facility.

ASSISTED LIVING AND PERSONAL CARE

Assisted living units: 16
Personal care is covered by the continuing care contract: No
Residents may receive personal care in independent living units: No
Nonresidents may be admitted directly to assisted living units: No

NURSING CARE: Fee-for-Service Plan

Under this fee-for-service plan, guaranteed access to nursing care is covered by the continuing care contract. Residents pay the full per diem rate for nursing care.

Intermediate beds: 36. Cost per day: private $43.50, semi-private $39.50.

Nursing beds are certified by Medicaid. Nonresidents may not be admitted directly to the nursing care facility.

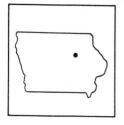

WESTERN HOME
420 East 11th Street, Cedar Falls, IA 50613
Telephone: (319) 277-2141

Opened in 1912 • One high-rise building on four acres • Current resident population is 240 • Waiting list may apply for some units

AAHA
Member

HOUSING AND SERVICES

Living Units	No.	Square Feet	No. of Persons	Entrance Fee	Monthly Fee
Studio	107	245	1	$1,200	$565
One Bedroom	5	500	1	$1,200	$650
			2	$1,800	
Two Bedroom	0	—	—	—	—
Larger Units	0	—	—	—	—
Total	112 Units				

Entrance fees are nonrefundable.

These fees include three meals per day, weekly housekeeping, scheduled transportation, and utilities. Special features of this community are presented in the Special Features Index at the back of the book. Ask about additional residential and health care services that may be available. Fees and services subject to change; verify with facility.

ASSISTED LIVING AND PERSONAL CARE

Assisted living units: 76
Personal care is covered by the continuing care contract: No
Residents may receive personal care in independent living units: Yes
Nonresidents may be admitted directly to assisted living units: Yes

NURSING CARE: Fee-for-Service Plan

Under this fee-for-service plan, guaranteed access to nursing care is covered by the continuing care contract. Residents pay the full per diem rate for nursing care.

Intermediate beds: 68. Cost per day: private $43.00, semi-private $39.00.
Nursing beds are certified by Medicaid. Nonresidents may be admitted directly to the nursing care facility.

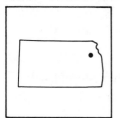

ALDERSGATE VILLAGE
7220 Asbury Drive, Topeka, KS 66614
Telephone: (913) 478-9440

Opened in 1979 • Mixed single-level and low-rise buildings on 242 acres • Current resident population is 297 • Waiting list

AAHA Member

HOUSING AND SERVICES

Living Units	No.	Square Feet	No. of Persons	Entrance Fee	Monthly Fee
Studio	6	541	1	$4,000	$590
One Bedroom	99	674–1,075	1, 2	$4,000	$670–$970
Two Bedroom	58	894–1,400	1, 2	$4,000	$860–$1,135
Larger Units	0	——	——	——	——
Total	163 Units				

Entrance fee refunds decline over time.

These fees include housekeeping and scheduled transportation. Special features of this community are presented in the Special Features Index at the back of the book. Ask about additional residential and health care services that may be available. Fees and services subject to change; verify with facility.

ASSISTED LIVING AND PERSONAL CARE

Assisted living units: 55
Personal care is covered by the continuing care contract: Yes
Residents may receive personal care in independent living units: No
Nonresidents may be admitted directly to assisted living units: Yes

NURSING CARE: Fee-for-Service Plan

Under this fee-for-service plan, guaranteed access to nursing care is covered by the continuing care contract. Residents pay the full per diem rate for nursing care.

Skilled beds: 60. Cost per day: private $60.50, semi-private $50.50.

Nursing beds are not certified by Medicare or Medicaid. Nonresidents may be admitted directly to the nursing care facility.

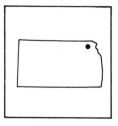

APOSTOLIC CHRISTIAN HOME
511 Paramount Street, Sabetha, KS 66534
Telephone: (913) 284-3471

Opened in 1983 • Predominantly single-level/garden apartments on 23 acres • Current resident population is 127 • Waiting list may apply for some units

AAHA
Member

HOUSING AND SERVICES

Living Units	No.	Square Feet	No. of Persons	Entrance Fee	Monthly Fee
Studio	2	449	1	$38,000	$38
One Bedroom	17	670–740	1	$51,500	$38
			2	$56,500	
Two Bedroom	11	800–923	1, 2	——	$38
Larger Units	0	——	——	——	——
Total	30 Units				

Entrance fees are partially refundable.

Special features of this community are presented in the Special Features Index at the back of the book. Ask about additional residential and health care services that may be available. Fees and services subject to change; verify with facility.

ASSISTED LIVING AND PERSONAL CARE

Assisted living units: 0
Personal care is covered by the continuing care contract: No
Residents may receive personal care in independent living units: No

NURSING CARE: Fee-for-Service Plan

Under this fee-for-service plan, guaranteed access to nursing care is covered by the continuing care contract. Residents pay the full per diem rate for nursing care.

Intermediate beds: 82. Cost per day: private $35.83, semi-private $30.83.

Nursing beds are certified by Medicaid. Nonresidents may be admitted directly to the nursing care facility.

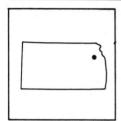

BREWSTER PLACE
1205 West 29th Street, Topeka, KS 66611
Telephone: (913) 267-1666

Opened in 1962 • Mixed single-level, low-rise, and high-rise buildings on 14 acres • Current resident population is 280 • Waiting list

AAHA
Member

HOUSING AND SERVICES

Living Units	No.	Square Feet	No. of Persons	Entrance Fee	Monthly Fee
Studio	40	200–300	1	$15,500–$28,800	$260–$339
One Bedroom	50	400–800	1, 2	$33,000–$43,700	$366–$661
Two Bedroom	90	900–1,150	1, 2	$41,000–$70,000	$471–$540
Larger Units	0	——	——	——	——
Total	180 Units				

Entrance fee refunds decline over time.

These fees include biweekly housekeeping and utilities. Special features of this community are presented in the Special Features Index at the back of the book. Ask about additional residential and health care services that may be available. Fees and services subject to change; verify with facility.

ASSISTED LIVING AND PERSONAL CARE

Assisted living units: 0
Personal care is covered by the continuing care contract: No
Residents may receive personal care in independent living units: No

NURSING CARE: Modified Plan

Under this modified plan, 15 or fewer days per year are covered by the continuing care contract. Once residents move permanently to the nursing unit, they pay the full per diem rate for nursing care.

Skilled beds: 77. Cost per day: private $60.17, semi-private $41.00.

Nursing beds are certified by both Medicare and Medicaid. Nonresidents may be admitted directly to the nursing care facility.

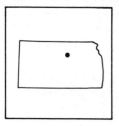

CLAY CENTER PRESBYTERIAN MANOR
924 Eighth Street, Clay Center, KS 67432
Telephone: (913) 632-5646

Opened in 1968 • One high-rise building on one acre • Current resident population is 54 • Waiting list may apply for some units

AAHA
Member

HOUSING AND SERVICES

Living Units	No.	Square Feet	No. of Persons	Entrance Fee	Monthly Fee
Studio	3	168	1	$3,000	$843
One Bedroom	28	650	1	$3,000	$1,108
			2	$6,000	$1,408
Two Bedroom	0	——	——	——	——
Larger Units	0	——	——	——	——
Total		31 Units			

Entrance fees are fully refundable.

These fees include three meals per day, housekeeping, and utilities. Special features of this community are presented in the Special Features Index at the back of the book. Ask about additional residential and health care services that may be available. Fees and services subject to change; verify with facility.

ASSISTED LIVING AND PERSONAL CARE

Assisted living units: 0
Personal care is covered by the continuing care contract: Yes
Residents may receive personal care in independent living units: Yes

NURSING CARE: Modified Plan

Under this modified plan, 12 days are covered by the continuing care contract. Thereafter, residents pay the full per diem rate for nursing care.

Intermediate beds: 25. Cost per day: private $46.36, semi-private $39.23.

Nursing beds are certified by Medicaid. Nonresidents may be admitted directly to the nursing care facility.

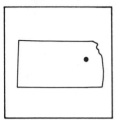

EMPORIA PRESBYTERIAN MANOR
2300 Industrial Road, Emporia, KS 66801
Telephone: (316) 343-2613

Opened in 1985 • Mixed single-level and low-rise buildings on 20 acres • Current resident population is 70 • Waiting list may apply for some units

AAHA
Member

HOUSING AND SERVICES

Living Units	No.	Square Feet	No. of Persons	Entrance Fee	Monthly Fee
Studio	4	379	1	$5,000	$670
One Bedroom	38	574	1	$5,000	$825
			2	$10,000	$1,100
Two Bedroom	21	779	1	$5,000	$1,145
			2	$10,000	$1,420
Larger Units	6	902	1	$5,000	$1,360
			2	$10,000	$1,635
Total		69 Units			

Entrance fee refunds decline over time.

These fees include one meal per day, monthly housekeeping, and scheduled transportation. Special features of this community are presented in the Special Features Index at the back of the book. Ask about additional residential and health care services that may be available. Fees and services subject to change; verify with facility.

ASSISTED LIVING AND PERSONAL CARE

Assisted living units: 0
Personal care is covered by the continuing care contract: No
Residents may receive personal care in independent living units: No

NURSING CARE: Modified Plan

Under this modified plan, 15 or fewer days per year are covered by the continuing care contract. Once residents move permanently to the nursing unit, they pay the full per diem rate for nursing care.

Intermediate beds. Cost per day: private $69.00, semi-private $46.00.

Skilled beds: 60. Cost per day: private $87.00, semi-private $58.00.

Nursing beds are not certified by Medicare or Medicaid. Nonresidents may be admitted directly to the nursing care facility.

KANSAS

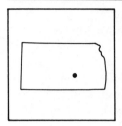

KANSAS CHRISTIAN HOME
1035 Southeast Third Street, Newton, KS 67114
Telephone: (316) 283-6600

Opened in 1962 • Predominantly single-level/garden
apartments on 30 acres • Current resident population
is 40 • Waiting list may apply for some units

AAHA
Member

HOUSING AND SERVICES

Living Units	No.	Square Feet	No. of Persons	Entrance Fee	Monthly Fee
Studio	0	——	——	——	——
One Bedroom	0	——	——	——	——
Two Bedroom	32	750–900	1, 2	$46,000	$120
Larger Units	1	1,200	1, 2	$62,000	$120
Total	33 Units				

Entrance fee refunds decline over time.

These fees include scheduled transportation. Special features of this community are presented in the Special Features Index at the back of the book. Ask
about additional residential and health care services that may be available. Fees
and services subject to change; verify with facility.

ASSISTED LIVING AND PERSONAL CARE

Assisted living units: 0
Personal care is covered by the continuing care contract: No
Residents may receive personal care in independent living units: No

NURSING CARE: Modified Plan

Under this modified plan, 15 or fewer days per year are covered by the continuing care contract. Once residents move permanently to the nursing unit, they
pay the full per diem rate for nursing care.

Intermediate beds: 115. Cost per day: private $46.00, semi-private $42.00.
Nursing beds are certified by Medicaid. Nonresidents may be admitted
directly to the nursing care facility.

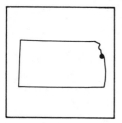

KANSAS CITY PRESBYTERIAN MANOR
7850 Freeman Street, Kansas City, KS 66112
Telephone: (913) 334-3666

Opened in 1967 • One high-rise building on four acres • Current resident population is 141 • Waiting list may apply for some units

AAHA
Member

HOUSING AND SERVICES

Living Units	No.	Square Feet	No. of Persons	Entrance Fee	Monthly Fee
Studio	33	180	1	$5,000	$900
One Bedroom	11	400	1	$10,000	$1,395
			2	$10,000	$2,095
Two Bedroom	0	——	——	——	——
Larger Units	0	——	——	——	——
Total	44 Units				

Entrance fee refunds decline over time.

These fees include three meals per day, weekly housekeeping, scheduled transportation, and utilities. Special features of this community are presented in the Special Features Index at the back of the book. Ask about additional residential and health care services that may be available. Fees and services subject to change; verify with facility.

ASSISTED LIVING AND PERSONAL CARE

Assisted living units: 44
Personal care is covered by the continuing care contract: No
Residents may receive personal care in independent living units: No
Nonresidents may be admitted directly to assisted living units: Yes

NURSING CARE: Modified Plan

Under this modified plan, 15 or fewer days per year are covered by the continuing care contract. Once residents move permanently to the nursing unit, they pay the full per diem rate for nursing care.

Intermediate beds: 43. Cost per day: private $69.00, semi-private $55.00.
Skilled beds: 21. Cost per day: private $75.00, semi-private $70.00.
Nursing beds are certified by both Medicare and Medicaid. Nonresidents may be admitted directly to the nursing care facility.

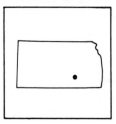

LARKSFIELD PLACE
650 North Carriage Parkway, Suite 135
Wichita, KS 67208
Telephone: (316) 686-7300

Opening in 1988 • Mixed single-level, low-rise, and high-rise buildings on 53 acres • Immediate availability

AAHA
Member

HOUSING AND SERVICES

Living Units	No.	Square Feet	No. of Persons	Entrance Fee	Monthly Fee
Studio	0	——	——	——	——
One Bedroom	99	475–750	1	$41,500–$62,500	$940–$1,255
			2	$41,500–$62,500	$1,310–$1,625
Two Bedroom	80	900–1,050	1	$73,000–$83,500	$1,360–$1,500
			2	$73,000–$83,500	$1,710–$1,870
Larger Units	0	——	——	——	——
Total	179 Units				

Entrance fees are fully refundable.

These fees include one meal per day, biweekly housekeeping, scheduled transportation, and utilities. Special features of this community are presented in the Special Features Index at the back of the book. Ask about additional residential and health care services that may be available. Fees and services subject to change; verify with facility.

ASSISTED LIVING AND PERSONAL CARE

Assisted living units: 0
Personal care is covered by the continuing care contract: Yes
Residents may receive personal care in independent living units: Yes

NURSING CARE: All-Inclusive Plan

Under this all-inclusive plan, unlimited nursing care is covered by the continuing care contract. When residents are in nursing care, they pay the same monthly fee they paid for their independent living unit.

Skilled beds: 60. Cost per day: not applicable.

Nursing beds are certified by Medicare. Nonresidents may not be admitted directly to the nursing care facility.

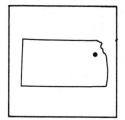

LAWRENCE PRESBYTERIAN MANOR
1429 Kasold Drive, Lawrence, KS 66044
Telephone: (913) 841-4262

Opened in 1976 • Mixed single-level, low-rise, and high-rise buildings on 16 acres • Current resident population is 129 • Waiting list

AAHA Member

HOUSING AND SERVICES

Living Units	No.	Square Feet	No. of Persons	Entrance Fee	Monthly Fee
Studio	48	500	1	$5,000	$846
One Bedroom	16	1,000	1	$5,000	$1,116
			2		$1,557
Two Bedroom	1	1,500	1, 2	$5,000	$1,682
Larger Units	16	1,300	1, 2	$5,000*	$238
Total	81 Units				

*In addition to the entrance fee, residents of larger units also pay a $60,000 life-use fee.

Entrance fee refunds decline over time.

These fees include three meals per day, scheduled transportation, and utilities. Special features of this community are presented in the Special Features Index at the back of the book. Ask about additional residential and health care services that may be available. Fees and services subject to change; verify with facility.

ASSISTED LIVING AND PERSONAL CARE

Assisted living units: 15
Personal care is covered by the continuing care contract: No
Residents may receive personal care in independent living units: Yes
Nonresidents may be admitted directly to assisted living units: Yes

NURSING CARE: Modified Plan

Under this modified plan, 30 days are covered by the continuing care contract. Once residents move permanently to the nursing unit, they pay the full per diem rate for nursing care.

Intermediate beds. Cost per day: private $66.00, semi-private $56.00.

Skilled beds: 43. Cost per day: private $54.63, semi-private $44.63.

Nursing beds are certified by Medicaid. Nonresidents may be admitted directly to the nursing care facility.

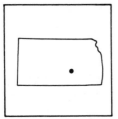

NEWTON PRESBYTERIAN MANOR
1200 East Seventh Street, Newton, KS 67114
Telephone: (316) 283-5400

Opened in 1949 • Mixed single-level and low-rise buildings on 23 acres • Current resident population is 140 • Immediate availability

---

HOUSING AND SERVICES

Living Units	No.	Square Feet	No. of Persons	Entrance Fee	Monthly Fee
Studio	0	——	——	——	——
One Bedroom	28	550–750	1	$3,000	$426–$618
			2	$6,000	$426–$618
Two Bedroom	6	900–1,050	1	$3,000	$632–$824
			2	$6,000	$632–$824
Larger Units	11	——	1	$3,000	$550–$650
			2	$6,000	

Total   45 Units

Entrance fees are nonrefundable.

These fees include utilities. Special features of this community are presented in the Special Features Index at the back of the book. Ask about additional residential and health care services that may be available. Fees and services subject to change; verify with facility.

ASSISTED LIVING AND PERSONAL CARE

Assisted living units: 46
Personal care is covered by the continuing care contract: Yes
Residents may receive personal care in independent living units: No
Nonresidents may be admitted directly to assisted living units: Yes

NURSING CARE: Modified Plan

Under this modified plan, 15 or fewer days are covered by the continuing care contract. Once residents move permanently to the nursing unit, they pay the full per diem rate for nursing care.

Intermediate beds: 46. Cost per day: private $49.50, semi-private $41.80.

Nursing beds are certified by Medicaid. Nonresidents may be admitted directly to the nursing care facility.

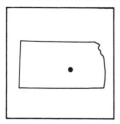

PARKSIDE HOMES
200 Willow Road, Hillsboro, KS 67063
Telephone: (316) 947-5700

Opened in 1962 • Predominantly single-level/garden apartments • Current resident population is 22 • Waiting list may apply for some units

AAHA
Member

HOUSING AND SERVICES

Living Units	No.	Square Feet	No. of Persons	Entrance Fee	Monthly Fee
Studio	0	——	——	——	——
One Bedroom	7	552	1	$1,000	$275–$285
			2	$1,500	$275–$285
Two Bedroom	12	772	1	$1,000	$315–$325
			2	$1,500	$315–$325
Larger Units	0	——	——	——	——
Total	19 Units				

Entrance fees are nonrefundable.

Special features of this community are presented in the Special Features Index at the back of the book. Ask about additional residential and health care services that may be available. Fees and services subject to change; verify with facility.

ASSISTED LIVING AND PERSONAL CARE

Assisted living units: 0
Personal care is covered by the continuing care contract: No
Residents may receive personal care in independent living units: No

NURSING CARE: Fee-for-Service Plan

Under this fee-for-service plan, guaranteed access to nursing care is covered by the continuing care contract. Residents pay the full per diem rate for nursing care.

Intermediate beds: 50. Cost per day: private $42.00, semi-private $38.00.
Nursing beds are certified by Medicaid. Nonresidents may be admitted directly to the nursing care facility.

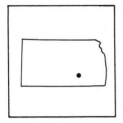

SCHOWALTER VILLA
200 West Cedar, P.O. Box 5000, Hesston, KS 67062
Telephone: (316) 327-4261

Opened in 1961 • Predominantly single-level/garden apartments on 15 acres • Current resident population is 186 • Waiting list may apply for some units

AAHA
Member

HOUSING AND SERVICES

Living Units	No.	Square Feet	No. of Persons	Entrance Fee	Monthly Fee
Studio	0	——	——	——	——
One Bedroom	30	767	1	$21,600	$280
			2	$21,600	$305
Two Bedroom	39	1,000	1	$27,900	$310
			2	$27,900	$335
Larger Units	0	——	——	——	——
Total		69 Units			

Entrance fees are partially refundable.

Special features of this community are presented in the Special Features Index at the back of the book. Ask about additional residential and health care services that may be available. Fees and services subject to change; verify with facility.

ASSISTED LIVING AND PERSONAL CARE

Assisted living units: 41
Personal care is covered by the continuing care contract: No
Residents may receive personal care in independent living units: No
Nonresidents may be admitted directly to assisted living units: Yes

NURSING CARE: Fee-for-Service Plan

Under this fee-for-service plan, guaranteed access to nursing care is covered by the continuing care contract. Residents pay the full per diem rate for nursing care.

Intermediate beds: 57. Cost per day: private $53.00, semi-private $48.00.

Nursing beds are certified by Medicaid. Nonresidents may be admitted directly to the nursing care facility.

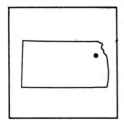

TOPEKA PRESBYTERIAN MANOR
4712 West Sixth Street, Topeka, KS 66606
Telephone: (913) 272-6510

Opened in 1962 • Mixed single-level, low-rise, and high-rise buildings on 17 acres • Current resident population is 212 • Waiting list may apply for some units

AAHA
Member

HOUSING AND SERVICES

Living Units	No.	Square Feet	No. of Persons	Entrance Fee	Monthly Fee
Studio	3	492	1	$25,850	$375
One Bedroom	16	524–710	1, 2	$32,000–$33,500	$380–$418
Two Bedroom	7	813–1,200	1	$35,750–$44,000	$526
			2	$35,750–$44,000	
Larger Units	0	—	—	—	—
Total	26 Units				

Entrance fee refunds decline over time.

These fees include weekly housekeeping and utilities. Special features of this community are presented in the Special Features Index at the back of the book. Ask about additional residential and health care services that may be available. Fees and services subject to change; verify with facility.

ASSISTED LIVING AND PERSONAL CARE

Assisted living units: 79
Personal care is covered by the continuing care contract: No
Residents may receive personal care in independent living units: Yes
Nonresidents may be admitted directly to assisted living units: Yes

NURSING CARE: Fee-for-Service Plan

Under this fee-for-service plan, guaranteed access to nursing care is covered by the continuing care contract. Residents pay the full per diem rate for nursing care.

Intermediate beds: 65. Cost per day: private $50.72, semi-private $40.36.

Skilled beds: 46. Cost per day: private $61.58, semi-private $51.23.

Nursing beds are certified by Medicaid. Nonresidents may be admitted directly to the nursing care facility.

KANSAS

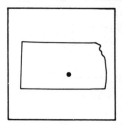

WESLEY TOWERS
700 Monterey Place, Hutchinson, KS 67502
Telephone: (316) 663-9175

Opened in 1969 • Mixed single-level, low-rise, and high-rise buildings on 75 acres • Current resident population is 263 • Immediate availability

AAHA
Member

HOUSING AND SERVICES

Living Units	No.	Square Feet	No. of Persons	Entrance Fee	Monthly Fee
Studio	86	280	1	$1,500	$684
One Bedroom	69	560	1	$1,500	$1,093
			2	$1,500	$1,255
Two Bedroom	0	——	——	——	——
Larger Units	12	1,200	1, 2	$81,500	$373
Total	167 Units				

Entrance fee refunds decline over time.

These fees include one meal per day, housekeeping, scheduled transportation, and utilities. Special features of this community are presented in the Special Features Index at the back of the book. Ask about additional residential and health care services that may be available. Fees and services subject to change; verify with facility.

ASSISTED LIVING AND PERSONAL CARE

Assisted living units: 60
Personal care is covered by the continuing care contract: Yes
Residents may receive personal care in independent living units: Yes
Nonresidents may be admitted directly to assisted living units: Yes

NURSING CARE: Fee-for-Service Plan

Under this fee-for-service plan, guaranteed access to nursing care is covered by the continuing care contract. Residents pay the full per diem rate for nursing care.

Intermediate beds: 70. Cost per day: private $50.56, semi-private $40.56.

Nursing beds are not certified by Medicare or Medicaid. Nonresidents may be admitted directly to the nursing care facility.

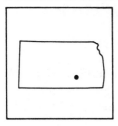

WICHITA PRESBYTERIAN MANOR
4700 West 13th Street, Wichita, KS 67212
Telephone: (316) 942-7456

Opened in 1970 • Mixed single-level and low-rise buildings on 13 acres • Current resident population is 182 • Waiting list may apply for some units

AAHA Member

HOUSING AND SERVICES

Living Units	No.	Square Feet	No. of Persons	Entrance Fee	Monthly Fee
Studio	0	—	—	—	—
One Bedroom	58	531–662	1,2	$36,000*	$195–$755
Two Bedroom	36	800–1,200	1,2	$45,000–$49,500*	$215–$890
Larger Units	0	—	—	—	—
Total	94 Units				

*These figures are "life use fees," which cover extended health care and are paid by most residents. In addition, a $5,000 entrance fee is required of all residents.

Residents have a choice of entrance fee refund plans.

Special features of this community are presented in the Special Features Index at the back of the book. Ask about additional residential and health care services that may be available. Fees and services subject to change; verify with facility.

ASSISTED LIVING AND PERSONAL CARE

Assisted living units: 30
Personal care is covered by the continuing care contract: Yes
Residents may receive personal care in independent living units: No
Nonresidents may be admitted directly to assisted living units: Yes

NURSING CARE: Modified Plan

Under this modified plan, 60 or more days are covered by the continuing care contract; the resident receives credit for nursing care based on the "life use fee." Once residents move permanently to the nursing unit, they pay the same monthly fee they paid for their independent living unit.

Skilled beds: 60. Cost per day: private $51.00, semi-private $44.50.

Nursing beds are certified by Medicaid. Nonresidents may be admitted directly to the nursing care facility.

MASONIC WIDOWS AND ORPHANS HOME
Masonic Home, KY 40041
Telephone: (502) 897-3344

Opened in 1927 • Mixed single-level and low-rise buildings on 179 acres • Current resident population is 238 • Located one mile from Louisville, KY • Waiting list may apply for some units

AAHA
Member

HOUSING AND SERVICES

The lifecare contract is given in exchange for an assumption of the widow's assets upon her admission. There are no monthly or other fees thereafter. Housing starts at the assisted living level.

Entrance fees are nonrefundable.

Services include three meals per day, housekeeping, scheduled transportation, and utilities. Special features of this community are presented in the Special Features Index at the back of the book. Ask about additional residential and health care services that may be available. Fees and services subject to change; verify with facility.

ASSISTED LIVING AND PERSONAL CARE

Assisted living units: 95
Personal care is covered by the continuing care contract: Yes
Residents may receive personal care in independent living units: No
Nonresidents may be admitted directly to assisted living units: Yes

NURSING CARE: All-Inclusive Plan

Under this all-inclusive plan, unlimited nursing care is covered by the continuing care contract. There is no charge for nursing care.

Intermediate beds: 130. Cost per day: not applicable.

Skilled beds: 38. Cost per day: not applicable.

Nursing beds are not certified by Medicare or Medicaid. Nonresidents may not be admitted directly to the nursing care facility.

WESTMINSTER TERRACE
2116 Buechel Bank Road, Louisville, KY 40218
Telephone: (502) 499-9383

Opened in 1966 • Mixed single-level and low-rise buildings on five acres • Current resident population is 202 • Waiting list may apply for some units

AAHA
Member

HOUSING AND SERVICES

Living Units	No.	Square Feet	No. of Persons	Entrance Fee	Monthly Fee
Studio	67	323	1	$10,000–$11,500	$675
One Bedroom	21	640	1	$15,000–$22,500	$1,040
			2	$15,000–$22,500	$1,240
Two Bedroom	0	——	——	——	——
Larger Units	0	——	——	——	——
Total		88 Units			

Entrance fee refunds decline over time.

These fees include three meals per day, housekeeping, scheduled transportation, and utilities. Special features of this community are presented in the Special Features Index at the back of the book. Ask about additional residential and health care services that may be available. Fees and services subject to change; verify with facility.

ASSISTED LIVING AND PERSONAL CARE

Assisted living units: 0
Personal care is covered by the continuing care contract: No
Residents may receive personal care in independent living units: No

NURSING CARE: Modified Plan

Under this modified plan, 16–59 days of nursing care are covered by the continuing care contract. Once residents move permanently to the nursing unit, they pay the basic monthly fee for the studio (smallest) unit plus 42 percent of the per diem rate for nursing care.

Intermediate beds: 81. Cost per day: private $65.00, semi-private $50.00.

Skilled beds: 31. Cost per day: private $66.00, semi-private $60.00.

Nursing beds are certified by both Medicare and Medicaid. Nonresidents may be admitted directly to the nursing care facility.

LIVE OAK RETIREMENT CENTER
600 East Flournoy-Lucas Road, Shreveport, LA 71115
Telephone: (318) 797-1900

Opened in 1982 • Predominantly single-level/garden apartments on 37 acres • Current resident population is 216 • Immediate availability

AAHA
Member

HOUSING AND SERVICES

Living Units	No.	Square Feet	No. of Persons	Entrance Fee	Monthly Fee
Studio	10	415	1	$4,400	$544
One Bedroom	78	480–682	1	$8,800–$13,200	$635–$819
			2		$725–$909
Two Bedroom	32	770	1	$16,500	$902
			2		$992
Larger Units	0	—	—	—	—
Total	120 Units				

Entrance fees are fully refundable.

These fees include one meal per day. Special features of this community are presented in the Special Features Index at the back of the book. Ask about additional residential and health care services that may be available. Fees and services subject to change; verify with facility.

ASSISTED LIVING AND PERSONAL CARE

Assisted living units: 0
Personal care is covered by the continuing care contract: No
Residents may receive personal care in independent living units: No

NURSING CARE: Fee-for-Service

Under this fee-for-service plan, guaranteed access to nursing care is covered by the continuing care contract. Residents pay the full per diem rate for nursing care.

Intermediate beds: 130. Cost per day: private $56.70, semi-private $38.40.

Nursing beds are certified by Medicaid. Nonresidents may be admitted directly to the nursing care facility.

LOUISIANA

SAINT JAMES PLACE
333 Lee Drive, Baton Rouge, LA 70808
Telephone: (504) 769-1407

Opened in 1983 • Mixed single-level and low-rise buildings on 40 acres • Current resident population is 223 • Immediate availability

HOUSING AND SERVICES

Living Units	No.	Square Feet	No. of Persons	Entrance Fee	Monthly Fee
Studio	25	401	1	$31,900	$522
One Bedroom	72	619–802	1	$46,900–$63,900	$606–$798
			2	$50,400–$67,400	$945–$1,137
Two Bedroom	86	872–1,020	1	$65,900–$85,900	$716–$884
			2	$69,400–$89,400	$1,055–$1,223
Larger Units	7	1,238–	1	$93,900–$121,900	$964–$1,151
		1,583	2	$97,400–$125,400	$1,303–$1,642
Total	190 Units				

Entrance fee refunds decline over time.

These fees include one meal per day, biweekly housekeeping, scheduled transportation, and utilities. Special features of this community are presented in the Special Features Index at the back of the book. Ask about additional residential and health care services that may be available. Fees and services subject to change; verify with facility.

ASSISTED LIVING AND PERSONAL CARE

Assisted living units: 0
Personal care is covered by the continuing care contract: No
Residents may receive personal care in independent living units: No

NURSING CARE: All-Inclusive Plan

Under this all-inclusive plan, unlimited nursing care is covered by the continuing care contract. When in nursing care, residents pay the same monthly fee they paid for their independent living unit.

Skilled beds: 60. Cost per day: semi-private $50.00.

Nursing beds are not certified by Medicare or Medicaid. Nonresidents may be admitted directly to the nursing care facility.

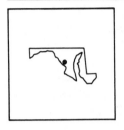

ASBURY METHODIST VILLAGE
201 Russell Avenue, Gaithersburg, MD 20877
Telephone: (301) 330-3000

Opened in 1926 • Predominantly high-rise buildings on 130 acres • Current resident population is 500 • Located 15 miles from Washington, DC • Waiting list

AAHA Member

HOUSING AND SERVICES

Living Units	No.	Square Feet	No. of Persons	Entrance Fee	Monthly Fee
Studio	99	538–688	1	$25,500–$32,400	$418–$490
One Bedroom	194	790–935	1	$37,000–$44,900	$539–$608
			2		$700–$770
Two Bedroom	100	1,030–1,107	1	$48,600–$53,200	$654–$690
			2		$817–$852
Larger Units	0	—	—	—	—
Total	393 Units				

Entrance fee refunds decline over time.

These fees include one meal per day, scheduled transportation, and utilities. Special features of this community are presented in the Special Features Index at the back of the book. Ask about additional residential and health care services that may be available. Fees and services subject to change; verify with facility.

ASSISTED LIVING AND PERSONAL CARE

Assisted living units: 197
Personal care is covered by the continuing care contract: Yes
Residents may receive personal care in independent living units: Yes
Nonresidents may be admitted directly to assisted living units: Yes

NURSING CARE: Fee-for-Service Plan

Under this fee-for-service plan, guaranteed access to nursing care is covered by the continuing care contract. Residents pay the full per diem rate for nursing care.

Dual-certified beds: 279. Cost per day: private $67.00, semi-private $62.00. Nursing beds are certified by both Medicare and Medicaid. Nonresidents may be admitted directly to the nursing care facility.

BROADMEAD
13801 York Road, Cockeysville, MD 21030
Telephone: (301) 628-6900

Opened in 1979 • Predominantly single-level/garden apartments on 80 acres • Current resident population is 380 • Located 12 miles from Baltimore, MD • Long waiting list; make reservations in advance • Accredited by the AAHA Continuing Care Accreditation Commission

AAHA Member

HOUSING AND SERVICES

Living Units	No.	Square Feet	No. of Persons	Entrance Fee	Monthly Fee
Studio	32	485	1	$44,000	$1,037
One Bedroom	77	700	1	$66,000	$1,244
			2	$76,000	$1,866
Two Bedroom	35	870	1	$84,000	$1,451
			2	$94,000	$2,074
Larger Units	96	875–1,040	1	$84,000–$102,000	$1,451–$1,659
			2	$94,000–$112,000	$2,074–$2,280
Total	240 Units				

Entrance fee refunds decline over time.

These fees include three meals per day, weekly housekeeping, scheduled transportation, and utilities. Special features of this community are presented in the Special Features Index at the back of the book. Ask about additional residential and health care services that may be available. Fees and services subject to change; verify with facility.

ASSISTED LIVING AND PERSONAL CARE

Assisted living units: 35
Personal care is covered by the continuing care contract: Yes
Residents may receive personal care in independent living units: No
Nonresidents may be admitted directly to assisted living units: Yes

NURSING CARE: All-Inclusive Plan

Under this all-inclusive plan, unlimited nursing care is covered by the continuing care contract. When residents are in nursing care, they pay the basic monthly fee for the studio (smallest) unit.

Dual-certified beds: 66. Cost per day: private $95.00, semi-private $89.00.

Nursing beds are certified by Medicare. Nonresidents may be admitted directly to the nursing care facility.

MARYLAND

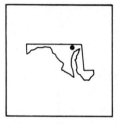

CARROLL LUTHERAN VILLAGE
200 Saint Luke Circle, Westminster, MD 21157
Telephone: (301) 848-0090

Opened in 1983 • One high-rise building on 70 acres
• Current resident population is 258 • Waiting list
may apply for some units

AAHA
Member

HOUSING AND SERVICES

Living Units	No.	Square Feet	No. of Persons	Entrance Fee	Monthly Fee
Studio	9	420	1	$34,000	$234
One Bedroom	34	624	1	$53,750	$276
			2		$386
Two Bedroom	17	960	1	$66,750	$302
			2		$412
Larger Units	8	1,152	1	$78,750	$338
			2		$448
Total		68 Units			

Residents have a choice of entrance fee refund plans.

These fees include one meal on weekdays and scheduled transportation. Special features of this community are presented in the Special Features Index at the back of the book. Ask about additional residential and health care services that may be available. Fees and services subject to change; verify with facility.

ASSISTED LIVING AND PERSONAL CARE

Assisted living units: 0
Personal care is covered by the continuing care contract: No
Residents may receive personal care in independent living units: No

NURSING CARE: Fee-for-Service Plan

Under this fee-for-service plan, guaranteed access to nursing care is covered by the continuing care contract. Residents pay the full per diem rate for nursing care.

Dual-certified beds: 99. Cost per day: private $67.00–$82.00, semi-private $54.00–$69.00

Nursing beds are certified by both Medicare and Medicaid. Nonresidents may be admitted directly to the nursing care facility.

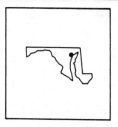

CHARLESTOWN RETIREMENT COMMUNITY
711 Maiden Choice Lane, Baltimore, MD 21228
Telephone: (301) 247-3400

Opened in 1984 • Mixed single-level and low-rise buildings on 110 acres • Current resident population is 360 • Waiting list may apply for some units

AAHA
Member

HOUSING AND SERVICES

Living Units	No.	Square Feet	No. of Persons	Entrance Fee	Monthly Fee
Studio	81	——	1	$52,400	$621
One Bedroom	105	——	1	$74,000	$682
			2		$951
Two Bedroom	56	——	1	$87,000	$799
			2		$1,068
Larger Units	3	——	1	$124,000	$942
			2		$1,211
Total	245 Units				

Entrance fees are fully refundable.

These fees include one meal per day, scheduled transportation, and utilities. Special features of this community are presented in the Special Features Index at the back of the book. Ask about additional residential and health care services that may be available. Fees and services subject to change; verify with facility.

ASSISTED LIVING AND PERSONAL CARE

Assisted living units: 77
Personal care is covered by the continuing care contract: Yes
Residents may receive personal care in independent living units: Yes
Nonresidents may be admitted directly to assisted living units: Yes

NURSING CARE: Fee-for-Service Plan

Under this fee-for-service plan, guaranteed access to nursing care is covered by the continuing care contract. Residents pay the full per diem rate for nursing care.

Skilled beds: 60. Cost per day: private $115.00, semi-private $64.00.

Nursing beds are not certified by Medicare or Medicaid. Nonresidents may not be admitted directly to the nursing care facility.

COLLINGTON EPISCOPAL LIFE CARE COMMUNITY
10001 Martin Luther King Jr. Highway
Lanham, MD 20706
Telephone: (301) 731-6040

Opening in 1988 • Mixed single-level and low-rise buildings on 128 acres • Located 10 miles from Washington, DC • Immediate availability

AAHA
Member

HOUSING AND SERVICES

Living Units	No.	Square Feet	No. of Persons	Entrance Fee	Monthly Fee
Studio	41	487–521	1	$46,760–$60,750	$1,050–$1,150
One Bedroom	198	660–911	1	$74,600–$121,050	$1,225–$1,560
			2	$86,600–$133,050	$1,875–$2,210
Two Bedroom	61	957–1,115	1	$106,040–$142,700	$1,600–$1,700
			2	$118,040–$154,700	$2,250–$2,350
Larger Units	0	——	——	——	——
Total		300 Units			

Residents have a choice of entrance fee refund plans.

These fees include three meals per day, biweekly housekeeping, scheduled transportation, and utilities. Special features of this community are presented in the Special Features Index at the back of the book. Ask about additional residential and health care services that may be available. Fees and services subject to change; verify with facility.

ASSISTED LIVING AND PERSONAL CARE

Assisted living units: 40
Personal care is covered by the continuing care contract: Yes
Residents may receive personal care in independent living units: No
Nonresidents may be admitted directly to assisted living units: No

NURSING CARE: All-Inclusive Plan

Under this all-inclusive plan, unlimited nursing care is covered by the continuing care contract. When in nursing care, residents pay the same monthly fee they paid for their independent living unit.

Skilled beds: 30. Cost per day: private $105.00.

Nursing beds are certified by Medicaid. Nonresidents may be admitted directly to the nursing care facility.

EDENWALD
800 Southerly Road, Towson, MD 21204–8403
Telephone: (301) 339-6000

Opened in 1985 • Predominantly high-rise buildings on five acres • Current resident population is 376 • Located ten miles from Baltimore, MD • Waiting list may apply for some units

AAHA Member

HOUSING AND SERVICES

Living Units	No.	Square Feet	No. of Persons	Entrance Fee	Monthly Fee
Studio	29	530	1	$49,568	$810
One Bedroom	116	620	1	$62,370	$972
			2	$65,070	$1,404
Two Bedroom	90	765–975	1	$76,140–$92,070	$1,080–$1,242
			2	$78,840–$94,770	$1,512–$1,674
Larger Units	6	1,275	1	$130,950	$1,512
			2	$133,650	$1,944
Total	241 Units				

Entrance fee refunds decline over time.

These fees include one meal per day, biweekly housekeeping, scheduled transportation, and utilities. Special features of this community are presented in the Special Features Index at the back of the book. Ask about additional residential and health care services that may be available. Fees and services subject to change; verify with facility.

ASSISTED LIVING AND PERSONAL CARE

Assisted living units: 68
Personal care is covered by the continuing care contract: Yes
Residents may receive personal care in independent living units: No
Nonresidents may be admitted directly to assisted living units: Yes

NURSING CARE: All-Inclusive Plan

Under this all-inclusive plan, unlimited nursing care is covered by the continuing care contract. When in nursing care, residents pay the same monthly fee they paid for their independent living unit.

Intermediate beds: 47. Cost per day: private $86.00, semi-private—not applicable.

Nursing beds are not certified by Medicare or Medicaid. Nonresidents may not be admitted directly to the nursing care facility.

MARYLAND

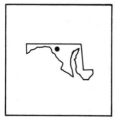

FAHRNEY-KEEDY MEMORIAL HOME
Boonsboro, MD 21713
Telephone: (301) 733-6284

Opened in 1962 • Predominantly single-level/garden apartments on 20 acres • Current resident population is 205 • Waiting list may apply for some units

AAHA Member

HOUSING AND SERVICES

Living Units	No.	Square Feet	No. of Persons	Entrance Fee	Monthly Fee
Studio	0	—	—	—	—
One Bedroom	4	520	1, 2	$25,000	$20
Two Bedroom	8	590–750	1, 2	$28,000–$31,000	$20
Larger Units	21	1,000–1,500	1, 2	$50,000–$55,000	$20
Total		33 Units			

Entrance fee refunds decline over time.

These fees include scheduled transportation. Special features of this community are presented in the Special Features Index at the back of the book. Ask about additional residential and health care services that may be available. Fees and services subject to change; verify with facility.

ASSISTED LIVING AND PERSONAL CARE

Assisted living units: 40
Personal care is covered by the continuing care contract: No
Residents may receive personal care in independent living units: No
Nonresidents may be admitted directly to assisted living units: Yes

NURSING CARE: Fee-for-Service Plan

Under this fee-for-service plan, guaranteed access to nursing care is covered by the continuing care contract. Residents pay the full per diem rate for nursing care.

Intermediate beds: 100. Cost per day: private $46.19, semi-private $43.89.

Nursing beds are certified by Medicaid. Nonresidents may be admitted directly to the nursing care facility.

FAIRHAVEN
7200 Third Avenue, Sykesville, MD 21784
Telephone: (301) 795-8800

Opened in 1980 • Mixed single-level and low-rise buildings on 300 acres • Current resident population is 381 • Located 25 miles from Baltimore, MD • Waiting list

AAHA
Member

HOUSING AND SERVICES

Living Units	No.	Square Feet	No. of Persons	Entrance Fee	Monthly Fee
Studio	48	300–445	1	$36,000–$46,000	$950–$1,035
One Bedroom	48	550–665	1	$57,000–$64,000	$1,140–$1,285
			2	$69,000–$76,000	$1,900–$2,045
Two Bedroom	12	855	1	$71,000	$1,425
			2	$83,000	$2,185
Larger Units	132	765–1,275	1	$61,000–$86,000	$1,165–$1,560
			2	$73,000–$98,000	$1,925–$2,320

Total   240 Units

Entrance fee refunds decline over time.

These fees include three meals per day, weekly housekeeping, scheduled transportation, and utilities. Special features of this community are presented in the Special Features Index at the back of the book. Ask about additional residential and health care services that may be available. Fees and services subject to change; verify with facility.

ASSISTED LIVING AND PERSONAL CARE

Assisted living units: 0
Personal care is covered by the continuing care contract: No
Residents may receive personal care in independent living units: No

NURSING CARE: All-Inclusive Plan

Under this all-inclusive plan, unlimited nursing care is covered by the continuing care contract. When in nursing care, residents pay the same monthly fee they paid for their independent living unit.

Skilled beds: 99. Cost per day: private $94.00, semi-private—not applicable.

Nursing beds are certified by Medicare. Nonresidents may not be admitted directly to the nursing care facility.

MARYLAND

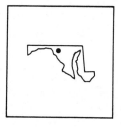

HOMEWOOD RETIREMENT CENTER
2750 Virginia Avenue, Williamsport, MD 21795
Telephone: (301) 582-1750

Opened in 1981 • Mixed single-level and low-rise buildings on 27 acres • Current resident population is 214 • Located six miles from Hagerstown, MD • Long waiting list; make reservations in advance

AAHA
Member

HOUSING AND SERVICES

Living Units	No.	Square Feet	No. of Persons	Entrance Fee	Monthly Fee
Studio	9	435	1	$27,600	$90
One Bedroom	62	605–890	1, 2	$39,800–$50,400	$90
Two Bedroom	55	775–1,000	1, 2	$49,300–$55,000	$90
Larger Units	30	1,250	1, 2	$64,800	$90
Total	156 Units				

Entrance fees are partially refundable.

Special features of this community are presented in the Special Features Index at the back of the book. Ask about additional residential and health care services that may be available. Fees and services subject to change; verify with facility.

ASSISTED LIVING AND PERSONAL CARE

Assisted living units: 43
Personal care is covered by the continuing care contract: No
Residents may receive personal care in independent living units: No
Nonresidents may be admitted directly to assisted living units: Yes

NURSING CARE: Fee-for-Service Plan

Under this fee-for-service plan, guaranteed access to nursing care is covered by the continuing care contract. Residents pay the full per diem rate for nursing care.

Intermediate beds: 93. Cost per day: private $49.50, semi-private $49.50.

Nursing beds are certified by Medicaid. Nonresidents may be admitted directly to the nursing care facility.

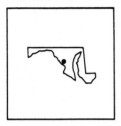

NATIONAL LUTHERAN HOME FOR AGED
9701 Viers Drive, Rockville, MD 20850
Telephone: (301) 424-9560

Opened in 1890 • Mixed single-level, low-rise, and high-rise buildings on 26 acres • Current resident population is 375 • Immediate availability

AAHA
Member

HOUSING AND SERVICES

Living Units	No.	Square Feet	No. of Persons	Entrance Fee	Monthly Fee
Studio	0	——	——	——	——
One Bedroom	17	875	1, 2	$58,500	$175
Two Bedroom	34	925	1, 2	$61,000–$63,000	$100
Larger Units	0	——	——	——	——
Total		51 Units			

Entrance fee refunds decline over time.

Special features of this community are presented in the Special Features Index at the back of the book. Ask about additional residential and health care services that may be available. Fees and services subject to change; verify with facility.

ASSISTED LIVING AND PERSONAL CARE

Assisted living units: 0
Personal care is covered by the continuing care contract: No
Residents may receive personal care in independent living units: No

NURSING CARE: Fee-for-Service

Under this fee-for-service plan, guaranteed access to nursing care is covered by the continuing care contract. When residents are in nursing care, they pay a ten-year discounted per diem rate based on a credit from the entrance fee.

Dual-certified beds: 300. Cost per day: private $68.00, semi-private $68.00.
Nursing beds are certified by both Medicare and Medicaid. Nonresidents may be admitted directly to the nursing care facility.

NOTCHCLIFF
11630 Glen Arm Road, Glen Arm, MD 21057
Telephone: (301) 592-5310

Opened in 1987 • Mixed single-level, low-rise, and high-rise buildings on 483 acres • Located 20 miles from Baltimore, MD • Immediate availability

---

HOUSING AND SERVICES

Living Units	No.	Square Feet	No. of Persons	Entrance Fee	Monthly Fee
Studio	45	315–615	1	$32,000–$59,000	$840–$1,065
One Bedroom	133	750–850	1	$56,000–$66,000	$1,035–$1,135
			2	$63,000–$73,000	$1,635–$1,730
Two Bedroom	27	1,060	1	$71,000	$1,235
			2	$78,000	$1,835
Larger Units	10	1,110	1	$81,000	$1,315
			2	$88,000	$1,915
Total	215 Units				

Entrance fee refunds decline over time.

These fees include one meal per day, housekeeping, scheduled transportation, and utilities. Special features of this community are presented in the Special Features Index at the back of the book. Ask about additional residential and health care services that may be available. Fees and services subject to change; verify with facility.

ASSISTED LIVING AND PERSONAL CARE

Assisted living units: 16 are planned for 1988.
Personal care is covered by the continuing care contract: Yes
Residents may receive personal care in independent living units: No
Nonresidents may be admitted directly to assisted living units: No

NURSING CARE: All-Inclusive Plan

Under this all-inclusive plan, unlimited nursing care is covered by the continuing care contract. When in nursing care, residents pay the same monthly fee they paid for their independent living unit.

Skilled beds: 43. The nursing care center is under construction; completion is set for 1989.

Nursing beds are expected to be certified by both Medicare and Medicaid. Nonresidents may not be admitted directly to the nursing care facility.

MARYLAND

RAVENWOOD LUTHERAN VILLAGE
1183 Luther Drive, Hagerstown, MD 21740
Telephone: (301) 790-1000

Opened in 1978 • Predominantly single-level/garden apartments on 30 acres • Current resident population is 128 • Waiting list may apply for some units

AAHA
Member

HOUSING AND SERVICES

Living Units	No.	Square Feet	No. of Persons	Entrance Fee	Monthly Fee
Studio	0	——	——	——	——
One Bedroom	8	900	1	$43,000	$132.50
			2	$43,100	$132.50
Two Bedroom	24	1,200	1, 2	$60,000	$116.50
Larger Units	0	——	——	——	——
Total	32 Units				

Entrance fees are partially refundable.

Special features of this community are presented in the Special Features Index at the back of the book. Ask about additional residential and health care services that may be available. Fees and services subject to change; verify with facility.

ASSISTED LIVING AND PERSONAL CARE

Assisted living units: 0
Personal care is covered by the continuing care contract: No
Residents may receive personal care in independent living units: No

NURSING CARE: Fee-for-Service Plan

Under this fee-for-service plan, guaranteed access to nursing care is covered by the continuing care contract. Residents pay the full per diem rate for nursing care.

Intermediate beds: 55. Cost per day: private $66.00, semi-private $52.00.

Skilled beds: 31. Cost per day: private $66.00, semi-private $58.00.

Nursing beds are certified by both Medicare and Medicaid. Nonresidents may be admitted directly to the nursing care facility.

MARYLAND

WESLEYAN HERITAGE COMMUNITY
P.O. Box 454, Camp Road, Denton, MD 21629
Telephone: (301) 479-4400

Opened in 1983 • Mixed single-level and low-rise buildings on 100 acres • Current resident population is 133 • Waiting list may apply for some units

HOUSING AND SERVICES

Living Units	No.	Square Feet	No. of Persons	Entrance Fee	Monthly Fee
Studio	1	487	1	$40,000	$125
One Bedroom	4	708	1	$50,000	$150
			2	$50,000	$175
Two Bedroom	9	896	1	$55,000	$175
			2	$55,000	$200
Larger Units	0	—	—	—	—
Total		14 Units			

Entrance fee refunds decline over time.

These fees include scheduled transportation. Special features of this community are presented in the Special Features Index at the back of the book. Ask about additional residential and health care services that may be available. Fees and services subject to change; verify with facility.

ASSISTED LIVING AND PERSONAL CARE

Assisted living units: 100
Personal care is covered by the continuing care contract: No
Residents may receive personal care in independent living units: No
Nonresidents may be admitted directly to assisted living units: Yes

NURSING CARE: Modified Plan

Under this modified plan, 30 days of nursing care are covered by the continuing care contract. Once residents move permanently to the nursing unit, they pay the full per diem rate for nursing care.

Intermediate beds: 120. Cost per day: private $63.00, semi-private $56.00.

Nursing beds are certified by both Medicare and Medicaid. Nonresidents may be admitted directly to the nursing care facility.

MARYLAND

WILLIAM HILL MANOR
501 Dutchman's Lane, Easton, MD 21601
Telephone: (301) 822-8888

Opened in 1981 • Mixed single-level and low-rise buildings on 27 acres • Current resident population is 183 • Waiting list may apply for some units

HOUSING AND SERVICES

Living Units	No.	Square Feet	No. of Persons	Entrance Fee	Monthly Fee
Studio	24	260–337	1	$3,600	$1,200
One Bedroom	42	525–900	1	$2,480–$10,080	$1,240–$1,680
			2	$3,080–$12,930	$1,540–$2,155
Two Bedroom	18	756–1,176	1	$2,800–$11,400	$1,400–$1,900
			2	$3,400–$14,250	$1,700–$2,375
Larger Units	20	1,530	1	$1,630–$3,490	$1,565–$1,745
			2	$3,730–$4,090	$1,865–$2,045

Total   104 Units

Entrance fees are fully refundable.

These fees include three meals per day, weekly housekeeping, scheduled transportation, and utilities. Special features of this community are presented in the Special Features Index at the back of the book. Ask about additional residential and health care services that may be available. Fees and services subject to change; verify with facility.

ASSISTED LIVING AND PERSONAL CARE

Assisted living units: 0
Personal care is covered by the continuing care contract: No
Residents may receive personal care in independent living units: No

NURSING CARE: Modified Plan

Under this modified plan, 60 days or more are covered by the continuing care contract over a resident's lifetime. Once residents move permanently to the nursing unit, they pay the full per diem rate for nursing care.

Dual-certified beds: 60. Cost per day: private $77.00, semi-private $64.50.

Nursing beds are certified by both Medicare and Medicaid. Nonresidents may be admitted directly to the nursing care facility.

MASSACHUSETTS

CARLETON-WILLARD HOMES
100 Old Billerica Road, Bedford, MA 01730
Telephone: (617) 275-8700

Opened in 1982 • Mixed single-level and low-rise buildings on 65 acres • Current resident population is 355 • Long waiting list; make reservations in advance

AAHA
Member

HOUSING AND SERVICES

Living Units	No.	Square Feet	No. of Persons	Entrance Fee	Monthly Fee
Studio	3	395	1	$45,000	$770
One Bedroom	91	612–791	1	$60,000–$90,000	$880–$998
			2	$65,000–$95,000	$1,360–$1,478
Two Bedroom	37	758–1,150	1	$80,000–$120,000	$992–$1,218
			2	$85,000–$125,000	$1,472–$1,698
Larger Units	6	1,340	1	$165,000	$1,442
			2	$170,000	$1,922
Total	137 Units				

Entrance fee refunds decline over time.

These fees include one meal per day, weekly housekeeping, scheduled transportation, and utilities. Special features of this community are presented in the Special Features Index at the back of the book. Ask about additional residential and health care services that may be available. Fees and services subject to change; verify with facility.

ASSISTED LIVING AND PERSONAL CARE

Assisted living units: 80
Personal care is covered by the continuing care contract: Yes
Residents may receive personal care in independent living units: No
Nonresidents may be admitted directly to assisted living units: Yes

NURSING CARE: Modified Plan

Under this modified plan, 60 days per year are covered by the continuing care contract. Once residents move permanently to a nursing unit, they pay 80 percent of the per diem rate for nursing care.

Intermediate beds: 40. Cost per day: private $110.00, semi-private $100.00.

Skilled beds: 80. Cost per day: private $120.00, semi-private $110.00.

Nursing beds are certified by both Medicare and Medicaid. Nonresidents may be admitted directly to the nursing care facility.

MASSACHUSETTS

LOOMIS HOUSE RETIREMENT COMMUNITY
298 Jarvis Avenue, Holyoke, MA 01040
Telephone: (413) 538-7551

Opened in 1981 • Mixed single-level and low-rise buildings on six acres • Current resident population is 148 • Located ten miles from Springfield, MA • Waiting list may apply for some units

AAHA
Member

HOUSING AND SERVICES

Living Units	No.	Square Feet	No. of Persons	Entrance Fee	Monthly Fee
Studio	14	270–368	1	$18,900–$23,920	$495–$535
One Bedroom	28	425–638	1	$27,625–$41,470	$605–$825
			2	$30,625–$44,470	$775–$995
Two Bedroom	6	746–940	1	$48,490–$61,100	$900–$1,335
			2	$51,490–$64,100	$1,070–$1,505
Larger Units	4	850	1	$55,250	$920
			2	$58,250	$1,090
Total		52 Units			

Entrance fee refunds decline over time.

These fees include one meal per day, weekly housekeeping, scheduled transportation, and utilities. Special features of this community are presented in the Special Features Index at the back of the book. Ask about additional residential and health care services that may be available. Fees and services subject to change; verify with facility.

ASSISTED LIVING AND PERSONAL CARE

Assisted living units: 8
Personal care is covered by the continuing care contract: Yes
Residents may receive personal care in independent living units: No
Nonresidents may be admitted directly to assisted living units: Yes

NURSING CARE: Modified Plan

Under this modified plan, 15 or fewer days per year are covered by the continuing care contract. Once residents move permanently to the nursing unit, they pay 80–95 percent of the per diem rate for nursing care; the lower rates apply for residents with longer previous stays in the independent or assisted living units.

Intermediate beds: 39. Cost per day: private $84.00, semi-private $73.00.

Skilled beds: 41. Cost per day: private $87.00, semi-private $75.00.

Nursing beds are certified by both Medicare and Medicaid. Nonresidents may be admitted directly to the nursing care facility.

MASSACHUSETTS

NORTH HILL
865 Central Avenue, Needham, MA 02192
Telephone: (617) 444-9910

Opened in 1984 • One high-rise building on 59 acres
• Current resident population is 475 • Long waiting
list; make reservations in advance

**AAHA
Member**

HOUSING AND SERVICES

Living Units	No.	Square Feet	No. of Persons	Entrance Fee	Monthly Fee
Studio	34	450	1	$102,000	$594
One Bedroom	129	600–775	1	$128,000	$653
			2		$1,117
Two Bedroom	132	940–1,000	1	$170,000	$772
			2		$1,236
Larger Units	46	1,200–	1	$244,000	$940
		1,250	2		$1,404
Total	341 Units				

Entrance fees are fully refundable.

These fees include one meal per day, weekly housekeeping, scheduled transportation, and utilities. Special features of this community are presented in the
Special Features Index at the back of the book. Ask about additional residential
and health care services that may be available. Fees and services subject to
change; verify with facility.

ASSISTED LIVING AND PERSONAL CARE

Assisted living units: 0
Personal care is covered by the continuing care contract: No
Residents may receive personal care in independent living units: No

NURSING CARE: All-Inclusive Plan

Under this all-inclusive plan, unlimited nursing care is covered by the continuing care contract. When residents are in nursing care, they pay the same
monthly fee they paid for their independent living unit.

Intermediate beds: 20. Cost per day: private $125.00, semi-private $80.00.

Skilled beds: 40. Cost per day: private $125.00, semi-private $80.00.

Nursing beds are certified by both Medicare and Medicaid. Nonresidents may
be admitted directly to the nursing care facility.

THE WILLOWS AT WESTBOROUGH
1 Lyman Street, Westborough, MA 01581
Telephone: (617) 366-4730

Opened in 1987 • One high-rise building on 12 acres
• Immediate availability

HOUSING AND SERVICES

Living Units	No.	Square Feet	No. of Persons	Entrance Fee	Monthly Fee
Studio	26	330–377	1	$58,000	$625
One Bedroom	142	728–750	1	$105,000	$825
			2	$117,500	$1,250
Two Bedroom	34	1,033–1,136	1	$160,000	$995
			2	$167,500	$1,420
Larger Units	0	—	—	—	—
Total		202 Units			

Entrance fees are fully refundable.

These fees include one meal per day, weekly housekeeping, scheduled transportation, and utilities. Special features of this community are presented in the Special Features Index at the back of the book. Ask about additional residential and health care services that may be available. Fees and services subject to change; verify with facility.

ASSISTED LIVING AND PERSONAL CARE

Assisted living units: 0
Personal care is covered by the continuing care contract: No
Residents may receive personal care in independent living units: Yes

NURSING CARE: Modified Plan

Under this modified plan, 15 or fewer days per year are covered by the continuing care contract. Once residents move permanently to the nursing unit, they pay the full per diem rate for nursing care.

Intermediate beds: 60. Cost per day: private $115.00, semi-private $88.00.

Skilled beds: 80. Cost per day: private $120.00, semi-private $98.00.

Nursing beds are certified by both Medicare and Medicaid. Nonresidents may be admitted directly to the nursing care facility.

FRIENDSHIP VILLAGE
1400 North Drake Road, Kalamazoo, MI 49007
Telephone: (616) 638-1560

Opened in 1975 • Mixed single-level and low-rise buildings on 24 acres • Current resident population is 350 • Waiting list

HOUSING AND SERVICES

Living Units	No.	Square Feet	No. of Persons	Entrance Fee	Monthly Fee
Studio	107	285–415	1	$27,000–$39,500	$590–$625
One Bedroom	99	570	1	$58,000	$705
			2	$63,000	
Two Bedroom	47	815	1	$72,000	$744
			2	$77,000	
Larger Units	0	——	——	——	——
Total	253 Units				

Entrance fee refunds decline over time.

These fees include one meal per day, biweekly housekeeping, scheduled transportation, and utilities. Special features of this community are presented in the Special Features Index at the back of the book. Ask about additional residential and health care services that may be available. Fees and services subject to change; verify with facility.

ASSISTED LIVING AND PERSONAL CARE

Assisted living units: 0
Personal care is covered by the continuing care contract: No
Residents may receive personal care in independent living units: Yes

NURSING CARE: All-Inclusive Plan

Under this all-inclusive plan, unlimited nursing care is covered by the continuing care contract. When residents are in nursing care, they pay the basic monthly fee for the studio (smallest) unit.

Dual-certified beds: 57. Cost per day: semi-private $65.00.

Nursing beds are certified by both Medicare and Medicaid. Nonresidents may be admitted directly to the nursing care facility.

GLACIER HILLS
1200 Earhart Road, Ann Arbor, MI 48105
Telephone: (313) 769-6410

Opened in 1973 • One mid-rise building on 33 acres • Current resident population is 309 • Waiting list may apply for some units

AAHA
Member

HOUSING AND SERVICES

Living Units	No.	Square Feet	No. of Persons	Entrance Fee*	Monthly Fee
Studio	148	260–334	1	$23,970–$34,540	$717–$810
One Bedroom	39	364–454	1, 2	$37,760–$45,970	$841–$946
Two Bedroom	38	487–637	1, 2	$49,760–$62,970	$995–$1,198
Larger Units	0	——	——	——	——
Total	225 Units				

*Residents have the option, at an additional cost, to enter into a lifecare plan that covers extended health care needs.
Entrance fee refunds decline over time.

These fees include three meals per day, biweekly housekeeping, scheduled transportation, and utilities. Special features of this community are presented in the Special Features Index at the back of the book. Ask about additional residential and health care services that may be available. Fees and services subject to change; verify with facility.

ASSISTED LIVING AND PERSONAL CARE

Assisted living units: 0
Personal care is covered by the continuing care contract: No
Residents may receive personal care in independent living units: Yes

NURSING CARE: Modified Plan

Under this modified plan, 15 or fewer days per year are covered by the continuing care contract. Once residents move permanently to the nursing unit, they pay 50 percent of the per diem rate if they are lifecare residents and the full per diem rate if they are nonlifecare residents.

Skilled beds: 89. Cost per day: semi-private $89.00.

Nursing beds are certified by both Medicare and Medicaid. Nonresidents may be admitted directly to the nursing care facility.

VISTA GRANDE VILLA
2251 Springport Road, Jackson, MI 49202
Telephone: (517) 787-0222

Opened in 1972 • Mixed single-level and low-rise buildings on 20 acres • Current resident population is 305 • Waiting list may apply for some units

AAHA
Member

HOUSING AND SERVICES

Living Units	No.	Square Feet	No. of Persons	Entrance Fee	Monthly Fee
Studio	17	317	1	$29,000	$561
One Bedroom	168	465	1	$39,000–$49,000	$683
			2	$49,000–$59,000	$920
Two Bedroom	39	737	1	$69,000	$674
			2	$79,000	$965
Larger Units	0	——	——	——	——
Total	224 Units				

Entrance fee refunds decline over time.

These fees include one meal per day, biweekly housekeeping, scheduled transportation, and utilities. Special features of this community are presented in the Special Features Index at the back of the book. Ask about additional residential and health care services that may be available. Fees and services subject to change; verify with facility.

ASSISTED LIVING AND PERSONAL CARE

Assisted living units: 0
Personal care is covered by the continuing care contract: No
Residents may receive personal care in independent living units: No

NURSING CARE: All-Inclusive Plan

Under this all-inclusive plan, unlimited nursing care is covered by the continuing care contract. When residents are in nursing care, they pay the same monthly fee they paid for their independent living unit.

Skilled beds: 60. Cost per day: private $72.20, semi-private $63.20.

Nursing beds are certified by both Medicare and Medicaid. Nonresidents may be admitted directly to the nursing care facility.

BETHANY COVENANT HOME
2309 Hayes Street N.E., Minneapolis, MN 55418
Telephone: (612) 781-2691

Opened in 1976 • Mixed single-level and low-rise buildings on one acre • Current resident population is 83 • Waiting list

AAHA
Member

HOUSING AND SERVICES

Living Units	No.	Square Feet	No. of Persons	Entrance Fee	Monthly Fee
Studio	14	310	1	$2,000–$20,000	$835–$1,260
One Bedroom	2	625	1, 2	$3,000–$30,000	$872–$1,386
Two Bedroom	0	——	——	——	——
Larger Units	0	——	——	——	——
Total	16 Units				

Residents have a choice of entrance fee refund plans.

These fees include three meals per day, scheduled transportation, and utilities. Special features of this community are presented in the Special Features Index at the back of the book. Ask about additional residential and health care services that may be available. Fees and services subject to change; verify with facility.

ASSISTED LIVING AND PERSONAL CARE

Assisted living units: 0
Personal care is covered by the continuing care contract: No
Residents may receive personal care in independent living units: Yes

NURSING CARE: Fee-for-Service Plan

Under this fee-for-service plan, guaranteed access to nursing care is covered by the continuing care contract. Residents pay the full per diem rate for nursing care.

Intermediate beds: 66. Cost per day: private $44.62–$76.52, semi-private $34.62–$65.52.

Nursing beds are certified by Medicaid. Nonresidents may be admitted directly to the nursing care facility.

COVENANT MANOR AND COLONIAL ACRES
5800 Saint Croix Avenue, Minneapolis, MN 55422
Telephone: (612) 546-6125

Opened in 1980 • Mixed single-level, low-rise, and high-rise buildings on 14 acres • Current resident population is 116 • Immediate availability

AAHA
Member

HOUSING AND SERVICES

Living Units	No.	Square Feet	No. of Persons	Entrance Fee	Monthly Fee
Studio	17	490	1	$49,000	$557
One Bedroom	49	600–715	1	$64,000–$72,000	$662
			2	$64,000–$72,000	$992
Two Bedroom	27	820–1,090	1	$75,000–$82,000	$741
			2	$75,000–$82,000	$1,071
Larger Units	4	1,200	1	$108,000	$999
			2	$108,000	$1,329
Total	97 Units				

Entrance fee refunds decline over time.

These fees include one meal per day, biweekly housekeeping, scheduled transportation, and utilities. Special features of this community are presented in the Special Features Index at the back of the book. Ask about additional residential and health care services that may be available. Fees and services subject to change; verify with facility.

ASSISTED LIVING AND PERSONAL CARE

Assisted living units: 16
Personal care is covered by the continuing care contract: Yes
Residents may receive personal care in independent living units: No
Nonresidents may be admitted directly to assisted living units: Yes

NURSING CARE: Modified Plan

Under this modified plan, 16–59 days over a resident's lifetime are covered by the continuing care contract. When residents are in nursing care, they pay the same monthly fee they paid for their independent living unit until their health subsidy is depleted; thereafter, residents pay 90 percent of the per diem rate for nursing care.

Intermediate beds: 20. Cost per day: private $58.00, semi-private $48.41.

Skilled beds: 85. Cost per day: private $76.00, semi-private $54.58.

Nursing beds are certified by Medicare. Nonresidents may be admitted directly to the nursing care facility.

THORNE CREST RETIREMENT CENTER
1201 Garfield Avenue, Albert Lea, MN 56007
Telephone: (507) 373-2311

Opened in 1974 • Mixed single-level and low-rise
buildings on three acres • Current resident population
is 170 • Waiting list may apply for some units

AAHA
Member

HOUSING AND SERVICES

Living Units	No.	Square Feet	No. of Persons	Entrance Fee	Monthly Fee
Studio	13	414–498	1	$14,500–$16,300	$436–$445
One Bedroom	69	543–719	1	$18,000–$22,700	$527–$544
			2	$21,500–$26,200	$651–$769
Two Bedroom	16	704–1,113	1	$24,500–$30,800	$598–$748
			2	$28,000–$34,300	$722–$872
Larger Units	0	—	—	—	—
Total	98 Units				

Entrance fee refunds decline over time.

These fees include one meal per day, scheduled transportation, and utilities.
Special features of this community are presented in the Special Features Index
at the back of the book. Ask about additional residential and health care services
that may be available. Fees and services subject to change; verify with facility.

ASSISTED LIVING AND PERSONAL CARE

Assisted living units: 0
Personal care is covered by the continuing care contract: No
Residents may receive personal care in independent living units: Yes

NURSING CARE: Fee-for-Service Plan

Under this fee-for-service plan, guaranteed access to nursing care is covered by
the continuing care contract. Residents pay the full per diem rate for nursing
care.

Dual-certified beds: 52. Cost per day: private $63.50–$71.00, semi-private—
varies.

Nursing beds are certified by Medicaid. Nonresidents may be admitted
directly to the nursing care facility.

CHATEAU GIRARDEAU
3120 Independence Street, Cape Girardeau, MO 63701
Telephone: (314) 335-1281

Opened in 1979 • Mixed single-level and low-rise buildings on 40 acres • Current resident population is 228 • Located 100 miles from Saint Louis, MO • Waiting list may apply for some units

AAHA
Member

HOUSING AND SERVICES

Living Units	No.	Square Feet	No. of Persons	Entrance Fee	Monthly Fee
Studio	3	228	1	$17,250	$492
One Bedroom	91	450–522	1	$32,950–$37,600	$502–$518
			2	$34,950–$39,600	$748–$764
Two Bedroom	57	648	1	$50,250	$569
			2	$52,250	$816
Larger Units	0	——	——	——	——
Total		151 Units			

Entrance fee refunds decline over time.

These fees include one meal per day, biweekly housekeeping, and utilities. Special features of this community are presented in the Special Features Index at the back of the book. Ask about additional residential and health care services that may be available. Fees and services subject to change; verify with facility.

ASSISTED LIVING AND PERSONAL CARE

Assisted living units: 0
Personal care is covered by the continuing care contract: No
Residents may receive personal care in independent living units: No

NURSING CARE: Modified Plan

Under this modified plan, 60 days or more of nursing care per year are covered by the continuing care contract. Once residents move permanently to the nursing unit, they pay the full per diem rate for nursing care. All residents are guaranteed full nursing care even though they may become unable to pay.

Skilled beds: 38. Cost per day: private $60.50, semi-private $52.00.

Nursing beds are certified by Medicare. Nonresidents may be admitted directly to the nursing care facility.

FRIENDSHIP VILLAGE OF SOUTH COUNTY
12503 Village Circle Drive, Saint Louis, MO 63127
Telephone: (314) 842-6840

Opened in 1978 • Mixed single-level, low-rise, and high-rise buildings on 40 acres • Current resident population is 517 • Waiting list may apply for some units

AAHA
Member

HOUSING AND SERVICES

Living Units	No.	Square Feet	No. of Persons	Entrance Fee	Monthly Fee
Studio	158	288–432	1	$26,950–$35,300	$496–$565
One Bedroom	133	576	1	$53,975	$671
			2		$999
Two Bedroom	64	864–1,008	1	$69,400–$75,300	$757–$812
			2		$1,085–$1,140
Larger Units	40	1,103	1	$82,950	$865
			2		$1,200
Total		395 Units			

Entrance fee refunds decline over time.

These fees include one meal per day, biweekly housekeeping, scheduled transportation, and utilities. Special features of this community are presented in the Special Features Index at the back of the book. Ask about additional residential and health care services that may be available. Fees and services subject to change; verify with facility.

ASSISTED LIVING AND PERSONAL CARE

Assisted living units: 0
Personal care is covered by the continuing care contract: No
Residents may receive personal care in independent living units: Yes

NURSING CARE: All-Inclusive Plan

Under this all-inclusive plan, unlimited nursing care is covered by the continuing care contract. When residents are in nursing care, they pay the same monthly fee they paid for their independent living unit.

Dual-certified beds: 60. Cost per day: private $68.00, semi-private $60.00.

Nursing beds are certified by both Medicare and Medicaid. Nonresidents may be admitted directly to the nursing care facility.

FRIENDSHIP VILLAGE OF WEST COUNTY
15201 Olive Street, Chesterfield, MO 63017
Telephone: (314) 532-1515

Opened in 1975 • Mixed single-level and low-rise buildings on 34 acres • Current resident population is 336 • Located 20 miles from Saint Louis, MO • Waiting list may apply in some units

AAHA Member

HOUSING AND SERVICES

Living Units	No.	Square Feet	No. of Persons	Entrance Fee	Monthly Fee
Studio	138	305–457	1	$27,000	$575
One Bedroom	122	609	1	$47,000	$769
			2	$47,000	$1,143
Two Bedroom	29	726	1	$55,000	$867
			2	$55,000	$1,241
Larger Units	5	1,066–	1	$72,000	$1,240
		1,250	2	$72,000	$1,614
Total		294 Units			

Entrance fees are partially refundable.

These fees include one meal per day, biweekly housekeeping, scheduled transportation, and utilities. Special features of this community are presented in the Special Features Index at the back of the book. Ask about additional residential and health care services that may be available. Fees and services subject to change; verify with facility.

ASSISTED LIVING AND PERSONAL CARE

Assisted living units: 0
Personal care is covered by the continuing care contract: No
Residents may receive personal care in independent living units: Yes

NURSING CARE: All-Inclusive Plan

Under this all-inclusive plan, unlimited nursing care is covered by the continuing care contract. When in nursing care, residents pay the same monthly fee they paid for their independent living unit.

Dual-certified beds: 60. Cost per day: private $118.50, semi-private $62.00.
Nursing beds are certified by Medicare. Nonresidents may be admitted directly to the nursing care facility.

GOOD SAMARITAN HOME

5200 South Broadway, Saint Louis, MO 63111
Telephone: (314) 352-2400

Opened in 1958 • One high-rise building on eight acres • Current resident population is 230 • Immediate availability

AAHA
Member

HOUSING AND SERVICES

Living Units	No.	Square Feet	No. of Persons	Entrance Fee	Monthly Fee
Studio	109	171–213	1	$28,440–$43,200	$645
One Bedroom	16	342–550	1	$28,440–$43,200	$1,118
			2	$42,660–$64,800	$1,440
Two Bedroom	1	895	1	$28,440–$43,200	$1,118
			2	$42,660–$64,800	$1,440
Larger Units	0	——	—	—	——
Total	126 Units				

Entrance fee refunds decline over time.

These fees include three meals per day, biweekly housekeeping, and utilities. Special features of this community are presented in the Special Features Index at the back of the book. Ask about additional residential and health care services that may be available. Fees and services subject to change; verify with facility.

ASSISTED LIVING AND PERSONAL CARE

Assisted living units: 67
Personal care is covered by the continuing care contract: Yes
Residents may receive personal care in independent living units: No
Nonresidents may be admitted directly to assisted living units: Yes

NURSING CARE: All-Inclusive Plan

Under this all-inclusive plan, unlimited nursing care is covered by the continuing care contract. When residents are in nursing care, they pay the basic monthly fee for the studio (smallest) unit.

Intermediate beds: 86. Cost per day: private $46.00, semi-private $46.00.

Nursing beds are not certified by Medicare or Medicaid. Nonresidents may be admitted directly to the nursing care facility.

KINGSWOOD MANOR
10000 Wornall Road, Kansas City, MO 64114
Telephone: (816) 942-0994

Opened in 1982 • Mixed single-level and low-rise buildings on 20 acres • Current population is 303 • Immediate availability

AAHA
Member

HOUSING AND SERVICES

Living Units	No.	Square Feet	No. of Persons	Entrance Fee	Monthly Fee
Studio	31	310–429	1	$24,633	$491
One Bedroom	190	542–970	1	$47,170	$739
			2		$939
Two Bedroom	46	834–1,860	1	$71,366	$992
			2		$1,192
Larger Units	0	—	—	—	—
Total		267 Units			

Entrance fee refunds decline over time.

These fees include one meal per day, biweekly housekeeping, and utilities. Special features of this community are presented in the Special Features Index at the back of the book. Ask about additional residential and health care services that may be available. Fees and services subject to change; verify with facility.

ASSISTED LIVING AND PERSONAL CARE

Assisted living units: 0
Personal care is covered by the continuing care contract: No
Residents may receive personal care in independent living units: No

NURSING CARE: Modified Plan

Under this modified plan, 15 or fewer days are covered by the continuing care contract. Once residents move permanently to the nursing unit, they pay the full per diem rate for nursing care.

Skilled beds: 41. Cost per day: semi-private $66.00.

Nursing beds are certified by Medicare. Nonresidents may be admitted directly to the nursing care facility.

LENOIR RETIREMENT CENTER
Highway 63 South, Columbia, MO 65201
Telephone: (314) 443-4561

Opened in 1962 • Mixed single-level and low-rise buildings on 106 acres • Current resident population is 280 • Waiting list may apply for some units

AAHA
Member

HOUSING AND SERVICES

Living Units	No.	Square Feet	No. of Persons	Entrance Fee	Monthly Fee
Studio	0	——	——	——	——
One Bedroom	7	1,100	1	$25,000–$32,000	$160
			2		$185
Two Bedroom	48	1,300	1	$32,000–$36,000	$185
			2		$210
Larger Units	65	1,600	1	$45,000–$65,000	$200
			2		$225

Total   120 Units

Entrance fee refunds decline over time.

These fees include scheduled transportation. Special features of this community are presented in the Special Features Index at the back of the book. Ask about additional residential and health care services that may be available. Fees and services subject to change; verify with facility.

ASSISTED LIVING AND PERSONAL CARE

Assisted living units: 47
Personal care is covered by the continuing care contract: Yes
Residents may receive personal care in independent living units: No
Nonresidents may be admitted directly to assisted living units: Yes

NURSING CARE: Modified Plan

Under this modified plan, 30 days per year are covered by the continuing care contract. Once residents move permanently to the nursing unit, they pay 75 percent of the per diem rate for nursing care.

Intermediate beds. Cost per day: semi-private $51.00.

Skilled beds: 60. Cost per day: semi-private $55.00.

Nursing beds are not certified by Medicare or Medicaid. Nonresidents may be admitted directly to the nursing care facility.

MISSOURI

PRESBYTERIAN MANOR AT FARMINGTON

Manor Court, Farmington, MO 63640
Telephone: (314) 756-6768

Opened in 1961 • Predominantly single-level/garden apartments on 15 acres • Current resident population is 155 • Immediate availability

AAHA Member

HOUSING AND SERVICES

Living Units	No.	Square Feet	No. of Persons	Entrance Fee	Monthly Fee
Studio	0	——	——	——	——
One Bedroom	15	——	1	$5,000	$428
			2	$10,000	$428
Two Bedroom	20	——	1	$5,000	$478
			2	$10,000	$478
Larger Units	1	——	1	$5,000	$478
			2	$10,000	$478
Total	36 Units				

Entrance fee refunds decline over time.

These fees include weekly housekeeping, scheduled transportation, and utilities. Special features of this community are presented in the Special Features Index at the back of the book. Ask about additional residential and health care services that may be available. Fees and services subject to change; verify with facility.

ASSISTED LIVING AND PERSONAL CARE

Assisted living units: 40
Personal care is covered by the continuing care contract: Yes
Residents may receive personal care in independent living units: Yes
Nonresidents may be admitted directly to assisted living units: Yes

NURSING CARE: Modified Plan

Under this modified plan, 15 or fewer days per year are covered by the continuing care contract. Once residents move permanently to the nursing unit, they pay the full per diem rate for nursing care.

Intermediate beds: 79. Cost per day: private $50.00, semi-private $40.60.

Nursing beds are certified by Medicaid. Nonresidents may be admitted directly to the nursing care facility.

VILLAGE NORTH
11160 Village North Drive, Saint Louis, MO 63136
Telephone: (314) 355-8010

Opened in 1982 • Mixed single-level and low-rise buildings on 44 acres • Current resident population is 211 • Waiting list may apply for some units

AAHA
Member

HOUSING AND SERVICES

Living Units	No.	Square Feet	No. of Persons	Entrance Fee	Monthly Fee
Studio	39	376	1	$30,820	$572
One Bedroom	114	582	1	$46,500	$780
			2	$48,940	$1,158
Two Bedroom	60	787	1	$58,400	$853
			2	$60,840	$1,231
Larger Units	0	——	——	——	——
Total	213 Units				

Entrance fee refunds decline over time.

These fees include one meal per day, weekly housekeeping, scheduled transportation, and utilities. Special features of this community are presented in the Special Features Index at the back of the book. Ask about additional residential and health care services that may be available. Fees and services subject to change; verify with facility.

ASSISTED LIVING AND PERSONAL CARE

Assisted living units: 0
Personal care is covered by the continuing care contract: Yes
Residents may receive personal care in independent living units: Yes

NURSING CARE: All-Inclusive Plan

Under this all-inclusive plan, unlimited nursing care is covered by the continuing care contract. When residents are in nursing care, they pay the same monthly fee they paid for their independent living unit.

Dual-certified beds: 60. Cost per day: private $72.00, semi-private $67.00.

Nursing beds are certified by both Medicare and Medicaid. Nonresidents may be admitted directly to the nursing care facility.

NEBRASKA

GATEWAY MANOR
225 North 56th Street, Lincoln, NE 68504
Telephone: (402) 464-6371

Opened in 1963 • One high-rise building on seven
acres • Current resident population is 84 • Waiting
list may apply for some units

AAHA
Member

HOUSING AND SERVICES

Living Units	No.	Square Feet	No. of Persons	Entrance Fee	Monthly Fee
Studio	34	352–525	1	$23,500–$34,000	$460–$565
One Bedroom	33	704–762	1	$45,000–$51,000	$700
			2	$47,000–$53,000	$925
Two Bedroom	3	1,075	1	$68,000–$73,000	$925
			2	$70,000–$75,000	$1,195
Larger Units	0	——	——	——	——
Total		70 Units			

Entrance fee refunds decline over time.

These fees include one meal per day, weekly housekeeping, and utilities. Special features of this community are presented in the Special Features Index at the back of the book. Ask about additional residential and health care services that may be available. Fees and services subject to change; verify with facility.

ASSISTED LIVING AND PERSONAL CARE

Assisted living units: 0
Personal care is covered by the continuing care contract: No
Residents may receive personal care in independent living units: Yes

NURSING CARE: Modified Plan

Under this modified plan, 30 days of nursing care are covered by the continuing care contract. Once residents move permanently to the nursing unit, they pay the full per diem rate for nursing care.

Dual-certified beds: 18. Cost per day: private $45.00.

Nursing beds are certified by Medicaid. Nonresidents may not be admitted directly to the nursing care facility.

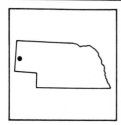

NORTHFIELD VILLA
2250 21st Street, Gering, NE 69241
Telephone: (308) 436-3101

Opened in 1974 • Predominantly single-level/garden apartments on 22 acres • Current resident population is 115 • Waiting list

HOUSING AND SERVICES

Living Units	No.	Square Feet	No. of Persons	Entrance Fee	Monthly Fee
Studio	24	450	1	$26,950	$466
One Bedroom	50	624	1	$39,950	$516
			2		$782
Two Bedroom	24	864	1	$49,950	$549
			2		$815
Larger Units	0	—	—	—	—
Total	98 Units				

Entrance fee refunds decline over time.

These fees include one meal per day, housekeeping, scheduled transportation, and utilities. Special features of this community are presented in the Special Features Index at the back of the book. Ask about additional residential and health care services that may be available. Fees and services subject to change; verify with facility.

ASSISTED LIVING AND PERSONAL CARE

Assisted living units: 0
Personal care is covered by the continuing care contract: No
Residents may receive personal care in independent living units: No

NURSING CARE: All-Inclusive Plan

Under this all-inclusive plan, unlimited nursing care is covered by the continuing care contract. When in nursing care, residents pay the same monthly fee they paid for their independent living unit.

Skilled beds: 41. Cost per day: semi-private $52.50.

Nursing beds are certified by both Medicare and Medicaid. Nonresidents may be admitted directly to the nursing care facility.

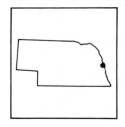

SKYLINE MANOR
7300 Graceland Drive, Omaha, NE 68134
Telephone: (402) 572-5753

Opened in 1969 • Mixed single-level, low-rise, and high-rise buildings on 14 acres • Current resident population is 550 • Waiting list may apply for some units

AAHA
Member

HOUSING AND SERVICES

Living Units	No.	Square Feet	No. of Persons	Entrance Fee	Monthly Fee
Studio	86	277–380	1	$23,999–$31,796	$439–$544
One Bedroom	235	450–632	1, 2	$37,858–$56,834	$455–$630
Two Bedroom	18	——	1	——	$630–$899
			2	——	$897–$1,009
Larger Units	0	——	——	——	——
Total	339 Units				

Entrance fee refunds decline over time.

These fees include one meal per day, biweekly housekeeping, scheduled transportation, and utilities. Special features of this community are presented in the Special Features Index at the back of the book. Ask about additional residential and health care services that may be available. Fees and services subject to change; verify with facility.

ASSISTED LIVING AND PERSONAL CARE

Assisted living units: 20
Personal care is covered by the continuing care contract: Yes
Residents may receive personal care in independent living units: Yes
Nonresidents may be admitted directly to assisted living units: No

NURSING CARE: All-Inclusive Plan

Under this all-inclusive plan, unlimited nursing care is covered by the continuing care contract. When in nursing care, residents pay the same monthly fee they paid for their independent living unit.

Intermediate beds: 84. Cost per day: not applicable.

Nursing beds are not certified by Medicare or Medicaid. Nonresidents may not be admitted directly to the nursing care facility.

NEW HAMPSHIRE

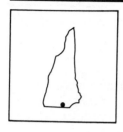

HUNT COMMUNITY
10 Allds Street, Nashua, NH 03060
Telephone: (603) 882-6511

Opened in 1984 • One high-rise building on 14 acres
• Current resident population is 160 • Waiting list
may apply for some units

HOUSING AND SERVICES

Living Units	No.	Square Feet	No. of Persons	Entrance Fee	Monthly Fee
Studio	8	410	1	$23,100	$715
One Bedroom	56	612–640	1	$36,500–$38,500	$810
			2		$1,090
Two Bedroom	10	980	1	$55,000	——
			2		$1,330
Larger Units	0	——	——	——	——
Total	74 Units				

Entrance fee refunds decline over time.

These fees include one meal per day, housekeeping, scheduled transportation, and some utilities. Special features of this community are presented in the Special Features Index at the back of the book. Ask about additional residential and health care services that may be available. Fees and services subject to change; verify with facility.

ASSISTED LIVING AND PERSONAL CARE

Assisted living units: 40
Personal care is covered by the continuing care contract: No
Residents may receive personal care in independent living units: No
Nonresidents may be admitted directly to assisted living units: Yes

NURSING CARE: Modified Plan

Under this modified plan, ten days are covered by the continuing care contract. Thereafter, residents pay the full per diem rate for nursing care.

Intermediate beds: 40. Cost per day: private $75.00, semi-private $65.00. Skilled beds: 0.

Nursing beds are not certified by Medicare or Medicaid. Nonresidents may not be admitted directly to the nursing care facility.

CADBURY
2150 Route 38, Cherry Hill, NJ 08002
Telephone: (609) 667-4550

Opened in 1978 • Mixed single-level and low-rise buildings on 13 acres • Current resident population is 300 • Waiting list may apply for some units • Accredited by the AAHA Continuing Care Accreditation Commission

HOUSING AND SERVICES

Living Units	No.	Square Feet	No. of Persons	Entrance Fee	Monthly Fee
Studio	143	308	1	$32,000–$39,000	$780
One Bedroom	31	532	1	$56,000	$1,154
			2	$68,000	$1,594
Two Bedroom	17	690	1	$67,000	$1,298
			2	$79,000	$1,796
Larger Units	2	——	1, 2	——	——
Total	193 Units				

Entrance fees are nonrefundable.

These fees include three meals per day, biweekly housekeeping, scheduled transportation, and utilities. Special features of this community are presented in the Special Features Index at the back of the book. Ask about additional residential and health care services that may be available. Fees and services subject to change; verify with facility.

ASSISTED LIVING AND PERSONAL CARE

Assisted living units: 0
Personal care is covered by the continuing care contract: No
Residents may receive personal care in independent living units: No

NURSING CARE: All-Inclusive Plan

Under this all-inclusive plan, unlimited nursing care is covered by the continuing care contract. When residents are in nursing care, they pay the same monthly fee they paid for their independent living unit.

Intermediate beds: 55. Cost per day: private $125.00, semi-private $75.00.

Skilled beds: 60. Cost per day: private $125.00, semi-private $75.00.

Nursing beds are certified by both Medicare and Medicaid. Nonresidents may be admitted directly to the nursing care facility.

HARROGATE
525 Route 70 West
Northern Ocean Professional Plaza
Lakewood, NJ 08701
Telephone: (201) 363-5099

Opening in 1988 • Mixed single-level and low-rise
buildings on 40 acres • Waiting list

AAHA
Member

HOUSING AND SERVICES

Living Units	No.	Square Feet	No. of Persons	Entrance Fee	Monthly Fee
Studio	30	450	1	$51,000	$917
One Bedroom	220	600	1	$62,300	$1,012
			2	$66,300	$1,470
Two Bedroom	28	900	1	$84,000	$1,199
			2	$88,000	$1,669
Larger Units	22	1,050	1	$95,000	$1,294
			2	$99,000	$1,764
Total	300 Units				

Residents have a choice of entrance fee refund plans.

These fees include one meal per day, weekly housekeeping, scheduled transportation, and utilities. Special features of this community are presented in the Special Features Index at the back of the book. Ask about additional residential and health care services that may be available. Fees and services subject to change; verify with facility.

ASSISTED LIVING AND PERSONAL CARE

Assisted living units: 0
Personal care is covered by the continuing care contract: Yes
Residents may receive personal care in independent living units: Yes

NURSING CARE: All-Inclusive Plan

Under this all-inclusive plan, unlimited nursing care is covered by the continuing care contract. When residents are in nursing care, they pay the basic monthly fee for the studio (smallest) unit.

Nursing beds: Nursing unit is under development; rates for outside admissions are not yet set.

Nursing beds will be certified by Medicare. Nonresidents may be admitted directly to the nursing care facility.

MEADOW LAKES
P.O. Box 70, Etra Road, Hightstown, NJ 08520
Telephone: (609) 448-4100

Opened in 1965 • Mixed single-level and low-rise buildings on 103 acres • Current resident population is 400 • Located 50 miles from New York, NY • Waiting list • Accredited by the AAHA Continuing Care Accreditation Commission

AAHA
Member

HOUSING AND SERVICES

Living Units	No.	Square Feet	No. of Persons	Entrance Fee	Monthly Fee
Studio	66	373	1	$40,125	$1,461
One Bedroom	179	572	1	$80,400	$1,806
			2	$88,425	$2,919
Two Bedroom	59	893	1	$103,583	$2,045
			2	$114,000	$3,159
Larger Units	4	1,875	1	$181,900	$3,069
			2	$200,900	$4,182
Total		308 Units			

Residents have a choice of entrance fee refund plans.

These fees include one meal per day, weekly housekeeping, scheduled transportation, and utilities. Special features of this community are presented in the Special Features Index at the back of the book. Ask about additional residential and health care services that may be available. Fees and services subject to change; verify with facility.

ASSISTED LIVING AND PERSONAL CARE

Assisted living units: 0
Personal care is covered by the continuing care contract: No
Residents may receive personal care in independent living units: No

NURSING CARE: All-Inclusive Plan

Under this all-inclusive plan, unlimited nursing care is covered by the continuing care contract. When in nursing care, residents pay the same monthly fee they paid for their independent living unit.

Dual-certified beds: 90. Cost per day: private $115.50, semi-private $101.50.

Nursing beds are certified by both Medicare and Medicaid. Nonresidents may be admitted directly to the nursing care facility.

MEDFORD LEAS RETIREMENT COMMUNITY
Route 70, Medford, NJ 08055
Telephone: (609) 654-3000

Opened in 1971 • Mixed single-level and low-rise
buildings on 214 acres • Current resident population
is 500 • Located 18 miles from Philadelphia, PA •
Long waiting list; make reservations in advance

AAHA
Member

HOUSING AND SERVICES

Living Units	No.	Square Feet	No. of Persons	Entrance Fee	Monthly Fee
Studio	72	330–417	1	$27,000–$34,500	$950
One Bedroom	142	557–968	1	$51,500–$73,500	$575–$1,135
			2	$61,000–$87,500	$915–$1,915
Two Bedroom	85	1,010–	1	$85,500–$104,500	$775–$1,515
		2,213	2	$97,000–$127,500	$1,120–$2,035
Larger Units	0	—	—	—	—
Total	299 Units				

Entrance fee refunds decline over time.

These fees include three meals per day, weekly housekeeping, scheduled transportation, and utilities. Special features of this community are presented in the
Special Features Index at the back of the book. Ask about additional residential
and health care services that may be available. Fees and services subject to
change; verify with facility.

ASSISTED LIVING AND PERSONAL CARE

Assisted living units: 36
Personal care is covered by the continuing care contract: Yes
Residents may receive personal care in independent living units: No
Nonresidents may be admitted directly to assisted living units: Yes

NURSING CARE: All-Inclusive Plan

Under this all-inclusive plan, unlimited nursing care is covered by the continuing care contract. When in nursing care, residents pay the monthly studio rate
for a semi-private room and the monthly one-bedroom rate for a private room.

Intermediate beds: 87. Cost per day: private $110.00, semi-private $95.00.

Skilled beds: 22. Cost per day: private $128.00, semi-private $113.00.

Nursing beds are certified by Medicare. Nonresidents may be admitted
directly to the nursing care facility.

WESTMONT HOME
265 Totowa Avenue, Paterson, NJ 07502
Telephone: (201) 595-7403

Opened in 1875 • Mixed single-level and low-rise
buildings on two acres • Current resident population
is 42 • Immediate availability

AAHA
Member

HOUSING AND SERVICES

Living Units	No.	Square Feet	No. of Persons	Entrance Fee	Monthly Fee
Studio	53	168	1	$55,000	$1,650
One Bedroom	0	——	——	——	——
Two Bedroom	0	——	——	——	——
Larger Units	0	——	——	——	——
Total		53 Units			

Entrance fees are nonrefundable.

These fees include three meals per day, housekeeping, scheduled transportation, and utilities. Special features of this community are presented in the Special Features Index at the back of the book. Ask about additional residential and health care services that may be available. Fees and services subject to change; verify with facility.

ASSISTED LIVING AND PERSONAL CARE

Assisted living units: 0
Personal care is covered by the continuing care contract: No
Residents may receive personal care in independent living units: No

NURSING CARE: All-Inclusive Plan

Under this all-inclusive plan, unlimited nursing care is covered by the continuing care contract. When residents are in nursing care, they pay the same monthly fee they paid for their independent living unit.

Skilled beds: 12. Cost per day: not applicable.

Nursing beds are not certified by Medicare or Medicaid. Nonresidents may not be admitted directly to the nursing care facility.

NEW MEXICO

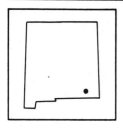

LANDSUN HOMES
1900 Landsun Drive, Carlsbad, NM 88220
Telephone: (505) 887-2894

Opened in 1965 • Mixed single-level, low-rise, and high-rise buildings on 22 acres • Current resident population is 187 • Waiting list may apply for some units

AAHA
Member

HOUSING AND SERVICES

Living Units	No.	Square Feet	No. of Persons	Entrance Fee	Monthly Fee
Studio	56	336–400	1	$22,000–$35,000	$713–$767
One Bedroom	13	750–900	1	$22,000–$35,000	$353–$750
	4*	480	2		$1,215
Two Bedroom	13	1,000–1,150	1, 2	$22,000–$35,000	$750
Larger Units	0	——	——	——	——
Total	86 Units				

*These units are available for couples only.
Entrance fee refunds decline over time.

These fees (except for townhome units) include three meals per day, weekly housekeeping, scheduled transportation, and utilities. Special features of this community are presented in the Special Features Index at the back of the book. Ask about additional residential and health care services that may be available. Fees and services subject to change; verify with facility.

ASSISTED LIVING AND PERSONAL CARE

Assisted living units: 64
Personal care is covered by the continuing care contract: No
Residents may receive personal care in independent living units: No
Nonresidents may be admitted directly to assisted living units: Yes

---

NURSING CARE: Modified Plan

Under this modified plan, 16–59 days per year are covered by the continuing care contract. Once residents move permanently to the nursing unit, they pay the full per diem rate for nursing care.

Intermediate beds: 64. Cost per day: private—not applicable, semi-private $66.00.

Nursing beds are certified by Medicaid. Nonresidents may not be admitted directly to the nursing care facility.

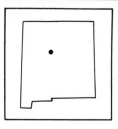

LA VIDA LLENA
10501 Lagrima De Oro, Albuquerque, NM 87111
Telephone: (505) 296-6700

Opening in 1983 • Mixed single-level and low-rise buildings on 16 acres • Current resident population is 281 • Immediate availability

AAHA
Member

HOUSING AND SERVICES

Living Units	No.	Square Feet	No. of Persons	Entrance Fee	Monthly Fee
Studio	29	385	1	$30,250	$600
One Bedroom	79	576	1	$45,500	$704
			2	$48,500	$1,094
Two Bedroom	148	798–1,077	1	$62,500–$84,500	$835–$1,018
			2	$65,500–$87,500	$1,225–$1,408
Larger Units	0	—	—	—	—
Total	256 Units				

Residents have a choice of entrance fee refund plans.

These fees include one meal per day, biweekly housekeeping, scheduled transportation, and utilities. Special features of this community are presented in the Special Features Index at the back of the book. Ask about additional residential and health care services that may be available. Fees and services subject to change; verify with facility.

ASSISTED LIVING AND PERSONAL CARE

Assisted living units: 11
Personal care is covered by the continuing care contract: Yes
Residents may receive personal care in independent living units: Yes
Nonresidents may be admitted directly to assisted living units: Yes

NURSING CARE: All-Inclusive Plan

Under this all-inclusive plan, unlimited nursing care is covered by the continuing care contract. When residents are in nursing care, they pay the same monthly fee they paid for their independent living unit.

Intermediate beds: 60. Cost per day: private $75.00, semi-private $65.00.

Skilled beds: 18. Cost per day: private $125.00, semi-private $115.00.

Nursing beds are certified by both Medicare and Medicaid. Nonresidents may be admitted directly to the nursing care facility.

EDDY MEMORIAL GERIATRIC CENTER
2256 Burdett Avenue, Troy, NY 12180
Telephone: (518) 274-9890

Opened in 1985 • Mixed single-level and low-rise
buildings on six acres • Current resident population is
182 • Waiting list may apply for some units

AAHA
Member

HOUSING AND SERVICES

Living Units	No.	Square Feet	No. of Persons	Entrance Fee	Monthly Fee
Studio	3	400–450	1	$52,900	$575
One Bedroom	45	500–525	1	$62,900	$625
			2	$62,900	$850
Two Bedroom	12	700–825	1	$75,900	$760
			2	$75,900	$985
Larger Units	0	——	——	——	——
Total	60 Units				

Entrance fees are fully refundable.

These fees include one meal per day, scheduled transportation, and utilities.
Special features of this community are presented in the Special Features Index
at the back of the book. Ask about additional residential and health care services
that may be available. Fees and services subject to change; verify with facility.

ASSISTED LIVING AND PERSONAL CARE

Assisted living units: 40
Personal care is covered by the continuing care contract: No
Residents may receive personal care in independent living units: No
Nonresidents may be admitted directly to assisted living units: Yes

NURSING CARE: Fee-for-Service Plan

Under this fee-for-service plan, guaranteed access to nursing care is covered by
the continuing care contract. Residents pay the full per diem rate for nursing
care.

Intermediate beds: 30. Cost per day: private $96.00, semi-private $92.00.

Skilled beds: 30. Cost per day: private $109.00, semi-private $105.00.

Nursing beds are certified by both Medicare and Medicaid. Nonresidents may
be admitted directly to the nursing care facility.

GREERCREST
P.O. Box 2000, Millbrook, NY 12545
Telephone: (914) 677-5041

Opened in 1986 • Mixed single-level and low-rise buildings on 200 acres • Current resident population is 82 • Located 20 miles from Poughkeepsie, NY • Waiting list may apply for some units

AAHA
Member

HOUSING AND SERVICES

Living Units	No.	Square Feet	No. of Persons	Entrance Fee	Monthly Fee
Studio	4	560	1	$40,000	$500
One Bedroom	30	800	1	$65,000	$750
			2	$65,000	——
Two Bedroom	104	1,100	1	$95,000	$950
			2	$95,000	$1,100
Larger Units	0	——	——	——	——
Total	138 Units				

Entrance fees are fully refundable.

These fees include one meal per day, weekly housekeeping, scheduled transportation, and utilities. Special features of this community are presented in the Special Features Index at the back of the book. Ask about additional residential and health care services that may be available. Fees and services subject to change; verify with facility.

ASSISTED LIVING AND PERSONAL CARE

Assisted living units: 0
Personal care is covered by the continuing care contract: No
Residents may receive personal care in independent living units: No

NURSING CARE: Fee-for-Service Plan

Under this fee-for-service plan, guaranteed access to nursing care is covered by the continuing care contract. Residents are required to hold private insurance to pay for nursing care.

Intermediate beds: 40.*

Skilled beds: 120.*

*The nursing unit is under development; per diem rates not yet set.
Nursing beds are certified by both Medicare and Medicaid. Nonresidents may be admitted directly to the nursing care facility.

NORTH CAROLINA

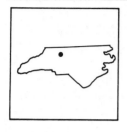

BAPTIST RETIREMENT HOMES OF NORTH CAROLINA

2900 Reynolds Park Road, Winston-Salem, NC 27107
Telephone: (919) 788-2441

Opened in 1957 • Mixed single-level and low-rise buildings on 40 acres • Current resident population is 140 • Waiting list may apply for some units

AAHA
Member

HOUSING AND SERVICES

Living Units	No.	Square Feet	No. of Persons	Entrance Fee	Monthly Fee
Studio	0	——	——	——	——
One Bedroom	1	900	1, 2	——	$250
Two Bedroom	20	1,250	1, 2	$60,000–$75,000	$250
Larger Units	0	——	——	——	——
Total	21 Units				

Entrance fee refunds decline over time.

These fees include scheduled transportation and utilities. Special features of this community are presented in the Special Features Index at the back of the book. Ask about additional residential and health care services that may be available. Fees and services subject to change; verify with facility.

ASSISTED LIVING AND PERSONAL CARE

Assisted living units: 30
Personal care is covered by the continuing care contract: No
Residents may receive personal care in independent living units: No
Nonresidents may be admitted directly to assisted living units: Yes

NURSING CARE: Fee-for-Service Plan

Under this fee-for-service plan, guaranteed access to nursing care is covered by the continuing care contract. Residents pay the full per diem rate for nursing care.

Intermediate beds: 58. Cost per day: private $57.00, semi-private $57.00.

Skilled beds: 27. Cost per day: private—not applicable, semi-private $67.00.

Nursing beds are certified by both Medicare and Medicaid. Nonresidents may be admitted directly to the nursing care facility.

CAROL WOODS
750 Weaver Dairy Road, Chapel Hill, NC 27514
Telephone: (919) 968-4511

Opened in 1979 • Mixed single-level and low-rise buildings on 104 acres • Current resident population is 327 • Waiting list may apply for some units

AAHA
Member

HOUSING AND SERVICES

Living Units	No.	Square Feet	No. of Persons	Entrance Fee	Monthly Fee
Studio	21	447	1	$23,300	$981
One Bedroom	125	681	1	$48,450	$1,053
			2	$50,300	$1,460
Two Bedroom	84	961	1	$70,223	$1,319
			2	$70,223	$1,706
Larger Units	0	——	——	——	——
Total	230 Units				

Entrance fee refunds decline over time.

These fees include one or three meals per day, weekly housekeeping, scheduled transportation, and utilities. Special features of this community are presented in the Special Features Index at the back of the book. Ask about additional residential and health care services that may be available. Fees and services subject to change; verify with facility.

ASSISTED LIVING AND PERSONAL CARE

Assisted living units: 30
Personal care is covered by the continuing care contract: No
Residents may receive personal care in independent living units: No
Nonresidents may be admitted directly to assisted living units: No

NURSING CARE: Modified Plan

Under this modified plan, 60 days or more are covered by the continuing care contract. Once residents move permanently to the nursing unit, they pay a discounted per diem rate for nursing care.

Skilled beds: 30. Cost per day: private $97.34, semi-private $80.00.

Nursing beds are certified by Medicare. Nonresidents may be admitted directly to the nursing care facility.

NORTH CAROLINA

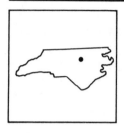

CAROLINA MEADOWS
P.O. Box 3484
Chapel Hill, NC 27514
Telephone: (919) 968-9423

Opened in 1985 • Mixed single-level and low-rise buildings on 80 acres • Current resident population is 72 • Immediate availability

AAHA
Member

HOUSING AND SERVICES

Living Units	No.	Square Feet	No. of Persons	Entrance Fee	Monthly Fee
Studio	4	504	1	$53,000	$500
One Bedroom	47	605–1,276	1	$63,000–$130,400	$500
			2	$63,000–$130,400	$625
Two Bedroom	74	1,075–	1	$119,800–$171,700	$500
		1,674	2	$119,800–$171,700	$625
Larger Units	0	——	——	——	——
Total		125 Units			

Entrance fees are fully refundable.

These fees include a meal allowance and scheduled transportation. Special features of this community are presented in the Special Features Index at the back of the book. Ask about additional residential and health care services that may be available. Fees and services subject to change; verify with facility.

ASSISTED LIVING AND PERSONAL CARE

Assisted living units: 40
Personal care is covered by the continuing care contract: No
Residents may receive personal care in independent living units: Yes
Nonresidents may be admitted directly to assisted living units: Yes

NURSING CARE: Fee-for-Service Plan

Under this fee-for-service plan, guaranteed access to nursing care is covered by the continuing care contract. Residents pay the full per diem rate for nursing care.

Skilled beds: 10. Health care center is scheduled for completion in late 1988; per diem rates not yet set.

Nursing beds are not yet certified. Nonresidents may not be admitted directly to the nursing care facility.

CAROLINA VILLAGE
600 Carolina Village Road, Hendersonville, NC 28739
Telephone: (704) 692-6275

Opened in 1974 • Mixed single-level and low-rise
buildings on 40 acres • Current resident population is
332 • Waiting list may apply for some units

AAHA
Member

HOUSING AND SERVICES

Living Units	No.	Square Feet	No. of Persons	Entrance Fee	Monthly Fee
Studio	76	400	1	$20,500–$26,500	$499–$563
One Bedroom	72	610	1	$35,500–$43,000	$650–738
			2	$40,500–$48,000	$984–$1,027
Two Bedroom	65	740	1	$48,000–$74,000	$738–$865
			2	$53,000–$79,000	$1,027–$1,154
Larger Units	27	1,200	1	$62,000–$80,500	$850–$924
			2	$67,000–$85,500	$1,149–$1,223

Total   240 Units

Entrance fee refunds decline over time.

These fees include one meal per day, biweekly housekeeping, scheduled transportation, and utilities. Special features of this community are presented in the Special Features Index at the back of the book. Ask about additional residential and health care services that may be available. Fees and services subject to change; verify with facility.

ASSISTED LIVING AND PERSONAL CARE

Assisted living units: 0
Personal care is covered by the continuing care contract: No
Residents may receive personal care in independent living units: Yes

NURSING CARE: All-Inclusive Plan

Under this all-inclusive plan, unlimited nursing care is covered by the continuing care contract. When residents are in nursing care, they pay the same monthly fee they paid for their independent living unit.

Skilled beds: 58. Cost per day: private—not applicable, semi-private $65.00.

Nursing beds are certified by both Medicare and Medicaid. Nonresidents may be admitted directly to the nursing care facility.

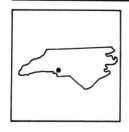

COVENANT VILLAGE
1351 Robinwood Road, Gastonia, NC 28054
Telephone: (704) 867-2319

Opened in 1982 • One mid-rise building on 32 acres •
Current resident population is 167 • Waiting list

AAHA
Member

HOUSING AND SERVICES

Living Units	No.	Square Feet	No. of Persons	Entrance Fee	Monthly Fee
Studio	73	351	1	$21,500–$26,500	$751
One Bedroom	38	750	1	$49,500	$866
			2	$49,500	$1,732
Two Bedroom	10	1,100	1, 2	$65,000	$1,718
Larger Units	0	——	——	——	——
Total	121 Units				

Entrance fees are refundable during first year of occupancy only.

These fees include three meals per day, weekly housekeeping, scheduled transportation, and utilities. Special features of this community are presented in the Special Features Index at the back of the book. Ask about additional residential and health care services that may be available. Fees and services subject to change; verify with facility.

ASSISTED LIVING AND PERSONAL CARE

Assisted living units: 0
Personal care is covered by the continuing care contract: No
Residents may receive personal care in independent living units: Yes

NURSING CARE: All-Inclusive Plan

Under this all-inclusive plan, unlimited nursing care is covered by the continuing care contract. When residents are in nursing care, they pay the same monthly fee they paid for their independent living unit.

Intermediate beds: 4. Cost per day: semi-private—not applicable.

Skilled beds: 36. Cost per day: semi-private—not applicable.

Nursing beds are not certified by Medicare or Medicaid. Nonresidents may not be admitted directly to the nursing care facility.

NORTH CAROLINA

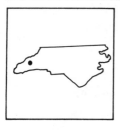

DEERFIELD EPISCOPAL RETIREMENT COMMUNITY
1617 Hendersonville Road, Asheville, NC 28803
Telephone: (704) 274-1531

Opened in 1955 • Mixed single-level and low-rise buildings on 30 acres • Current resident population is 114 • Waiting list

AAHA Member

HOUSING AND SERVICES

Living Units	No.	Square Feet	No. of Persons	Entrance Fee	Monthly Fee
Studio	26	160	1	$4,000	$960*–$995*
One Bedroom	4	320	1	$4,000	$1,650*
			2	$8,000	$1,850*
Two Bedroom	34	1,200–1,700	1, 2	$50,000–$110,00	$184
Larger Units	0	——	——	——	——
Total		64 Units			

Entrance fee refunds decline over time.

*These fees include three meals per day, weekly housekeeping, and utilities. Special features of this community are presented in the Special Features Index at the back of the book. Ask about additional residential and health care services that may be available. Fees and services subject to change; verify with facility.

ASSISTED LIVING AND PERSONAL CARE

Assisted living units: 0
Personal care is covered by the continuing care contract: No
Residents may receive personal care in independent living units: No

NURSING CARE: Fee-for-Service Plan

Under this fee-for-service plan, guaranteed access to nursing care is covered by the continuing care contract. Residents pay the full per diem rate for nursing care.

Intermediate beds: 8. Cost per day: private $56.67, semi-private—not applicable.

Skilled beds: 31. Cost per day: private $75.50, semi-private $55.00.

Nursing beds are not certified by Medicare or Medicaid. Nonresidents may be admitted directly to the nursing care facility.

NORTH CAROLINA

EPISCOPAL HOME FOR THE AGEING
P.O. Box 2001, Southern Pines, NC 28387
Telephone: (919) 692-0300

Opened in 1964 • Mixed single-level and low-rise buildings on 24 acres • Current resident population is 201 • Waiting list

HOUSING AND SERVICES

Living Units	No.	Square Feet	No. of Persons	Entrance Fee	Monthly Fee
Studio	86	200	1	$25,000	$623–$825
One Bedroom	27	407	1	$50,000	$819–$1,350
			2		$1,161–$1,692
Two Bedroom	30	1,500	1	$75,000	$923–$2,000
			2		$1,423–$2,500
Larger Units	0	——	——	——	——
Total	143 Units				

Entrance fees are nonrefundable.

These fees include three meals per day, biweekly housekeeping, scheduled transportation, and utilities. Special features of this community are presented in the Special Features Index at the back of the book. Ask about additional residential and health care services that may be available. Fees and services subject to change; verify with facility.

ASSISTED LIVING AND PERSONAL CARE

Assisted living units: 42
Personal care is covered by the continuing care contract: Yes
Residents may receive personal care in independent living units: Yes
Nonresidents may be admitted directly to assisted living units: Yes

NURSING CARE: Modified Plan

Under this modified plan, 15 or fewer days per illness are covered by the continuing care contract. Once residents move permanently to the nursing unit, they pay the full per diem rate for nursing care.

Skilled beds: 33. Cost per day: private $56.00, semi-private $50.00.

Nursing beds are certified by both Medicare and Medicaid. Nonresidents are rarely admitted directly to the nursing care facility.

NORTH CAROLINA

FRIENDS HOME
925 New Garden Road, Greensboro, NC 27410
Telephone: (919) 292-8187

Opened in 1968 • Mixed single-level, low-rise, and high-rise buildings on 16 acres • Current resident population is 323 • Long waiting list; make reservations in advance

AAHA
Member

HOUSING AND SERVICES

Living Units	No.	Square Feet	No. of Persons	Entrance Fee	Monthly Fee
Studio	89	240	1	$15,000–$16,500	$407–$537
One Bedroom	74	456	1	$25,000–$27,500	$578–$803
			2		$783–$1,008
Two Bedroom	17	660	1	$37,500–$41,250	$750–$1,075
			2		$955–$1,280
Larger Units	4	1,600	1	$40,000–$60,000	$600 (no meals)

Total   184 Units

Residents have a choice of entrance fee refund plans.

These fees include two meals per day, scheduled transportation, and utilities. Special features of this community are presented in the Special Features Index at the back of the book. Ask about additional residential and health care services that may be available. Fees and services subject to change; verify with facility.

ASSISTED LIVING AND PERSONAL CARE

Assisted living units: 60
Personal care is covered by the continuing care contract: No
Residents may receive personal care in independent living units: No
Nonresidents may be admitted directly to assisted living units: Yes

NURSING CARE: Fee-for-Service Plan

Under this fee-for-service plan, guaranteed access to nursing care is covered by the continuing care contract. Residents pay the full per diem rate for nursing care.

Intermediate beds: 37. Cost per day: private $53.00, semi-private $48.00.

Skilled beds: 32. Cost per day: private $58.00, semi-private $54.00.

Dual-certified beds: 26. Cost per day: private $58.00, semi-private $54.00. Nursing beds are certified by both Medicare and Medicaid. Nonresidents may be admitted directly to the nursing care facility.

NORTH CAROLINA

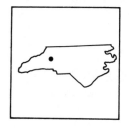

J. W. ABERNETHY CENTER
UNITED CHURCH RETIREMENT HOMES
100 Leonard Avenue, Newton, NC 28658
Telephone: (704) 464-8260

Opened in 1971 • Predominantly single-level/garden apartments on 120 acres • Current resident population is 206 • Waiting list

AAHA
Member

HOUSING AND SERVICES

Living Units	No.	Square Feet	No. of Persons	Entrance Fee	Monthly Fee
Studio	0	——	——	——	——
One Bedroom	2	900	1	$38,500	$200
			2	$38,500	$250
Two Bedroom	16	1,050	1	$48,500	$270
			2	$48,500	$320
Larger Units	42	1,100–1,400	1	$58,500–$78,500	$295
			2	$58,500–$78,500	$345
Total		60 Units			

Entrance fees are partially refundable.

Special features of this community are presented in the Special Features Index at the back of the book. Ask about additional residential and health care services that may be available. Fees and services subject to change; verify with facility.

ASSISTED LIVING AND PERSONAL CARE

Assisted living units: 33
Personal care is covered by the continuing care contract: Yes
Residents may receive personal care in independent living units: Yes
Nonresidents may be admitted directly to assisted living units: Yes

NURSING CARE: Modified Plan

Under this modified plan, 15 or fewer days are covered by the continuing care contract. Thereafter, residents pay the full per diem rate for nursing care.

Intermediate beds: 67. Cost per day: private $63.50, semi-private $53.00.

Skilled beds: 31. Cost per day: private $72.00, semi-private $65.00.

Nursing beds are certified by both Medicare and Medicaid. Nonresidents may be admitted directly to the nursing care facility.

MARYFIELD NURSING HOME
1315 Greensboro Road, High Point, NC 27260
Telephone: (919) 454-5313

Opened in 1978 • Predominantly single-level/garden apartments on 25 acres • Current resident population is 23 • Waiting list

AAHA
Member

HOUSING AND SERVICES

Living Units	No.	Square Feet	No. of Persons	Entrance Fee	Monthly Fee
Studio	0	——	——	——	——
One Bedroom	7	731–938	1	$28,500–$36,500	$490–$550
			2		$680–$740
Two Bedroom	10	1,265–1,501	1	$53,000–$75,000	$600–$625
			2		$790–$815
Larger Units	0	——	——	——	——
Total	17 Units				

Entrance fees are nonrefundable.

These fees include one meal per day, weekly housekeeping, scheduled transportation, and utilities. Special features of this community are presented in the Special Features Index at the back of the book. Ask about additional residential and health care services that may be available. Fees and services subject to change; verify with facility.

ASSISTED LIVING AND PERSONAL CARE

Assisted living units: 115
Personal care is covered by the continuing care contract: Yes
Residents may receive personal care in independent living units: No
Nonresidents may be admitted directly to assisted living units: Yes

NURSING CARE: Modified Plan

Under this modified plan, 100 days of nursing care are covered by the continuing care contract. Thereafter, residents pay the full per diem rate for nursing care.

Intermediate beds: 4. Cost per day: semi-private $39.00.

Skilled beds: 111. Cost per day: private $48.00, semi-private $42.00.

Nursing beds are certified by both Medicare and Medicaid. Nonresidents may be admitted directly to the nursing care facility.

NORTH CAROLINA

THE METHODIST HOME FOR THE AGED
3420 Shamrock Drive, Charlotte, NC 28215
Telephone: (704) 537-9731

Opened in 1948 • Mixed single-level and low-rise
buildings on 225 acres • Current resident population
is 586 • Waiting list may apply for some units

HOUSING AND SERVICES

Living Units	No.	Square Feet	No. of Persons	Entrance Fee	Monthly Fee
Studio	0	——	——	——	——
One Bedroom	14	600	1, 2	$30,000–$60,000	$950
Two Bedroom	47	800	1, 2	$30,000–$60,000	$950
Larger Units	3	1,000	1, 2	$30,000–$60,000	$950

Total   64 Units

Entrance fee refunds decline over time.

These fees include three meals per day, housekeeping, scheduled transportation, and utilities. Special features of this community are presented in the Special Features Index at the back of the book. Ask about additional residential and health care services that may be available. Fees and services subject to change; verify with facility.

ASSISTED LIVING AND PERSONAL CARE

Assisted living units: 135
Personal care is covered by the continuing care contract: Yes
Residents may receive personal care in independent living units: Yes
Nonresidents may be admitted directly to assisted living units: No

NURSING CARE: Modified Plan

Under this modified plan, 90 days are covered by the continuing care contract. Once residents move permanently to the nursing unit, they pay 80 percent of the per diem rate for nursing care.

Intermediate beds: 100. Cost per day: private $69.00.

Skilled beds: 289. Cost per day: private $78.00, semi-private $72.00.

Nursing beds are certified by both Medicare and Medicaid. Nonresidents may be admitted directly to the nursing care facility.

NORTH CAROLINA

MORAVIAN HOME
5401 Indiana Avenue, Winston-Salem, NC 27106
Telephone: (919) 767-8130

Opened in 1972 • Mixed single-level and low-rise buildings on 32 acres • Current resident population is 274 • Waiting list may apply for some units

AAHA
Member

HOUSING AND SERVICES

Living Units	No.	Square Feet	No. of Persons	Entrance Fee	Monthly Fee
Studio	179	167	1	0	$860
One Bedroom	0	——	——	——	——
Two Bedroom	16	1,250	1	$65,000	$860
			2	$65,000	$1,620
Larger Units	0	——	——	——	——
Total	195 Units				

Entrance fee refunds decline over time.

These fees include three meals per day, weekly housekeeping, scheduled transportation, and utilities. Special features of this community are presented in the Special Features Index at the back of the book. Ask about additional residential and health care services that may be available. Fees and services subject to change; verify with facility.

ASSISTED LIVING AND PERSONAL CARE

Assisted living units: 0
Personal care is covered by the continuing care contract: Yes
Residents may receive personal care in independent living units: Yes

NURSING CARE: Fee-for-Service Plan

Under this fee-for-service plan, guaranteed access to nursing care is covered by the continuing care contract. Residents pay the full per diem rate for nursing care.

Intermediate beds: 64. Cost per day: private $60.00, semi-private $50.00.

Skilled beds: 20. Cost per day: private $60.00, semi-private $50.00.

Nursing beds are not certified by Medicare or Medicaid. Nonresidents may be admitted directly to the nursing care facility.

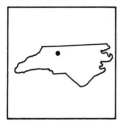

**PIEDMONT CENTER UNITED CHURCH
RETIREMENT HOMES**
100 Hedrick Drive, Thomasville, NC 28360
Telephone: (919) 476-4182

Opened in 1986 • Predominantly single-level/garden
apartments on 49 acres • Current resident population
is 44 • Waiting list may apply for some units

**AAHA
Member**

HOUSING AND SERVICES

Living Units	No.	Square Feet	No. of Persons	Entrance Fee	Monthly Fee
Studio	0	——	——	——	——
One Bedroom	6	900	1	$38,500	$200
			2	$38,500	$250
Two Bedroom	34	1,050	1	$48,500	$270
			2	$48,500	$320
Larger Units	6	1,100–	1	$58,500	$295
		1,400	2	$78,500	$345
Total		46 Units			

Entrance fees are partially refundable.

Special features of this community are presented in the Special Features Index
at the back of the book. Ask about additional residential and health care services
that may be available. Fees and services subject to change; verify with facility.

ASSISTED LIVING AND PERSONAL CARE

Assisted living units: 72
Personal care is covered by the continuing care contract: Yes
Residents may receive personal care in independent living units: Yes
Nonresidents may be admitted directly to assisted living units: Yes

NURSING CARE: Modified Plan

Under this modified plan, 15 or fewer days are covered by the continuing care
contract. Once residents move permanently to the nursing unit, they pay the
full per diem rate for nursing care.

Intermediate beds: 24. Cost per day: private $63.50, semi-private $53.00.

Skilled beds: 24. Cost per day: private $72.00, semi-private $65.00.

Nursing beds are not certified by Medicare or Medicaid. Nonresidents may not
be admitted directly to the nursing care facility.

THE PINES AT DAVIDSON
P.O. Box 118, Davidson, NC 28036
Telephone: (704) 892-5004

Opening in 1988 • Mixed single-level and low-rise buildings on 47 acres • Immediate availability

HOUSING AND SERVICES

Living Units	No.	Square Feet	No. of Persons	Entrance Fee	Monthly Fee
Studio	50	418–527	1	$32,500–$41,000	$800–$1,290
One Bedroom	91	722	1	$62,800	$950
			2		$1,500
Two Bedroom	20	975	1	$82,500	$1,050
			2		$1,650
Larger Units	0	—	—	—	—
Total	161 Units				

Entrance fee refunds decline over time.

These fees include one meal per day, housekeeping, scheduled transportation, and utilities. Special features of this community are presented in the Special Features Index at the back of the book. Ask about additional residential and health care services that may be available. Fees and services subject to change; verify with facility.

ASSISTED LIVING AND PERSONAL CARE

Assisted living units: 20
Personal care is covered by the continuing care contract: Yes
Residents may receive personal care in independent living units: Yes
Nonresidents may be admitted directly to assisted living units: Yes

NURSING CARE: Modified Plan

Under this modified plan, 15 or fewer days are covered by the continuing care contract. Once residents move permanently to a nursing unit, they pay 80 percent of the per diem rate for nursing care.

Intermediate beds: 20.*

Skilled beds: 20.*

*Nursing unit under construction; rates not yet set.

Nursing beds are not certified by Medicare or Medicaid. Nonresidents may be admitted directly to the nursing care facility.

NORTH CAROLINA

THE PRESBYTERIAN HOME AT CHARLOTTE
5100 Sharon Road, Charlotte, NC 28210
Telephone: (704) 553-1670

Opened in 1969 • Predominantly high-rise buildings
on 23 acres • Current resident population is 305 •
Waiting list

AAHA
Member

HOUSING AND SERVICES

Living Units	No.	Square Feet	No. of Persons	Entrance Fee	Monthly Fee
Studio	149	275	1	$24,500	$740
One Bedroom	24	550	1	$47,000	$885
			2		$1,480
Two Bedroom	5	825	1	$73,500	$945
			2		$1,570
Larger Units	28	1,200	1	$51,500–$76,000	$885
			2		$1,570

Total   206 Units

Entrance fees are fully refundable.

These fees include three meals per day, weekly housekeeping, scheduled transportation, and utilities. Special features of this community are presented in the Special Features Index at the back of the book. Ask about additional residential and health care services that may be available. Fees and services subject to change; verify with facility.

ASSISTED LIVING AND PERSONAL CARE

Assisted living units: 8
Personal care is covered by the continuing care contract: Yes
Residents may receive personal care in independent living units: No
Nonresidents may be admitted directly to assisted living units: No

NURSING CARE: All-Inclusive Plan

Under this all-inclusive plan, unlimited nursing care is covered by the continuing care contract. When residents are in nursing care, they pay the basic monthly fee for the studio (smallest) unit plus $15 per day.

Skilled beds: 96. Cost per day: not applicable.

Nursing beds are not certified by Medicare or Medicaid. Nonresidents may not be admitted directly to the nursing care facility.

THE PRESBYTERIAN HOME AT HIGH POINT
P.O. Box 2007, High Point, NC 27261
Telephone: (919) 883-9111

Opened in 1952 • Mixed single-level and low-rise buildings on 28 acres • Current resident population is 251 • Long waiting list; make reservations in advance

AAHA
Member

HOUSING AND SERVICES

Living Units	No.	Square Feet	No. of Persons	Entrance Fee	Monthly Fee
Studio	8	216	1	——	$835
One Bedroom	34	600	1	$26,000	$835
			2		$1,670
Two Bedroom	64	1,121	1	$40,000	$835
			2		$1,670
Larger Units	1	3,046	1	$106,000	$835
			2		$1,670
Total	107 Units				

Entrance fees are nonrefundable.

These fees include three meals per day, weekly housekeeping, scheduled transportation, and utilities. Special features of this community are presented in the Special Features Index at the back of the book. Ask about additional residential and health care services that may be available. Fees and services subject to change; verify with facility.

ASSISTED LIVING AND PERSONAL CARE

Assisted living units: 75
Personal care is covered by the continuing care contract: Yes
Residents may receive personal care in independent living units: Yes
Nonresidents may be admitted directly to assisted living units: Yes

NURSING CARE: All-Inclusive Plan

Under this all-inclusive plan, unlimited nursing care is covered by the continuing care contract. When residents are in nursing care, they pay the basic monthly fee for the studio (smallest) unit.

Intermediate beds: 10. Cost per day: semi-private $50.00.

Skilled beds: 68. Cost per day: semi-private $60.00.

Nursing beds are certified by both Medicare and Medicaid. Nonresidents may be admitted directly to the nursing care facility.

TRIAD UNITED METHODIST HOME
1240 Arbor Road, Winston-Salem, NC 27104
Telephone: (919) 724-7921

Opened in 1980 • Mixed single-level and low-rise
buildings on 70 acres • Current resident population is
276 • Waiting list

AAHA
Member

HOUSING AND SERVICES

Living Units	No.	Square Feet	No. of Persons	Entrance Fee	Monthly Fee
Studio	141	359–400	1	$19,500	$840
One Bedroom	8	560–1,000	1	$32,000–$50,000	$570–$595
			2	$32,000–$50,000	$635–$660
Two Bedroom	42	800–1,200	1	$45,000–$65,000	$595–$605
			2	$45,000–$65,000	$660–$670
Larger Units	11	1,200– 1,500	1	$85,000–$120,000	$635
			2	$85,000–$120,000	$690
Total	202 Units				

Entrance fee refunds decline over time.

These fees include weekly housekeeping, scheduled transportation, and utilities. Special features of this community are presented in the Special Features Index at the back of the book. Ask about additional residential and health care services that may be available. Fees and services subject to change; verify with facility.

ASSISTED LIVING AND PERSONAL CARE

Assisted living units: 19
Personal care is covered by the continuing care contract: No
Residents may receive personal care in independent living units: Yes
Nonresidents may be admitted directly to assisted living units: No

NURSING CARE: Modified Plan

Under this modified plan, 5 days (renewable after 90 days without nursing care) are covered by the continuing care contract. Once residents move permanently to the nursing unit, they pay the full per diem rate for nursing care.

Intermediate beds: 36. Cost per day: private $69.00, semi-private $62.00.

Skilled beds: 24. Cost per day: private $69.00, semi-private $62.00.

Nursing beds are not certified by Medicare or Medicaid. Nonresidents may be admitted directly to the nursing care facility.

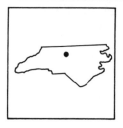

TWIN LAKES CENTER
100 Wade Coble Drive, Burlington, NC 27215
Telephone: (919) 538-1400

Opened in 1983 • Mixed single-level and low-rise buildings on 70 acres • Current resident population is 207 • Waiting list may apply for some units

AAHA
Member

HOUSING AND SERVICES

Living Units	No.	Square Feet	No. of Persons	Entrance Fee	Monthly Fee
Studio	30	320	1	0	$1,050 (no meals)
One Bedroom	24	600	1, 2	$32,000	$370
Two Bedroom	24	850	1, 2	$42,000	$470
Larger Units	16	1,200	1, 2	$50,000	$475
Total	94 Units				

Entrance fee refunds decline over time.

These fees include scheduled transportation and utilities. Special features of this community are presented in the Special Features Index at the back of the book. Ask about additional residential and health care services that may be available. Fees and services subject to change; verify with facility.

ASSISTED LIVING AND PERSONAL CARE

Assisted living units: 30
Personal care is covered by the continuing care contract: Yes
Residents may receive personal care in independent living units: No
Nonresidents may be admitted directly to assisted living units: Yes

NURSING CARE: Modified Plan

Under this modified plan, 15 or fewer days per year are covered by the continuing care contract. Once residents move permanently to the nursing unit, they pay the full per diem rate for nursing care.

Intermediate beds: 37. Cost per day: private $56.00, semi-private $51.00.

Skilled beds: 36. Cost per day: private $69.00, semi-private $65.00.

Nursing beds are certified by both Medicare and Medicaid. Nonresidents may be admitted directly to the nursing care facility.

WESLEY PINES
100 Wesley Pines Road, Lumberton, NC 28358
Telephone: (919) 738-9691

Opened in 1977 • Predominantly single-level/garden apartments on 49 acres • Current resident population is 80 • Waiting list may apply for some units

AAHA
Member

HOUSING AND SERVICES

Living Units	No.	Square Feet	No. of Persons	Entrance Fee	Monthly Fee
Studio	34	165	1	$6,000	$815
One Bedroom	0	——	——	——	——
Two Bedroom	12	1,200	1	$6,000	$815
			2	$12,000	$1,630
Larger Units	2	1,300	1	$6,000	$815
			2	$12,000	$1,630
Total		48 Units			

Entrance fee refunds decline over time.

These fees include three meals per day, weekly housekeeping, scheduled transportation, and utilities. Special features of this community are presented in the Special Features Index at the back of the book. Ask about additional residential and health care services that may be available. Fees and services subject to change; verify with facility.

ASSISTED LIVING AND PERSONAL CARE

Assisted living units: 15
Personal care is covered by the continuing care contract: Yes
Residents may receive personal care in independent living units: No
Nonresidents may be admitted directly to assisted living units: No

NURSING CARE: Fee-for-Service Plan

Under this fee-for-service plan, guaranteed access to nursing care is covered by the continuing care contract. Residents pay the full per diem rate for nursing care.

Intermediate beds: 23. Cost per day: private $68.50, semi-private $66.00.
Skilled beds: 18. Cost per day: private $76.00, semi-private $71.00.
Nursing beds are certified by both Medicare and Medicaid. Nonresidents may be admitted directly to the nursing care facility.

BRECKENRIDGE VILLAGE
36855 Ridge Road, Willoughby, OH 44094
Telephone: (216) 942-4342

Opened in 1979 • Predominantly single-level/garden apartments on 40 acres • Current resident population is 63 • Long waiting list; make reservations in advance

AAHA
Member

HOUSING AND SERVICES

Living Units	No.	Square Feet	No. of Persons	Entrance Fee	Monthly Fee
Studio	0	——	——	——	——
One Bedroom	0	——	——	——	——
Two Bedroom	44	1,350	1	$75,000	$255
			2	$75,000	$355
Larger Units	0	——	——	——	——
Total	44	Units			

Entrance fee refunds decline over time.

These fees include utilities. Special features of this community are presented in the Special Features Index at the back of the book. Ask about additional residential and health care services that may be available. Fees and services subject to change; verify with facility.

ASSISTED LIVING AND PERSONAL CARE

Assisted living units: 0
Personal care is covered by the continuing care contract: No
Residents may receive personal care in independent living units: Yes

NURSING CARE: Fee-for-Service Plan

Under this fee-for-service plan, guaranteed access to nursing care is covered by the continuing care contract. Residents pay the full per diem rate for nursing care.

Intermediate beds: 50. Cost per day: private $81.25, semi-private $55.25.

Dual-certified beds: 50. Cost per day: private $122.56, semi-private $83.50.

Nursing beds are certified by both Medicare and Medicaid. Nonresidents may be admitted directly to the nursing care facility.

BRETHREN CARE
2000 Center Street, Ashland, OH 44805
Telephone: (419) 289-1585

Opened in 1972 • Predominantly single-level/garden apartments on 12 acres • Current resident population is 98 • Waiting list

AAHA
Member

HOUSING AND SERVICES

Living Units	No.	Square Feet	No. of Persons	Entrance Fee	Monthly Fee
Studio	0	—	—	—	—
One Bedroom	3	630	1	$8,400	$335
			2		$355
Two Bedroom	4	1,000	1	$12,600	$515
			2		$535
Larger Units	0	—	—	—	—
Total		7 Units			

Entrance fee refunds decline over time.

These fees include utilities. Special features of this community are presented in the Special Features Index at the back of the book. Ask about additional residential and health care services that may be available. Fees and services subject to change; verify with facility.

ASSISTED LIVING AND PERSONAL CARE

Assisted living units: 0
Personal care is covered by the continuing care contract: No
Residents may receive personal care in independent living units: No

NURSING CARE: Fee-for-Service Plan

Under this fee-for-service plan, guaranteed access to nursing care is covered by the continuing care contract. Residents pay the full per diem rate for nursing care.

Intermediate beds: 91. Cost per day: private $58.00, semi-private $47.00.

Nursing beds are certified by Medicaid. Nonresidents may be admitted directly to the nursing care facility.

AAHA
Member

COPELAND OAKS AND CRANDALL MEDICAL CENTER
800 South 15th Street, Sebring, OH 44672
Telephone: (216) 938-6126

Opened in 1968 • Mixed single-level and low-rise buildings on 260 acres • Current resident population is 520 • Waiting list may apply for some units • Accredited by the AAHA Continuing Care Accreditation Commission

HOUSING AND SERVICES

Living Units	No.	Square Feet	No. of Persons	Entrance Fee	Monthly Fee
Studio	215	323–384	1	$18,000–$22,300	$890–$908
One Bedroom	93	455–650	1	$29,000–$35,000	$1,022–$1,093
			2	$29,000–$35,000	$1,834–$1,946
Two Bedroom	50	1,702–3,508	1	$35,600–$56,400	$633–$883
			2	$35,600–$56,400	$814–$1,064
Larger Units	0	—	—	—	—
Total	358 Units				

Entrance fee refunds decline over time.

These fees include three meals per day, biweekly housekeeping, scheduled transportation, and utilities. Special features of this community are presented in the Special Features Index at the back of the book. Ask about additional residential and health care services that may be available. Fees and services subject to change; verify with facility.

ASSISTED LIVING AND PERSONAL CARE

Assisted living units: 0
Personal care is covered by the continuing care contract: Yes
Residents may receive personal care in independent living units: Yes

NURSING CARE: Fee-for-Service Plan

Under this fee-for-service plan, guaranteed access to nursing care is covered by the continuing care contract. Residents pay the full per diem rate for nursing care.

Dual-certified beds: 192. Cost per day: private $63.00, semi-private $63.00.

Nursing beds are certified by both Medicare and Medicaid. Nonresidents may be admitted directly to the nursing care facility.

DUPREE HOUSE EAST
3939 Erie Avenue, Cincinnati, OH 45208
Telephone: (513) 561-6363

Opened in 1982 • One low-rise building on 11 acres •
Current resident population is 117 • Waiting list may
apply for some units

AAHA
Member

HOUSING AND SERVICES

Living Units	No.	Square Feet	No. of Persons	Entrance Fee	Monthly Fee
Studio	3	545	1	$32,500	$499
One Bedroom	32	903–978	1	$50,000–$60,500	$734–$780
			2	$55,000–$64,500	$871–$917
Two Bedroom	42	1,168	1	$70,000–$73,000	$909
			2	$75,000–$78,000	$1,046
Larger Units	12	1,189–2,071	1	$78,000–$125,000	$926–$1,247
			2	$83,000–$135,000	$1,063–$1,384
Total		89 Units			

Entrance fee refunds decline over time.

These fees include one meal per day, scheduled transportation, and utilities.
Special features of this community are presented in the Special Features Index
at the back of the book. Ask about additional residential and health care services
that may be available. Fees and services subject to change; verify with facility.

ASSISTED LIVING AND PERSONAL CARE

Assisted living units: 47*
Personal care is covered by the continuing care contract: No
Residents may receive personal care in independent living units: Yes
Nonresidents may be admitted directly to assisted living units: No

NURSING CARE: Modified Plan

Under this modified plan, 16–59 days per year are covered by the continuing
care contract. Once residents move permanently to the nursing unit, they pay a
discounted per diem rate for nursing care.

Intermediate beds: 72.* Cost per day: private $70.00, semi-private $60.00.

*Located at the Marjorie P. Lee Home (page 266)

Nursing beds are certified by Medicaid. Nonresidents may be admitted
directly to the nursing care facility.

FIRST COMMUNITY VILLAGE
1800 Riverside Drive, Columbus, OH 43212
Telephone: (614) 486-9511

Opened in 1963 • Mixed single-level, low-rise, and high-rise buildings on 34 acres • Current resident population is 420 • Waiting list may apply for some units • Accredited by the AAHA Continuing Care Accreditation Commission

AAHA
Member

HOUSING AND SERVICES

Living Units	No.	Square Feet	No. of Persons	Entrance Fee	Monthly Fee
Studio	71	220–342	1	$21,900–$27,900	$542
One Bedroom	83	575–684	1	$39,900–$42,900	$658–$807
			2	$43,900–$46,900	$933–$1,142
Two Bedroom	9	660	1, 2	$60,900	$1,433
Larger Units	1	880	1, 2	$80,900	$1,615
Total	164 Units				

Entrance fee refunds decline over time.

These fees include weekly housekeeping, scheduled transportation, and utilities. Special features of this community are presented in the Special Features Index at the back of the book. Ask about additional residential and health care services that may be available. Fees and services subject to change; verify with facility.

ASSISTED LIVING AND PERSONAL CARE

Assisted living units: 104
Personal care is covered by the continuing care contract: Yes
Residents may receive personal care in independent living units: No
Nonresidents may be admitted directly to assisted living units: Yes

NURSING CARE: All-Inclusive Plan

Under this all-inclusive plan, unlimited nursing care is covered by the continuing care contract. Once residents move permanently to the nursing unit, they pay 50 percent of the per diem rate for nursing care.

Dual-certified beds: 154. Cost per day: private $71.00, semi-private $68.00.

Nursing beds are certified by both Medicare and Medicaid. Nonresidents may be admitted directly to the nursing care facility.

FRIENDSHIP VILLAGE OF COLUMBUS
5800 Forest Hills Boulevard, Columbus, OH 43229
Telephone: (614) 890-8282

Opened in 1978 • Mixed single-level and low-rise buildings on 20 acres • Current resident population is 375 • Waiting list may apply for some units

AAHA
Member

HOUSING AND SERVICES

Living Units	No.	Square Feet	No. of Persons	Entrance Fee	Monthly Fee
Studio	112	287–430	1	$26,425–$42,363	$528–$567
One Bedroom	129	574	1	$60,500	$605
			2	$60,500	$943
Two Bedroom	64	789–864	1	$74,700–$84,000	$718–$757
			2	$74,700–$84,000	$1,056–$1,805
Larger Units	0	—	—	—	—
Total	305 Units				

Entrance fee refunds decline over time.

These fees include one meal per day, biweekly housekeeping, scheduled transportation, and utilities. Special features of this community are presented in the Special Features Index at the back of the book. Ask about additional residential and health care services that may be available. Fees and services subject to change; verify with facility.

ASSISTED LIVING AND PERSONAL CARE

Assisted living units: 0
Personal care is covered by the continuing care contract: No
Residents may receive personal care in independent living units: Yes

NURSING CARE: All-Inclusive Plan

Under this all-inclusive plan, unlimited nursing care is covered by the continuing care contract. When residents are in nursing care, they pay the same monthly fee they paid for their independent living unit.

Skilled beds: 90. Cost per day: private $80.00, semi-private $75.00.

Nursing beds are certified by both Medicare and Medicaid. Nonresidents may be admitted directly to the nursing care facility.

JUDSON VILLAGE BAPTIST HOME AND CENTER
2373 Harrison Avenue, Cincinnati, OH 45211
Telephone: (513) 662-5880

Opened in 1946 • Predominantly mid-rise buildings
on 17 acres • Current resident population is 107 •
Waiting list may apply for some units

AAHA
Member

HOUSING AND SERVICES

Living Units	No.	Square Feet	No. of Persons	Entrance Fee	Monthly Fee
Studio	36	104	1	$12,500	$715
One Bedroom	10	533	1, 2	$15,000	$480
Two Bedroom	0	——	——	——	——
Larger Units	0	——	——	——	——
Total	46 Units				

Entrance fee refunds decline over time.

These fees include three meals per day, weekly housekeeping, and utilities. Special features of this community are presented in the Special Features Index at the back of the book. Ask about additional residential and health care services that may be available. Fees and services subject to change; verify with facility.

ASSISTED LIVING AND PERSONAL CARE

Assisted living units: 43
Personal care is covered by the continuing care contract: Yes
Residents may receive personal care in independent living units: Yes
Nonresidents may be admitted directly to assisted living units: Yes

NURSING CARE: Modified Plan

Under this modified plan, 15 or fewer days per year are covered by the continuing care contract. Once residents move permanently to the nursing unit, they pay the full per diem rate for nursing care.

Intermediate beds: 50. Cost per day: private $67.50, semi-private $61.00.

Nursing beds are certified by Medicaid. Nonresidents may be admitted directly to the nursing care facility.

LLANFAIR RETIREMENT COMMUNITY
1701 Llanfair Avenue, Cincinnati, OH 45224
Telephone: (513) 681-4230

Opened in 1956 • Mixed single-level and low-rise
buildings on 12 acres • Current resident population is
300 • Waiting list

AAHA Member

HOUSING AND SERVICES

Living Units	No.	Square Feet	No. of Persons	Entrance Fee	Monthly Fee
Studio	48	140–300	1	$8,200–$20,000	$807–$1,003
One Bedroom	67	536–696	1	$30,000–$43,400	$534–$1,216
			2		$858–$1,537
Two Bedroom	51	864–1,150	1	$51,645–$75,000	$476–$571
			2		$535–$895
Larger Units	3	7,800	1	$50,000	$421–$461
			2		$520

Total   169 Units

Entrance fee refunds decline over time.

These fees include housekeeping, scheduled transportation, and utilities. Special features of this community are presented in the Special Features Index at the back of the book. Ask about additional residential and health care services that may be available. Fees and services subject to change; verify with facility.

ASSISTED LIVING AND PERSONAL CARE

Assisted living units: 24
Personal care is covered by the continuing care contract: No
Residents may receive personal care in independent living units: Yes
Nonresidents may be admitted directly to assisted living units: Yes

NURSING CARE: Modified Plan

Under this modified plan, 15 or fewer days per year are covered by the continuing care contract. Once residents move permanently to the nursing unit, they pay 88 percent of the per diem rate for nursing care.

Dual-certified beds: 75. Cost per day: private $80.00, semi-private $70.00.

Nursing beds are certified by both Medicare and Medicaid. Nonresidents may be admitted directly to the nursing care facility.

MARJORIE P. LEE HOME
3550 Shaw Avenue, Cincinnati, OH 45208
Telephone: (513) 871-2090

Opened in 1962 • Predominantly mid-rise buildings on two acres • Current resident population is 235 • Waiting list

AAHA
Member

HOUSING AND SERVICES

Living Units	No.	Square Feet	No. of Persons	Entrance Fee	Monthly Fee
Studio	69	300–600	1	$16,000	$550
One Bedroom	40	750–800	1	$40,000	$868
			2	$43,000	$1,244
Two Bedroom	14	1,000	1	$58,000	$1,013
			2	$63,000	$1,388
Larger Units	0	—	—	—	—
Total		123 Units			

Entrance fee refunds decline over time.

These fees include three meals per day, housekeeping, scheduled transportation, and utilities. Special features of this community are presented in the Special Features Index at the back of the book. Ask about additional residential and health care services that may be available. Fees and services subject to change; verify with facility.

ASSISTED LIVING AND PERSONAL CARE

Assisted living units: 47
Personal care is covered by the continuing care contract: No
Residents may receive personal care in independent living units: No
Nonresidents may be admitted directly to assisted living units: Yes

NURSING CARE: Modified Plan

Under this modified plan, 16–59 days per year are covered by the continuing care contract. Once residents move permanently to the nursing unit, they pay a discounted per diem rate for nursing care.

Intermediate beds: 72.* Cost per day: private $70.00, semi-private $60.00.

*Dupree House East (see page 261) also uses these nursing facilities.

Nursing beds are certified by Medicaid. Nonresidents may be admitted directly to the nursing care facility.

MENNONITE MEMORIAL HOME
410 West Elm Street, Bluffton, OH 45817
Telephone: (419) 358-1015

Opened in 1955 • Mixed single-level and low-rise buildings on 15 acres • Current resident population is 146 • Waiting list

AAHA
Member

HOUSING AND SERVICES

Living Units	No.	Square Feet	No. of Persons	Entrance Fee	Monthly Fee
Studio	1	600	1	$34,000	$175
One Bedroom	1	800	1, 2	$38,000	$200
Two Bedroom	1	1,000	1, 2	$45,000	$250
Larger Units	4	1,300	1, 2	$50,000	$250
Total	7 Units				

Entrance fees are partially refundable.

These fees include housekeeping, scheduled transportation, and utilities. Special features of this community are presented in the Special Features Index at the back of the book. Ask about additional residential and health care services that may be available. Fees and services subject to change; verify with facility.

ASSISTED LIVING AND PERSONAL CARE

Assisted living units: 47
Personal care is covered by the continuing care contract: No
Residents may receive personal care in independent living units: No
Nonresidents may be admitted directly to assisted living units: Yes

NURSING CARE: Modified Plan

Under this modified plan, 15 or fewer days per year are covered by the continuing care contract. Once residents move permanently to the nursing unit, they pay the full per diem rate for nursing care.

Intermediate beds: 92. Cost per day: private—not applicable, semi-private $44.25.
Nursing beds are certified by Medicaid. Nonresidents may be admitted directly to the nursing care facility.

MOUNT PLEASANT RETIREMENT VILLAGE
225 Britton Lane, Monroe, OH 45050
Telephone: (513) 539-7391

Opened in 1953 • Mixed single-level and low-rise buildings on 43 acres • Current resident population is 240 • Waiting list

AAHA
Member

HOUSING AND SERVICES

Living Units	No.	Square Feet	No. of Persons	Entrance Fee	Monthly Fee
Studio	46	——	1	$18,500	$800
One Bedroom	0	——	——	——	——
Two Bedroom	93	1,400	1, 2	$40,000–$60,000	$350
Larger Units	0	——	——	——	——
Total	139 Units				

Entrance fee refunds decline over time.

Special features of this community are presented in the Special Features Index at the back of the book. Ask about additional residential and health care services that may be available. Fees and services subject to change; verify with facility.

ASSISTED LIVING AND PERSONAL CARE

Assisted living units: 0
Personal care is covered by the continuing care contract: No
Residents may receive personal care in independent living units: No

NURSING CARE: Fee-for-Service Plan

Under this fee-for-service plan, 15 or fewer days per year are covered by the continuing care contract. Once residents move permanently to the nursing unit, they pay the full per diem rate for nursing care.

Intermediate beds: 29. Cost per day: private $42.00, semi-private—not applicable.

Skilled beds: 70. Cost per day: private $66.25, semi-private $64.75.

Nursing beds are certified by both Medicare and Medicaid. Nonresidents may be admitted directly to the nursing care facility.

PARK VISTA RETIREMENT COMMUNITY
1216 Fifth Avenue, Youngstown, OH 44504
Telephone: (216) 746-2944

Opened in 1970 • Mixed single-level, low-rise, and high-rise buildings on three acres • Current resident population is 325 • Waiting list may apply for some units

AAHA
Member

HOUSING AND SERVICES

Living Units	No.	Square Feet	No. of Persons	Entrance Fee	Monthly Fee
Studio	90	221	1	$19,000	$735
One Bedroom	67	442–625	1	$22,900–$38,000	$313–$1,007
			2	$22,900–$38,000	$432–$1,007
Two Bedroom	22	1,010	1	$30,600	$413
			2	$30,600	$556
Larger Units	22	1,125	1	$40,700	$444
			2	$40,700	$598
Total	201 Units				

Entrance fee refunds decline over time.

These fees include three meals per day, weekly housekeeping, scheduled transportation, and utilities. Special features of this community are presented in the Special Features Index at the back of the book. Ask about additional residential and health care services that may be available. Fees and services subject to change; verify with facility.

ASSISTED LIVING AND PERSONAL CARE

Assisted living units: 27
Personal care is covered by the continuing care contract: Yes
Residents may receive personal care in independent living units: Yes
Nonresidents may be admitted directly to assisted living units: No

NURSING CARE: Fee-for-Service

Under this fee-for-service plan, guaranteed access to nursing care is covered by the continuing care contract. Residents pay the full per diem rate for nursing care.

Dual-certified beds: 98. Cost per day: private $133.00, semi-private $66.00.
Nursing beds are certified by both Medicare and Medicaid. Nonresidents may be admitted directly to the nursing care facility.

ROCKYNOL RETIREMENT COMMUNITY
1150 West Market Street, Akron, OH 44313
Telephone: (216) 867-2150

Opened in 1966 • Mixed single-level, low-rise, and high-rise buildings on ten acres • Current resident population is 153 • Waiting list may apply for some units

AAHA
Member

HOUSING AND SERVICES

Living Units	No.	Square Feet	No. of Persons	Entrance Fee	Monthly Fee
Studio	0	—	—	—	—
One Bedroom	43	294	1	$26,000	$820
			2	$52,000	—
Two Bedroom	17	588	1	$52,000	$1,145
			2	$104,000	$1,510
Larger Units	0	—	—	—	—
Total	60 Units				

Entrance fee refunds decline over time.

These fees include three meals per day, housekeeping, scheduled transportation, and utilities. Special features of this community are presented in the Special Features Index at the back of the book. Ask about additional residential and health care services that may be available. Fees and services subject to change; verify with facility.

ASSISTED LIVING AND PERSONAL CARE

Assisted living units: 24
Personal care is covered by the continuing care contract: Yes
Residents may receive personal care in independent living units: No
Nonresidents may be admitted directly to assisted living units: Yes

NURSING CARE: Modified Plan

Under this modified plan, seven days per year are covered by the continuing care contract. Once residents move permanently to the nursing unit, they pay the full per diem rate for nursing care.

Skilled beds: 72. Cost per day: private $108.00, semi-private $65.00.

Nursing beds are certified by both Medicare and Medicaid. Nonresidents may be admitted directly to the nursing care facility.

SCHRODER MANOR
1302 Millville Avenue, Hamilton, OH 45013
Telephone: (513) 867-1300

Opened in 1972 • Mixed single-level, low-rise, and high-rise buildings on 16 acres • Current resident population is 103 • Waiting list may apply for some units

AAHA
Member

HOUSING AND SERVICES

Living Units	No.	Square Feet	No. of Persons	Entrance Fee	Monthly Fee
Studio	0	——	——	——	——
One Bedroom	0	——	——	——	——
Two Bedroom	18	1,340	1, 2	$64,000–$72,000	$200
Larger Units	0	——	——	——	——
Total	18 Units				

Entrance fee refunds decline over time.

These fees include weekly housekeeping, scheduled transportation, and utilities. Special features of this community are presented in the Special Features Index at the back of the book. Ask about additional residential and health care services that may be available. Fees and services subject to change; verify with facility.

ASSISTED LIVING AND PERSONAL CARE

Assisted living units: 45
Personal care is covered by the continuing care contract: Yes
Residents may receive personal care in independent living units: No
Nonresidents may be admitted directly to assisted living units: Yes

NURSING CARE: Modified Plan

Under this modified plan, emergency care is covered by the continuing care contract. Residents pay a discounted per diem rate for nursing care.

Skilled beds: 23. Cost per day: private $84.25, semi-private $62.50.

Nursing beds are certified by Medicare. Nonresidents may be admitted directly to the nursing care facility.

TRINITY HOME
3218 Indian Ripple Road, Dayton, OH 45440
Telephone: (513) 426-8481

Opened in 1974 • Mixed single-level and low-rise buildings on 32 acres • Current resident population is 164 • Immediate availability

AAHA
Member

HOUSING AND SERVICES

Living Units	No.	Square Feet	No. of Persons	Entrance Fee	Monthly Fee
Studio	0	——	——	——	——
One Bedroom	68	276–776	1	$10,000	$845
			2	$15,000	$1,250
Two Bedroom	0	——	——	——	——
Larger Units	0	——	——	——	——
Total	68 Units				

Residents have a choice of entrance fee refund plans.

These fees include three meals per day, weekly housekeeping, scheduled transportation, and utilities. Special features of this community are presented in the Special Features Index at the back of the book. Ask about additional residential and health care services that may be available. Fees and services subject to change; verify with facility.

ASSISTED LIVING AND PERSONAL CARE

Assisted living units: 36
Personal care is covered by the continuing care contract: No
Residents may receive personal care in independent living units: No
Nonresidents may be admitted directly to assisted living units: No

NURSING CARE: Modified Plan

Under this modified plan, 15 or fewer days are covered by the continuing care contract. Once residents move permanently to the nursing unit, they pay the full per diem rate for nursing care.

Intermediate beds: 22. Cost per day: private $62.03, semi-private $52.69.

Skilled beds: 50. Cost per day: private $81.43, semi-private $69.55.

Nursing beds are certified by both Medicare and Medicaid. Nonresidents may be admitted directly to the nursing care facility.

WESLEY GLEN
5155 North High Street, Columbus, OH 43214
Telephone: (614) 888-7492

Opened in 1969 • Predominantly high-rise buildings on 12 acres • Current resident population is 275 • Waiting list

AAHA
Member

HOUSING AND SERVICES

Living Units	No.	Square Feet	No. of Persons	Entrance Fee	Monthly Fee
Studio	76	275	1	$20,000	$524
One Bedroom	92	450	1, 2	$40,000	$669
Two Bedroom	0	——	——	——	——
Larger Units	0	——	——	——	——
Total	168 Units				

Entrance fee refunds decline over time.

These fees include three meals per day, weekly housekeeping, and utilities. Special features of this community are presented in the Special Features Index at the back of the book. Ask about additional residential and health care services that may be available. Fees and services subject to change; verify with facility.

ASSISTED LIVING AND PERSONAL CARE

Assisted living units: 14
Personal care is covered by the continuing care contract: Yes
Residents may receive personal care in independent living units: No
Nonresidents may be admitted directly to assisted living units: Yes

NURSING CARE: Fee-for-Service Plan

Under this fee-for-service plan, guaranteed access to nursing care is covered by the continuing care contract. When residents are in nursing care, they pay the fee for the studio (smallest) unit plus $25.00 per day.

Dual-certified beds: 82. Cost per day: private—not applicable, semi-private $66.00.

Nursing beds are certified by both Medicare and Medicaid. Nonresidents may be admitted directly to the nursing care facility.

WESTMINSTER TERRACE
717 Neil Avenue, Columbus, OH 43215
Telephone: (614) 228-8888

Opened in 1965 • Predominantly high-rise buildings on ten acres • Current resident population is 350 • Waiting list may apply for some units

AAHA
Member

HOUSING AND SERVICES

Living Units	No.	Square Feet	No. of Persons	Entrance Fee	Monthly Fee
Studio	39	446	1	$20,000	$316
One Bedroom	80	567	1	$39,000	$361
			2		$421
Two Bedroom	58	890	1	$49,500–$56,000	$421
			2		$481
Larger Units	1	1,134	1, 2	$85,000	$720
Total		178 Units			

Entrance fee refunds decline over time.

These fees include biweekly housekeeping, scheduled transportation, and utilities. Special features of this community are presented in the Special Features Index at the back of the book. Ask about additional residential and health care services that may be available. Fees and services subject to change; verify with facility.

ASSISTED LIVING AND PERSONAL CARE

Assisted living units: 89
Personal care is covered by the continuing care contract: Yes
Residents may receive personal care in independent living units: No
Nonresidents may be admitted directly to assisted living units: Yes

NURSING CARE: Modified Plan

Under this modified plan, 15 or fewer days per year are covered by the continuing care contract. Thereafter, residents pay the full per diem rate for nursing care.

Dual-certified beds: 92. Cost per day: private—not applicable, semi-private $65.50.

Nursing beds are certified by both Medicare and Medicaid. Nonresidents may be admitted directly to the nursing care facility.

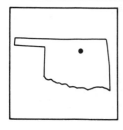

FRANCISCAN VILLA
17110 East 51st Street, Tulsa, OK 74012
Telephone: (918) 355-1596

Opened in 1979 • Predominantly single-level/garden apartments on eight acres • Current resident population is 128 • Waiting list may apply for some units

HOUSING AND SERVICES

Living Units	No.	Square Feet	No. of Persons	Entrance Fee	Monthly Fee
Studio	24	420	1	$500	$860
One Bedroom	37	580	1	$500	$1,114
			2		$1,364
Two Bedroom	5	800	1	$500	$1,800
			2		$2,050
Larger Units	0	——	——	——	——
Total		66 Units			

Entrance fees are nonrefundable.

These fees include three meals per day, weekly housekeeping, scheduled transportation, and utilities. Special features of this community are presented in the Special Features Index at the back of the book. Ask about additional residential and health care services that may be available. Fees and services subject to change; verify with facility.

ASSISTED LIVING AND PERSONAL CARE

Assisted living units: 22
Personal care is covered by the continuing care contract: No
Residents may receive personal care in independent living units: Yes
Nonresidents may be admitted directly to assisted living units: Yes

NURSING CARE: Fee-for-Service Plan

Under this fee-for-service plan, emergency or temporary infirmary care is covered by the continuing care contract. Residents pay the full per diem rate for other nursing care.

Intermediate beds: 60. Cost per day: private $59.00, semi-private $46.00.
Nursing beds are certified by Medicaid. Nonresidents may be admitted directly to the nursing care facility.

OKLAHOMA

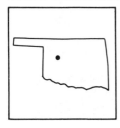

SPANISH COVE
1401 Cornwell, Yukon, OK 73099
Telephone: (405) 354-1901

Opened in 1974 • Predominantly single-level/garden apartments on 12 acres • Current resident population is 188 • Located ten miles from Oklahoma City, OK • Immediate availability

HOUSING AND SERVICES

Living Units	No.	Square Feet	No. of Persons	Entrance Fee	Monthly Fee
Studio	2	358	1	$37,000	$541
One Bedroom	52	517–702	1	$54,000–$66,000	$590–$642
			2		$924–$976
Two Bedroom	114	875	1	$81,000	$697
			2		$1,031
Larger Units	24	1,015	1	$96,000	$750
			2		$1,084

Total 192 Units

Entrance fee refunds decline over time.

These fees include one meal per day, biweekly housekeeping, scheduled transportation, and utilities. Special features of this community are presented in the Special Features Index at the back of the book. Ask about additional residential and health care services that may be available. Fees and services subject to change; verify with facility.

ASSISTED LIVING AND PERSONAL CARE

Assisted living units: 0
Personal care is covered by the continuing care contract: Yes
Residents may receive personal care in independent living units: Yes

NURSING CARE: All-Inclusive Plan

Under this all-inclusive plan, unlimited nursing care is covered by the continuing care contract. When residents are in nursing care, they pay the same monthly fee they paid for their independent living unit.

Skilled beds: 29. Cost per day: not applicable.

Nursing beds are certified by Medicare. Nonresidents may not be admitted directly to the nursing care facility.

OKLAHOMA

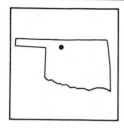

WESTMINSTER VILLAGE
1601 Academy Road, Ponca City, OK 74604
Telephone: (405) 762-6641

Opened in 1985 • Mixed single-level, low-rise, and high-rise buildings on 23 acres • Current resident population is 62 • Immediate availability

AAHA
Member

HOUSING AND SERVICES

Living Units	No.	Square Feet	No. of Persons	Entrance Fee	Monthly Fee
Studio	0	—	—	—	—
One Bedroom	12	580	1	$2,500	$300
			2	$2,500	—
Two Bedroom	26	880	1	$2,500	$350
			2	$2,500	$500
Larger Units	8	1,080	1	$2,500	$400
			2	—	$550
Total	46 Units				

Entrance fees are partially refundable.

These fees include scheduled transportation and utilities. Special features of this community are presented in the Special Features Index at the back of the book. Ask about additional residential and health care services that may be available. Fees and services subject to change; verify with facility.

ASSISTED LIVING AND PERSONAL CARE

Assisted living units: 20
Personal care is covered by the continuing care contract: No
Residents may receive personal care in independent living units: No
Nonresidents may be admitted directly to assisted living units: Yes

NURSING CARE: Modified Plan

Under this modified plan, 15 or fewer days of nursing care per year are covered by the continuing care contract. Once residents move permanently to the nursing unit, they pay the full per diem rate for nursing care.

Intermediate beds: 18. Cost per day: private $55.00, semi-private $40.00.

Nursing beds are not certified by Medicare or Medicaid. Nonresidents may be admitted directly to the nursing care facility.

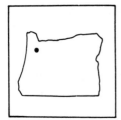

CAPITAL MANOR
P.O. Box 5000, Salem, OR 97304
Telephone: (503) 362-4101

Opened in 1963 • One high-rise building on 30 acres • Current resident population is 320 • Waiting list may apply for some units

AAHA
Member

HOUSING AND SERVICES

Living Units	No.	Square Feet	No. of Persons	Entrance Fee	Monthly Fee
Studio	147	338–507	1	$15,000–$25,500	$858–$1,000
One Bedroom	89	519–778	1, 2	$26,500–$42,500	$1,004–$1,258
Two Bedroom	0	——	——	——	——
Larger Units	0	——	——	——	——
Total	236 Units				

Entrance fee refunds decline over time.

These fees include three meals per day, biweekly housekeeping, and utilities. Special features of this community are presented in the Special Features Index at the back of the book. Ask about additional residential and health care services that may be available. Fees and services subject to change; verify with facility.

ASSISTED LIVING AND PERSONAL CARE

Assisted living units: 0
Personal care is covered by the continuing care contract: No
Residents may receive personal care in independent living units: No

NURSING CARE: All-Inclusive Plan

Under this all-inclusive plan, unlimited nursing care is covered by the continuing care contract. Once residents move permanently to the nursing unit, they pay the monthly fee for the studio (smallest) unit plus $8 per day.

Intermediate beds: 43. Cost per day: not applicable.

Nursing beds are not certified by Medicare or Medicaid. Nonresidents may not be admitted directly to the nursing care facility.

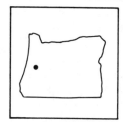

CASCADE MANOR
65 West 30th Street, Eugene, OR 97405
Telephone: (503) 342-5901

Opened in 1967 • One high-rise building on five acres • Current resident population is 112 • Long waiting list; make reservations in advance

AAHA Member

HOUSING AND SERVICES

Living Units	No.	Square Feet	No. of Persons	Entrance Fee	Monthly Fee
Studio	32	428	1	$28,500	$464
One Bedroom	30	857	1	$56,500	$678
			2	$56,500	$928
Two Bedroom	6	1,258	1	$84,500	$892
			2	$84,500	$1,142
Larger Units	21	642–1,090	1	$41,000–$69,500	$571–$785
			2		$821–$1,035
Total		89 Units			

Entrance fee refunds decline over time.

These fees include one meal per day, biweekly housekeeping, scheduled transportation, and utilities. Special features of this community are presented in the Special Features Index at the back of the book. Ask about additional residential and health care services that may be available. Fees and services subject to change; verify with facility.

ASSISTED LIVING AND PERSONAL CARE

Assisted living units: 0
Personal care is covered by the continuing care contract: No
Residents may receive personal care in independent living units: Yes

NURSING CARE: Fee-for-Service Plan

Under this fee-for-service plan, guaranteed access to nursing care is covered by the continuing care contract. Residents pay the full per diem rate for nursing care.

Skilled beds: 21. Cost per day: semi-private $35.00.

Nursing beds are not certified by Medicare or Medicaid. Nonresidents may not be admitted directly to the nursing care facility.

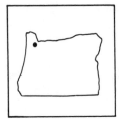

FRIENDSVIEW MANOR
1301 East Fulton Street, Newberg, OR 97132
Telephone: (503) 538-3144

Opened in 1961 • One high-rise building on 17 acres • Current resident population is 225 • Long waiting list; make reservations in advance

AAHA
Member

HOUSING AND SERVICES

Living Units	No.	Square Feet	No. of Persons	Entrance Fee	Monthly Fee
Studio	126	293	1	$16,600	$424–$744
One Bedroom	2	900	1	$28,200	$222
			2	$28,200	$307
Two Bedroom	11	1,000	1	$32,200	$222
			2	$32,200	$307
Larger Units	2	1,200	1	$35,200	$222
			2	$35,200	$307

Total   141 Units

Entrance fee refunds decline over time.

For studio residents, these fees include three meals per day, biweekly house-keeping, and utilities. Special features of this community are presented in the Special Features Index at the back of the book. Ask about additional residential and health care services that may be available. Fees and services subject to change; verify with facility.

ASSISTED LIVING AND PERSONAL CARE

Assisted living units: 15
Personal care is covered by the continuing care contract: Yes
Residents may receive personal care in independent living units: No
Nonresidents may be admitted directly to assisted living units: No

NURSING CARE: All-Inclusive Plan

Under this all-inclusive plan, unlimited nursing care is covered by the continuing care contract. When residents are in nursing care, they pay the basic monthly fee for the studio (smallest) unit.

Intermediate beds: 34. Cost per day: not applicable.

Nursing beds are not certified by Medicare or Medicaid. Nonresidents may not be admitted directly to the nursing care facility.

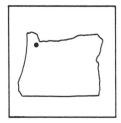

HILLSIDE MANOR
900 North Hill Road, McMinnville, OR 97128
Telephone: (503) 472-9534

Opened in 1983 • Mixed single-level and low-rise buildings on ten acres • Current resident population is 114 • Located 30 miles from Portland, OR • Immediate availability

AAHA
Member

HOUSING AND SERVICES

Living Units	No.	Square Feet	No. of Persons	Entrance Fee	Monthly Fee
Studio	9	333	1	$31,200	$530–$820
One Bedroom	71	500–666	1	$43,600–$60,000	$745–$990
			2	$43,600–$60,000	$1,032–$1,244
Two Bedroom	13	666–833	1	$60,000–$75,000	$1,144–$1,356
			2	$60,000–$75,000	$1,244–$1,456
Larger Units	0	—	—	—	—
Total	93 Units				

Entrance fee refunds decline over time.

These fees include three meals per day, biweekly housekeeping, scheduled transportation, and utilities. Special features of this community are presented in the Special Features Index at the back of the book. Ask about additional residential and health care services that may be available. Fees and services subject to change; verify with facility.

ASSISTED LIVING AND PERSONAL CARE

Assisted living units: 0
Personal care is covered by the continuing care contract: No
Residents may receive personal care in independent living units: Yes

NURSING CARE: All-Inclusive Plan

Under this all-inclusive plan, unlimited nursing care is covered by the continuing care contract. When residents are in nursing care, they pay for a single-occupancy one-bedroom unit.

Intermediate beds: 15. Cost per day: not applicable.

Nursing beds are not certified by Medicare or Medicaid. Nonresidents may not be admitted directly to the nursing care facility.

PENNSYLVANIA

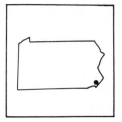

BEAUMONT AT BRYN MAWR
601 North Ithan Avenue, Bryn Mawr, PA 19010
Telephone: (215) 527-8840

Opened in 1987 • Mixed single-level and low-rise
buildings on 50 acres • Immediate availability

AAHA
Member

HOUSING AND SERVICES

Living Units	No.	Square Feet	No. of Persons	Entrance Fee	Monthly Fee
Studio	0	——	——	——	——
One Bedroom	20	1,029–1,163	1	$151,700–$163,900	$1,321–$1,379
			2	$151,700–$163,900	$1,881–$1,939
Two Bedroom	109	1,298–3,634	1	$178,400–$255,300	$1,462–$1,683
			2	$178,400–$255,300	$2,022–$2,243
Larger Units	29	1,970–3,940	1	$251,100–$268,100	$1,772–$1,862
			2	$251,100–$268,100	$2,332–$2,422
Total	158 Units				

Entrance fees are fully refundable.

These fees include one meal per day, weekly housekeeping, scheduled transportation, and utilities. Special features of this community are presented in the Special Features Index at the back of the book. Ask about additional residential and health care services that may be available. Fees and services subject to change; verify with facility.

ASSISTED LIVING AND PERSONAL CARE

Assisted living units: 22
Personal care is covered by the continuing care contract: Yes
Residents may receive personal care in independent living units: Yes
Nonresidents may be admitted directly to assisted living units: Yes

NURSING CARE: All-Inclusive Plan

Under this all-inclusive plan, unlimited nursing care is covered by the continuing care contract. When residents are in nursing care, they pay nothing for the first six months; thereafter, they pay the same monthly fee they paid for their independent living unit.

Dual-certified beds: 28. Cost per day: semi-private $50.00.

Nursing beds are certified by Medicare. Nonresidents may be admitted directly to the nursing care facility.

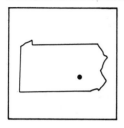

BETHANY VILLAGE RETIREMENT CENTER
325 Wesley Drive, Mechanicsburg, PA 17055
Telephone: (717) 766-0279

Opened in 1964 • Mixed single-level and low-rise buildings on 55 acres • Current resident population is 352 • Located eight miles from Harrisburg, PA • Waiting list may apply for some units

AAHA
Member

HOUSING AND SERVICES

Living Units	No.	Square Feet	No. of Persons	Entrance Fee	Monthly Fee
Studio	71	132–196	1	$15,000–$22,000	$806
One Bedroom	24	356	1		$1,128
			2	$30,000–$35,000	$1,612
Two Bedroom	95	960–1,300	1, 2	$38,000–$53,000	$155 + utilities
Larger Units	0	—	—	—	—
Total	190 Units				

Entrance fee refunds decline over time.

These fees include three meals per day (for studio and one-bedroom units only), biweekly housekeeping, scheduled transportation, and utilities. Special features of this community are presented in the Special Features Index at the back of the book. Ask about additional residential and health care services that may be available. Fees and services subject to change; verify with facility.

ASSISTED LIVING AND PERSONAL CARE

Assisted living units: 31
Personal care is covered by the continuing care contract: Yes
Residents may receive personal care in independent living units: No
Nonresidents may be admitted directly to assisted living units: Yes

NURSING CARE: Modified Plan

Under this modified plan, guaranteed access to nursing care is covered by the continuing care contract. When residents are in nursing care, they pay 86 percent of the per diem rate until their entrance fee credit is depleted; thereafter, they pay the full per diem rate for nursing care.

Intermediate beds: 34. Cost per day: private $62.00, semi-private $55.00.

Skilled beds: 35. Cost per day: private $74.00, semi-private $67.00.

Nursing beds are certified by both Medicare and Medicaid. Nonresidents may be admitted directly to the nursing care facility.

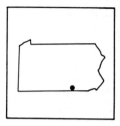

THE BRETHREN HOME
2990 Carlisle Pike, P.O. Box 128
New Oxford, PA 17350
Telephone: (717) 624-2161

Opened in 1952 • Mixed single-level and low-rise buildings on 180 acres • Current resident population is 284 • Waiting list

AAHA
Member

HOUSING AND SERVICES

Living Units	No.	Square Feet	No. of Persons	Entrance Fee	Monthly Fee
Studio	17	288–524	1	$20,000–$26,500	$116–$685
One Bedroom	50	576–742	1	$33,000–$38,340	$126–$642
			2		$883
Two Bedroom	52	1,022	1, 2	$53,525	$136
Larger Units	0	——	——	——	——
Total	119 Units				

Entrance fee refunds decline over time.

These fees include weekly housekeeping and scheduled transportation. Special features of this community are presented in the Special Features Index at the back of the book. Ask about additional residential and health care services that may be available. Fees and services subject to change; verify with facility.

ASSISTED LIVING AND PERSONAL CARE

Assisted living units: 12
Personal care is covered by the continuing care contract: Yes
Residents may receive personal care in independent living units: Apartments only
Nonresidents may be admitted directly to assisted living units: Yes

NURSING CARE: Fee-for-Service Plan

Under this fee-for-service plan, guaranteed access to nursing care is covered by the continuing care contract. Residents pay the full per diem rate for nursing care.

Intermediate beds: 191. Cost per day: private $53.92, semi-private $47.50.

Skilled beds: 85. Cost per day: private $62.50, semi-private $54.50.

Nursing beds are certified by both Medicare and Medicaid. Nonresidents may be admitted directly to the nursing care facility.

PENNSYLVANIA

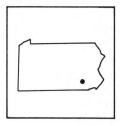

CALVARY FELLOWSHIP HOMES
502 Elizabeth Drive, Lancaster, PA 17601
Telephone: (717) 393-0711

Opened in 1963 • Predominantly single-level/garden apartments and cottages on 20 acres • Current resident population is 260 • Long waiting list; make reservations in advance

HOUSING AND SERVICES

Living Units	No.	Square Feet	No. of Persons	Entrance Fee	Monthly Fee
Studio	54	342	1	$22,900	$340*
One Bedroom	23	638	1	$36,300	$400*
			2	$36,300	$545*
Two Bedroom	70	1,222	1, 2	$46,680	$325
Larger Units	2	1,650	1, 2	$60,000	$325
Total	149 Units				

*One meal per day included.
Entrance fee refunds decline over time.

These fees include scheduled transportation. Special features of this community are presented in the Special Features Index at the back of the book. Ask about additional residential and health care services that may be available. Fees and services subject to change; verify with facility.

ASSISTED LIVING AND PERSONAL CARE

Assisted living units: 16
Personal care is covered by the continuing care contract: Yes
Residents may receive personal care in independent living units: No
Nonresidents may be admitted directly to assisted living units: Yes

NURSING CARE: Modified Plan

Under this modified plan, guaranteed access to nursing care is covered by the continuing care contract. Residents pay 50 percent of the per diem rate for nursing care.

Skilled beds: 45. Cost per day: private $54.00, semi-private $27.00.

Nursing beds are certified by both Medicare and Medicaid. Nonresidents may be admitted directly to the nursing care facility.

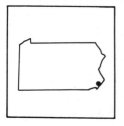

CATHEDRAL VILLAGE
600 East Cathedral Road, Philadelphia, PA 19128
Telephone: (215) 487-1300

Opened in 1979 • Mixed single-level and low-rise buildings on 34 acres • Current resident population is 401 • Long waiting list; make reservations in advance • Accredited by the AAHA Continuing Care Accreditation Commission.

AAHA
Member

HOUSING AND SERVICES

Living Units	No.	Square Feet	No. of Persons	Entrance Fee	Monthly Fee
Studio	45	382	1	$28,500	$808
One Bedroom	120	710	1	$54,500	$1,069
			2	$58,600	$1,721
Two Bedroom	45	1,032	1	$75,000	$1,452
			2	$80,600	$2,095
Larger Units	15	1,242	1	$90,000	$1,676
			2	$96,800	$2,326
Total	225 Units				

Entrance fee refunds decline over time.

These fees include three meals per day, weekly housekeeping, scheduled transportation, and utilities. Special features of this community are presented in the Special Features Index at the back of the book. Ask about additional residential and health care services that may be available. Fees and services subject to change; verify with facility.

ASSISTED LIVING AND PERSONAL CARE

Assisted living units: 0
Personal care is covered by the continuing care contract: No
Residents may receive personal care in independent living units: No

NURSING CARE: All-Inclusive Plan

Under this all-inclusive plan, unlimited nursing care is covered by the continuing care contract. When residents are in nursing care, they pay the same monthly fee they paid for their independent living unit.

Intermediate beds. Cost per day: private $88.00, semi-private $68.00.

Skilled beds: 146. Cost per day: private $96.00, semi-private $76.00.

Nursing beds are certified by both Medicare and Medicaid. Nonresidents may be admitted directly to the nursing care facility.

PENNSYLVANIA

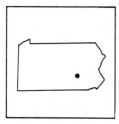

CORNWALL MANOR
P.O. Box 125, Cornwall, PA 17016
Telephone: (717) 273-2647

Opened in 1949 • Mixed single-level and low-rise buildings on 85 acres • Current resident population is 393 • Located five miles from Lebanon, PA • Immediate availability

AAHA
Member

HOUSING AND SERVICES

Living Units	No.	Square Feet	No. of Persons	Entrance Fee	Monthly Fee
Studio	39	300–400	1	$15,000	$745
One Bedroom	120	470–700	1	$35,000	$715
			2		$855
Two Bedroom	34	870–1,400	1	$57,000	$900
			2		$1,040
Larger Units	27	700–1,510	1	$71,000	$600
			2		$650

Total 220 Units

Entrance fee refunds decline over time.

These fees include monthly housekeeping and scheduled transportation. Special features of this community are presented in the Special Features Index at the back of the book. Ask about additional residential and health care services that may be available. Fees and services subject to change; verify with facility.

ASSISTED LIVING AND PERSONAL CARE

Assisted living units: 0
Personal care is covered by the continuing care contract: Yes
Residents may receive personal care in independent living units: Yes

NURSING CARE: Fee-for-Service Plan

Under this fee-for-service plan, guaranteed access to nursing care is covered by the continuing care contract. Residents pay the full per diem rate for nursing care.

Intermediate beds: 78. Cost per day: private $75.50, semi-private $66.00.

Skilled beds: 47. Cost per day: private $83.50, semi-private $83.50.

Nursing beds are certified by both Medicare and Medicaid. The nursing center is accredited by the Joint Commission on Accreditation of Hospitals. Nonresidents may be admitted directly to the nursing care facility.

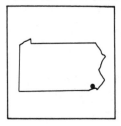

AAHA
Member

CROSSLANDS
P.O. Box 100, Kennett Square, PA 19348
Telephone: (215) 388-1441

Opened in 1977 • Mixed single-level and low-rise buildings on 125 acres • Current resident population is 378 • Located 30 miles from Philadelphia, PA • Long waiting list; make reservations in advance • Accredited by the AAHA Continuing Care Accreditation Commission

HOUSING AND SERVICES

Living Units	No.	Square Feet	No. of Persons	Entrance Fee	Monthly Fee
Studio	16	300	1	$41,000	$953
One Bedroom	210	620–890	1	$41,500–$81,500	$978–$1,334
			2	$41,500–$88,000	$1,600–$1,778
Two Bedroom	40	975	1	$83,000	$1,555
			2	$89,500	$1,955
Larger Units	0	—	—	—	—
Total		266 Units			

Entrance fee refunds decline over time.

These fees include three meals per day, weekly housekeeping, scheduled transportation, and utilities. Special features of this community are presented in the Special Features Index at the back of the book. Ask about additional residential and health care services that may be available. Fees and services subject to change; verify with facility.

ASSISTED LIVING AND PERSONAL CARE

Assisted living units: 0
Personal care is covered by the continuing care contract: No
Residents may receive personal care in independent living units: No

NURSING CARE: All-Inclusive Plan

Under this all-inclusive plan, unlimited nursing care is covered by the continuing care contract. When residents are in nursing care, they pay the same monthly fee they paid for their independent living unit.

Intermediate beds: 33. Cost per day: private $59.00.

Skilled beds: 40. Cost per day: private $74.00.

Nursing beds are certified by Medicare. Nonresidents may be admitted directly to the nursing care facility.

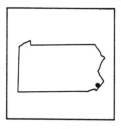

DUNWOODY VILLAGE
3500 West Chester Pike, Newtown Square, PA 19073
Telephone: (215) 359-4400

Opened in 1974 • Mixed single-level and low-rise buildings on 83 acres • Current resident population is 360 • Located ten miles from Philadelphia, PA • Waiting list • Accredited by the AAHA Continuing Care Accreditation Commission

 AAHA Member

HOUSING AND SERVICES

Living Units	No.	Square Feet	No. of Persons	Entrance Fee	Monthly Fee
Studio	62	420	1	$32,500	$994
One Bedroom	107	720	1	$55,500	$1,148
			2	$61,000	$1,986
Two Bedroom	94	1,050–1,750	1	$83,500–$139,500	$1,657–$2,200
			2	$90,000–$147,500	$2,451–$2,950
Larger Units	0	——	——	——	——
Total		263 Units			

Entrance fee refunds decline over time.

These fees include three meals per day, weekly housekeeping, scheduled transportation, and utilities. Special features of this community are presented in the Special Features Index at the back of the book. Ask about additional residential and health care services that may be available. Fees and services subject to change; verify with facility.

ASSISTED LIVING AND PERSONAL CARE

Assisted living units: 21
Personal care is covered by the continuing care contract: Yes
Residents may receive personal care in independent living units: No
Nonresidents may be admitted directly to assisted living units: No

NURSING CARE: All-Inclusive Plan

Under this all-inclusive plan, unlimited nursing care is covered by the continuing care contract. When residents are in nursing care, they pay the same monthly fee they paid for their independent living unit.

Skilled beds: 71. Cost per day: semi-private $75.00.

Nursing beds are certified by Medicare. Nonresidents may be admitted directly to the nursing care facility.

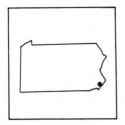

EVANGELICAL MANOR
8401 Roosevelt Boulevard, Philadelphia, PA 19152
Telephone: (215) 624-5800

Opened in 1930 • Low-rise buildings on 13 acres •
Current resident population is 310 • Waiting list

AAHA
Member

HOUSING AND SERVICES

Living Units	No.	Square Feet	No. of Persons	Entrance Fee	Monthly Fee
Studio	166	360	1	$16,000–$18,000	$660–$990
One Bedroom	28	720	1	$25,000–$38,000	$885
			2	$25,000–$38,000	$1,140
Two Bedroom	0	——	——	——	——
Larger Units	0	——	——	——	——
Total	194 Units				

Entrance fee refunds decline over time.

These fees include three meals per day, weekly housekeeping, and utilities. Special features of this community are presented in the Special Features Index at the back of the book. Ask about additional residential and health care services that may be available. Fees and services subject to change; verify with facility.

ASSISTED LIVING AND PERSONAL CARE

Assisted living units: 0
Personal care is covered by the continuing care contract: No
Residents may receive personal care in independent living units: No

NURSING CARE: Fee-for-Service Plan

Under this fee-for-service plan, guaranteed access to nursing care is covered by the continuing care contract. Residents pay the full per diem rate for nursing care.

Intermediate beds: 60. Cost per day: private $55.00, semi-private $55.00.

Skilled beds: 60. Cost per day: private $65.00, semi-private $65.00.

Nursing beds are certified by both Medicare and Medicaid. Nonresidents may be admitted directly to the nursing care facility.

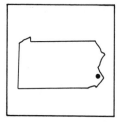

FORT WASHINGTON ESTATES
Fort Washington and Susquehanna Roads
Fort Washington, PA 19034
Telephone: (215) 542-8787

Opened in 1972 • Predominantly single-level/garden apartments on 16 acres • Current resident population is 122 • Located 30 miles from Philadelphia, PA • Waiting list may apply for some units

HOUSING AND SERVICES

Living Units	No.	Square Feet	No. of Persons	Entrance Fee	Monthly Fee
Studio	20	375	1	$32,000	$557
One Bedroom	75	530	1	$48,000	$632
			2		$1,074
Two Bedroom	13	810	1	$62,000	$716
			2		$1,217
Larger Units	0	—	—	—	—
Total	108 Units				

Entrance fee refunds decline over time.

These fees include two meals per day, scheduled transportation, and utilities. Special features of this community are presented in the Special Features Index at the back of the book. Ask about additional residential and health care services that may be available. Fees and services subject to change; verify with facility.

ASSISTED LIVING AND PERSONAL CARE

Assisted living units: 0
Personal care is covered by the continuing care contract: Yes
Residents may receive personal care in independent living units: Yes

NURSING CARE: All-Inclusive Plan

Under this all-inclusive plan, unlimited nursing care is covered by the continuing care contract. When residents are in nursing care, they pay the same monthly fee they paid for their independent living unit.

Skilled beds: 60.* Cost per day: private $90.00, semi-private $67.00.

*Residents of Gwynedd Estates (page 296) also use this nursing facility.

Nursing beds are certified by Medicare. Nonresidents may be admitted directly to the nursing care facility.

PENNSYLVANIA

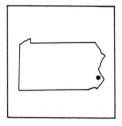

FOULKEWAYS AT GWYNEDD
Meeting House Road, Gwynedd, PA 19436
Telephone: (215) 643-2200

Opened in 1967 • Predominantly single-level/garden apartments on 83 acres • Current resident population is 358 • Located 20 miles from Philadelphia • Long waiting list; make reservations in advance • Accredited by the AAHA Continuing Care Accreditation Commission

AAHA
Member

HOUSING AND SERVICES

Living Units	No.	Square Feet	No. of Persons	Entrance Fee	Monthly Fee
Studio	41	458	1	$23,500	$890
One Bedroom	127	626	1	$49,500	$1,068
			2	$58,000	$1,780
Two Bedroom	64	1,063	1	$74,500	$1,557
			2	$83,700	$2,002
Larger Units	0	——	——	——	——
Total		232 Units			

Entrance fee refunds decline over time.

These fees include three meals per day, weekly housekeeping, scheduled transportation, and utilities. Special features of this community are presented in the Special Features Index at the back of the book. Ask about additional residential and health care services that may be available. Fees and services subject to change; verify with facility.

ASSISTED LIVING AND PERSONAL CARE

Assisted living units: 32
Personal care is covered by the continuing care contract: Yes
Residents may receive personal care in independent living units: No
Nonresidents may be admitted directly to assisted living units: No

NURSING CARE: All-Inclusive Plan

Under this all-inclusive plan, unlimited nursing care is covered by the continuing care contract. When residents are in nursing care, they pay the basic monthly fee for the studio (smallest) unit.

Intermediate beds: 32. Cost per day: private $28.17, semi-private $28.17.

Skilled beds: 62. Cost per day: private $28.17, semi-private $28.17.

Nursing beds are certified by Medicare. Nonresidents may be admitted directly to the nursing care facility.

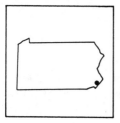

GRANITE FARMS ESTATES
Route 1, Lima, PA 19037
Telephone: (215) 565-2206

Opened in 1986 • Mixed single-level and low-rise buildings on 26 acres • Current resident population is 500 • Located 25 miles from Philadelphia, PA • Waiting list may apply for some units

HOUSING AND SERVICES

Living Units	No.	Square Feet	No. of Persons	Entrance Fee	Monthly Fee
Studio	24	455	1	$52,000	$588
One Bedroom	152	585	1	$81,000	$632
			2		$1,074
Two Bedroom	148	820–970	1	$110,500	$716
			2		$1,217
Larger Units	36	1,290	1	$128,000	$753
			2		$1,258

Total   360 Units

Entrance fee refunds decline over time.

These fees include two meals per day, scheduled transportation, and utilities. Special features of this community are presented in the Special Features Index at the back of the book. Ask about additional residential and health care services that may be available. Fees and services subject to change; verify with facility.

ASSISTED LIVING AND PERSONAL CARE

Assisted living units: 40
Personal care is covered by the continuing care contract: Yes
Residents may receive personal care in independent living units: Yes
Nonresidents may be admitted directly to assisted living units: Yes

NURSING CARE: All-Inclusive Plan

Under this all-inclusive plan, unlimited nursing care is covered by the continuing care contract. When residents are in nursing care, they pay the same monthly fee they paid for their independent living unit.

Skilled beds: 60. Cost per day: private $90.00, semi-private $67.00.

Nursing beds are certified by Medicare. Nonresidents may be admitted directly to the nursing care facility.

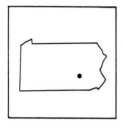

GREEN RIDGE VILLAGE
Big Spring Road, Newville, PA 17241
Telephone: (717) 776-3192

Opened in 1978 • Predominantly single-level/garden apartments on 135 acres • Current resident population is 170 • Located 12 miles from Carlisle, PA • Waiting list • Accredited by the AAHA Continuing Care Accreditation Commission

AAHA Member

HOUSING AND SERVICES

Living Units	No.	Square Feet	No. of Persons	Entrance Fee	Monthly Fee
Studio	4	468	1	$35,000	$605
One Bedroom	19	676–1,300	1	$50,000	$630
			2	$65,000	$970
Two Bedroom	45	1,040–1,700	1	$60,000	$660
			2	$85,000	$1,015
Larger Units	0	—	—	—	—
Total	68 Units				

Entrance fee refunds decline over time.

These fees include one meal per day and scheduled transportation. Special features of this community are presented in the Special Features Index at the back of the book. Ask about additional residential and health care services that may be available. Fees and services subject to change; verify with facility.

ASSISTED LIVING AND PERSONAL CARE

Assisted living units: 14
Personal care is covered by the continuing care contract: Yes
Residents may receive personal care in independent living units: No
Nonresidents may be admitted directly to assisted living units: No

NURSING CARE: All-Inclusive Plan

Under this all-inclusive plan, unlimited nursing care is covered by the continuing care contract. When residents are in nursing care, they pay the basic monthly fee for a one-bedroom apartment.

Dual-certified beds: 60. Cost per day: private $72.00, semi-private $66.00.
Nursing beds are certified by both Medicare and Medicaid. Nonresidents may be admitted directly to the nursing care facility.

PENNSYLVANIA

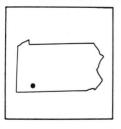

GREENSBURG HOME OF THE PRESBYTERY OF REDSTONE
6 Garden Center Drive, Greensburg, PA 15601
Telephone: (412) 832-8400

Opened in 1980 • Mixed single-level and low-rise buildings on three acres • Current resident population is 100 • Waiting list may apply for some units

AAHA
Member

HOUSING AND SERVICES

Living Units	No.	Square Feet	No. of Persons	Entrance Fee	Monthly Fee
Studio	0	——	——	——	——
One Bedroom	63	386	1, 2	$500–$30,000*	$840
Two Bedroom	0	——	——	——	——
Larger Units	0	——	——	——	——
Total		63 Units			

*Five percent of the resident's first $50,000 of assets, 10 percent of remaining assets over $50,000.
Entrance fee refunds decline over time.

These fees include three meals per day, weekly housekeeping, scheduled transportation, and utilities. Special features of this community are presented in the Special Features Index at the back of the book. Ask about additional residential and health care services that may be available. Fees and services subject to change; verify with facility.

ASSISTED LIVING AND PERSONAL CARE

Assisted living units: 0
Personal care is covered by the continuing care contract: No
Residents may receive personal care in independent living units: Yes

NURSING CARE: Fee-for-Service Plan

Under this fee-for-service plan, guaranteed access to nursing care is covered by the continuing care contract. Residents pay the full per diem rate for nursing care.

Intermediate beds: 30. Cost per day: private—not applicable, semi-private $45.00.

Nursing beds are certified by Medicaid. Nonresidents may be admitted directly to the nursing care facility.

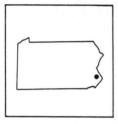

GWYNEDD ESTATES
Norristown Road and Tennis Avenue
Spring House, PA 19477
Telephone: (215) 628-8840

Opened in 1976 • Mixed single-level and low-rise buildings on 20 acres • Current resident population is 201 • Located 30 miles from Philadelphia, PA • Waiting list

HOUSING AND SERVICES

Living Units	No.	Square Feet	No. of Persons	Entrance Fee	Monthly Fee
Studio	10	375	1	$34,000	$588
One Bedroom	91	530	1	$61,000	$632
			2		$1,074
Two Bedroom	52	810	1	$79,000	$716
			2		$1,217
Larger Units	12	1,130	1	$96,000	$753
			2		$1,258
Total	165 Units				

Entrance fee refunds decline over time.

These fees include two meals per day, scheduled transportation, and utilities. Special features of this community are presented in the Special Features Index at the back of the book. Ask about additional residential and health care services that may be available. Fees and services subject to change; verify with facility.

ASSISTED LIVING AND PERSONAL CARE

Assisted living units: 0
Personal care is covered by the continuing care contract: Yes
Residents may receive personal care in independent living units: Yes

NURSING CARE: All-Inclusive Plan

Under this all-inclusive plan, unlimited nursing care is covered by the continuing care contract. When residents are in nursing care, they pay the same monthly fee they paid for their independent living unit.

Skilled beds: 60.* Cost per day: private $90.00, semi-private $67.00.

*Nursing care is provided five miles from Gwynedd Estates at Fort Washington Estates (page 291).

Nursing beds are certified by Medicare. Nonresidents may be admitted directly to the nursing care facility.

PENNSYLVANIA

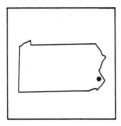

HERITAGE TOWERS
200 Veterans Lane, Doylestown, PA 18901
Telephone: (215) 345-4300

Opened in 1981 • One high-rise building on eight acres • Current resident population is 148 • Immediate availability

AAHA
Member

HOUSING AND SERVICES

Living Units	No.	Square Feet	No. of Persons	Entrance Fee	Monthly Fee
Studio	98	390	1	$25,700	$695
One Bedroom	105	560	1	$40,220	$865
			2	$40,220	$1,264
Two Bedroom	35	1,015	1	$58,370	$1,300
			2	$58,370	$1,700
Larger Units	0	——	——	——	——
Total	238 Units				

Entrance fee refunds decline over time.

These fees include one meal per day, weekly housekeeping, scheduled transportation, and utilities. Special features of this community are presented in the Special Features Index at the back of the book. Ask about additional residential and health care services that may be available. Fees and services subject to change; verify with facility.

ASSISTED LIVING AND PERSONAL CARE

Assisted living units: 0
Personal care is covered by the continuing care contract: No
Residents may receive personal care in independent living units: No

NURSING CARE: Fee-for-Service Plan

Under this fee-for-service plan, guaranteed access to nursing care is covered by the continuing care contract. Residents pay the full per diem rate for nursing care.

Skilled beds: 60. Cost per day: private—not applicable, semi-private $65.00.

Nursing beds are certified by both Medicare and Medicaid. Nonresidents may not be admitted directly to the nursing care facility.

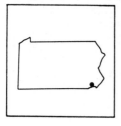

AAHA
Member

KENDAL AT LONGWOOD
P.O. Box 100, Kennett Square, PA 19348
Telephone: (215) 388-7001

Opened in 1973 • Predominantly single-level/garden apartments on 85 acres • Current resident population is 356 • Located 30 miles from Philadelphia, PA • Long waiting list; make reservations in advance • Accredited by the AAHA Continuing Care Accreditation Commission

HOUSING AND SERVICES

Living Units	No.	Square Feet	No. of Persons	Entrance Fee	Monthly Fee
Studio	65	300–351	1	$27,500–$41,000	$889–$953
One Bedroom	125	630	1	$53,500	$1,067
			2	$59,500–$81,750	$1,778
Two Bedroom	53	837	1	$83,000	$1,244
			2	$89,500	$1,867
Larger Units	0	——	——	——	——
Total	243 Units				

Entrance fee refunds decline over time.

These fees include three meals per day, weekly housekeeping, scheduled transportation and utilities. Special features of this community are presented in the Special Features Index at the back of the book. Ask about additional residential and health care services that may be available. Fees and services subject to change; verify with facility.

ASSISTED LIVING AND PERSONAL CARE

Assisted living units: 0
Personal care is covered by the continuing care contract: No
Residents may receive personal care in independent living units: No

NURSING CARE: All-Inclusive Plan

Under this all-inclusive plan, unlimited nursing care is covered by the continuing care contract. When residents are in nursing care, they pay the same monthly fee they paid for their independent living unit.

Intermediate beds: 32. Cost per day: private $59.18.

Skilled beds: 56. Cost per day: private $73.98.

Nursing beds are certified by Medicare. Nonresidents may be admitted directly to the nursing care facility.

PENNSYLVANIA

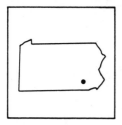

LANDIS HOMES RETIREMENT COMMUNITY
Route Three, Lititz, PA 17543
Telephone: (717) 569-3271

Opened in 1964 • Predominantly single-level/garden apartments on 50 acres • Current resident population is 344 • Long waiting list; make reservations in advance

AAHA
Member

HOUSING AND SERVICES

Living Units	No.	Square Feet	No. of Persons	Entrance Fee	Monthly Fee
Studio	4	306	1	$12,300	$195
One Bedroom	36	660	1, 2	$15,000–$27,000	$202–$241
Two Bedroom	57	1,050	1, 2	$20,250–$38,000	$361
Larger Units	2	1,171	1, 2	$41,700	$361
Total	99 Units				

Entrance fee refunds decline over time.

These fees include utilities. Special features of this community are presented in the Special Features Index at the back of the book. Ask about additional residential and health care services that may be available. Fees and services subject to change; verify with facility.

ASSISTED LIVING AND PERSONAL CARE

Assisted living units: 28
Personal care is covered by the continuing care contract: No
Residents may receive personal care in independent living units: No
Nonresidents may be admitted directly to assisted living units: Yes

NURSING CARE: Fee-for-Service Plan

Under this fee-for-service plan, guaranteed access to nursing care is covered by the continuing care contract. Residents pay the full per diem rate for nursing care.

Intermediate beds: 62. Cost per day: private $41.50, semi-private $41.50.

Skilled beds: 49. Cost per day: private $47.00, semi-private $47.00.

Nursing beds are certified by Medicaid. Nonresidents may be admitted directly to the nursing care facility.

PENNSYLVANIA

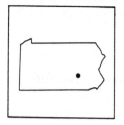

LEBANON VALLEY BRETHREN HOME
1200 Grubb Street, Palmyra, PA 17078
Telephone: (717) 838-5406

Opened in 1979 • Mixed single-level and low-rise
buildings on 60 acres • Current resident population is
253 • Waiting list may apply for some units

AAHA
Member

HOUSING AND SERVICES

Living Units	No.	Square Feet	No. of Persons	Entrance Fee	Monthly Fee
Studio	3	——	1	$19,500	$125
One Bedroom	22	——	1, 2	$35,000	$140
Two Bedroom	53	——	1, 2	$47,650–$59,900	$155–$170
Larger Units	0	——	——	——	——
Total	78 Units				

Entrance fee refunds decline over time.

These fees include scheduled transportation and utilities. Special features of
this community are presented in the Special Features Index at the back of the
book. Ask about additional residential and health care services that may be
available. Fees and services subject to change; verify with facility.

ASSISTED LIVING AND PERSONAL CARE

Assisted living units: 40
Personal care is covered by the continuing care contract: No
Residents may receive personal care in independent living units: No
Nonresidents may be admitted directly to assisted living units: Yes

NURSING CARE: Fee-for-Service Plan

Under this fee-for-service plan, guaranteed access to nursing care is covered by
the continuing care contract. Residents pay the full per diem rate for nursing
care.

Intermediate beds: 58. Cost per day: private $57.00, semi-private $48.00.

Skilled beds: 42. Cost per day: private $62.50, semi-private $53.00.

Nursing beds are certified by both Medicare and Medicaid. Nonresidents may
be admitted directly to the nursing care facility.

PENNSYLVANIA

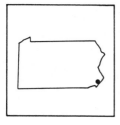

LIMA ESTATES
411 North Middletown Road, Lima, PA 19037
Telephone: (215) 565-7020

Opened in 1979 • Mixed single-level and low-rise buildings on 50 acres • Current resident population is 355 • Located 25 miles from Philadelphia, PA • Waiting list

HOUSING AND SERVICES

Living Units	No.	Square Feet	No. of Persons	Entrance Fee	Monthly Fee
Studio	26	375	1	$37,000	$588
One Bedroom	148	549	1	$64,000	$632
			2		$1,074
Two Bedroom	100	810	1	$82,000	$716
			2		$1,217
Larger Units	26	1,130	1	$101,000	$753
			2		$1,258
Total	300 Units				

Entrance fee refunds decline over time.

These fees include two meals per day, scheduled transportation, and utilities. Special features of this community are presented in the Special Features Index at the back of the book. Ask about additional residential and health care services that may be available. Fees and services subject to change; verify with facility.

ASSISTED LIVING AND PERSONAL CARE

Assisted living units: 0
Personal care is covered by the continuing care contract: No
Residents may receive personal care in independent living units: No

NURSING CARE: All-Inclusive Plan

Under this all-inclusive plan, unlimited nursing care is covered by the continuing care contract. When in nursing care, residents pay the same monthly fee they paid for their independent living unit.

Skilled beds: 60. Cost per day: private $90.00, semi-private $67.00.

Nursing beds are certified by Medicare. Nonresidents may be admitted directly to the nursing care facility.

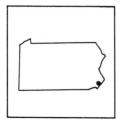

LOGAN SQUARE EAST
Two Franklin Town Boulevard, Philadelphia, PA 19103
Telephone: (215) 563-1800

Opened in 1984 • One high-rise building on one acre
• Current resident population is 300 • Immediate
availability

AAHA
Member

HOUSING AND SERVICES

Living Units	No.	Square Feet	No. of Persons	Entrance Fee	Monthly Fee
Studio	40	375	1	$54,000	$885
One Bedroom	180	667	1	$63,000	$1,105
			2	$63,000	$1,595
Two Bedroom	80	945	1	$71,000	$1,380
			2	$71,000	$1,870
Larger Units	20	1,000	1	$93,000	$1,515
			2	$93,000	$2,005
Total		320 Units			

Residents have a choice of entrance fee refund plans.

These fees include one meal per day, weekly housekeeping, scheduled transportation, and utilities. Special features of this community are presented in the Special Features Index at the back of the book. Ask about additional residential and health care services that may be available. Fees and services subject to change; verify with facility.

ASSISTED LIVING AND PERSONAL CARE

Assisted living units: 0
Personal care is covered by the continuing care contract: No
Residents may receive personal care in independent living units: No

NURSING CARE: All-Inclusive Plan

Under this all-inclusive plan, unlimited nursing care is covered by the continuing care contract. When in nursing care, residents pay the same monthly fee they paid for their independent living unit.

Intermediate beds: 47. Cost per day: private $95.00, semi-private $75.00.

Skilled beds: 101. Cost per day: private $95.00, semi-private $75.00.

Nursing beds are certified by both Medicare and Medicaid. Nonresidents may be admitted directly to the nursing care facility.

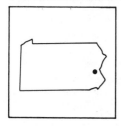

LUTHER CREST
800 Hausman Road, Allentown, PA 18103
Telephone: (215) 398-8011

Opened in 1983 • Mixed single-level, low-rise, and high-rise buildings on 50 acres • Current resident population is 381 • Waiting list may apply for some units

HOUSING AND SERVICES

Living Units	No.	Square Feet	No. of Persons	Entrance Fee	Monthly Fee
Studio	36	——	1	$43,900	$830
One Bedroom	196	——	1	$54,900	$1,097
			2	$54,900	$1,638
Two Bedroom	62	——	1	$85,900	$1,292
			2	$85,900	$1,838
Larger Units	8	——	1	$118,000	$1,600
			2	$118,000	$2,200
Total	302 Units				

Residents have a choice of entrance fee refund plans.

These fees include one meal per day, biweekly housekeeping, scheduled transportation, and utilities. Special features of this community are presented in the Special Features Index at the back of the book. Ask about additional residential and health care services that may be available. Fees and services subject to change; verify with facility.

ASSISTED LIVING AND PERSONAL CARE

Assisted living units: 0
Personal care is covered by the continuing care contract: No
Residents may receive personal care in independent living units: No

NURSING CARE: All-Inclusive Plan

Under this all-inclusive plan, unlimited nursing care is covered by the continuing care contract. When in nursing care, residents pay the same monthly fee they paid for their independent living unit.

Skilled beds: 60. Cost per day: private $32.00, semi-private $14.00.

Nursing beds are certified by both Medicare and Medicaid. Nonresidents may be admitted directly to the nursing care facility.

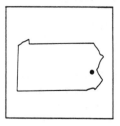

THE LUTHERAN HOME
Topton, PA 19562
Telephone: (215) 682-2145

Opened in 1983 • Mixed single-level and low-rise buildings on 50 acres • Current resident population is 428 • Located one mile from Allentown, PA • Waiting list may apply for some units

AAHA
Member

HOUSING AND SERVICES

Living Units	No.	Square Feet	No. of Persons	Entrance Fee	Monthly Fee
Studio	36	500	1	$45,900	$897
One Bedroom	204	750	1	$59,900	$1,185
			2	$59,900	$1,770
Two Bedroom	62	1,000	1	$85,900	$1,396
			2	$85,900	$1,986
Larger Units	8	1,500	1	$118,000	$1,706
			2	$118,000	$2,296
Total		310 Units			

Residents have a choice of entrance fee refund plans.

These fees include one meal per day, biweekly housekeeping, scheduled transportation, and utilities. Special features of this community are presented in the Special Features Index at the back of the book. Ask about additional residential and health care services that may be available. Fees and services subject to change; verify with facility.

ASSISTED LIVING AND PERSONAL CARE

Assisted living units: 0
Personal care is covered by the continuing care contract: Yes
Residents may receive personal care in independent living units: Yes

NURSING CARE: All-Inclusive Plan

Under this all-inclusive plan, unlimited nursing care is covered by the continuing care contract. When residents are in nursing care, they pay the same monthly fee they paid for their independent living unit.

Skilled beds: 60. Cost per day: private $79.00, semi-private $70.00.

Nursing beds are certified by both Medicare and Medicaid. Nonresidents may be admitted directly to the nursing care facility.

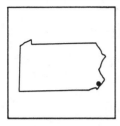

AAHA
Member

MARTINS RUN
11 Martins Run, Marple Township, Media, PA 19063
Telephone: (215) 353-7660

Opened in 1980 • Predominantly single-level/garden apartments on 22 acres • Current resident population is 225 • Located 12 miles from Philadelphia, PA • Waiting list may apply for some units • Accredited by the AAHA Continuing Care Accreditation Commission

HOUSING AND SERVICES

Living Units	No.	Square Feet	No. of Persons	Entrance Fee	Monthly Fee
Studio	51	518	1	$39,000	$1,015
One Bedroom	126	656	1	$50,000	$1,080
			2	$55,000	$1,785
Two Bedroom	25	748	1	$65,000	$1,505
			2	$70,000	$2,150
Larger Units	0	—	—	—	—
Total		202 Units			

Entrance fee refunds decline over time.

These fees include one meal per day, weekly housekeeping, scheduled transportation, and utilities. Special features of this community are presented in the Special Features Index at the back of the book. Ask about additional residential and health care services that may be available. Fees and services subject to change; verify with facility.

ASSISTED LIVING AND PERSONAL CARE

Assisted living units: 0
Personal care is covered by the continuing care contract: No
Residents may receive personal care in independent living units: No

NURSING CARE: All-Inclusive Plan

Under this all-inclusive plan, unlimited nursing care is covered by the continuing care contract. When in nursing care, residents pay the basic monthly fee for a one-bedroom apartment.

Skilled beds: 60. Cost per day: private $72.00, semi-private $63.00.

Nursing beds are certified by both Medicare and Medicaid. Nonresidents may be admitted directly to the nursing care facility.

PENNSYLVANIA

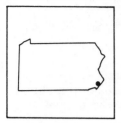

MEADOWOOD
3205 Skippack Pike, Worcester, PA 19490
Telephone: (215) 584-1000

Opened in 1987 • Predominantly single-level/garden apartments on 110 acres • Located 25 miles from Philadelphia, PA • Immediate availability

AAHA
Member

HOUSING AND SERVICES

Living Units	No.	Square Feet	No. of Persons	Entrance Fee	Monthly Fee
Studio	0	—	—	—	—
One Bedroom	164	585–900	1	$74,900–$104,900	$1,080–$1,430
			2	$84,900–$114,900	$1,702–$2,052
Two Bedroom	70	910–1,050	1	$104,900–$124,900	$1,430–$1,650
			2	$114,900–$134,900	$2,052–$2,272
Larger Units	24	1,230–1,440	1	$144,900–$169,000	$1,845–$2,140
			2	$154,900–$179,000	$2,467–$2,762
Total		258 Units			

Entrance fees are fully refundable.

These fees include one meal per day, weekly housekeeping, scheduled transportation, and utilities. Special features of this community are presented in the Special Features Index at the back of the book. Ask about additional residential and health care services that may be available. Fees and services subject to change; verify with facility.

ASSISTED LIVING AND PERSONAL CARE

Assisted living units: 50
Personal care is covered by the continuing care contract: Yes
Residents may receive personal care in independent living units: Yes
Nonresidents may be admitted directly to assisted living units: Yes

NURSING CARE: All-Inclusive Plan

Under this all-inclusive plan, unlimited nursing care is covered by the continuing care contract. When in nursing care, residents pay the same monthly fee they paid for their independent living unit.

Skilled beds: 32.* Cost per day: private—not applicable, semi-private $94.00.

*The nursing center is under construction; it will initially have 32 beds and expand to 60 beds as needs increase. Private rooms are reserved for residents.

Nursing beds will be certified by Medicare. Nonresidents may be admitted directly to the nursing care facility.

PENNSYLVANIA

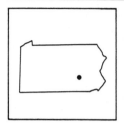

MENNO-HAVEN/MENNO-VILLAGE
2075 Scotland Avenue, Chambersburg, PA 17201
Telephone: (717) 263-8545

Opened in 1964 • Predominantly single-level/garden apartments on 65 acres • Current resident population is 401 • Waiting list

AAHA Member

HOUSING AND SERVICES

Living Units	No.	Square Feet	No. of Persons	Entrance Fee	Monthly Fee
Studio	1	430	1	$24,900	$70
One Bedroom	6	600–640	1, 2	$38,500–$41,800	$70
Two Bedroom	159	790–1,070	1, 2	$47,400–$69,500	$70
Larger Units	0	——	——	——	——
Total	166 Units				

Entrance fee refunds decline over time.

Special features of this community are presented in the Special Features Index at the back of the book. Ask about additional residential and health care services that may be available. Fees and services subject to change; verify with facility.

ASSISTED LIVING AND PERSONAL CARE

Assisted living units: 29
Personal care is covered by the continuing care contract: Yes
Residents may receive personal care in independent living units: No
Nonresidents may be admitted directly to assisted living units: Yes

NURSING CARE: Fee-for-Service Plan

Under this fee-for-service plan, guaranteed access to nursing care is covered by the continuing care contrct. Residents pay the full per diem rate for nursing care.

Intermediate beds. Cost per day: private $57.00, semi-private $48.00.

Skilled beds: 132. Cost per day: private $62.00, semi-private $53.00.

Nursing beds are certified by both Medicare and Medicaid. Nonresidents may be admitted directly to the nursing care facility.

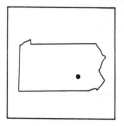

MESSIAH VILLAGE
100 Mount Allen Drive, Mechanicsburg, PA 17055
Telephone: (717) 697-4666

Opened in 1977 • Mixed single-level and low-rise buildings on 72 acres • Current resident population is 391 • Located ten miles from Harrisburg, PA • Waiting list may apply for some units

AAHA
Member

HOUSING AND SERVICES

Living Units	No.	Square Feet	No. of Persons	Entrance Fee	Monthly Fee
Studio	7	522	1	$39,000	$150
One Bedroom	52	688	1, 2	$54,500	$185
Two Bedroom	130	1,026	1, 2	$83,500	$245
Larger Units	7	1,136	1, 2	$91,500	$255

Total 196 Units

Entrance fees are nonrefundable, but the resident owns the unit.

These fees include biweekly housekeeping and utilities. Special features of this community are presented in the Special Features Index at the back of the book. Ask about additional residential and health care services that may be available. Fees and services subject to change; verify with facility.

ASSISTED LIVING AND PERSONAL CARE

Assisted living units: 100
Personal care is covered by the continuing care contract: No
Residents may receive personal care in independent living units: No
Nonresidents may be admitted directly to assisted living units: Yes

NURSING CARE: Fee-for-Service Plan

Under this fee-for-service plan, guaranteed access to nursing care is covered by the continuing care contract. Residents pay the full per diem rate for nursing care.

Skilled beds: 90. Cost per day: private $59.50, semi-private $59.50.

Nursing beds are certified by both Medicare and Medicaid. Nonresidents may be admitted directly to the nursing care facility.

PENNSYLVANIA

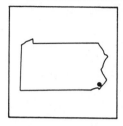

NORMANDY FARMS ESTATES
1801 Morris Road, Blue Bell, PA 19422
Telephone: (215) 699-8721

Opened in 1983 • Mixed single-level and low-rise buildings on 90 acres • Current resident population is 501 • Located 35 miles from Philadelphia, PA • Waiting list may apply for some units

HOUSING AND SERVICES

Living Units	No.	Square Feet	No. of Persons	Entrance Fee	Monthly Fee
Studio	24	390	1	$43,000	$588
One Bedroom	148	558	1	$67,000	$632
			2		$1,074
Two Bedroom	144	822–913	1	$92,000	$716
			2		$1,217
Larger Units	34	1,169	1	$107,000	$753
			2		$1,258
Total		350 Units			

Entrance fee refunds decline over time.

These fees include two meals per day, scheduled transportation, and utilities. Special features of this community are presented in the Special Features Index at the back of the book. Ask about additional residential and health care services that may be available. Fees and services subject to change; verify with facility.

ASSISTED LIVING AND PERSONAL CARE

Assisted living units: 0
Personal care is covered by the continuing care contract: Yes
Residents may receive personal care in independent living units: Yes

NURSING CARE: All-Inclusive Plan

Under this all-inclusive plan, unlimited nursing care is covered by the continuing care contract. When in nursing care, residents pay the same monthly fee they paid for their independent living unit.

Skilled beds: 60. Cost per day: private $90.00, semi-private $67.00.

Nursing beds are certified by Medicare. Nonresidents may be admitted directly to the nursing care facility.

PENNSYLVANIA

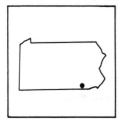

OXFORD MANOR-STEWARD HOME
7 Locust Street, Oxford, PA 19363
Telephone: (215) 932-2900

Opened in 1986 • Predominantly single-level/garden apartments on 14 acres • Current resident population is 161 • Immediate availability

AAHA
Member

HOUSING AND SERVICES

Living Units	No.	Square Feet	No. of Persons	Entrance Fee	Monthly Fee
Studio	0	——	——	——	——
One Bedroom	5	660	1	$58,000	$900
			2	$58,000	$1,200
Two Bedroom	8	972	1	$73,000	$1,100
			2	$73,000	$1,450
Larger Units	0	——	——	——	——
Total		13 Units			

Entrance fees are partially refundable.

These fees include one meal per day, biweekly housekeeping, scheduled transportation, and utilities. Special features of this community are presented in the Special Features Index at the back of the book. Ask about additional residential and health care services that may be available. Fees and services subject to change; verify with facility.

ASSISTED LIVING AND PERSONAL CARE

Assisted living units: 40
Personal care is covered by the continuing care contract: Yes
Residents may receive personal care in independent living units: No
Nonresidents may be admitted directly to assisted living units: No

NURSING CARE: All-Inclusive Plan

Under this all-inclusive plan, unlimited nursing care is covered by the continuing care contract. When residents are in nursing care, they pay the same monthly fee they paid for their independent living unit.

Skilled beds: 100. Cost per day: private $72.00, semi-private $62.00.

Nursing beds are certified by both Medicare and Medicaid. Nonresidents may be admitted directly to the nursing care facility.

PENNSYLVANIA

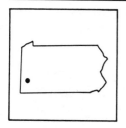

PASSAVANT RETIREMENT AND HEALTH CENTER
401 South Main Street, Zelienople, PA 16063
Telephone: (412) 452-5400

Opened in 1905 • Mixed single-level, low-rise, and
high-rise buildings on 40 acres • Current resident
population is 458 • Located 30 miles from Pittsburgh,
PA • Waiting list may apply for some units

AAHA
Member

HOUSING AND SERVICES

Living Units	No.	Square Feet	No. of Persons	Entrance Fee	Monthly Fee
Studio	17	155–414	1	$5,000	$175–$411
One Bedroom	158	600–750	1, 2	$10,000	$411–$522
Two Bedroom	63	768–1,296	1, 2	$10,000	$472–$705
Larger Units	2	1,296	1, 2	$10,000	$705
Total	240 Units				

Entrance fee refunds decline over time.

These fees include scheduled transportation. Special features of this community are presented in the Special Features Index at the back of the book. Ask about additional residential and health care services that may be available. Fees and services subject to change; verify with facility.

ASSISTED LIVING AND PERSONAL CARE

Assisted living units: 30
Personal care is covered by the continuing care contract: No
Residents may receive personal care in independent living units: Yes
Nonresidents may be admitted directly to assisted living units: Yes

NURSING CARE: Fee-for-Service Plan

Under this fee-for-service plan, guaranteed access to nursing care is covered by the continuing care contract. Residents pay the full per diem rate for nursing care.

Intermediate beds: 162. Cost per day: semi-private $65.00.

Skilled beds: 22. Cost per day: semi-private $70.00.

Nursing beds are certified by both Medicare and Medicaid. Nonresidents may be admitted directly to the nursing care facility.

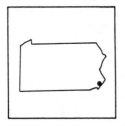

PAUL'S RUN RETIREMENT COMMUNITY
9896 Bustleton Avenue, Philadelphia, PA 19115
Telephone: (215) 934-3000

Opened in 1981 • Predominantly high-rise buildings
on 14 acres • Current resident population is 270 •
Immediate availability

AAHA
Member

HOUSING AND SERVICES

Living Units	No.	Square Feet	No. of Persons	Entrance Fee	Monthly Fee
Studio	122	250–485	1	$28,500–$41,000	$809–$910
One Bedroom	160	550–782	1	$41,500–$56,500	$972–$1,036
			2	$47,500–$62,500	$1,565–$1,665
Two Bedroom	39	800–1,000	1	$59,500–$66,500	$1,260
			2	$65,500–$72,500	$1,896–$2,174
Larger Units	0	—	—	—	—
Total		321 Units			

Entrance fee refunds decline over time.

These fees include two meals per day, monthly housekeeping, scheduled transportation, and utilities. Special features of this community are presented in the Special Features Index at the back of the book. Ask about additional residential and health care services that may be available. Fees and services subject to change; verify with facility.

ASSISTED LIVING AND PERSONAL CARE

Assisted living units: 0
Personal care is covered by the continuing care contract: No
Residents may receive personal care in independent living units: No

NURSING CARE: All-Inclusive Plan

Under this all-inclusive plan, unlimited nursing care is covered by the continuing care contract. When in nursing care, residents pay the same monthly fee they paid for their independent living unit.

Skilled beds: 120.* Cost per day: private $75.00, semi-private $69.00.

*Some residents of Wood River Village Association in Bensalem (see page 333) also use this nursing facility.

Nursing beds are certified by Medicare. Nonresidents may be admitted directly to the nursing care facility.

PENNSYLVANIA

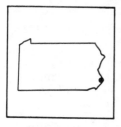

PENNSWOOD VILLAGE
Route 413, Newtown, PA 18940
Telephone: (215) 968-9110

Opened in 1980 • Mixed single-level and low-rise buildings on 82 acres • Current resident population is 375 • Located 20 miles from Philadelphia, PA • Long waiting list; make reservations in advance • Accredited by the AAHA Continuing Care Accreditation Commission

**AAHA
Member**

HOUSING AND SERVICES

Living Units	No.	Square Feet	No. of Persons	Entrance Fee	Monthly Fee
Studio	24	504	1	$36,050	$820
One Bedroom	190	576–1,032	1	$47,000–$86,000	$984–$1,312
			2	$54,000–$98,900	$1,476–$1,804
Two Bedroom	38	1,064	1	$86,000	$1,312
			2	$98,900	$1,804
Larger Units	0	—	—	—	—
Total	252 Units				

Entrance fee refunds decline over time.

These fees include two meals per day, housekeeping, scheduled transportation, and utilities. Special features of this community are presented in the Special Features Index at the back of the book. Ask about additional residential and health care services that may be available. Fees and services subject to change; verify with facility.

ASSISTED LIVING AND PERSONAL CARE
Assisted living units: 41
Personal care is covered by the continuing care contract: Yes
Residents may receive personal care in independent living units: No
Nonresidents may be admitted directly to assisted living units: No

NURSING CARE: All-Inclusive Plan

Under this all-inclusive plan, unlimited nursing care is covered by the continuing care contract. When residents are in nursing care, they pay the basic monthly fee for the studio (smallest) unit.

Skilled beds: 45. Cost per day: private $130.00, semi-private $120.00.

Nursing beds are certified by Medicare. Nonresidents may be admitted directly to the nursing care facility.

PENNSYLVANIA

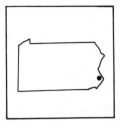

PETER BECKER COMMUNITY
Maple Avenue and Yoder Road, Harleysville, PA 19438
Telephone: (215) 256-9501

Opened in 1971 • Mixed single-level, low-rise, and high-rise buildings on 21 acres • Current resident population is 260 • Located 25 miles from Philadelphia and from Allentown, PA • Long waiting list; make reservations in advance

AAHA Member

HOUSING AND SERVICES

Living Units	No.	Square Feet	No. of Persons	Entrance Fee	Monthly Fee
Studio	39	300–436	1	$19,000–$27,000	$251–$765
One Bedroom	42	618	1, 2	$37,000	$281
Two Bedroom	7	765	1	$45,500	$315
			2	$46,200	$315
Larger Units	0	——	——	——	——
Total	88 Units				

Residents have a choice of entrance fee refund plans.

These fees include weekly housekeeping and utilities. Special features of this community are presented in the Special Features Index at the back of the book. Ask about additional residential and health care services that may be available. Fees and services subject to change; verify with facility.

ASSISTED LIVING AND PERSONAL CARE

Assisted living units: 35
Personal care is covered by the continuing care contract: Yes
Residents may receive personal care in independent living units: No
Nonresidents may be admitted directly to assisted living units: Yes

NURSING CARE: Modified Plan

Under this modified plan, 60 days or more are covered by the continuing care contract. When residents are in nursing care, they pay the full per diem rate after a credit consisting of 25 percent of the entrance fee expires.

Skilled beds: 81. Cost per day: private $64.00, semi-private $56.00.

Nursing beds are certified by both Medicare and Medicaid. Nonresidents may be admitted directly to the nursing care facility.

PENNSYLVANIA

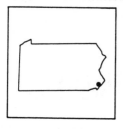

PHILADELPHIA PROTESTANT HOME
6500 Tabor Road, Philadelphia, PA 19111
Telephone: (215) 697-8000

Opened in 1890 • Predominantly high-rise buildings on 14 acres • Current resident population is 600 • Waiting list

HOUSING AND SERVICES

Living Units	No.	Square Feet	No. of Persons	Entrance Fee	Monthly Fee
Studio	94	——	1	$33,428	$255
One Bedroom	167	——	1	$47,853	$303
			2		$365
Two Bedroom	16	——	1	$67,986	$342
			2		$412
Larger Units	0	——	——	——	——
Total	277 Units				

Entrance fee refunds decline over time.

These fees include scheduled transportation and utilities. Special features of this community are presented in the Special Features Index at the back of the book. Ask about additional residential and health care services that may be available. Fees and services subject to change; verify with facility.

ASSISTED LIVING AND PERSONAL CARE

Assisted living units: 84
Personal care is covered by the continuing care contract: No
Residents may receive personal care in independent living units: No
Nonresidents may be admitted directly to assisted living units: No

NURSING CARE: Fee-for-Service Plan

Under this fee-for-service plan, guaranteed access to nursing care is covered by the continuing care contract. Residents pay the full per diem rate for nursing care.

Intermediate beds: 53. Cost per day: semi-private $54.60.

Skilled beds: 53. Cost per day: semi-private $54.97.

Nursing beds are certified by both Medicare and Medicaid. Nonresidents may not be admitted directly to the nursing care facility.

PENNSYLVANIA

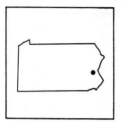

PHOEBE TERRACE
1940 Turner Street, Allentown, PA 18104
Telephone: (215) 820-9081

Opened in 1984 • One high-rise building on two acres • Current resident population is 110 • Waiting list may apply for some units

AAHA
Member

HOUSING AND SERVICES

Living Units	No.	Square Feet	No. of Persons	Entrance Fee	Monthly Fee
Studio	14	450	1	$39,000	$675
One Bedroom	44	590	1	$48,000	$850
			2	$48,000	$1,250
Two Bedroom	30	950	1	$73,000	$975
			2	$73,000	$1,450
Larger Units	0	—	—	—	—
Total		88 Units			

Entrance fee refunds decline over time.

These fees include one meal per day, weekly housekeeping, and utilities. Special features of this community are presented in the Special Features Index at the back of the book. Ask about additional residential and health care services that may be available. Fees and services subject to change; verify with facility.

ASSISTED LIVING AND PERSONAL CARE

Assisted living units: 0
Personal care is covered by the continuing care contract: No
Residents may receive personal care in independent living units: No

NURSING CARE: All-Inclusive Plan

Under this all-inclusive plan, unlimited nursing care is covered by the continuing care contract. When in nursing care, residents pay the same monthly fee they paid for their independent living unit.

Intermediate beds: 286. Cost per day: private $72.00, semi-private $65.00.

Skilled beds: 102. Cost per day: private $86.00, semi-private $72.00.

Nursing beds are certified by both Medicare and Medicaid. Nonresidents may be admitted directly to the nursing care facility.

PENNSYLVANIA

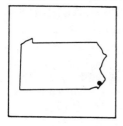

PRESBYTERIAN HOME AT 58TH STREET
Greenway Avenue and 58th Street
Philadelphia, PA 19143
Telephone: (215) 724-2218

Opened in 1872 • Eleven single-level and low-rise buildings on ten acres • Current resident population is 194 • Immediate availability

HOUSING AND SERVICES

Living Units	No.	Square Feet	No. of Persons	Entrance Fee	Monthly Fee
Studio	176	142–150	1	$7,500–$12,000	$635–$750
One Bedroom	0	——	——	——	——
Two Bedroom	0	——	——	——	——
Larger Units	0	——	——	——	——
Total	176 Units				

Entrance fee refunds decline over time.

These fees include three meals per day, monthly housekeeping, and utilities. Special features of this community are presented in the Special Features Index at the back of the book. Ask about additional residential and health care services that may be available. Fees and services subject to change; verify with facility.

ASSISTED LIVING AND PERSONAL CARE

Assisted living units: 0
Personal care is covered by the continuing care contract: Yes
Residents may receive personal care in independent living units: Yes

NURSING CARE: Fee-for-Service Plan

Under this fee-for-service plan, guaranteed access to nursing care is covered by the continuing care contract. Residents pay the full per diem rate for nursing care.

Skilled beds: 50. Cost per day: private $90.00, semi-private $80.00.

Nursing beds are certified by both Medicare and Medicaid. Nonresidents may not be admitted directly to the nursing care facility.

PENNSYLVANIA

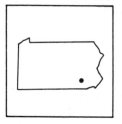

THE QUARRYVILLE PRESBYTERIAN HOME
R.D. 2, Box 20, Quarryville, PA 17566
Telephone: (717) 786-7321

Opened in 1948 • Predominantly high-rise buildings on 160 acres • Current resident population is 285 • Located 15 miles from Lancaster, PA • Waiting list

AAHA
Member

HOUSING AND SERVICES

Living Units	No.	Square Feet	No. of Persons	Entrance Fee	Monthly Fee
Studio	80	224–529	1	$500*	$404–$510
One Bedroom	42	558	1	$500*	$645–$684
			2	$500*	$919–$958
Two Bedroom	15	781	1	$500*	$742–$794
			2	$500*	$1,016–$1,068
Larger Units	—	——	1	$500*	$404–$798
			2	$500*	$919–$1,068

Total   137 Units

*Fee is $500 plus a partial turnover of assets.

Entrance fee refunds decline over time.

These fees include three meals per day, scheduled transportation, and utilities. Special features of this community are presented in the Special Features Index at the back of the book. Ask about additional residential and health care services that may be available. Fees and services subject to change; verify with facility.

ASSISTED LIVING AND PERSONAL CARE

Assisted living units: 0
Personal care is covered by the continuing care contract: No
Residents may receive personal care in independent living units: Yes

NURSING CARE: Modified Plan

Under this modified plan, guaranteed access to nursing care is covered by the continuing care contract. Residents pay 87 percent of the per diem rate for nursing care.

Skilled beds: 120. Cost per day: private $86.25, semi-private $57.50.

Dual-certified beds: 40. Cost per day: private $86.25, semi-private $57.50.

Nursing beds are certified by both Medicare and Medicaid. Nonresidents may be admitted directly to the nursing care facility.

PENNSYLVANIA

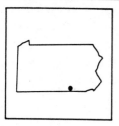

QUINCY UNITED METHODIST HOME
P.O. Box 217, Quincy, PA 17247
Telephone: (717) 749-3151

Opened in 1975 • Predominantly single-level/garden apartments on 360 acres • Current resident population is 36 • Located four miles from Waynesboro, PA • Immediate availability

AAHA
Member

HOUSING AND SERVICES

Living Units	No.	Square Feet	No. of Persons	Entrance Fee	Monthly Fee
Studio	0	——	——	—	——
One Bedroom	8	1,000	1, 2	$30,000	$375–$525
Two Bedroom	20	1,034–1,039	1, 2	$30,000	$475–$600
Larger Units	0	——	——	——	——
Total		28 Units			

Entrance fee refunds decline over time.

These fees include scheduled transportation. Special features of this community are presented in the Special Features Index at the back of the book. Ask about additional residential and health care services that may be available. Fees and services subject to change; verify with facility.

ASSISTED LIVING AND PERSONAL CARE

Assisted living units: 0
Personal care is covered by the continuing care contract: No
Residents may receive personal care in independent living units: No

NURSING CARE: Fee-for-Service Plan

Under this fee-for-service plan, guaranteed access to nursing care is covered by the continuing care contract. Residents pay the full per diem rate for nursing care.

Intermediate beds: 101. Cost per day: private $56.00, semi-private $52.00.

Skilled beds: 94. Cost per day: private $67.00, semi-private $58.00.

Nursing beds are certified by both Medicare and Medicaid. The nursing center is accredited by the Joint Commission on Accreditation of Hospitals. Nonresidents may be admitted directly to the nursing care facility.

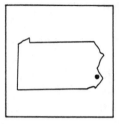

PENNSYLVANIA

ROCKHILL MENNONITE COMMUNITY
Box 21, Route 152, Sellersville, PA 18960
Telephone: (215) 257-2751

Opened in 1978 • One high-rise building on 40 acres • Current resident population is 165 • Located 30 miles from Philadelphia, PA • Waiting list

AAHA
Member

HOUSING AND SERVICES

Living Units	No.	Square Feet	No. of Persons	Entrance Fee	Monthly Fee
Studio	32	340	1	$30,000	$326
One Bedroom	92	530	1, 2	$45,000	$387
Two Bedroom	11	820	1, 2	$60,000	$465
Larger Units	0	——	——	——	——
Total	135 Units				

Entrance fee refunds decline over time.

These fees include scheduled transportation and utilities. Special features of this community are presented in the Special Features Index at the back of the book. Ask about additional residential and health care services that may be available. Fees and services subject to change; verify with facility.

ASSISTED LIVING AND PERSONAL CARE

Assisted living units: 0
Personal care is covered by the continuing care contract: No
Residents may receive personal care in independent living units: No

NURSING CARE: Fee-for-Service Plan

Under this fee-for-service plan, guaranteed access to nursing care is covered by the continuing care contract. Residents pay the full per diem rate for nursing care.

Skilled beds: 96. Cost per day: private $65.00, semi-private $55.00.

Nursing beds are certified by both Medicare and Medicaid. Nonresidents may be admitted directly to the nursing care facility.

PENNSYLVANIA

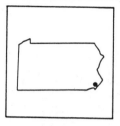

ROSEMONT PRESBYTERIAN VILLAGE
404 Cheswick Place, Rosemont, PA 19010
Telephone: (215) 527-6500

Opened in 1956 • Mixed single-level and low-rise buildings on ten acres • Current resident population is 225 • Located 15 miles from Philadelphia, PA • Long waiting list; make reservations in advance • Accredited by the AAHA Continuing Care Accreditation Commission

AAHA Member

HOUSING AND SERVICES

Living Units	No.	Square Feet	No. of Persons	Entrance Fee	Monthly Fee
Studio	126	312–506	1	$16,300–$32,700	$628
One Bedroom	61	448–728	1	$29,300–$41,100	$755
			2	$34,000–$47,700	$1,196
Two Bedroom	15	804–853	1	$39,300–$45,000	$1,060
			2	$45,600–$52,200	$1,336
Larger Units	0	—	—	—	—
Total	202 Units				

Entrance fee refunds decline over time.

These fees include three meals per day, weekly housekeeping, scheduled transportation, and utilities. Special features of this community are presented in the Special Features Index at the back of the book. Ask about additional residential and health care services that may be available. Fees and services subject to change; verify with facility.

ASSISTED LIVING AND PERSONAL CARE
Assisted living units: 0
Personal care is covered by the continuing care contract: No
Residents may receive personal care in independent living units: No

NURSING CARE: Fee-for-Service Plan

Under this fee-for-service plan, guaranteed access to nursing care is covered by the continuing care contract. Residents pay the full per diem rate for nursing care.

Skilled beds: 147.* Cost per day: private $76.00, semi-private $64.00.

*The nursing facility is Broomall Presbyterian Home, located approximately three miles away.

Nursing beds are certified by both Medicare and Medicaid. Nonresidents may be admitted directly to the nursing care facility.

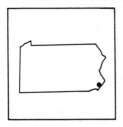

RYDAL PARK
1515 on the Fairway, Rydal, PA 19046
Telephone: (215) 885-6800

Opened in 1974 • Predominantly high-rise buildings on 13 acres • Current resident population is 440 • Located five miles from Philadelphia, PA • Long waiting list; make reservations in advance • Accredited by the AAHA Continuing Care Accreditation Commission

AAHA
Member

HOUSING AND SERVICES

Living Units	No.	Square Feet	No. of Persons	Entrance Fee	Monthly Fee
Studio	105	316	1	$26,000	$865
One Bedroom	190	554	1	$41,500–$51,400	$1,039–$1,081
			2	$48,800–$60,400	$1,704–$1,763
Two Bedroom	28	760	1	$67,100–$74,700	$1,352–$1,385
			2	$78,800–$87,800	$1,837–$1,887
Larger Units	0	—	—	—	—
Total	323 Units				

Entrance fee refunds decline over time.

These fees include three meals per day, weekly housekeeping, and utilities. Special features of this community are presented in the Special Features Index at the back of the book. Ask about additional residential and health care services that may be available. Fees and services subject to change; verify with facility.

ASSISTED LIVING AND PERSONAL CARE

Assisted living units: 0
Personal care is covered by the continuing care contract: No
Residents may receive personal care in independent living units: No

NURSING CARE: All-Inclusive Plan

Under this all-inclusive plan, unlimited nursing care is covered by the continuing care contract. When residents are in nursing care, they pay the same monthly fee they paid for their independent living unit.

Skilled beds: 120. Cost per day: private $81.00, semi-private $74.00.

Nursing beds are certified by both Medicare and Medicaid. Nonresidents may be admitted directly to the nursing care facility.

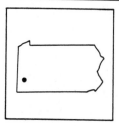

SAINT BARNABAS RETIREMENT VILLAGE
5850 Meridian Road, Gibsonia, PA 15044
Telephone: (412) 443-0700

Opened in 1980 • Predominantly high-rise buildings on 270 acres • Current resident population is 310 • Located 15 miles from Pittsburgh, PA • Waiting list may apply for some units

AAHA Member

HOUSING AND SERVICES

Living Units	No.	Square Feet	No. of Persons	Entrance Fee	Monthly Fee
Studio	0	—	—	—	—
One Bedroom	144	700	1	$1,000	$971
			2	$1,000	$1,295
Two Bedroom	104	1,400	1	$1,000	$1,581
			2	$1,000	$1,870
Larger Units	4	1,500	1	$2,000	$1,581
			2	$2,000	$1,870
Total		152 Units			

Entrance fee refunds decline over time.

These fees include one meal per day, monthly housekeeping, scheduled transportation, and utilities. Special features of this community are presented in the Special Features Index at the back of the book. Ask about additional residential and health care services that may be available. Fees and services subject to change; verify with facility.

ASSISTED LIVING AND PERSONAL CARE

Assisted living units: 0
Personal care is covered by the continuing care contract: No
Residents may receive personal care in independent living units: No

NURSING CARE: Fee-for-Service Plan

Under this fee-for-service plan, guaranteed access to nursing care is covered by the continuing care contract. Residents pay the full per diem rate for nursing care.

Skilled beds: 107. Cost per day: private $65.00, semi-private $60.00.

Nursing beds are certified by both Medicare and Medicaid. Nonresidents may be admitted directly to the nursing care facility.

PENNSYLVANIA

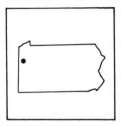

SAINT PAUL HOMES
339 East Jamestown Road, Greenville, PA 16125
Telephone: (412) 588-4070

Opened in 1973 • Predominantly single-level/garden apartments on 622 acres • Current resident population is 280 • Waiting list may apply for some units

AAHA
Member

HOUSING AND SERVICES

Living Units	No.	Square Feet	No. of Persons	Entrance Fee	Monthly Fee
Studio	0	——	——	——	——
One Bedroom	0	——	——	——	——
Two Bedroom	24	1,050	1, 2	$65,000	$280
Larger Units*	—	——	——	——	——
Total		24 Units			

*Duplex homes can be custom built for residents who then earn equity over time.

Entrance fees are partially refundable.

These fees include utilities. Special features of this community are presented in the Special Features Index at the back of the book. Ask about additional residential and health care services that may be available. Fees and services subject to change; verify with facility.

ASSISTED LIVING AND PERSONAL CARE

Assisted living units: 26
Personal care is covered by the continuing care contract: No
Residents may receive personal care in independent living units: No
Nonresidents may be admitted directly to assisted living units: No

NURSING CARE: Fee-for-Service Plan

Under this fee-for-service plan, guaranteed access to nursing care is covered by the continuing care contract. When residents are in nursing care, they pay the full per diem rate after any equity credit on the previous unit is expended.

Intermediate beds: 197. Cost per day: semi-private $70.00.

Skilled beds: 29. Cost per day: semi-private $70.00.

Nursing beds are certified by both Medicare and Medicaid. Nonresidents may be admitted directly to the nursing care facility.

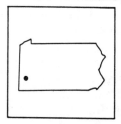

SHERWOOD OAKS
100 Norman Drive, Mars, PA 16046
Telephone: (412) 776-8100

Opened in 1982 • Predominantly single-level/garden apartments on 85 acres • Current resident population is 247 • Located 23 miles from Pittsburgh, PA • Immediate availability

AAHA Member

HOUSING AND SERVICES

Living Units	No.	Square Feet	No. of Persons	Entrance Fee	Monthly Fee
Studio	25	579	1	$48,875	$890
One Bedroom	124	739–904	1	$78,650	$1,120–$1,260
			2	$78,650	$1,620–$1,760
Two Bedroom	91	916–1,069	1	$78,650–$95,150	$1,275–$1,775
			2	$78,650	$1,425–$1,925
Larger Units	20	1,110	1	$99,750	$1,625
			2	$99,750	$2,125
Total	260 Units				

Entrance fee refunds decline over time.

These fees include one meal per day, weekly housekeeping, scheduled transportation, and utilities. Special features of this community are presented in the Special Features Index at the back of the book. Ask about additional residential and health care services that may be available. Fees and services subject to change; verify with facility.

ASSISTED LIVING AND PERSONAL CARE

Assisted living units: 37
Personal care is covered by the continuing care contract: Yes
Residents may receive personal care in independent living units: Yes
Nonresidents may be admitted directly to assisted living units: Yes

NURSING CARE: All-Inclusive Plan

Under this all-inclusive plan, unlimited nursing care is covered by the continuing care contract. When residents are in nursing care, they pay the same monthly fee they paid for their independent living unit.

Dual-certified beds: 59. Cost per day: private $94.00, semi-private $72.00.

Nursing beds are certified by both Medicare and Medicaid. Nonresidents may be admitted directly to the nursing care facility.

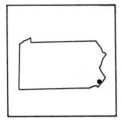

SOUTHAMPTON ESTATES
238 Street Road, Southampton, PA 18966
Telephone: (215) 364-0500

Opened in 1979 • Mixed single-level and low-rise buildings on 85 acres • Current resident population is 466 • Located 20 miles from Philadelphia, PA • Waiting list

HOUSING AND SERVICES

Living Units	No.	Square Feet	No. of Persons	Entrance Fee	Monthly Fee
Studio	84	375	1	$37,000	$588
One Bedroom	193	549	1	$64,000	$632
			2		$1,074
Two Bedroom	84	810	1	$82,000	$716
			2		$1,217
Larger Units	16	1,130	1	$101,000	$753
			2		$1,258

Total 377 Units

Entrance fee refunds decline over time.

These fees include two meals per day, scheduled transportation, and utilities. Special features of this community are presented in the Special Features Index at the back of the book. Ask about additional residential and health care services that may be available. Fees and services subject to change; verify with facility.

ASSISTED LIVING AND PERSONAL CARE

Assisted living units: 22
Personal care is covered by the continuing care contract: Yes
Residents may receive personal care in independent living units: Yes
Nonresidents may be admitted directly to assisted living units: No

NURSING CARE: All-Inclusive Plan

Under this all-inclusive plan, unlimited nursing care is covered by the continuing care contract. When residents are in nursing care, they pay the same monthly fee they paid for their independent living unit.

Skilled beds: 60. Cost per day: private $90.00, semi-private $67.00.

Nursing beds are certified by Medicare. Nonresidents may be admitted directly to the nursing care facility.

PENNSYLVANIA

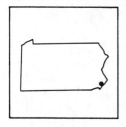

SPRINGFIELD RETIREMENT RESIDENCE
ALL SAINTS' REHABILITATION HOSPITAL
551 East Evergreen Avenue, Wyndmoor, PA 19118
Telephone: (215) 233-6300

Opened in 1975 • One low-rise building on 11 acres •
Current resident population is 160 • Located one mile
from Philadelphia, PA • Waiting list may apply for
some units

AAHA
Member

HOUSING AND SERVICES

Living Units	No.	Square Feet	No. of Persons	Entrance Fee	Monthly Fee
Studio	100	306–434	1	$30,900–$37,800	$850–$995
One Bedroom	28	702–826	1	$51,975–$69,280	$1,075–$1,300
			2	$60,810–$80,680	$1,515–$1,830
Two Bedroom	2	918	1, 2	$89,500	$2,050
Larger Units	0	——	——	——	——
Total	130 Units				

Entrance fee refunds decline over time.

These fees include three meals per day, weekly housekeeping, scheduled transportation, and utilities. Special features of this community are presented in the Special Features Index at the back of the book. Ask about additional residential and health care services that may be available. Fees and services subject to change; verify with facility.

ASSISTED LIVING AND PERSONAL CARE

Assisted living units: 0
Personal care is covered by the continuing care contract: Yes
Residents may receive personal care in independent living units: Yes

NURSING CARE: All-Inclusive Plan

Under this all-inclusive plan, unlimited nursing care is covered by the continuing care contract. When residents are in nursing care, they pay the same monthly fee they paid for their independent living unit.

Skilled beds: 31. Cost per day: private $130.00, semi-private $130.00.

Nursing beds are certified by both Medicare and Medicaid. The nursing center is accredited by the Joint Commission on Accreditation of Hospitals. Nonresidents may be admitted directly to the nursing care facility.

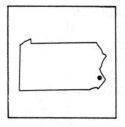

SPRINGHOUSE ESTATES
Norristown and McKean Roads
Springhouse, PA 19477
Telephone: (215) 542-9937

Opened in 1977 • Mixed single-level and low-rise buildings on 58 acres • Current resident population is 500 • Located 30 miles from Philadelphia, PA • Waiting list may apply for some units

AAHA
Member

HOUSING AND SERVICES

Living Units	No.	Square Feet	No. of Persons	Entrance Fee	Monthly Fee
Studio	25	375	1	$37,000	$588
One Bedroom	180	549	1	$64,000	$632
			2		$1,074
Two Bedroom	103	810	1	$82,000	$716
			2		$1,217
Larger Units	20	1,130	1	$101,000	$753
			2		$1,258

Total   328 Units

Entrance fee refunds decline over time.

These fees include two meals per day, scheduled transportation, and utilities. Special features of this community are presented in the Special Features Index at the back of the book. Ask about additional residential and health care services that may be available. Fees and services subject to change; verify with facility.

ASSISTED LIVING AND PERSONAL CARE
Assisted living units: 22
Personal care is covered by the continuing care contract: Yes
Residents may receive personal care in independent living units: Yes
Nonresidents may be admitted directly to assisted living units: No

NURSING CARE: All-Inclusive Plan

Under this all-inclusive plan, unlimited nursing care is covered by the continuing care contract. When residents are in nursing care, they pay the same monthly fee they paid for their independent living unit.

Skilled beds: 60. Cost per day: private $90.00, semi-private $67.00.

Nursing beds are certified by Medicare. Nonresidents may be admitted directly to the nursing care facility.

PENNSYLVANIA

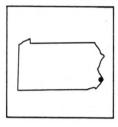

TWINING VILLAGE
280 Middle Holland Road, Holland, PA 18966
Telephone: (215) 322-6100

Opened in 1978 • Mixed single-level and low-rise buildings on 46 acres • Current resident population is 270 • Located 20 miles from Philadelphia, PA • Waiting list may apply for some units

HOUSING AND SERVICES

Living Units	No.	Square Feet	No. of Persons	Entrance Fee	Monthly Fee
Studio	5	292	1	$48,600	$877
One Bedroom	169	463–622	1	$58,400–$68,300	$984–$1,304
			2	$69,600–$77,300	$1,726–$1,944
Two Bedroom	51	945	1	$88,300	$1,632
			2	$99,300	$2,274
Larger Units	0	—	—	—	—
Total		225 Units			

Entrance fee refunds decline over time.

These fees include three meals per day, weekly housekeeping, scheduled transportation, and utilities. Special features of this community are presented in the Special Features Index at the back of the book. Ask about additional residential and health care services that may be available. Fees and services subject to change; verify with facility.

ASSISTED LIVING AND PERSONAL CARE

Assisted living units: 60
Personal care is covered by the continuing care contract: Yes
Residents may receive personal care in independent living units: No
Nonresidents may be admitted directly to assisted living units: Yes

NURSING CARE: All-Inclusive Plan

Under this all-inclusive plan, unlimited nursing care is covered by the continuing care contract. When residents are in nursing care, they pay the same monthly fee they paid for their independent living unit.

Skilled beds: 82. Cost per day: private $112.00, semi-private $87.00.

Nursing beds are certified by Medicare. Nonresidents may be admitted directly to the nursing care facility.

PENNSYLVANIA

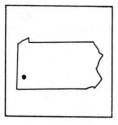

THE UNITED METHODIST HOME
700 Bower Hill Road, Pittsburgh, PA 15243
Telephone: (412) 341-1030

Opened in 1908 • Mixed single-level and low-rise
buildings on 27 acres • Current resident population is
224 • Located four miles from Pittsburgh, PA •
Waiting list may apply for some units

AAHA
Member

HOUSING AND SERVICES

Living Units	No.	Square Feet	No. of Persons	Entrance Fee	Monthly Fee
Studio	0	——	——	——	——
One Bedroom	—	——	1	$15,000–$68,000	$525–$1,020
			2		$825–$1,320
Two Bedroom	—	——	1, 2	$15,000–$98,000	$620–$1,260
Larger Units	0	——	——	——	——
Total	148 Units				

Residents have a choice of entrance fee refund plans.

These fees include one, two, or three meals per day; weekly housekeeping; and
utilities. Special features of this community are presented in the Special Features Index at the back of the book. Ask about additional residential and health
care services that may be available. Fees and services subject to change; verify
with facility.

ASSISTED LIVING AND PERSONAL CARE

Assisted living units: 10
Personal care is covered by the continuing care contract: No
Residents may receive personal care in independent living units: No
Nonresidents may be admitted directly to assisted living units: No

NURSING CARE: Modified Plan

Under this modified plan, 15 or fewer days are covered by the continuing care
contract. Once residents move permanently to the nursing unit, they pay the
full per diem rate for nursing care.

Intermediate beds: 81. Cost per day: private $75.00, semi-private $67.50.

Skilled beds: 42. Cost per day: private $87.50, semi-private $75.00.

Nursing beds are certified by both Medicare and Medicaid. Nonresidents may
be admitted directly to the nursing care facility.

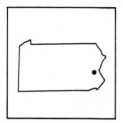

WESTMINSTER VILLAGE
803 North Wahneta Street, Allentown, PA 18103
Telephone: (215) 434-6245

Opened in 1983 • One high-rise building on one acre
• Current resident population is 47 • Waiting list

AAHA
Member

HOUSING AND SERVICES

Living Units	No.	Square Feet	No. of Persons	Entrance Fee	Monthly Fee
Studio	0	——	——	——	——
One Bedroom	34	——	1	$45,000	$894
			2	$45,000	$1,326
Two Bedroom	8	——	1	$61,600	$978
			2	$61,600	$1,410
Larger Units	0	——	——	——	——
Total	42 Units				

Entrance fee refunds decline over time.

These fees include one meal per day, housekeeping, scheduled transportation, and utilities. Special features of this community are presented in the Special Features Index at the back of the book. Ask about additional residential and health care services that may be available. Fees and services subject to change; verify with facility.

ASSISTED LIVING AND PERSONAL CARE

Assisted living units: 0
Personal care is covered by the continuing care contract: Yes
Residents may receive personal care in independent living units: Yes

NURSING CARE: All-Inclusive Plan

Under this all-inclusive plan, unlimited nursing care is covered by the continuing care contract. When residents are in nursing care, they pay the same monthly fee they paid for their independent living unit.

Intermediate beds: 55. Cost per day: private $82.00, semi-private $72.00.

Skilled beds: 56. Cost per day: private $82.00, semi-private $72.00.

Nursing beds are certified by both Medicare and Medicaid. Nonresidents may be admitted directly to the nursing care facility.

PENNSYLVANIA

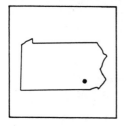

WILLOW VALLEY MANOR
211 Willow Valley Square, Lancaster, PA 17602
Telephone: (717) 464-5478

Opened in 1984 • Mixed single-level and low-rise buildings on 30 acres • Current resident population is 513 • Located three miles from Lancaster, PA • Waiting list

**AAHA
Member**

HOUSING AND SERVICES

Living Units	No.	Square Feet	No. of Persons	Entrance Fee	Monthly Fee
Studio	51	430	1	$50,900	$587–$865
One Bedroom	111	625	1	$64,900	$633
			2	$64,900	$911
Two Bedroom	87	905	1	$82,900	$680
			2	$82,900	$958
Larger Units	93	——	1	$92,900	$703
			2	$92,900	$981
Total	342 Units				

Entrance fee refunds decline over time.

These fees include two meals per day, housekeeping, scheduled transportation, and utilities. Special features of this community are presented in the Special Features Index at the back of the book. Ask about additional residential and health care services that may be available. Fees and services subject to change; verify with facility.

ASSISTED LIVING AND PERSONAL CARE

Assisted living units: 10
Personal care is covered by the continuing care contract: Yes
Residents may receive personal care in independent living units: No
Nonresidents may be admitted directly to assisted living units: Yes

NURSING CARE: All-Inclusive Plan

Under this all-inclusive plan, unlimited nursing care is covered by the continuing care contract. When residents are in nursing care, they pay the same monthly fee they paid for their independent living unit.

Skilled beds: 50. Cost per day: private $85.00, semi-private $60.00.

Nursing beds are certified by Medicare. Nonresidents may be admitted directly to the nursing care facility.

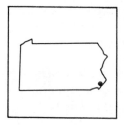

WOOD RIVER VILLAGE
3200 Bensalem Boulevard, Bensalem, PA 19020
Telephone: (215) 752-2370

Opened in 1981 • Predominantly low-rise buildings on 20 acres • Current resident population is 290 • Located 20 miles from the center of Philadelphia, PA • Immediate availability

AAHA
Member

HOUSING AND SERVICES

Living Units	No.	Square Feet	No. of Persons	Entrance Fee	Monthly Fee
Studio	54	433	1	$54,500	$688
One Bedroom	190	623	1	$71,000	$908
			2	$73,000	$1,513
Two Bedroom	65	843	1	$85,000	$1,144
			2	$87,000	$1,755
Larger Units	0	—	—	—	—
Total	309 Units				

Entrance fee refunds decline over time.

These fees include one meal per day, scheduled transportation, and utilities. Special features of this community are presented in the Special Features Index at the back of the book. Ask about additional residential and health care services that may be available. Fees and services subject to change; verify with facility.

ASSISTED LIVING AND PERSONAL CARE
Assisted living units: 18
Personal care is covered by the continuing care contract: Yes
Residents may receive personal care in independent living units: Yes
Nonresidents may be admitted directly to assisted living units: No

NURSING CARE: All-Inclusive Plan

Under this all-inclusive plan, unlimited nursing care is covered by the continuing care contract. When residents are in nursing care, they pay the same monthly fee they paid for their independent living unit.

Intermediate beds: 120.* Cost per day: not applicable.
Skilled beds: 60*/120.** Cost per day: not applicable.

Residents have guaranteed access to one of two nursing centers within a ten-mile radius of Bensalem: *Attleboro Nursing and Rehabilitation Center, 300 East Winchester Avenue, Langhorne, PA 19047, (215) 757-3739; and **Paul's Run (page 312) in Philadelphia, PA.

Nursing beds are certified by Medicare. Nonresidents may not be admitted directly to the nursing care facility.

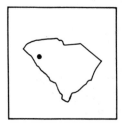

HERITAGE HILLS RETIREMENT COMMUNITY
GREENWOOD METHODIST HOME
1110 Marshall Road, Greenwood, SC 29646
Telephone: (803) 227-1220

Opened in 1971 • Predominantly single-level/garden apartments on 100 acres • Current resident population is 145 • Waiting list

AAHA
Member

HOUSING AND SERVICES

Living Units	No.	Square Feet	No. of Persons	Entrance Fee	Monthly Fee
Studio	1	825	1	——	——
One Bedroom	13	775–1,000	1	$49,500	$175
			2	$49,500	$240
Two Bedroom	16	1,150–2,000	1	$68,000	$175
			2	$68,000	$240
Larger Units	0	——	——	——	——
Total	30 Units				

Entrance fees are partially refundable.

These fees include scheduled transportation and some utilities. Special features of this community are presented in the Special Features Index at the back of the book. Ask about additional residential and health care services that may be available. Fees and services subject to change; verify with facility.

ASSISTED LIVING AND PERSONAL CARE

Assisted living units: 0
Personal care is covered by the continuing care contract: No
Residents may receive personal care in independent living units: No

NURSING CARE: Fee-for-Service Plan

Under this fee-for-service plan guaranteed access to nursing care is covered by the continuing care contract. Residents pay the full per diem rate for nursing care.

Dual-certified beds: 102. Cost per day: private $55.00.

Nursing beds are certified by both Medicare and Medicaid. Nonresidents may be admitted directly to the nursing care facility.

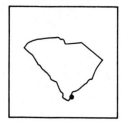

SEABROOK OF HILTON HEAD
300 Woodhaven Drive, Hilton Head Island, SC 29928
Telephone: (803) 842-3747

Opened in 1982 • Mixed single-level and mid-rise buildings on 12 acres • Current resident population is 170 • Located 35 miles from Savannah, GA • Waiting list may apply for some units

HOUSING AND SERVICES

Living Units	No.	Square Feet	No. of Persons	Entrance Fee	Monthly Fee
Studio	20	467	1	$49,200–$55,000	$513
One Bedroom	47	700	1	$71,500–$78,500	$636
			2		$931
Two Bedroom	79	1,167–	1	$115,000–$149,000	$866
		1,400	2		$1,225
Larger Units	0	——	——	——	——
Total	146 Units				

Entrance fees include purchase of apartment as well as prepaid health care; resident may sell apartment at vacancy.

These fees include one meal per day and scheduled transportation. Special features of this community are presented in the Special Features Index at the back of the book. Ask about additional residential and health care services that may be available. Fees and services subject to change; verify with facility.

ASSISTED LIVING AND PERSONAL CARE

Assisted living units: 0
Personal care is covered by the continuing care contract: No
Residents may receive personal care in independent living units: No

NURSING CARE: Modified Plan

Under this modified plan, 15 or fewer days per year are covered by the continuing care contract. Thereafter, residents pay the full per diem rate for nursing care.

Dual-certified beds: 44. Cost per day: private $65.00–$70.00.

Nursing beds are certified by Medicare. Nonresidents may be admitted directly to the nursing care facility.

WESTHILLS VILLAGE
255 Texas Street, Rapid City, SD 57701
Telephone: (605) 342-0255

Opened in 1984 • Mixed single-level and low-rise buildings on 16 acres • Current resident population is 180 • Immediate availability

HOUSING AND SERVICES

Living Units	No.	Square Feet	No. of Persons	Entrance Fee	Monthly Fee
Studio	10	447	1	$40,500	$432
One Bedroom	65	526	1	$52,300	$486
			2	$52,300	$666
Two Bedroom	53	781–1,056	1, 2	rates vary	rates vary
Larger Units	73	1,376–1,400	1, 2	rates vary	rates vary
Total		201 Units			

Residents have a choice of entrance fee refund plans.

These fees include one meal per day, biweekly housekeeping, scheduled transportation, and utilities. Special features of this community are presented in the Special Features Index at the back of the book. Ask about additional residential and health care services that may be available. Fees and services subject to change; verify with facility.

ASSISTED LIVING AND PERSONAL CARE

Assisted living units: 44
Personal care is covered by the continuing care contract: Yes
Residents may receive personal care in independent living units: Yes
Nonresidents may be admitted directly to assisted living units: No

NURSING CARE: Modified Plan

Under this modified plan, a percentage of the cost of nursing care, as a credit based on the entrance fee, is covered by the continuing care contract. When in nursing care, residents pay any remaining balance.

Intermediate beds: 16. Cost per day: private $37.00, semi-private $34.00.

Skilled beds: 28. Cost per day: private $57.00, semi-private $54.00.

Nursing beds are certified by Medicare. Nonresidents may be admitted directly to the nursing care facility.

TENNESSEE

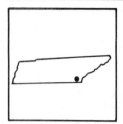

ALEXIAN VILLAGE OF TENNESSEE
100 James Boulevard, Signal Mountain, TN 37377
Telephone: (615) 870-0100

Opened in 1984 • Mixed single-level and low-rise buildings on 32 acres • Current resident population is 123 • Located eight miles from Chattanooga, TN • Waiting list may apply for some units

AAHA Member

HOUSING AND SERVICES

Living Units	No.	Square Feet	No. of Persons	Entrance Fee	Monthly Fee
Studio	26	414	1	$41,400	$537
One Bedroom	99	613	1	$64,400–$88,000	$589–$679
			2		$862–$952
Two Bedroom	54	941	1	$98,800	$689
			2		$962
Larger Units	20	941	1	$116,000	$948
			2		$1,221

Total 199 Units

Entrance fee refunds decline over time.

These fees include one meal per day, biweekly housekeeping, scheduled transportation, and utilities. Special features of this community are presented in the Special Features Index at the back of the book. Ask about additional residential and health care services that may be available. Fees and services subject to change; verify with facility.

ASSISTED LIVING AND PERSONAL CARE

Assisted living units: 0
Personal care is covered by the continuing care contract: No
Residents may receive personal care in independent living units: No

---

NURSING CARE: All-Inclusive Plan

Under this all-inclusive plan, unlimited nursing care is covered by the continuing care contract. When residents are in nursing care, they pay the same monthly fee they paid for their independent living unit.

Intermediate beds: 112. Cost per day: private $92.50, semi-private $52.00.

Skilled beds: 12. Cost per day: private $170.00, semi-private $85.00.

Nursing beds are certified by both Medicare and Medicaid. Nonresidents may be admitted directly to the nursing care facility.

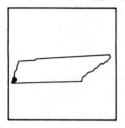

TREZEVANT MANOR AND ALLEN MORGAN NURSING CENTER
177 North Highland Street, Memphis, TN 38111
Telephone: (901) 452-4021

Opened in 1976 • One high-rise building on six acres • Current resident population is 200 • Waiting list may apply for some units

AAHA
Member

HOUSING AND SERVICES

Living Units	No.	Square Feet	No. of Persons	Entrance Fee	Monthly Fee
Studio	18	303	1	$29,769	$490
One Bedroom	99	538	1	$50,100	$560
			2	$54,100	$900
Two Bedroom	56	878	1	$85,433	$795
			2	$89,433	$1,135
Larger Units	3	1,338	1	$128,380	$1,356
			2	$132,300	$1,696

Total 176 Units

Entrance fee refunds decline over time.

These fees include one meal per day, biweekly housekeeping, scheduled transportation, and utilities. Special features of this community are presented in the Special Features Index at the back of the book. Ask about additional residential and health care services that may be available. Fees and services subject to change; verify with facility.

ASSISTED LIVING AND PERSONAL CARE

Assisted living units: 0
Personal care is covered by the continuing care contract: No
Residents may receive personal care in independent living units: No

NURSING CARE: All-Inclusive Plan

Under this all-inclusive plan, unlimited nursing care is covered by the continuing care contract. When residents are in nursing care, they pay the same monthly fee they paid for their independent living unit.

Skilled beds: 60. Cost per day: private $71.00, semi-private $51.00.

Nursing beds are certified by Medicare. Nonresidents may be admitted directly to the nursing care facility.

AIR FORCE VILLAGE
4917 Ravenswood Drive, San Antonio, TX 78227
Telephone: (512) 673-2761

Opened in 1970 • Mixed single-level, low-rise, and high-rise buildings on 21 acres • Current resident population is 580 • Waiting list

AAHA
Member

HOUSING AND SERVICES

Living Units	No.	Square Feet	No. of Persons	Entrance Fee	Monthly Fee
Studio	0	——	——	——	——
One Bedroom	166	410–725	1	$26,240–$49,300	$315–$557
Two Bedroom	210	870–1,100	1, 2	$50,285–$70,400	$669–$761
Larger Units	3	1,160–1,275	1, 2	$74,240–$81,600	$892–$980
Total	379 Units				

Entrance fee refunds decline over time.

These fees include weekly housekeeping, scheduled transportation, and utilities. Special features of this community are presented in the Special Features Index at the back of the book. Ask about additional residential and health care services that may be available. Fees and services subject to change; verify with facility.

ASSISTED LIVING AND PERSONAL CARE
Assisted living units: 0
Personal care is covered by the continuing care contract: No
Residents may receive personal care in independent living units: No

NURSING CARE: Fee-for-Service Plan

Under this fee-for-service plan, guaranteed access to nursing care is covered by the continuing care contract. Residents pay the full per diem rate for nursing care.

Intermediate beds: 68. Cost per day: private $33.00–$39.00, semi-private $25.00–$29.00.

Nursing beds are not certified by Medicare or Medicaid. Nonresidents may not be admitted directly to the nursing care facility.

BAYOU MANOR
4141 South Braeswood Boulevard, Houston, TX 77025
Telephone: (713) 666-2651

Opened in 1963 • Mixed single-level, low-rise, and high-rise buildings on six acres • Current resident population is 240 • Waiting list

AAHA
Member

HOUSING AND SERVICES

Living Units	No.	Square Feet	No. of Persons	Entrance Fee	Monthly Fee
Studio	115	377	1	$23,400	$730
One Bedroom	87	690	1	$40,000	$925
			2	$45,000	$1,270
Two Bedroom	8	1,125	1	$83,000	$1,290
			2	$83,000	$1,535
Larger Units	0	——	——	——	——
Total	210 Units				

Entrance fee refunds decline over time.

These fees include two meals per day, weekly housekeeping, scheduled transportation, and utilities. Special features of this community are presented in the Special Features Index at the back of the book. Ask about additional residential and health care services that may be available. Fees and services subject to change; verify with facility.

ASSISTED LIVING AND PERSONAL CARE

Assisted living units: 0
Personal care is covered by the continuing care contract: No
Residents may receive personal care in independent living units: No

NURSING CARE: Fee-for-Service Plan

Under this fee-for-service plan, guaranteed access to nursing care is covered by the continuing care contract. Residents pay the full per diem rate for nursing care.

Skilled beds: 25. Cost per day: private—not applicable, semi-private $34.00.

Nursing beds are not certified by Medicare or Medicaid. Nonresidents may not be admitted directly to the nursing care facility.

BUCKNER RETIREMENT VILLAGE
1101 East Braker Lane, Austin, TX 78753
Telephone: (512) 836-1515

Opening in 1988 • Predominantly single-level/garden apartments on 27 acres • Current resident population is 95 • Waiting list may apply for some units

**AAHA
Member**

HOUSING AND SERVICES

Living Units	No.	Square Feet	No. of Persons	Entrance Fee	Monthly Fee
Studio	0 —				
One Bedroom	0 —				
Two Bedroom	8	1,090	1	$85,000	$225
			2	$85,000	$250
Larger Units	0 —				
Total	8 Units				

Entrance fees are fully refundable.

These fees include monthly housekeeping, scheduled transportation, and utilities. Special features of this community are presented in the Special Features Index at the back of the book. Ask about additional residential and health care services that may be available. Fees and services subject to change; verify with facility.

ASSISTED LIVING AND PERSONAL CARE

Assisted living units: 30
Personal care is covered by the continuing care contract: No
Residents may receive personal care in independent living units: No
Nonresidents may be admitted directly to assisted living units: Yes

NURSING CARE: Fee-for-Service Plan

Under this fee-for-service plan, guaranteed access to nursing care is covered by the continuing care contract. Residents pay the full per diem rate for nursing care.

Intermediate beds: 123. Cost per day: private $60.00, semi-private $48.50.

Nursing beds are certified by Medicaid. Nonresidents may be admitted directly to the nursing care facility.

EDEN HOME
631 Lakeview Boulevard, New Braunfels, TX 78130
Telephone: (512) 625-6291

Opened in 1956 • Predominantly single-level/garden apartments on 60 acres • Current resident population is 213 • Waiting list

AAHA
Member

HOUSING AND SERVICES

Living Units	No.	Square Feet	No. of Persons	Entrance Fee	Monthly Fee
Studio	0	——	——	——	——
One Bedroom	8	815	1, 2	$33,000–$42,000	$75
Two Bedroom	16	1,019	1, 2	$46,000–$50,500	$75
Larger Units	0	——	——	——	——
Total	24 Units				

Entrance fees are partially refundable.

These fees include scheduled transportation. Special features of this community are presented in the Special Features Index at the back of the book. Ask about additional residential and health care services that may be available. Fees and services subject to change; verify with facility.

ASSISTED LIVING AND PERSONAL CARE

Assisted living units: 0
Personal care is covered by the continuing care contract: No
Residents may receive personal care in independent living units: No

NURSING CARE: Fee-for-Service Plan

Under this fee-for-service plan, guaranteed access to nursing care is covered by the continuing care contract. Residents pay the full per diem rate for nursing care.

Intermediate beds: 132. Cost per day: semi-private $40.00.

Skilled beds: 46. Cost per day: semi-private $50.00.

Nursing beds are certified by both Medicare and Medicaid. Nonresidents may be admitted directly to the nursing care facility.

GOOD SAMARITAN VILLAGE
2500 Hinkle Drive, Denton, TX 76201
Telephone: (817) 383-2651

Opened in 1976 • Mixed single-level, low-rise, and high-rise buildings on 27 acres • Current resident population is 295 • Immediate availability

AAHA
Member

HOUSING AND SERVICES

Living Units	No.	Square Feet	No. of Persons	Entrance Fee	Monthly Fee
Studio	30	450	1	$24,000	$460
One Bedroom	28	600	1	$35,000	$560
			2		$777
Two Bedroom	60	960	1	$45,000	$610
			2		$827
Larger Units	30	1,300	1, 2	$60,000	$230
Total		148 Units			

Entrance fee refunds decline over time.

These fees include one meal per day, housekeeping, scheduled transportation, and utilities. Special features of this community are presented in the Special Features Index at the back of the book. Ask about additional residential and health care services that may be available. Fees and services subject to change; verify with facility.

ASSISTED LIVING AND PERSONAL CARE

Assisted living units: 0
Personal care is covered by the continuing care contract: No
Residents may receive personal care in independent living units: No

NURSING CARE: Modified Plan

Under this modified plan, 15 or fewer days are covered by the continuing care contract. Once residents move permanently to the nursing unit, they pay the full per diem rate for nursing care.

Dual-certified beds: 92. Cost per day: semi-private $70.00.

Nursing beds are certified by both Medicare and Medicaid. Nonresidents may be admitted directly to the nursing care facility.

THE HALLMARK
4718 Hallmark, Houston, TX 77056
Telephone: (713) 622-6633

Opened in 1972 • Predominantly high-rise buildings on two acres • Current resident population is 176 • Waiting list may apply for some units

AAHA
Member

HOUSING AND SERVICES

Living Units	No.	Square Feet	No. of Persons	Entrance Fee	Monthly Fee
Studio	4	450	1	$22,500	$675
One Bedroom	84	900	1	$58,000	$1,025
			2	$64,000	$1,345
Two Bedroom	55	1,300	1	$97,000	$1,340
			2	$97,000	$1,660
Larger Units	9	1,750	1	$130,000	$1,695
			2	$130,000	$2,015

Total   152 Units

Entrance fee refunds decline over time.

These fees include one meal per day, weekly housekeeping, scheduled transportation, and utilities. Special features of this community are presented in the Special Features Index at the back of the book. Ask about additional residential and health care services that may be available. Fees and services subject to change; verify with facility.

ASSISTED LIVING AND PERSONAL CARE

Assisted living units: 0
Personal care is covered by the continuing care contract: No
Residents may receive personal care in independent living units: No

NURSING CARE: Modified Plan

Under this modified plan, 30–45 days are covered by the continuing care contract. Once residents move permanently to the nursing unit, they pay the full per diem rate for nursing care.

Intermediate beds: 42. Cost per day: private $57.00, semi-private $43.00.

Nursing beds are not certified by Medicare or Medicaid. Nonresidents may not be admitted directly to the nursing care facility.

JOHN KNOX VILLAGE OF THE RIO GRANDE VALLEY

1300 South Border Avenue, Weslaco, TX 78596
Telephone: (512) 968-4575

Opened in 1977 • Mixed single-level and low-rise buildings on 40 acres • Current resident population is 335 • Waiting list may apply for some units

AAHA
Member

HOUSING AND SERVICES

Living Units	No.	Square Feet	No. of Persons	Entrance Fee	Monthly Fee
Studio	74	350	1	$27,950	$519
One Bedroom	111	528–950	1	$40,950–$52,950	$438–$683
			2	$44,950–$55,950	$676–$1,007
Two Bedroom	66	792–925	1	$50,950–$56,950	$465–$699
			2	$53,950–$59,950	$703–$1,038
Larger Units	3	725–926	1	$55,950–$59,950	$759–$774
			2	$58,950–$62,950	$1,098–$1,545
Total	254 Units				

Entrance fee refunds decline over time.

These fees include housekeeping, scheduled transportation, and utilities. Special features of this community are presented in the Special Features Index at the back of the book. Ask about additional residential and health care services that may be available. Fees and services subject to change; verify with facility.

ASSISTED LIVING AND PERSONAL CARE

Assisted living units: 0
Personal care is covered by the continuing care contract: No
Residents may receive personal care in independent living units: Yes

NURSING CARE: All-Inclusive Plan

Under this all-inclusive plan, unlimited nursing care is covered by the continuing care contract. When residents are in nursing care, they pay the same monthly fee they paid for their independent living unit.

Skilled beds: 31. Cost per day: not applicable.

Nursing beds are certified by Medicare. Nonresidents may not be admitted directly to the nursing care facility.

JOHN KNOX VILLAGE OF WEST TEXAS
1717 Norfolk Street, Lubbock, TX 79416
Telephone: (806) 797-4305

Opened in 1976 • Mixed single-level, low-rise, and high-rise buildings on 26 acres • Current resident population is 400 • Waiting list may apply for some units

HOUSING AND SERVICES

Living Units	No.	Square Feet	No. of Persons	Entrance Fee	Monthly Fee
Studio	51	216	1	$11,500	$322
One Bedroom	214	561	1	$24,000	$411
			2		$553
Two Bedroom	89	790	1	$36,950	$499
			2		$657
Larger Units	0	—	—	—	—
Total	354 Units				

Entrance fee refunds decline over time.

These fees include biweekly housekeeping, scheduled transportation, and utilities. Special features of this community are presented in the Special Features Index at the back of the book. Ask about additional residential and health care services that may be available. Fees and services subject to change; verify with facility.

ASSISTED LIVING AND PERSONAL CARE

Assisted living units: 0
Personal care is covered by the continuing care contract: No
Residents may receive personal care in independent living units: No

NURSING CARE: Modified Plan

Under this modified plan, 60 days or more are covered by the continuing care contract. Once residents move permanently to the nursing unit, they pay $18.50 per day for nursing care.

Skilled beds: 60. Cost per day: private $75.00, semi-private $50.00.

Nursing beds are not certified by Medicare or Medicaid. Nonresidents may be admitted directly to the nursing care facility.

LAKEWOOD VILLAGE
5100 Randol Mill Road, Fort Worth, TX 76112
Telephone: (817) 451-8001

Opened in 1982 • Predominantly high-rise buildings on 36 acres • Current resident population is 167 • Waiting list may apply for some units

AAHA Member

HOUSING AND SERVICES

Living Units	No.	Square Feet	No. of Persons	Entrance Fee	Monthly Fee
Studio	5	380	1	$17,800	$330
One Bedroom	44	557	1	$31,640	$438
			2		$638
Two Bedroom	39	847	1	$44,680	$503
			2		$703
Larger Units	20	1,088	1	$58,000	$562
			2		$762
Total		108 Units			

Entrance fee refunds decline over time.

These fees include one meal per day, housekeeping, scheduled transportation, and utilities. Special features of this community are presented in the Special Features Index at the back of the book. Ask about additional residential and health care services that may be available. Fees and services subject to change; verify with facility.

ASSISTED LIVING AND PERSONAL CARE

Assisted living units: 0
Personal care is covered by the continuing care contract: No
Residents may receive personal care in independent living units: Yes

NURSING CARE: All-Inclusive Plan

Under this all-inclusive plan, unlimited nursing care is covered by the continuing care contract. When residents are in nursing care, they pay approximately the same monthly fee they paid for their independent living unit.

Skilled beds: 30. Cost per day: private—not applicable, semi-private $48.00.
Nursing beds are certified by Medicare. Nonresidents may be admitted directly to the nursing care facility.

TEXAS

MESA SPRINGS
4149 Forrest Hill Road, Abilene, TX 79605
Telephone: (915) 692-8080

Opening in 1987 • Mixed single-level and low-rise
buildings on 15 acres • Immediate availability

AAHA
Member

HOUSING AND SERVICES

Living Units	No.	Square Feet	No. of Persons	Entrance Fee	Monthly Fee
Studio	0	—	—	—	—
One Bedroom	4	717–958	1	$17,950–$22,950	$695–$895
			2	$17,950–$22,950	$895–$1,095
Two Bedroom	4	1,006–1,171	1	$23,450–$24,950	$895–$995
			2	$23,450–$24,950	$1,095–$1,195
Larger Units	2	1,282	1	$27,450	$1,250
			2	$27,450	$1,450
Total	10 Units				

Entrance fees are fully refundable.

These fees include one meal per day, weekly housekeeping, and scheduled transportation. Special features of this community are presented in the Special Features Index at the back of the book. Ask about additional residential and health care services that may be available. Fees and services subject to change; verify with facility.

ASSISTED LIVING AND PERSONAL CARE

Assisted living units: 0
Personal care is covered by the continuing care contract: Yes
Residents may receive personal care in independent living units: Yes

NURSING CARE: Fee-for-Service Plan

Under this fee-for-service plan, guaranteed access to nursing care is covered by the continuing care contract. Residents pay the full per diem rate for nursing care.

Intermediate beds: 90. Cost per day: private $60.00, semi-private $30.00.

Nursing beds are not certified by Medicare or Medicaid. Nonresidents may be admitted directly to the nursing care facility.

PRESBYTERIAN MANOR
4600 Taft Boulevard, Wichita Falls, TX 76308
Telephone: (817) 691-1710

Opened in 1980 • Mixed single-level and low-rise buildings on 13 acres • Current resident population is 275 • Long waiting list; make reservations in advance

AAHA
Member

HOUSING AND SERVICES

Living Units	No.	Square Feet	No. of Persons	Entrance Fee	Monthly Fee
Studio	49	344–516	1	$9,350–$13,750	$450–$555
One Bedroom	72	594–781	1	$16,500–$21,000	$530–$590
			2	$16,500–$21,000	$830–$905
Two Bedroom	79	957–1,031	1	$27,500	$350–$665
			2	$27,500	$485–$965
Larger Units	0	——	——	——	——
Total		200 Units			

Entrance fee refunds decline over time.

These fees include one meal per day, weekly housekeeping, scheduled transportation, and utilities. Special features of this community are presented in the Special Features Index at the back of the book. Ask about additional residential and health care services that may be available. Fees and services subject to change; verify with facility.

ASSISTED LIVING AND PERSONAL CARE

Assisted living units: 0
Personal care is covered by the continuing care contract: No
Residents may receive personal care in independent living units: No

NURSING CARE: Modified Plan

Under this modified plan, 15 or fewer days per year are covered by the continuing care contract. Once residents move permanently to the nursing unit, they pay the full per diem rate for nursing care.

Intermediate beds: 14. Cost per day: private $44.00.

Skilled beds: 43. Cost per day: private $50.50.

Nursing beds are not certified by Medicare or Medicaid. Nonresidents may not be admitted directly to the nursing care facility.

PRESBYTERIAN VILLAGE
550 East Ann Arbor, Dallas, TX 75216
Telephone: (214) 376-1701

Opened in 1962 • Mixed single-level and low-rise buildings on 20 acres • Current resident population is 330 • Waiting list may apply for some units

AAHA
Member

HOUSING AND SERVICES

Living Units	No.	Square Feet	No. of Persons	Entrance Fee	Monthly Fee
Studio	60	245	1	——	$745–$1,275
One Bedroom	25	500	1	$25,000–$30,000	$275–$288
			2		$320
Two Bedroom	15	900	1	$35,000–$37,000	$335
			2		$365
Larger Units	5	1,200	1	$53,000	$365
			2		$400
Total		105 Units			

Entrance fee refunds decline over time.

These fees include utilities. Special features of this community are presented in the Special Features Index at the back of the book. Ask about additional residential and health care services that may be available. Fees and services subject to change; verify with facility.

ASSISTED LIVING AND PERSONAL CARE

Assisted living units: 36
Personal care is covered by the continuing care contract: Yes
Residents may receive personal care in independent living units: No
Nonresidents may be admitted directly to assisted living units: Yes

NURSING CARE: Modified Plan

Under this modified plan, 16–59 days per year are covered by the continuing care contract. Thereafter, residents pay a discounted per diem rate for nursing care.

Intermediate beds: 125. Cost per day: private $54.08, semi-private $49.31.
Skilled beds: 35. Cost per day: private $64.11, semi-private $58.19.
Nursing beds are certified by both Medicare and Medicaid. Nonresidents may be admitted directly to the nursing care facility.

TEXAS

ROLLING MEADOWS
3006 McNeil, Wichita Falls, TX 76309
Telephone: (817) 691-7511

Opened in 1985 • Mixed single-level and low-rise buildings on 33 acres • Current resident population is 120 • Immediate availability

HOUSING AND SERVICES

Living Units	No.	Square Feet	No. of Persons	Entrance Fee	Monthly Fee
Studio	4	490	1	$32,000*	$794
One Bedroom	48	729	1	$49,500*	$1,077
			2		$1,477
Two Bedroom	64	975	1	$67,500*	$1,365
			2		$1,765
Larger Units	54	1,336	1	$75,000*	$1,525
			2		$1,925
Total		170 Units			

*These units are lease-purchased by means of the monthly fee over a period of eight years, four months. For example, the one-bedroom monthly fee of $1,077 represents a monthly payment of $582 toward rent plus a payment of $495 toward the purchase of the unit (equal to 1 percent of the purchase price of the contract).

Residents have a choice of entrance fee refund plans.

These fees include one meal per day, biweekly housekeeping, scheduled transportation, and utilities. Special features of this community are presented in the Special Features Index at the back of the book. Ask about additional residential and health care services that may be available. Fees and services subject to change; verify with facility.

ASSISTED LIVING AND PERSONAL CARE

Assisted living units: 8
Personal care is covered by the continuing care contract: Yes
Residents may receive personal care in independent living units: Yes
Nonresidents may be admitted directly to assisted living units: Yes

NURSING CARE: Modified Plan

Under this modified plan, 16–59 days per year are covered by the continuing care contract. Once residents move permanently to the nursing unit, they pay the full per diem rate for nursing care.

Intermediate beds.* Cost per day: private $67.50, semi-private $45.00.

Skilled beds.* Cost per day: private $75.00, semi-private $50.00.

Dual-certified beds.* Cost per day: private $60.00, semi-private $40.00.

*There are a total of 76 beds.

Nursing beds are not certified by Medicare or Medicaid. Nonresidents may be admitted directly to the nursing care facility.

TRINITY TERRACE
1600 Texas Street, Fort Worth, TX 76102
Telephone: (817) 338-2400

Opened in 1983 • One high-rise building on 2 acres • Current resident population is 338 • Waiting list may apply for some units

AAHA
Member

HOUSING AND SERVICES

Living Units	No.	Square Feet	No. of Persons	Entrance Fee	Monthly Fee
Studio	107	——	1	$25,650–$35,900	$579–$692
One Bedroom	125	——	1	$55,150	$692
			2	$58,150	$1,051
Two Bedroom	62	——	1	$76,950	$772
			2	$79,950	$1,131
Larger Units	0	——	——	——	——
Total	294 Units				

Entrance fee refunds decline over time.

These fees include one meal per day, biweekly housekeeping, scheduled transportation, and utilities. Special features of this community are presented in the Special Features Index at the back of the book. Ask about additional residential and health care services that may be available. Fees and services subject to change; verify with facility.

ASSISTED LIVING AND PERSONAL CARE

Assisted living units: 0
Personal care is covered by the continuing care contract: No
Residents may receive personal care in independent living units: No

NURSING CARE: All-Inclusive Plan

Under this all-inclusive plan, unlimited nursing care is covered by the continuing care contract. When residents are in nursing care, they pay the same monthly fee they paid for their independent living unit.

Skilled beds: 60. Cost per day: private $110.00, semi-private $67.50.

Nursing beds are not certified by Medicare or Medicaid. Nonresidents may be admitted directly to the nursing care facility.

TRINITY TOWERS MANOR PARK
2208 North Loop 250 West, Midland, TX 79707
Telephone: (915) 689-9898

Opened in 1983 • Mixed single-level and low-rise buildings on 40 acres • Current resident population is 170 • Immediate availability

AAHA
Member

HOUSING AND SERVICES

Living Units	No.	Square Feet	No. of Persons	Entrance Fee	Monthly Fee
Studio	8	516	1	$34,250–$35,750	$275–$440
One Bedroom	40	693–882	1	$44,500–$72,500	$320–$520
			2	$44,500–$72,500	$380–$690
Two Bedroom	71	1,078–1,336	1	$82,000–$109,000	$400–$595
			2	$82,000–$109,000	$460–$765
Larger Units	4	2,390	1	$196,500	$535
			2	$196,500	$595
Total	123 Units				

Prospective residents should inquire about the entrance fee refund plan.

These fees include weekly housekeeping. Special features of this community are presented in the Special Features Index at the back of the book. Ask about additional residential and health care services that may be available. Fees and services subject to change; verify with facility.

ASSISTED LIVING AND PERSONAL CARE

Assisted living units: 180.
Personal care is covered by the continuing care contract: No
Residents may receive personal care in independent living units: No
Nonresidents may be admitted directly to assisted living units: No

NURSING CARE: Modified Plan

Under this modified plan, 15 or fewer days are covered by the continuing care contract. Once residents move permanently to the nursing unit, they pay the full per diem rate for nursing care.

Intermediate beds: 120. Cost per day: private $50.00, semi-private $35.00.

Nursing beds are not certified by Medicare or Medicaid. Nonresidents may not be admitted directly to the nursing care facility.

WESTMINSTER MANOR
4100 Jackson Avenue, Austin, TX 78731
Telephone: (512) 454-4711

Opened in 1967 • One high-rise building on four
acres • Current resident population is 374 • Waiting
list may apply for some units

AAHA
Member

HOUSING AND SERVICES

Living Units	No.	Square Feet	No. of Persons	Entrance Fee	Monthly Fee
Studio	92	400	1	$32,628	$711
One Bedroom	147	600	1	$47,883	$861
			2		$1,307
Two Bedroom	64	880	1	$63,933	$1,008
			2		$1,454
Larger Units	0	—	—	—	—
Total		303 Units			

Entrance fee refunds decline over time.

These fees include one meal per day, weekly housekeeping, scheduled transportation, and utilities. Special features of this community are presented in the Special Features Index at the back of the book. Ask about additional residential and health care services that may be available. Fees and services subject to change; verify with facility.

ASSISTED LIVING AND PERSONAL CARE

Assisted living units: 0
Personal care is covered by the continuing care contract: Yes
Residents may receive personal care in independent living units: Yes

NURSING CARE: All-Inclusive Plan

Under this all-inclusive plan, unlimited nursing care is covered by the continuing care contract. When residents are in nursing care, they pay the same monthly fee they paid for their independent living unit.

Dual-certified beds: 90. Cost per day: private $74.00, semi-private $58.00.

Nursing beds are certified by Medicare. Nonresidents may be admitted directly to the nursing care facility.

BRANDERMILL WOODS

2203 Birch Glen Court, Midlothian, VA 23113
Telephone: (804) 744-1173

Opened in 1986 • Mixed single-level and low-rise buildings on 30 acres • Located 13 miles from Richmond, VA • Waiting list may apply for some units

HOUSING AND SERVICES

Living Units	No.	Square Feet	No. of Persons	Entrance Fee	Monthly Fee
Studio	0	—	—	—	—
One Bedroom	32	823–915	1	$74,900–$79,900	$575
			2	$74,900–$79,900	$725
Two Bedroom	108	1,020–1,078	1	$89,900–$96,900	$600
			2	$89,900–$96,900	$750
Larger Units	40	1,321–1,348	1	$115,000–$121,000	$625
			2	$115,000–$121,000	$725
Total	180 Units				

Entrance fees are fully refundable.

These fees include scheduled transportation and utilities. Special features of this community are presented in the Special Features Index at the back of the book. Ask about additional residential and health care services that may be available. Fees and services subject to change; verify with facility.

ASSISTED LIVING AND PERSONAL CARE

Assisted living units: 60
Personal care is covered by the continuing care contract: Yes
Residents may receive personal care in independent living units: Yes
Nonresidents may be admitted directly to assisted living units: No

NURSING CARE: Modified Plan

Under this modified plan, 16–59 days per year are covered by the continuing care contract. Once residents move permanently to the nursing unit, they pay the full per diem rate for nursing care.

Intermediate beds: 30. Cost per day: semi-private $52.00.

Skilled beds: 30. Cost per day: semi-private $65.00.

Nursing beds are certified by both Medicare and Medicaid. Nonresidents may be admitted directly to the nursing care facility.

GOODWIN HOUSE
4800 Fillmore Avenue, Alexandria, VA 22311
Telephone: (703) 578-1000

Opened in 1967 • One high-rise building on eight acres • Current resident population is 347 • Waiting list • Accredited by the Continuing Care Accreditation Commission

AAHA
Member

HOUSING AND SERVICES

Living Units	No.	Square Feet	No. of Persons	Entrance Fee	Monthly Fee
Studio	216	238	1	$39,000–$68,000	$850–$889
One Bedroom	62	401	1	$76,000	$963
			2	$76,000	$1,655
Two Bedroom	0	——	——	——	——
Larger Units	0	——	——	——	——
Total	278 Units				

Entrance fee refunds decline over time.

These fees include three meals per day, weekly housekeeping, and utilities. Special features of this community are presented in the Special Features Index at the back of the book. Ask about additional residential and health care services that may be available. Fees and services subject to change; verify with facility.

ASSISTED LIVING AND PERSONAL CARE

Assisted living units: 0
Personal care is covered by the continuing care contract: No
Residents may receive personal care in independent living units: Yes

NURSING CARE: All-Inclusive Plan

Under this all-inclusive plan, unlimited nursing care is covered by the continuing care contract. When residents are in nursing care, they pay the same monthly fee they paid for their independent living unit.

Intermediate beds: 34. Cost per day: private—not applicable, semi-private $65.00.

Skilled beds: 60. Cost per day: private—not applicable, semi-private $86.00.

Nursing beds are certified by both Medicare and Medicaid. The nursing unit is accredited by the Joint Commission on Accreditation of Hospitals. Nonresidents may be admitted directly to the nursing care facility.

GOODWIN HOUSE WEST
c/o Goodwin House, 4800 Fillmore Avenue
Alexandria, VA 22311
Telephone: (703) 824-1187

Opened in 1987 • One high-rise building on eight acres • Waiting list may apply for some units

AAHA Member

HOUSING AND SERVICES

Living Units	No.	Square Feet	No. of Persons	Entrance Fee	Monthly Fee
Studio	69	367	1	$56,700	$1,050
One Bedroom	213	570–932	1	$79,300–$93,500	$1,200–$1,250
			2	$79,300–$93,500	$2,000–$2,050
Two Bedroom	38	903	1	$136,000	$1,600
			2	$136,000	$2,400
Larger Units	0	—	—	—	—
Total	320 Units				

Entrance fee refunds decline over time.

These fees include three meals per day, weekly housekeeping, and utilities. Special features of this community are presented in the Special Features Index at the back of the book. Ask about additional residential and health care services that may be available. Fees and services subject to change; verify with facility.

ASSISTED LIVING AND PERSONAL CARE

Assisted living units: 60
Personal care is covered by the continuing care contract: Yes
Residents may receive personal care in independent living units: No
Nonresidents may be admitted directly to assisted living units: Yes

NURSING CARE: All-Inclusive Plan

Under this all-inclusive plan, unlimited nursing care is covered by the continuing care contract. When residents are in nursing care, they pay the same monthly fee they paid for their independent living unit.

Skilled beds: 72. Cost per day: not applicable.*

*Nursing center under construction; nonresident rates not yet set.

Nursing beds will be certified by both Medicare and Medicaid. Nonresidents may be admitted directly to the nursing care facility.

THE HERMITAGE
1600 Westwood Avenue, Richmond, VA 23227
Telephone: (804) 355-5721

Opened in 1949 • Mixed single-level and low-rise buildings on eight acres • Current resident population is 356 • Waiting list may apply for some units

AAHA Member

HOUSING AND SERVICES

Living Units	No.	Square Feet	No. of Persons	Entrance Fee	Monthly Fee
Studio	210	168	1	$30,000	$805
One Bedroom	11	336	1	$49,000	$1,207
			2	$49,000	$1,610
Two Bedroom	0	——	——	——	——
Larger Units	0	——	——	——	——
Total	221 Units				

Residents have a choice of entrance fee refund plans.

These fees include three meals per day, housekeeping, scheduled transportation, and utilities. Special features of this community are presented in the Special Features Index at the back of the book. Ask about additional residential and health care services that may be available. Fees and services subject to change; verify with facility.

ASSISTED LIVING AND PERSONAL CARE

Assisted living units: 41
Personal care is covered by the continuing care contract: Yes
Residents may receive personal care in independent living units: No
Nonresidents may be admitted directly to assisted living units: Yes

NURSING CARE: All-Inclusive Plan

Under this all-inclusive plan, unlimited nursing care is covered by the continuing care contract. When residents are in nursing care, they pay the basic monthly fee for the studio (smallest) unit after 30 free days.

Intermediate beds: 115. Cost per day: private $64.66, semi-private $58.00.

Nursing beds are not certified by Medicare or Medicaid. Nonresidents may be admitted directly to the nursing care facility.

HERMITAGE IN NORTHERN VIRGINIA
5000 Fairbanks Avenue, Alexandria, VA 22311
Telephone: (703) 820-2434

Opened in 1962 • Predominantly high-rise buildings
on 17 acres • Current resident population is 278 •
Waiting list may apply for some units

AAHA
Member

HOUSING AND SERVICES

Living Units	No.	Square Feet	No. of Persons	Entrance Fee	Monthly Fee
Studio	148	313	1	$34,000	$755
One Bedroom	39	518	1	$51,000	$960
			2	$51,000	$1,300
Two Bedroom	0	——	——	——	——
Larger Units	0	——	——	——	——
Total	187 Units				

Entrance fee refunds decline over time.

These fees include three meals per day, weekly housekeeping, and utilities. Special features of this community are presented in the Special Features Index at the back of the book. Ask about additional residential and health care services that may be available. Fees and services subject to change; verify with facility.

ASSISTED LIVING AND PERSONAL CARE

Assisted living units: 109
Personal care is covered by the continuing care contract: Yes
Residents may receive personal care in independent living units: Yes
Nonresidents may be admitted directly to assisted living units: Yes

---

NURSING CARE: Modified Plan

Under this modified plan, 16–59 days are covered by the continuing care contract. Once residents move permanently to the nursing unit, they pay 70 percent of the per diem rate for nursing care.

Dual-certified beds: 109. Cost per day: private $85.00, semi-private $75.00.

Nursing beds are not certified by Medicare or Medicaid. Nonresidents may be admitted directly to the nursing care facility.

VIRGINIA

HERMITAGE ON THE EASTERN SHORE
North Street Extended, Onancock, VA 23417
Telephone: (804) 787-4343

Opened in 1966 • Predominantly single-level/garden apartments on 70 acres • Current resident population is 106 • Waiting list

AAHA
Member

HOUSING AND SERVICES

Living Units	No.	Square Feet	No. of Persons	Entrance Fee	Monthly Fee
Studio	52	316	1	$31,900	$795
One Bedroom	10	632	1	$53,000	$1,192
			2	$53,000	$1,500
Two Bedroom	0	—	—	—	—
Larger Units	0	—	—	—	—
Total		62 Units			

Entrance fee refunds decline over time.

These fees include three meals per day, housekeeping, scheduled transportation, and utilities. Special features of this community are presented in the Special Features Index at the back of the book. Ask about additional residential and health care services that may be available. Fees and services subject to change; verify with facility.

ASSISTED LIVING AND PERSONAL CARE

Assisted living units: 8
Personal care is covered by the continuing care contract: Yes
Residents may receive personal care in independent living units: No
Nonresidents may be admitted directly to assisted living units: Yes

NURSING CARE: Modified Plan

Under this modified plan, 16–59 days per year are covered by the continuing care contract. Once residents move permanently to the nursing unit, they pay the full per diem rate for nursing care.

Intermediate beds: 35. Cost per day: private $67.00, semi-private $67.00.

Nursing beds are not certified by Medicare or Medicaid. Nonresidents may be admitted directly to the nursing care facility.

LAKEWOOD MANOR BAPTIST RETIREMENT COMMUNITY
1900 Lauderdale Drive, Richmond, VA 23233
Telephone: (804) 740-2900

Opened in 1977 • Mixed single-level and low-rise buildings on 68 acres • Current resident population is 374 • Waiting list

AAHA Member

HOUSING AND SERVICES

Living Units	No.	Square Feet	No. of Persons	Entrance Fee	Monthly Fee
Studio	160	411–472	1	$35,000–$40,500	$830–$935
One Bedroom	90	472–615	1	$42,000–$48,000	$935–$1,155
			2	$55,000	$1,533
Two Bedroom	45	874–937	1	$58,000–$60,000	$1,302
			2	$65,000–$67,000	$1,827
Larger Units	0	—	—	—	—
Total	295 Units				

Entrance fee refunds decline over time.

These fees include one meal per day, biweekly housekeeping, scheduled transportation, and utilities. Special features of this community are presented in the Special Features Index at the back of the book. Ask about additional residential and health care services that may be available. Fees and services subject to change; verify with facility.

ASSISTED LIVING AND PERSONAL CARE

Assisted living units: 0
Personal care is covered by the continuing care contract: No
Residents may receive personal care in independent living units: No

NURSING CARE: All-Inclusive Plan

Under this all-inclusive plan, unlimited nursing care is covered by the continuing care contract. When residents are in nursing care, they pay the same monthly fee they paid for their independent living unit.

Intermediate beds: 110. Cost per day: not applicable.

Nursing beds are not certified by Medicare or Medicaid. Nonresidents may not be admitted directly to the nursing care facility.

NEWPORT NEWS BAPTIST RETIREMENT COMMUNITY
P.O. Box 6010, Newport News, VA 23606
Telephone: (804) 599-4376

Opened in 1969 • Predominantly high-rise buildings on 34 acres • Current resident population is 239 • Waiting list may apply for some units

AAHA Member

HOUSING AND SERVICES

Living Units	No.	Square Feet	No. of Persons	Entrance Fee	Monthly Fee
Studio	182	190	1	$25,000	$655
One Bedroom	0	—			
Two Bedroom	14	366	1, 2	$40,000	$1,175
Larger Units	0	—			
Total		196 Units			

Residents have a choice of entrance fee refund plans.

These fees include three meals per day, weekly housekeeping, scheduled transportation, and utilities. Special features of this community are presented in the Special Features Index at the back of the book. Ask about additional residential and health care services that may be available. Fees and services subject to change; verify with facility.

ASSISTED LIVING AND PERSONAL CARE

Assisted living units: 18
Personal care is covered by the continuing care contract: No
Residents may receive personal care in independent living units: Yes
Nonresidents may be admitted directly to assisted living units: No

NURSING CARE: Modified Plan

Under this modified plan, 16–59 days per year are covered by the continuing care contract. Once residents move permanently to the nursing unit, they pay the full per diem rate for nursing care.

Intermediate beds: 52. Cost per day: private $60.00, semi-private $60.00.

Nursing beds are certified by Medicaid. Nonresidents may not be admitted directly to the nursing care facility.

VIRGINIA

RAPPAHANNOCK WESTMINSTER-CANTERBURY
P.O. Box 300, Irvington, VA 22480
Telephone: (804) 438-4000

Opened in 1985 • Mixed single-level and low-rise buildings on 113 acres • Current resident population is 88 • Located 75 miles from Richmond, VA • Waiting list may apply for some units

AAHA
Member

HOUSING AND SERVICES

Living Units	No.	Square Feet	No. of Persons	Entrance Fee	Monthly Fee
Studio	15	636–684	1	$58,200–$102,900	$1,020–$1,740
One Bedroom	48	852–853	1	$91,200	$1,315–$1,330
			2	$119,100–$121,500	$1,910–$1,925
Two Bedroom	55	1,077–	1	$109,600–$116,700	$1,488–$1,578
		1,094	2	$140,000–$149,050	$2,083–$2,173
Larger Units	0	—	—	—	—
Total	118 Units				

Entrance fee refunds decline over time.

These fees include three meals per day, housekeeping, scheduled transportation, and utilities. Special features of this community are presented in the Special Features Index at the back of the book. Ask about additional residential and health care services that may be available. Fees and services subject to change; verify with facility.

ASSISTED LIVING AND PERSONAL CARE

Assisted living units: 26
Personal care is covered by the continuing care contract: Yes
Residents may receive personal care in independent living units: No
Nonresidents may be admitted directly to assisted living units: Yes

NURSING CARE: All-Inclusive Plan

Under this all-inclusive plan, unlimited nursing care is covered by the continuing care contract. When residents are in nursing care, they pay the same monthly fee they paid for their independent living unit.

Intermediate beds: 24. Cost per day: private $91.00, semi-private $82.00.

Skilled beds: 10. Cost per day: private $97.00, semi-private $89.00.

Nursing beds are certified by both Medicare and Medicaid. Nonresidents may be admitted directly to the nursing care facility.

VIRGINIA

ROANOKE UNITED METHODIST HOME
P.O. Box 6339, Roanoke, VA 24017
Telephone: (703) 344-6248

Opened in 1964 • Mixed single-level and low-rise buildings on 11 acres • Current resident population is 150 • Waiting list

AAHA
Member

HOUSING AND SERVICES

Living Units	No.	Square Feet	No. of Persons	Entrance Fee	Monthly Fee
Studio	66	255–300	1	$30,000	$750
One Bedroom	4	729	1	$35,000	$200
Two Bedroom	22	942–1,024	1, 2	$65,000	$300
Larger Units	2	2,334–2,774	1, 2	$65,000	$300

Total 94 Units

Entrance fee refunds decline over time.

These fees include weekly housekeeping, scheduled transportation, and utilities. Special features of this community are presented in the Special Features Index at the back of the book. Ask about additional residential and health care services that may be available. Fees and services subject to change; verify with facility.

ASSISTED LIVING AND PERSONAL CARE

Assisted living units: 8
Personal care is covered by the continuing care contract: Yes
Residents may receive personal care in independent living units: No
Nonresidents may be admitted directly to assisted living units: Yes

NURSING CARE: Modified Plan

Under this modified plan, 30 days per year are covered by the continuing care contract. Thereafter, residents pay a discounted per diem rate for nursing care.

Intermediate beds: 40. Cost per day: private—not applicable, semi-private $50.00.

Nursing beds are not certified by Medicare or Medicaid. Nonresidents may be admitted directly to the nursing care facility.

VIRGINIA

SUNNYSIDE PRESBYTERIAN HOME
P.O. Box 928, Harrisonburg, VA 22801
Telephone: (703) 434-3801

Opened in 1955 • Mixed single-level and low-rise buildings on 57 acres • Current resident population is 305 • Waiting list

AAHA
Member

HOUSING AND SERVICES

Living Units	No.	Square Feet	No. of Persons	Entrance Fee	Monthly Fee
Studio	14	353–556	1	$37,900	$590
One Bedroom	20	490–867	1	$35,000–$54,000	$615
			2	$40,000–$59,000	$800
Two Bedroom	9	744–1,090	1	$67,900	$980
			2	$72,900	$1,190
Larger Units	30	940–1,190	1	$50,000	$100*
			2	$58,000	$100*

Total   73 Units

*Fee includes building maintenance only.
Entrance fee refunds decline over time.

These fees include one meal per day, weekly housekeeping, and scheduled transportation. Special features of this community are presented in the Special Features Index at the back of the book. Ask about additional residential and health care services that may be available. Fees and services subject to change; verify with facility.

ASSISTED LIVING AND PERSONAL CARE

Assisted living units: 10
Personal care is covered by the continuing care contract: No
Residents may receive personal care in independent living units: No
Nonresidents may be admitted directly to assisted living units: No

NURSING CARE: Modified Plan

Under this modified plan, 60 days or more of nursing care are covered by the continuing care contract because the unamortized entrance fee prepays nursing care. Once residents move permanently to the nursing unit and the entrance fee credit is exhausted, they pay the full per diem rate for nursing care.

Intermediate beds: 100. Cost per day: private $68.00, semi-private $62.00.
Nursing beds are certified by Medicaid. Nonresidents may be admitted directly to the nursing care facility.

THE VIRGINIAN
9229 Arlington Boulevard, Fairfax, VA 22031
Telephone: (703) 385-0555

Opened in 1980 • One high-rise building on 33 acres • Current resident population is 255 • Waiting list may apply for some units

AAHA
Member

HOUSING AND SERVICES

Living Units	No.	Square Feet	No. of Persons	Entrance Fee	Monthly Fee
Studio	0	——	——	——	——
One Bedroom	225	——	1	$69,000–$70,500	$987
			2	$97,000	$1,605
Two Bedroom	10	——	1	$78,000	$1,477
			2	$97,125	$2,046
Larger Units	24	——	1	$82,500	$1,530
			2	$102,125	$2,100

Total   259 Units

Entrance fee refunds decline over time.

These fees include two meals per day, biweekly housekeeping, scheduled transportation, and utilities. Special features of this community are presented in the Special Features Index at the back of the book. Ask about additional residential and health care services that may be available. Fees and services subject to change; verify with facility.

ASSISTED LIVING AND PERSONAL CARE

Assisted living units: 0
Personal care is covered by the continuing care contract: No
Residents may receive personal care in independent living units: No

NURSING CARE: Modified Plan

Under this modified plan, residents pay the per diem rate for nursing care. Nonresidents admitted to the nursing unit pay a higher rate.

Skilled beds: 100. Cost per day: semi-private $50.00.

Nursing beds are not certified by Medicare or Medicaid. Nonresidents may be admitted directly to the nursing care facility.

WARWICK FOREST
c/o Riverside Healthcare Association
606 Denbigh Boulevard, Suite 601
Newport News, VA 23602
Telephone: (804) 875-7500

Opened in 1987 • Mixed single-level and low-rise
buildings on ten acres • Immediate availability

HOUSING AND SERVICES

Living Units	No.	Square Feet	No. of Persons	Entrance Fee	Monthly Fee
Studio	6	500	1	$40,000–$90,000	$800–$1,500
One Bedroom	14	700	1, 2	$40,000–$90,000	$800–$1,500
Two Bedroom	30	900	1, 2	$40,000–$90,000	$800–$1,500
Larger Units	0	——	——	——	——
Total	50 Units				

Entrance fee refunds decline over time.

These fees include one meal per day, biweekly housekeeping, and utilities. Special features of this community are presented in the Special Features Index at the back of the book. Ask about additional residential and health care services that may be available. Fees and services subject to change; verify with facility.

ASSISTED LIVING AND PERSONAL CARE

Assisted living units: 0
Personal care is covered by the continuing care contract: No
Residents may receive personal care in independent living units: No

NURSING CARE: Modified Plan

Under this modified plan, nursing care is initially covered in the continuing care contract by a percentage of the resident's entrance fee. Residents pay the full per diem rate for nursing care once the entry fee credit is exhausted.

Intermediate beds: 300. Cost per day: private $79.00, semi-private $76.00.

Skilled beds: 65. Cost per day: private $89.00, semi-private $85.00.

Nursing beds are certified by both Medicare and Medicaid. The nursing unit is accredited by the Joint Commission on Accreditation of Hospitals. Nonresidents may be admitted directly to the nursing care facility.

THE WASHINGTON HOUSE
5100 Fillmore Avenue, Alexandria, VA 22311
Telephone: (703) 379-9000

Opened in 1972 • One high-rise building on five acres • Current resident population is 235 • Waiting list may apply for some units

AAHA Member

HOUSING AND SERVICES

Living Units	No.	Square Feet	No. of Persons	Entrance Fee	Monthly Fee
Studio	91	234–247	1	$43,000	$737
One Bedroom	70	398–449	1,2	$57,000	$899
Two Bedroom	24	580–737	1,2	$92,500	$1,202
Larger Units	0	——	——	——	——
Total	185 Units				

Entrance fee refunds decline over time.

These fees include two meals per day, biweekly housekeeping, and utilities. Special features of this community are presented in the Special Features Index at the back of the book. Ask about additional residential and health care services that may be available. Fees and services subject to change; verify with facility.

ASSISTED LIVING AND PERSONAL CARE

Assisted living units: 0
Personal care is covered by the continuing care contract: No
Residents may receive personal care in independent living units: Yes

NURSING CARE: Fee-for-Service Plan

Under this fee-for-service plan, guaranteed access to nursing care is covered by the continuing care contract. Residents pay $1,463 per month for nursing care, a discount of one-third off the per diem rate for nonresidents.

Intermediate beds: 17. Cost per day: private $85.00, semi-private $75.00.

Skilled beds: 28. Cost per day: private $85.00, semi-private $75.00.

Dual-certified beds: 23. Cost per day: private $85.00, semi-private $75.00.

Nursing beds are not certified by Medicare or Medicaid. Nonresidents may be admitted directly to the nursing care facility.

WESTMINSTER CANTERBURY HOUSE
1600 Westbrook Avenue, Richmond, VA 23227
Telephone: (804) 264-6000

Opened in 1975 • Mixed low-rise and high-rise buildings on 25 acres • Current resident population is 612 • Waiting list • Accredited by the AAHA Continuing Care Accreditation Commission

AAHA Member

HOUSING AND SERVICES

Living Units	No.	Square Feet	No. of Persons	Entrance Fee	Monthly Fee
Studio	250	380–522	1	$49,700–$56,700	$877–$994
One Bedroom	95	571–1,044	1	$59,100–$87,200	$1,033–$1,349
			2	$85,700–$126,500	$1,498–$1,956
Two Bedroom	30	810	1	$72,000	$1,201
			2	$104,400	$1,741
Larger Units	0	—	—	—	—
Total	375 Units				

Entrance fee refunds decline over time.

These fees include three meals per day, weekly housekeeping, and utilities. Special features of this community are presented in the Special Features Index at the back of the book. Ask about additional residential and health care services that may be available. Fees and services subject to change; verify with facility.

ASSISTED LIVING AND PERSONAL CARE

Assisted living units: 130
Personal care is covered by the continuing care contract: Yes
Residents may receive personal care in independent living units: No
Nonresidents may be admitted directly to assisted living units: Yes

NURSING CARE: All-Inclusive Plan

Under this all-inclusive plan, unlimited nursing care is covered by the continuing care contract. When in nursing care, residents pay the same monthly fee they paid for their independent living unit.

Intermediate beds: 74. Cost per day: private $99.00, semi-private—not applicable.

Skilled beds: 59. Cost per day: private $112.00, semi-private—not applicable.

Nursing beds are certified by both Medicare and Medicaid. Nonresidents may be admitted directly to the nursing care facility.

VIRGINIA

WESTMINSTER-CANTERBURY OF LYNCHBURG
501 Virginia Episcopal School Road
Lynchburg, VA 24503
Telephone: (804) 386-3500

Opened in 1980 • Predominantly high-rise buildings on 21 acres • Current resident population is 370 • Waiting list • Accredited by the AAHA Continuing Care Accreditation Commission

HOUSING AND SERVICES

Living Units	No.	Square Feet	No. of Persons	Entrance Fee	Monthly Fee
Studio	121	423–598	1	$46,350–$62,700	$808–$905
One Bedroom	66	684–846	1	$72,500–$92,700	$984–$1,132
			2	$72,500–$92,700	$1,462–$1,501
Two Bedroom	23	846–1,107	1	$92,700–$120,000	$1,132–$1,411
			2	$92,700–$120,000	$1,501–$1,683
Larger Units	0	—	—	—	—
Total	210 Units				

Entrance fee refunds decline over time.

These fees include three meals per day, weekly housekeeping, and utilities. Special features of this community are presented in the Special Features Index at the back of the book. Ask about additional residential and health care services that may be available. Fees and services subject to change; verify with facility.

ASSISTED LIVING AND PERSONAL CARE

Assisted living units: 40
Personal care is covered by the continuing care contract: Yes
Residents may receive personal care in independent living units: No
Nonresidents may be admitted directly to assisted living units: Yes

NURSING CARE: All-Inclusive Plan

Under this all-inclusive plan, unlimited nursing care is covered by the continuing care contract. When in nursing care, residents pay the same monthly fee they paid for their independent living unit.

Intermediate beds: 61. Cost per day: private $93.00, semi-private $62.00.

Skilled beds: 19. Cost per day: private $105.50, semi-private $67.00.

Nursing beds are certified by both Medicare and Medicaid. Nonresidents may be admitted directly to the nursing care facility.

WESTMINSTER-CANTERBURY IN VIRGINIA BEACH

3100 Shore Drive, Virginia Beach, VA 23451
Telephone: (804) 496-1100

Opened in 1982 • Mixed single-level, low-rise, and high-rise buildings on 14 acres • Current resident population is 461 • Waiting list may apply for some units • Accredited by the AAHA Continuing Care Accreditation Commission

AAHA
Member

HOUSING AND SERVICES

Living Units	No.	Square Feet	No. of Persons	Entrance Fee	Monthly Fee
Studio	158	432	1	$54,900–$72,100	$689–$1,126
One Bedroom	124	750	1	$90,400–$103,800	$922–$1,052
			2	$90,400–$103,800	$1,250–$1,380
Two Bedroom	57	1,048	1	$120,500–$146,500	$1,101–$1,285
			2	$120,500–$146,500	$1,429–$1,613
Larger Units	0	—	—	—	—
Total	339 Units				

Entrance fee refunds decline over time.

These fees include one meal per day, weekly housekeeping, and utilities. Special features of this community are presented in the Special Features Index at the back of the book. Ask about additional residential and health care services that may be available. Fees and services subject to change; verify with facility.

ASSISTED LIVING AND PERSONAL CARE

Assisted living units: 36
Personal care is covered by the continuing care contract: Yes
Residents may receive personal care in independent living units: No
Nonresidents may be admitted directly to assisted living units: Yes

NURSING CARE: All-Inclusive Plan

Under this all-inclusive plan, unlimited nursing care is covered by the continuing care contract. When residents are in nursing care, they pay the same monthly fee they paid for their independent living unit.

Intermediate beds: 46. Cost per day: private $105.00, semi-private $72.50.

Skilled beds: 15. Cost per day: private $140.00, semi-private $94.00.

Nursing beds are certified by both Medicare and Medicaid. Nonresidents may be admitted directly to the nursing care facility.

WESTMINSTER-CANTERBURY OF WINCHESTER
956 Westminster Canterbury Drive
Winchester, VA 22601
Telephone: (703) 665-0156

Opened in 1986 • One high-rise building on 40 acres
• Current resident population is 73 • Immediate
availability

AAHA
Member

HOUSING AND SERVICES

Living Units	No.	Square Feet	No. of Persons	Entrance Fee	Monthly Fee
Studio	21	485	1	$67,800	$1,002
One Bedroom	51	709	1	$91,700	$1,181
			2	$123,000	$1,755
Two Bedroom	25	970	1	$110,000	$1,390
			2	$143,000	$1,866
Larger Units	14	1,195	1	$132,000	$1,570
			2	$166,600	$2,146
Total	111 Units				

Entrance fee refunds decline over time.

These fees include one meal per day, biweekly housekeeping, scheduled transportation, and utilities. Special features of this community are presented in the Special Features Index at the back of the book. Ask about additional residential and health care services that may be available. Fees and services subject to change; verify with facility.

ASSISTED LIVING AND PERSONAL CARE

Assisted living units: 41
Personal care is covered by the continuing care contract: Yes
Residents may receive personal care in independent living units: No
Nonresidents may be admitted directly to assisted living units: Yes

NURSING CARE: All-Inclusive Plan

Under this all-inclusive plan, unlimited nursing care is covered by the continuing care contract. When residents are in nursing care, they pay the same monthly fee they paid for their independent living unit.

Intermediate beds: 25. Cost per day: private $77.00, semi-private $69.00.

Skilled beds: 15. Cost per day: private $88.00, semi-private $80.00.

Nursing beds are certified by both Medicare and Medicaid. Nonresidents may be admitted directly to the nursing care facility.

VIRGINIA

WILLIAMSBURG LANDING
5700 Williamsburg Landing Drive
Williamsburg, VA 23185
Telephone: (804) 253-0303

Opened in 1985 • Mixed single-level and low-rise buildings on 70 acres • Current resident population is 197 • Located one mile from Williamsburg, VA • Immediate availability

AAHA
Member

HOUSING AND SERVICES

Living Units	No.	Square Feet	No. of Persons	Entrance Fee	Monthly Fee
Studio	1	650	1	$82,700	$1,131–$1,510
One Bedroom	73	880–1,325	1	$87,700–$135,000	$1,159
			2	$87,700–$135,000	$1,529
Two Bedroom	68	1,080–1,663	1	$106,700–$149,300	$1,187
			2	$106,700–$149,300	$1,557
Larger Units	70	1,350–2,121	1	$122,600–$173,800	$935
			2	$122,600–$173,800	$1,305
Total	212 Units				

Entrance fees are fully refundable.

These fees include one meal per day and biweekly housekeeping. Special features of this community are presented in the Special Features Index at the back of the book. Ask about additional residential and health care services that may be available. Fees and services subject to change; verify with facility.

ASSISTED LIVING AND PERSONAL CARE

Assisted living units: 7
Personal care is covered by the continuing care contract: Yes
Residents may receive personal care in independent living units: No
Nonresidents may be admitted directly to assisted living units: Yes

NURSING CARE: Modified Plan

Under this modified plan, ten days of nursing care are covered by the continuing care contract. Once residents move permanently to the nursing unit, they pay the basic monthly fee for a one-bedroom unit for nursing care; in addition, residents are required to hold long-term care insurance with a private company.

Intermediate beds: 15. Cost per day: private $112.00, semi-private $78.50.

Nursing beds are not certified by Medicare or Medicaid. Nonresidents may be admitted directly to the nursing care facility.

BAYVIEW MANOR
11 West Aloha Street, Seattle, WA 98119
Telephone: (206) 284-7330

Opened in 1961 • One high-rise building on two acres
• Current resident population is 242 • Long waiting
list; make reservations in advance

AAHA
Member

HOUSING AND SERVICES

Living Units	No.	Square Feet	No. of Persons	Entrance Fee	Monthly Fee
Studio	140	——	1	$22,000	$600
One Bedroom	51	——	1	$44,000	$786
			2	$49,000	$1,211
Two Bedroom	0	——	——	——	——
Larger Units	0	——	——	——	——
Total	191 Units				

Entrance fee refunds decline over time.

These fees include three meals per day, weekly housekeeping, and utilities.
Special features of this community are presented in the Special Features Index
at the back of the book. Ask about additional residential and health care services
that may be available. Fees and services subject to change; verify with facility.

ASSISTED LIVING AND PERSONAL CARE

Assisted living units: 27
Personal care is covered by the continuing care contract: No
Residents may receive personal care in independent living units: No
Nonresidents may be admitted directly to assisted living units: No

NURSING CARE: Modified Plan

Under this modified plan, 16–59 days are covered by the continuing care contract. Once residents move permanently to the nursing unit, they pay the full
per diem rate for nursing care.

Skilled beds: 45. Cost per day: semi-private $34.00–$60.00.

Nursing beds are certified by both Medicare and Medicaid. Nonresidents may
not be admitted directly to the nursing care facility.

CRISTA SENIOR COMMUNITY
19303 Fremont Avenue North, Seattle, WA 98133
Telephone: (206) 546-7400

Opened in 1984 • Mixed single-level, low-rise, and high-rise buildings on 23 acres • Current resident population is 352 • Waiting list

AAHA
Member

HOUSING AND SERVICES

Living Units	No.	Square Feet	No. of Persons	Entrance Fee	Monthly Fee
Studio	51	300–452	1	vary up $40,950	$355–$535
One Bedroom	146	540–664	1	$14,875–$60,250	$420–$680
			2	$14,875–$60,250	$450–$930
Two Bedroom	80	751–1,286	1	$18,975–$118,350	$445–$1,100
			2	$18,975–$118,350	$475–$1,350
Larger Units	0	——	——	——	——
Total	277 Units				

Entrance fees are partially refundable.

These fees include one meal per day, monthly housekeeping, scheduled transportation, and utilities. Special features of this community are presented in the Special Features Index at the back of the book. Ask about additional residential and health care services that may be available. Fees and services subject to change; verify with facility.

ASSISTED LIVING AND PERSONAL CARE

Assisted living units: 16
Personal care is covered by the continuing care contract: No
Residents may receive personal care in independent living units: No
Nonresidents may be admitted directly to assisted living units: Yes

NURSING CARE: Modified Plan

Under this modified plan, 60 days or more are covered by the continuing care contract. Once residents move permanently to the nursing unit, they pay 80 percent of the per diem rate for nursing care.

Intermediate beds: 49. Cost per day: private $69.00, semi-private $58.25.

Skilled beds: 187. Cost per day: private $85.00, semi-private $74.00.

Nursing beds are certified by both Medicare and Medicaid. Nonresidents may be admitted directly to the nursing care facility.

EXETER HOUSE
720 Seneca Street, Seattle, WA 98101
Telephone: (206) 622-1300

Opened in 1962 • One high-rise building on one acre • Current resident population is 137 • Waiting list

AAHA
Member

HOUSING AND SERVICES

Living Units	No.	Square Feet	No. of Persons	Entrance Fee	Monthly Fee
Studio	84	370–490	1	$14,300–$31,350	$561–$1,121
One Bedroom	47	615–1,030	1	$31,900–$58,300	$687–$815
			2		$1,121–$1,249
Two Bedroom	0	——	——	——	——
Larger Units	0	——	——	——	——
Total	131 Units				

Entrance fee refunds decline over time.

These fees include three meals per day, housekeeping, and utilities. Special features of this community are presented in the Special Features Index at the back of the book. Ask about additional residential and health care services that may be available. Fees and services subject to change; verify with facility.

ASSISTED LIVING AND PERSONAL CARE

Assisted living units: 0
Personal care is covered by the continuing care contract: No
Residents may receive personal care in independent living units: Yes

NURSING CARE: Modified Plan

Under this modified plan, 15 or fewer days per year are covered by the continuing care contract. Once residents move permanently to the nursing unit, they pay the full per diem rate for nursing care.

Skilled beds: 20. Cost per day: private $50.00, semi-private $44.00.

Nursing beds are not certified by Medicare or Medicaid. Nonresidents may not be admitted directly to the nursing care facility.

WASHINGTON

THE HEARTHSTONE
6720 East Green Lake Way North, Seattle, WA 98103
Telephone: (206) 525-9666

Opened in 1966 • One high-rise building on one acre
• Current resident population is 288 • Long waiting
list; make reservations in advance • Accredited by the
AAHA Continuing Care Accreditation Commission

HOUSING AND SERVICES

Living Units	No.	Square Feet	No. of Persons	Entrance Fee	Monthly Fee
Studio	164	336–432	1	$16,000–$35,400	$565–$875
One Bedroom	64	576–672	1	$39,200–$51,600	$763–$1,073
			2		$822–$1,132
Two Bedroom	0	——	——	——	——
Larger Units	0	——	——	——	——
Total	228 Units				

Entrance fee refunds decline over time.

These fees include three meals per day, biweekly housekeeping, scheduled transportation, and utilities. Special features of this community are presented in the Special Features Index at the back of the book. Ask about additional residential and health care services that may be available. Fees and services subject to change; verify with facility.

ASSISTED LIVING AND PERSONAL CARE

Assisted living units: 0
Personal care is covered by the continuing care contract: No
Residents may receive personal care in independent living units: Yes

NURSING CARE: Modified Plan

Under this modified plan, 16–59 days per year are covered by the continuing care contract. Once residents move permanently to the nursing unit, they pay the full per diem rate for nursing care.

Dual-certified beds: 51. Cost per day: private $69.50, semi-private $69.50.

Nursing beds are certified by both Medicare and Medicaid. Nonresidents may be admitted directly to the nursing care facility.

WASHINGTON

HORIZON HOUSE
900 University Street, Seattle, WA 98101
Telephone: (206) 624-3700

Opened in 1961 • Predominantly high-rise buildings on three acres • Current resident population is 465 • Waiting list may apply for some units

AAHA
Member

HOUSING AND SERVICES

Living Units	No.	Square Feet	No. of Persons	Entrance Fee	Monthly Fee
Studio	36	400–421	1	$17,000–$44,000	$380
One Bedroom	179	530–785	1	$45,000–$106,000	$495
			2	$45,000–$106,000	$715
Two Bedroom	141	722–1,200	1	$79,000–$164,000	$665–$795
			2	$79,000–$164,000	$885–$1,015
Larger Units	0	—	—	—	—
Total	356 Units				

Entrance fee refunds decline over time.

These fees include utilities. Special features of this community are presented in the Special Features Index at the back of the book. Ask about additional residential and health care services that may be available. Fees and services subject to change; verify with facility.

ASSISTED LIVING AND PERSONAL CARE

Assisted living units: 31
Personal care is covered by the continuing care contract: Yes
Residents may receive personal care in independent living units: No
Nonresidents may be admitted directly to assisted living units: No

NURSING CARE: Modified Plan

Under this modified plan, 180 days are covered by the continuing care contract. Once residents move permanently to the nursing unit, they pay the basic monthly fee for the studio (smallest) unit plus $460 per month for nursing care.

Skilled beds: 22. Cost per day: not applicable.

Nursing beds are certified by Medicare. Nonresidents may not be admitted directly to the nursing care facility.

WASHINGTON

JUDSON PARK RETIREMENT RESIDENCE
23600 Marine View Drive South
Des Moines, WA 98198
Telephone: (206) 824-4000

Opened in 1963 • One low-rise building on nine acres
• Current resident population is 203 • Located
between Tacoma, WA, and Seattle, WA, and 15 miles
from both • Waiting list

AAHA
Member

HOUSING AND SERVICES

Living Units	No.	Square Feet	No. of Persons	Entrance Fee	Monthly Fee
Studio	150	371–570	1	$17,300–$36,190	$570–$650
One Bedroom	28	680–928	1	$46,600–$59,800	$695–$783
			2	$51,260–$65,780	$1,010–$1,098
Two Bedroom	0	——	——	——	——
Larger Units	0	——	——	——	——
Total	178 Units				

Entrance fee refunds decline over time.

These fees include one meal per day, weekly housekeeping, and utilities. Special features of this community are presented in the Special Features Index at the back of the book. Ask about additional residential and health care services that may be available. Fees and services subject to change; verify with facility.

ASSISTED LIVING AND PERSONAL CARE

Assisted living units: 18
Personal care is covered by the continuing care contract: Yes
Residents may receive personal care in independent living units: Yes
Nonresidents may be admitted directly to assisted living units: No

NURSING CARE: Modified Plan

Under this modified plan, 45 days of nursing care over a resident's lifetime are covered by the continuing care contract. Once residents move permanently to the nursing unit, they pay a discounted per diem rate for nursing care.

Skilled beds: 60. Cost per day: private $86.00, semi-private $69.00.

Dual-certified beds: 60. Cost per day: private $72.00, semi-private $55.00.

Nursing beds are certified by both Medicare and Medicaid. Nonresidents may be admitted directly to the nursing care facility.

WASHINGTON

NORSE HOME
5311 Phinney Avenue North, Seattle, WA 98103
Telephone: (206) 783-9600

Opened in 1957 • One high-rise building on one acre
• Current resident population is 170 • Waiting list
may apply for some units

HOUSING AND SERVICES

Living Units	No.	Square Feet	No. of Persons	Entrance Fee	Monthly Fee
Studio	96	250	1	$13,000–$21,500	$510
One Bedroom	7	500	1, 2	$34,000–$38,000	$1,020
Two Bedroom	0	——	——	——	——
Larger Units	0	——	——	——	——
Total	103 Units				

Entrance fee refunds decline over time.

These fees include three meals per day, weekly housekeeping, and utilities. Special features of this community are presented in the Special Features Index at the back of the book. Ask about additional residential and health care services that may be available. Fees and services subject to change; verify with facility.

ASSISTED LIVING AND PERSONAL CARE

Assisted living units: 19
Personal care is covered by the continuing care contract: No
Residents may receive personal care in independent living units: No
Nonresidents may be admitted directly to assisted living units: No

NURSING CARE: Modified Plan

Under this modified plan, 15 or fewer days per year are covered by the continuing care contract. Once residents move permanently to the nursing unit, they pay 80 percent of the per diem rate for nursing care.

Skilled beds: 51. Cost per day: semi-private $65.00.

Nursing beds are certified by Medicaid. Nonresidents may be admitted directly to the nursing care facility.

PARK SHORE

1630 43rd Avenue East, Seattle, WA 98112
Telephone: (206) 329-0770

Opened in 1963 • One high-rise building on one acre
• Current resident population is 228 • Waiting list

AAHA
Member

HOUSING AND SERVICES

Living Units	No.	Square Feet	No. of Persons	Entrance Fee	Monthly Fee
Studio	120	420–650	1	$20,700–$38,000	$609–$695
One Bedroom	60	700–925	1	$40,900–$57,100	$779
			2	$40,900–$57,100	$1,224
Two Bedroom	10	1,300	1	$69,000–$81,000	$948
			2	$69,000–$81,000	$1,393
Larger Units	0	—	—	—	—
Total	190 Units				

Entrance fee refunds decline over time.

These fees include three meals per day, weekly housekeeping, and utilities. Special features of this community are presented in the Special Features Index at the back of the book. Ask about additional residential and health care services that may be available. Fees and services subject to change; verify with facility.

ASSISTED LIVING AND PERSONAL CARE

Assisted living units: 0
Personal care is covered by the continuing care contract: No
Residents may receive personal care in independent living units: No

NURSING CARE: Fee-for-Service Plan

Under this fee-for-service plan, guaranteed access to nursing care is covered by the continuing care contract. Residents pay the full per diem rate for nursing care.

Dual-certified beds: 47. Cost per day: semi-private $50.00.

Nursing beds are not certified by Medicare or Medicaid. Nonresidents may not be admitted directly to the nursing care facility.

WASHINGTON

ROCKWOOD MANOR
2903 East 25th Avenue, Spokane, WA 99223
Telephone: (509) 536-6650

Opened in 1960 • One high-rise building on one acre
• Current resident population is 257 • Waiting list
may apply for some units

AAHA
Member

HOUSING AND SERVICES

Living Units	No.	Square Feet	No. of Persons	Entrance Fee	Monthly Fee
Studio	—	300	1	$19,000	$589
One Bedroom	—	600	1	$37,000	$883
			2	$37,000	$1,178
Two Bedroom	—	900	1	$55,000	$1,179
			2	$55,000	$1,474
Larger Units	0	—	—	—	—
Total	200 Units				

Entrance fee refunds decline over time.

These fees include three meals per day, weekly housekeeping, and utilities.
Special features of this community are presented in the Special Features Index
at the back of the book. Ask about additional residential and health care services
that may be available. Fees and services subject to change; verify with facility.

ASSISTED LIVING AND PERSONAL CARE

Assisted living units: 0
Personal care is covered by the continuing care contract: Yes
Residents may receive personal care in independent living units: Yes

NURSING CARE: All-Inclusive Plan

Under this all-inclusive plan, unlimited nursing care is covered by the continuing care contract. When residents are in nursing care, they pay the basic
monthly fee for the studio (smallest) unit.

Skilled beds: 44. Cost per day: not applicable.

Nursing beds are certified by Medicare. Nonresidents may not be admitted
directly to the nursing care facility.

WASHINGTON

THE SAMUEL AND JESSIE KENNEY PRESBYTERIAN HOME

7125 Fauntleroy Way Southwest, Seattle, WA 98136
Telephone: (206) 937-2800

Opened in 1909 • Mixed single-level and low-rise buildings on four acres • Current resident population is 132 • Waiting list may apply for some units

AAHA Member

HOUSING AND SERVICES

Living Units	No.	Square Feet	No. of Persons	Entrance Fee	Monthly Fee
Studio	74	200–300	1	$16,625–$22,875	$566–$700
One Bedroom	22	400–500	1	$28,300–$39,000	$814
			2		$1,117
Two Bedroom	0	——	——	——	——
Larger Units	0	——	——	——	——
Total	96 Units				

Entrance fees are nonrefundable.

These fees include three meals per day, weekly housekeeping, scheduled transportation, and utilities. Special features of this community are presented in the Special Features Index at the back of the book. Ask about additional residential and health care services that may be available. Fees and services subject to change; verify with facility.

ASSISTED LIVING AND PERSONAL CARE

Assisted living units: 10
Personal care is covered by the continuing care contract: Yes
Residents may receive personal care in independent living units: No
Nonresidents may be admitted directly to assisted living units: No

---

NURSING CARE: Modified Plan

Under this modified plan, 16–59 days over a resident's lifetime are covered by the continuing care contract. Once residents move permanently to the nursing unit, they pay the full per diem rate for nursing care.

Skilled beds: 53. Cost per day: private $57.00, semi-private $57.00.

Nursing beds are certified by Medicaid. Nonresidents may be admitted directly to the nursing care facility.

ALEXIAN VILLAGE OF MILWAUKEE
7979 West Glenbrook Road, Milwaukee, WI 53223
Telephone: (414) 355-9300

Opened in 1977 • Mixed single-level, low-rise, and high-rise buildings on 23 acres • Current resident population is 400 • Waiting list may apply for some units • Accredited by the AAHA Continuing Care Accreditation Commission

AAHA
Member

HOUSING AND SERVICES

Living Units	No.	Square Feet	No. of Persons	Entrance Fee	Monthly Fee
Studio	36	350–480	1	$33,900–$41,950	$550–$640
One Bedroom	169	600	1	$54,800	$673
			2	$66,800	$1,051
Two Bedroom	120	750–880	1	$63,800–$66,800	$728
			2	$75,800–$78,800	$1,106
Larger Units	6	1,000	1	$73,800	$793
			2	$85,800	$1,171
Total	331 Units				

Entrance fee refunds decline over time.

These fees include one meal per day, biweekly housekeeping, scheduled transportation, and utilities. Special features of this community are presented in the Special Features Index at the back of the book. Ask about additional residential and health care services that may be available. Fees and services subject to change; verify with facility.

ASSISTED LIVING AND PERSONAL CARE

Assisted living units: 0
Personal care is covered by the continuing care contract: No
Residents may receive personal care in independent living units: No

NURSING CARE: All-Inclusive Plan

Under this all-inclusive plan, unlimited nursing care is covered by the continuing care contract. When residents are in nursing care, they pay the same monthly fee they paid for their independent living unit.

Intermediate beds. Cost per day: semi-private $87.00.

Skilled beds: 61. Cost per day: semi-private $90.00.

Nursing beds are certified by Medicaid. Nonresidents may be admitted directly to the nursing care facility.

WISCONSIN

ATTIC ANGEL NURSING HOME AND TOWER
602–606 North Segoe Road, Madison, WI 53705
Telephone: (608) 238-8282

Opened in 1975 • Mixed single-level, low-rise, and high-rise buildings on three acres • Current resident population is 124 • Waiting list

AAHA Member

HOUSING AND SERVICES

Living Units	No.	Square Feet	No. of Persons	Entrance Fee	Monthly Fee
Studio	14	440	1	$10,000	$590
One Bedroom	56	620	1	$15,000	$645
			2	$20,000	$1,100
Two Bedroom	0	—	—	—	—
Larger Units	0	—	—	—	—
Total	70 Units				

Entrance fee refunds decline over time.

These fees include one meal per day, biweekly housekeeping, scheduled transportation, and utilities. Special features of this community are presented in the Special Features Index at the back of the book. Ask about additional residential and health care services that may be available. Fees and services subject to change; verify with facility.

ASSISTED LIVING AND PERSONAL CARE

Assisted living units: 0
Personal care is covered by the continuing care contract: No
Residents may receive personal care in independent living units: No

NURSING CARE: Modified Plan

Under this modified plan, 15 or fewer days are covered by the continuing care contract. Once residents move permanently to the nursing unit, they pay the full per diem rate for nursing care.

Intermediate beds. Cost per day: private $63.50, semi-private $53.50.

Skilled beds: 64. Cost per day: private $72.00, semi-private $62.00.

Nursing beds are not certified by Medicare or Medicaid. The nursing center is accredited by the Joint Commission on Accreditation of Hospitals. Nonresidents may be admitted directly to the nursing care facility.

WISCONSIN

**CEDAR LAKE HOME CAMPUS OF THE
BENEVOLENT CORPORATION**
5595 Highway Z, West Bend, WI 53095
Telephone: (414) 334-9487

Opened in 1986 • Mixed single-level and low-rise
buildings on 50 acres • Immediate availability

AAHA
Member

HOUSING AND SERVICES

Living Units	No.	Square Feet	No. of Persons	Entrance Fee	Monthly Fee
Studio	0	——	——	——	——
One Bedroom	54	686	1	$22,500	$300
			2	$24,500	$350
Two Bedroom	66	966	1	$27,500	$350
			2	$29,500	$400
Larger Units	0	——	——	——	——
Total	120 Units				

Residents have a choice of entrance fee refund plans.

These fees include monthly housekeeping and utilities. Special features of this community are presented in the Special Features Index at the back of the book. Ask about additional residential and health care services that may be available. Fees and services subject to change; verify with facility.

ASSISTED LIVING AND PERSONAL CARE

Assisted living units: 0
Personal care is covered by the continuing care contract: No
Residents may receive personal care in independent living units: No

NURSING CARE: Fee-for-Service Plan

Under this fee-for-service plan, guaranteed access to nursing care is covered by the continuing care contract. Residents pay the full per diem rate for nursing care.

Intermediate beds. Cost per day: private $34.55, semi-private $32.10.

Skilled beds: 415. Cost per day: private $52.00, semi-private $50.40.

Nursing beds are certified by Medicaid. Nonresidents may be admitted directly to the nursing care facility.

EVERGREEN MANOR
1130 North Westfield Street, Oshkosh, WI 54901
Telephone: (414) 233-2340

Opened in 1967 • Mixed single-level and low-rise
buildings on 26 acres • Current resident population is
255 • Waiting list may apply for some units

AAHA
Member

HOUSING AND SERVICES

Living Units	No.	Square Feet	No. of Persons	Entrance Fee	Monthly Fee
Studio	52	268–319	1	$10,000–$13,000	$470–$493
One Bedroom	20	587	1	$23,000	$769
			2	$23,000	$934
Two Bedroom	22	1,000	1	$46,000	$285
			2	$46,000	$360
Larger Units	1	1,344	1	$50,500	$285
			2	$50,500	$360
Total		95 Units			

Entrance fee refunds decline over time.

These fees include scheduled transportation. Special features of this community are presented in the Special Features Index at the back of the book. Ask about additional residential and health care services that may be available. Fees and services subject to change; verify with facility.

ASSISTED LIVING AND PERSONAL CARE

Assisted living units: 14
Personal care is covered by the continuing care contract: Yes
Residents may receive personal care in independent living units: Yes
Nonresidents may be admitted directly to assisted living units: Yes

NURSING CARE: Fee-for-Service Plan

Under this fee-for-service plan, guaranteed access to nursing care is covered by the continuing care contract. Residents pay the full per diem rate for nursing care.

Intermediate beds. Cost per day: private $64.83, semi-private $57.50.

Skilled beds: 106. Cost per day: private $71.33, semi-private $64.00.

Nursing beds are certified by Medicaid. Nonresidents may be admitted directly to the nursing care facility.

FAIRHAVEN
435 Starin Road, Whitewater, WI 53190
Telephone: (414) 473-2140

Opened in 1962 • Mixed single-level and low-rise buildings on ten acres • Current resident population is 260 • Waiting list may apply for some units

AAHA
Member

HOUSING AND SERVICES

Living Units	No.	Square Feet	No. of Persons	Entrance Fee	Monthly Fee
Studio	105	320–565	1	$10,000–$16,000	$225–$375
One Bedroom	44	561–785	1, 2	$16,500–$26,000	$404–$516
Two Bedroom	4	939	1, 2	$31,200	$599
Larger Units	0	—	—	—	—
Total	153 Units				

Entrance fee refunds decline over time.

These fees include monthly housekeeping, scheduled transportation, and utilities. Special features of this community are presented in the Special Features Index at the back of the book. Ask about additional residential and health care services that may be available. Fees and services subject to change; verify with facility.

ASSISTED LIVING AND PERSONAL CARE

Assisted living units: 0
Personal care is covered by the continuing care contract: No
Residents may receive personal care in independent living units: No

NURSING CARE: Fee-for-Service Plan

Under this fee-for-service plan, guaranteed access to nursing care is covered by the continuing care contract. Residents pay the full per diem rate for nursing care.

Intermediate beds: 25. Cost per day: private $51.00, semi-private $43.00.

Skilled beds: 59. Cost per day: private $80.50, semi-private $70.50.

Nursing beds are certified by Medicaid. Nonresidents may be admitted directly to the nursing care facility.

FRIENDSHIP VILLAGE OF GREATER MILWAUKEE
7300 West Dean Road, Milwaukee, WI 53223
Telephone: (414) 354-3700

Opened in 1973 • Mixed single-level and low-rise buildings on 13 acres • Current resident population is 472 • Waiting list

AAHA
Member

HOUSING AND SERVICES

Living Units	No.	Square Feet	No. of Persons	Entrance Fee	Monthly Fee
Studio	112	305–493	1	$23,000–$35,000	$440–$500
One Bedroom	132	610–690	1	$40,000–$46,000	$562
			2		$842
Two Bedroom	81	782–940	1	$50,000–$60,000	$630
			2		$910
Larger Units	0	——	——	——	——
Total	325 Units				

Entrance fee refunds decline over time.

These fees include one meal per day, biweekly housekeeping, scheduled transportation, and utilities. Special features of this community are presented in the Special Features Index at the back of the book. Ask about additional residential and health care services that may be available. Fees and services subject to change; verify with facility.

ASSISTED LIVING AND PERSONAL CARE

Assisted living units: 22
Personal care is covered by the continuing care contract: Yes
Residents may receive personal care in independent living units: Yes
Nonresidents may be admitted directly to assisted living units: No

NURSING CARE: All-Inclusive Plan

Under this all-inclusive plan, unlimited nursing care is covered by the continuing care contract. When residents are in nursing care, they pay the same fee they paid for their independent living unit.

Intermediate beds: 22. Cost per day: not applicable.

Skilled beds: 67. Cost per day: not applicable.

Nursing beds are not certified by Medicare or Medicaid. Nonresidents may not be admitted directly to the nursing care facility.

WISCONSIN

LUTHER MANOR
4545 North 92nd Street, Wauwatosa, WI 53225
Telephone: (414) 464-3880

Opened in 1973 • Mixed single-level and low-rise buildings on 28 acres • Current resident population is 640 • Long waiting list; make reservations in advance

AAHA
Member

HOUSING AND SERVICES

Living Units	No.	Square Feet	No. of Persons	Entrance Fee	Monthly Fee
Studio	64	400	1	$10,000	$245
One Bedroom	126	700	1	$18,000	$430
			2	$18,000	$480
Two Bedroom	28	1,000	1	$32,500	$585
			2	$32,500	$635
Larger Units	0	——	——	——	——
Total	218 Units				

Entrance fee refunds decline over time.

These fees include scheduled transportation and utilities. Special features of this community are presented in the Special Features Index at the back of the book. Ask about additional residential and health care services that may be available. Fees and services subject to change; verify with facility.

ASSISTED LIVING AND PERSONAL CARE

Assisted living units: 166
Personal care is covered by the continuing care contract: No
Residents may receive personal care in independent living units: No
Nonresidents may be admitted directly to assisted living units: Yes

NURSING CARE: Modified Plan

Under this modified plan, 16–59 days are covered by the continuing care contract. Once residents move permanently to the nursing unit, they pay the full per diem rate for nursing care.

Skilled beds: 201. Cost per day: private $80.00, semi-private $75.00.

Nursing beds are certified by Medicaid. Nonresidents may be admitted directly to the nursing care facility.

METHODIST MANOR
3023 South 84th Street, Milwaukee, WI 53227
Telephone: (414) 541-2600

Opened in 1960 • Mixed single-level, low-rise, and high-rise buildings on 20 acres • Current resident population is 590 • Waiting list may apply for some units

AAHA
Member

HOUSING AND SERVICES

Living Units	No.	Square Feet	No. of Persons	Entrance Fee	Monthly Fee
Studio	54	485	1	$38,624	$460
One Bedroom	139	660	1	$46,024	$558
			2	$60,376	$737
Two Bedroom	33	900	1	$52,824	$722
			2	$67,176	$908
Larger Units	0	—	—	—	—
Total	226 Units				

Entrance fee refunds decline over time.

These fees include scheduled transportation and utilities. Special features of this community are presented in the Special Features Index at the back of the book. Ask about additional residential and health care services that may be available. Fees and services subject to change; verify with facility.

ASSISTED LIVING AND PERSONAL CARE

Assisted living units: 174
Personal care is covered by the continuing care contract: Yes
Residents may receive personal care in independent living units: No
Nonresidents may be admitted directly to assisted living units: Yes

NURSING CARE: All-Inclusive Plan

Under this all-inclusive plan, unlimited nursing care is covered by the continuing care contract. When residents are in nursing care, they pay the same monthly fee they paid for their independent living unit.

Intermediate beds: 20. Cost per day: private $60.00, semi-private $52.00.

Skilled beds: 168. Cost per day: private $146.00, semi-private $80.50.

Nursing beds are certified by both Medicare and Medicaid. Nonresidents may be admitted directly to the nursing care facility.

MILWAUKEE CATHOLIC HOME

2462 North Prospect Avenue, Milwaukee, WI 53211
Telephone: (414) 224-9700

Opened in 1913 • One high-rise building on one acre
• Current resident population is 176 • Waiting list
may apply for some units

AAHA
Member

HOUSING AND SERVICES

Living Units	No.	Square Feet	No. of Persons	Entrance Fee	Monthly Fee
Studio	98	318	1	$14,600–$19,900	$520–$612
One Bedroom	52	566	1	$36,500	$837–$900
			2		$1,037–$1,100
Two Bedroom	1	828	1	$48,700	$1,056
			2		$1,256
Larger Units	0	——	——	——	——
Total	151 Units				

Entrance fee refunds decline over time.

These fees include three meals per day, biweekly housekeeping, and utilities. Special features of this community are presented in the Special Features Index at the back of the book. Ask about additional residential and health care services that may be available. Fees and services subject to change; verify with facility.

ASSISTED LIVING AND PERSONAL CARE

Assisted living units: 0
Personal care is covered by the continuing care contract: No
Residents may receive personal care in independent living units: No

NURSING CARE: Modified Plan

Under this modified plan, 15 or fewer days per year are covered by the continuing care contract. Once residents move permanently to the nursing unit, they pay the full per diem rate for nursing care.

Intermediate beds. Cost per day: private $82.00, semi-private $62.00.

Skilled beds: 44. Cost per day: private $94.00, semi-private $74.00.

Nursing beds are certified by Medicaid. Nonresidents may not be admitted directly to the nursing care facility.

WISCONSIN

MILWAUKEE PROTESTANT HOME—BRADFORD TERRACE DIVISION
2449 North Downer Avenue, Milwaukee, WI 53211
Telephone: (414) 332-8610

Opened in 1967 • Mixed single-level and low-rise buildings on six acres • Current resident population is 75 • Waiting list

AAHA
Member

HOUSING AND SERVICES

Living Units	No.	Square Feet	No. of Persons	Entrance Fee	Monthly Fee
Studio	10	210–343	1	$11,000–$20,000	$535–$570
One Bedroom	16	455	1, 2	$25,500	$725
Two Bedroom	2	679	1, 2	$45,000	$1,055
Larger Units	0	——	——	——	——
Total		28 Units			

Entrance fee refunds decline over time.

These fees include three meals per day, biweekly housekeeping, and utilities. Special features of this community are presented in the Special Features Index at the back of the book. Ask about additional residential and health care services that may be available. Fees and services subject to change; verify with facility.

ASSISTED LIVING AND PERSONAL CARE

Assisted living units: 0
Personal care is covered by the continuing care contract: No
Residents may receive personal care in independent living units: No

NURSING CARE: Modified Plan

Under this modified plan, unlimited days of nursing care are covered by the continuing care contract. Residents pay a discounted fee of $18 below the per diem rate for nursing care.

Skilled beds: 50. Cost per day: private $86.00, semi-private $76.00.

Nursing beds are certified by Medicare. Nonresidents may be admitted directly to the nursing care facility.

NEW GLARUS HOME
700 Second Avenue, New Glarus, WI 53574
Telephone: (608) 527-2126

Opened in 1983 • Mixed single-level and low-rise
buildings on five acres • Current resident population
is 96 • Immediate availability

**AAHA
Member**

HOUSING AND SERVICES

Living Units	No.	Square Feet	No. of Persons	Entrance Fee	Monthly Fee
Studio	0	——	——	——	——
One Bedroom	14	——	1, 2	$10,500	$260
Two Bedroom	8	——	1, 2	$12,500	$300
Larger Units	0	——	——	——	——
Total	22 Units				

Entrance fee refunds decline over time.

These fees include scheduled transportation and utilities. Special features of
this community are presented in the Special Features Index at the back of the
book. Ask about additional residential and health care services that may be
available. Fees and services subject to change; verify with facility.

ASSISTED LIVING AND PERSONAL CARE

Assisted living units: 0
Personal care is covered by the continuing care contract: No
Residents may receive personal care in independent living units: No

NURSING CARE: Fee-for-Service Plan

Under this fee-for-service plan, guaranteed access to nursing care is covered by
the continuing care contract. Residents pay the full per diem rate for nursing
care.

Dual-certified beds: 97. Cost per day: private $46.00, semi-private $43.00.

Nursing beds are certified by Medicaid. Nonresidents may be admitted
directly to the nursing care facility.

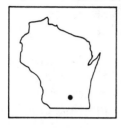

OAKWOOD LUTHERAN HOMES ASSOCIATION
OAKWOOD VILLAGE APARTMENTS
6201–09 Mineral Point Road, Madison, WI 53705
Telephone: (608) 231-3451

Opened in 1976 • Mixed single-level, low-rise, and high-rise buildings on 30 acres • Current resident population is 39 • Waiting list may apply for some units

AAHA
Member

HOUSING AND SERVICES

Living Units	No.	Square Feet	No. of Persons	Entrance Fee	Monthly Fee
Studio	16	430	1	$8,000	$452
One Bedroom	164	517–588	1, 2	$11,000–$11,500	$517–$579
Two Bedroom	18	660–735	1, 2	$16,000–$20,000	$595–$686
Larger Units	10	947–1,167	1, 2	$22,000–$24,000	$993–$1,079
Total	208 Units				

Entrance fee refunds decline over time.

These fees include scheduled transportation and utilities. Special features of this community are presented in the Special Features Index at the back of the book. Ask about additional residential and health care services that may be available. Fees and services subject to change; verify with facility.

ASSISTED LIVING AND PERSONAL CARE

Assisted living units: 15
Personal care is covered by the continuing care contract: No
Residents may receive personal care in independent living units: No
Nonresidents may be admitted directly to assisted living units: Yes

NURSING CARE: Modified Plan

Under this modified plan, 15 or fewer days of nursing care per year are covered by the continuing care contract. Once residents move permanently to the nursing unit, they pay the full per diem rate for nursing care.

Intermediate beds. Cost per day: private $66.50, semi-private $56.50.

Skilled beds: 137. Cost per day: private $80.00, semi-private $70.00.

Nursing beds are certified by both Medicare and Medicaid. Nonresidents may be admitted directly to the nursing care facility.

SAINT JOHN'S HOME OF MILWAUKEE
1840 North Prospect Avenue, Milwaukee, WI 53202
Telephone: (414) 272-2022

Opened in 1979 • Mixed single-level, low-rise, and high-rise buildings on four acres • Current resident population is 274 • Waiting list may apply for some units

HOUSING AND SERVICES

Living Units	No.	Square Feet	No. of Persons	Entrance Fee	Monthly Fee
Studio	44	446	1	$31,150	$452
One Bedroom	98	600	1	$44,100	$576
			2	$54,100	$666
Two Bedroom	31	875	1	$61,300	$834
			2	$71,300	$924
Larger Units	7	1,260	1	$73,000	$1,031
			2	$83,000	$1,121
Total	180 Units				

Entrance fee refunds decline over time.

These fees include scheduled transportation and utilities. Special features of this community are presented in the Special Features Index at the back of the book. Ask about additional residential and health care services that may be available. Fees and services subject to change; verify with facility.

ASSISTED LIVING AND PERSONAL CARE

Assisted living units: 0
Personal care is covered by the continuing care contract: No
Residents may receive personal care in independent living units: Yes

NURSING CARE: All-Inclusive Plan

Under this all-inclusive plan, unlimited nursing care is covered by the continuing care contract. When residents are in nursing care, they pay the same monthly fee they paid for their independent living unit.

Skilled beds: 95. Cost per day: semi-private $76.00.

Nursing beds are certified by Medicaid. Nonresidents may be admitted directly to the nursing care facility.

TUDOR OAKS RETIREMENT COMMUNITY
South 77 West 12929 McShane Road, Box 901
Hales Corners, WI 53130
Telephone: (414) 529-0100

Opened in 1975 • Low-rise buildings on 110 acres •
Current resident population is 277 • Located 15 miles
from Milwaukee, WI • Waiting list may apply for
some units

AAHA Member

HOUSING AND SERVICES

Living Units	No.	Square Feet	No. of Persons	Entrance Fee	Monthly Fee
Studio	60	300–450	1	$27,000–$33,500	$568–$616
One Bedroom	85	450–600	1	$36,000–$45,000	$636–$669
			2	$43,500–$52,500	$1,040–$1,073
Two Bedroom	48	750	1	$52,000	$740
			2	$59,500	$1,144
Larger Units	4	1,440	1	$72,000	$831
			2	$79,500	$1,235
Total	197 Units				

Entrance fee refunds decline over time.

These fees include one meal per day, biweekly housekeeping, scheduled transportation, and utilities. Special features of this community are presented in the Special Features Index at the back of the book. Ask about additional residential and health care services that may be available. Fees and services subject to change; verify with facility.

ASSISTED LIVING AND PERSONAL CARE

Assisted living units: 0
Personal care is covered by the continuing care contract: No
Residents may receive personal care in independent living units: Yes

NURSING CARE: All-Inclusive Plan

Under this all-inclusive-plan, unlimited nursing care is covered by the continuing care contract. When residents are in nursing care, they pay the same monthly fee they paid for their independent living unit.

Intermediate beds. Cost per day: semi-private $74.50.

Skilled beds: 61. Cost per day: $79.50.

Nursing beds are certified by both Medicare and Medicaid. Nonresidents may be admitted directly to the nursing care facility.

VILLA CLEMENT
3939 South 92nd Street, Greenfield, WI 53228
Telephone: (414) 321-1800

Opened in 1982 • Mixed single-level and low-rise buildings on 21 acres • Current resident population is 119 • Long waiting list; make reservations in advance

AAHA
Member

HOUSING AND SERVICES

Living Units	No.	Square Feet	No. of Persons	Entrance Fee	Monthly Fee
Studio	9	392	1	$11,000	$403
One Bedroom	70	630	1	$20,000	$502
			2	$22,000	$563
Two Bedroom	20	924	1	$24,000	$674
			2	$27,000	$734
Larger Units	0	—	—	—	—
Total		99 Units			

Entrance fee refunds decline over time.

These fees include scheduled transportation and utilities. Special features of this community are presented in the Special Features Index at the back of the book. Ask about additional residential and health care services that may be available. Fees and services subject to change; verify with facility.

ASSISTED LIVING AND PERSONAL CARE

Assisted living units: 0
Personal care is covered by the continuing care contract: No
Residents may receive personal care in independent living units: No

NURSING CARE: Modified Plan

Under this modified plan, 16–59 days are covered by the continuing care contract. Once residents move permanently to the nursing unit, they pay the full per diem rate for nursing care.

Intermediate beds. Cost per day: private $103.00, semi-private $90.00.

Skilled beds: 164. Cost per day: private $110.50, semi-private $97.50.

Nursing beds are certified by both Medicare and Medicaid. Nonresidents may be admitted directly to the nursing care facility.

Where to Get More Information

The following publications are available from the American Association of Homes for the Aging, 1129 20th Street, N.W., Suite 400, Washington, DC 20036, (202)296-5960:

Cloud, Deborah A., ed. *Continuing Care Issues for Nonprofit Providers.* Washington, D.C.: AAHA, revised 1985. $14.35, postage and handling included.

———. *The Continuing Care Retirement Community: A Guidebook for Consumers.* Washington, D.C.: AAHA, revised 1983. $2.00, postage and handling included.

Continuing Care Retirement Communities: An Industry in Action. Washington, D.C.: AAHA and Ernst & Whinney, 1987. $48.00, postage and handling included.

RELATED PUBLICATIONS AND ARTICLES

Carlin, Vivian F., and Ruth Mansberg. *If I Live to Be 100 . . . Congregate Housing for Later Life.* West Nyack, N.Y.: Parker Publishing Company, 1984. $8.95. This sociological study of one continuing care retirement community is quite readable, giving an inside look at resident life, staff development, the relationship of the community to the surrounding town, and more. The book discusses the retirement community as a model of successful old age and presents other communal housing choices for elderly consumers.

Carson, Gerald. "Odyssey at Eighty." *Blair & Ketchum's Country Journal* (August 1983). This is a heartwarming story of one couple's decision to move to a continuing care retirement community and what they found there.

Directory of the Presbyterian Association of Homes for the Aging. This national list of facilities (revised annually) related to the Presbyterian denomination may be obtained by sending $3.50 to Ronald A. Romeis, Philadelphia Presbytery Homes, Inc., P.O. Box 607, Villanova, PA 19085-0607.

Greenhouse, Steven. "Continuing Care Communities for the Elderly." *New York Times Personal Finance* (supplement) (September 14, 1986): 34–37.

Paulson, Morton C. "Sizing Up Life Care." *Changing Times* 41, no. 5 (May 1987): 65–70.

Rosenblatt, Robert A., and Jonathan Peterson. "Life Care: Insurance Against Age." *Los Angeles Times* (August 5, 1986).

Walters, Beth Resler. "Retirement's New Wave: A Short Look at the Long Haul." *PACE* (Piedmont Airlines publication) (February 1987): 42–50.

Winklevoss, Howard E., and Alwyn V. Powell. *Continuing Care Retirement Communities: An Empirical, Financial, and Legal Analysis.* Homewood, Ill.: Richard D. Irwin, 1984. Based on results of the first national study of continuing care retirement communities (CCRCs), this book is divided into three parts: a general overview and description of continuing care, financial and actuarial principles and methods required for managing and pricing CCRCs, and a discussion of various legal issues and laws related to continuing care at the time of publication. Intended primarily for managers, academics, regulators, and professionals such as actuaries, attorneys, and financial officers associated with CCRCs, the book is more technical than most consumers will want. Write Richard D. Irwin, Inc., 1818 Ridge Road, Homewood, IL 60430, or call (312) 798-6000.

RELATED PROGRAMS

Continuing Care Accreditation Commission
American Association of Homes for the Aging
1129 20th Street, N.W., Suite 400
Washington, DC 20036
(202) 296-5960

The Life Care at Home Plan   or   Health Policy Center
FRC Management, Inc.   Brandeis University
P.O. Box 81   Florence Heller Graduate School
Gwynedd, PA 19436   Waltham, MA 02154
(215) 628-8960   (617) 736-3901

National Continuing Care Data Base
American Association of Homes for the Aging
1129 20th Street, N.W., Suite 400
Washington, DC 20036
(202) 296-5960

Special Features Index

Special Features Index

State	Activities Director	Bank	Barber Shop	Beauty Salon	Cable TV	Chapel	Coffee Shop	Crafts Program	Exercise Program
ALABAMA									
Kirkwood by the River	x		x	x	x	x		x	
Westminster Village	x	x	x	x	x	x	x	x	
ARIZONA									
Pueblo Norte	x		x	x	x		x	x	x
Royal Oaks	x	x	x	x	x			x	x
Westminster Village	x	x	x	x	x	x	x	x	
ARKANSAS									
Butterfield Trail Village	x		x	x	x	x	x	x	x
Woodland Heights	x		x	x	x	x	x	x	x
CALIFORNIA									
Aldersly	x		x	x	x	x		x	x
Bixby Knolls Towers	x	x	x	x	x	x		x	x
Brethren Hillcrest Homes	x		x			x		x	x
Carmel Valley Manor	x		x	x	x	x		x	x
Casa Dorinda	x		x	x	x			x	x
Channing House	x	x	x					x	x
Covenant Village	x	x		x	x	x		x	x
Friends House					x			x	x
Grand Lake Gardens	x			x	x			x	x
Heritage	x			x		x		x	x
Hollenbeck Home	x	x		x	x	x	x	x	x
Inland Christian Home	x		x	x				x	x
Lake Park	x		x	x		x	x	x	x
La Serena	x		x	x	x	x	x	x	x
Los Gatos Meadows	x		x	x		x		x	x
Mount Miguel Covenant Village	x		x	x	x	x		x	x
Mount San Antonio Gardens	x	x	x	x		x		x	x
Piedmont Gardens	x		x	x		x		x	x
Pilgrim Haven	x		x	x		x		x	x
Quaker Gardens	x		x	x		x		x	x
Redwood Terrace	x		x	x	x			x	x
Rosewood	x			x		x	x	x	x
Saint Paul's Towers	x		x	x				x	x
Samarkand of Santa Barbara	x			x	x	x	x	x	x

Fireplaces	Game Room	Greenhouse	Guest Accommodations	Hiking/Walking Trails	Library	Master TV Antenna	Pharmacy	Private Dining Room	Religious Services	Resident Association	Sauna/Whirlpool	Security System	Store/Gift Shop	Swimming Pool-Indoor	Swimming Pool-Outdoor	Woodwork/Metal Shop
	x		x	x	x	x		x	x	x		x			x	
x	x		x		x	x		x	x	x		x	x			x
	x		x		x	x		x	x	x	x	x	x		x	x
					x	x			x	x	x	x	x		x	x
	x	x	x		x	x	x	x	x	x	x	x	x		x	x
x	x		x		x			x	x	x	x	x	x	x		x
x	x		x	x	x	x		x			x	x	x	x		x
	x	x	x		x			x				x				
	x		x		x	x	x	x	x			x				x
x	x		x		x			x	x	x	x	x	x			x
	x		x		x			x	x	x	x	x	x		x	x
x	x		x	x	x			x		x	x	x			x	x
x	x		x		x	x		x		x		x				x
x	x		x	x	x			x			x	x	x		x	x
x		x	x		x			x	x	x						
	x	x	x		x	x		x	x			x				
x		x	x	x	x	x		x				x				
	x	x	x		x	x		x	x	x	x	x	x			
	x				x			x	x	x	x	x				
x	x		x		x	x	x	x	x	x		x	x			x
	x		x		x	x	x	x	x	x	x	x	x		x	x
x	x		x	x	x	x	x	x	x	x		x	x			x
x	x	x	x	x	x	x		x	x	x	x	x	x		x	x
x	x		x		x	x	x		x	x	x	x	x		x	
	x		x		x	x			x	x		x				
	x		x		x				x	x			x			x
x	x		x		x	x		x	x	x		x	x			x
			x		x			x	x	x	x	x	x			
	x	x	x		x			x	x	x		x	x			x
	x		x		x	x	x	x	x	x		x				x
x	x		x	x	x			x	x	x	x	x	x			x

405

Special Features Index

State	Activities Director	Bank	Barber Shop	Beauty Salon	Cable TV	Chapel	Coffee Shop	Crafts Program	Exercise Program
CALIFORNIA (continued)									
San Joaquin Gardens	x	x	x	x		x	x	x	x
Scripps Home	x	x	x	x		x		x	x
Sequoias–San Francisco	x	x		x		x		x	x
Solheim Lutheran Homes			x	x		x		x	x
Sunny View Lutheran Home	x	x	x	x		x		x	x
Valle Verde	x		x	x	x	x	x	x	x
Villa Gardens	x		x	x	x		x	x	
Webster House					x		x		x
White Sands of La Jolla	x		x	x	x	x		x	x
Windsor Manor	x		x	x				x	x
COLORADO									
Medalion	x			x	x	x			x
Medalion West	x			x		x			x
Sunny Acres Villa	x			x	x	x			x
Villa Pueblo Towers	x			x		x		x	x
CONNECTICUT									
Covenant Village and Pilgrim Manor	x		x	x		x	x	x	x
Duncaster	x	x	x	x	x	x		x	x
Elim Park Baptist Home	x	x	x	x	x	x	x	x	
Masonic Home and Hospital	x		x	x	x			x	x
Thirty Thirty Park	x	x	x	x		x		x	x
Whitney Center	x		x	x	x			x	x
DELAWARE									
Cokesbury Village	x	x		x	x	x	x		
Methodist Country House	x		x	x	x	x	x	x	x
Methodist Manor House	x	x	x	x	x	x		x	x
DISTRICT OF COLUMBIA									
Thomas House	x			x		x	x	x	x
FLORIDA									
Abbey Delray	x		x	x	x	x		x	
Asbury Towers	x		x	x		x		x	x
Azalea Trace	x		x	x	x	x		x	x
Bay Village of Sarasota	x		x	x		x	x	x	x
Bradenton Manor	x		x	x		x		x	x
Canterbury Tower	x		x	x		x		x	x

Fireplaces	Game Room	Greenhouse	Guest Accommodations	Hiking/Walking Trails	Library	Master TV Antenna	Pharmacy	Private Dining Room	Religious Services	Resident Association	Sauna/Whirlpool	Security System	Store/Gift Shop	Swimming Pool-Indoor	Swimming Pool-Outdoor	Woodwork/Metal Shop
x	x	x	x		x	x		x	x	x	x	x	x			x
x			x	x	x	x	x		x	x	x	x				
	x			x	x			x	x	x		x	x			x
			x		x				x	x						
	x	x	x	x	x	x	x	x	x	x			x			x
x	x		x	x	x			x	x	x	x	x	x		x	x
			x		x					x		x	x			x
		x	x		x	x	x	x		x		x			x	
x			x		x	x	x		x	x		x			x	x
	x		x		x	x			x	x		x	x			
	x	x	x		x				x	x		x	x		x	
	x		x		x				x	x		x			x	
	x		x	x	x	x			x	x	x	x	x	x		
	x	x	x	x	x	x			x	x		x	x			x
x	x	x	x		x	x			x	x		x	x			x
	x	x	x	x	x			x		x		x	x			x
	x	x	x		x				x			x				x
x	x		x	x	x	x	x	x	x	x		x		x		
x	x		x	x	x	x	x	x	x	x		x	x			x
x	x		x	x	x			x	x	x	x	x				x
x	x	x	x	x	x	x	x	x	x	x	x	x		x	x	
x	x		x		x	x	x	x	x	x	x		x			x
	x		x	x	x		x	x	x	x		x	x			
	x		x		x	x	x	x	x	x		x	x		x	x
	x		x		x			x		x	x	x			x	x
	x			x	x		x	x	x		x	x				
	x	x	x	x	x	x		x	x	x		x		x		x
	x		x	x	x			x	x	x	x	x			x	x
			x	x	x	x			x	x		x	x			x
	x	x	x	x	x	x		x	x	x		x			x	

Special Features Index

State	Activities Director	Bank	Barber Shop	Beauty Salon	Cable TV	Chapel	Coffee Shop	Crafts Program	Exercise Program
FLORIDA (continued)									
Central Park Lodge	x		x	x	x			x	x
Covenant Village	x		x	x	x	x	x	x	x
Cross Keys Village	x	x	x	x	x	x	x	x	x
East Ridge	x	x	x	x		x		x	x
Edgewater Pointe	x	x	x	x	x		x	x	x
Florida United Presbyterian Homes	x	x		x	x	x			x
Freedom Village	x	x	x	x	x	x	x	x	x
Gulf Coast Village	x	x	x	x	x	x	x	x	x
Indian River Estates	x	x	x	x	x		x	x	x
John Knox Village of Central Florida	x	x	x	x	x	x	x	x	x
John Knox Village of Florida	x			x	x	x	x	x	x
Lake Pointe Woods	x		x	x	x		x	x	x
Mease Manor	x		x	x		x		x	x
Moorings Park	x	x	x	x	x	x			x
Oak Cove	x		x	x	x		x		x
Orlando Lutheran Towers	x		x	x	x	x		x	x
Palms	x		x	x	x	x		x	x
Palm Shores			x					x	
Plymouth Harbor	x		x	x	x	x	x	x	x
Saint Andrews North Estates	x	x	x	x	x	x	x	x	x
Saint Andrews South Estates	x	x	x	x	x	x	x	x	x
Saint Mark Village	x		x	x	x	x	x	x	x
Shell Point Village	x	x	x	x	x	x	x	x	x
South Port Square	x	x	x	x	x	x	x	x	x
Southwest Florida	x		x	x	x	x	x	x	x
Village on the Green	x	x		x	x			x	x
Waterford	x	x	x	x	x			x	x
Westminster Oaks	x			x	x			x	x
Westminster Towers	x		x	x	x			x	x
Winter Park Towers	x			x				x	x
GEORGIA									
Lenbrook Square	x		x	x	x		x	x	x

Fireplaces	Game Room	Greenhouse	Guest Accommodations	Hiking/Walking Trails	Library	Master TV Antenna	Pharmacy	Private Dining Room	Religious Services	Resident Association	Sauna/Whirlpool	Security System	Store/Gift Shop	Swimming Pool-Indoor	Swimming Pool-Outdoor	Woodwork/Metal Shop
	X		X	X	X	X		X	X	X	X	X			X	X
	X		X	X	X	X		X	X	X	X	X	X		X	
	X		X	X	X	X		X	X	X		X			X	X
	X		X	X				X	X	X			X		X	X
	X			X	X	X		X	X	X	X	X	X		X	X
			X		X	X		X	X			X			X	
X	X		X	X	X	X	X	X	X	X	X	X	X	X		X
	X		X	X	X	X		X	X	X	X	X	X		X	X
	X			X	X			X	X	X	X	X	X		X	X
	X	X	X	X	X	X		X	X	X	X	X	X		X	X
	X		X	X	X	X		X	X	X	X				X	
	X	X	X	X	X			X		X	X	X	X		X	X
	X		X		X	X		X	X	X		X				X
	X	X	X	X	X	X		X	X	X	X	X			X	X
	X		X		X	X			X	X		X				
	X	X	X		X	X		X	X	X	X	X	X			X
	X		X		X	X		X	X			X	X			
	X		X		X	X		X	X	X			X			X
	X		X			X	X	X	X	X	X			X		X
	X		X	X	X	X	X	X	X	X			X	X	X	X
	X			X		X		X	X	X	X	X	X		X	X
	X	X	X		X	X		X	X	X	X	X	X		X	X
	X	X	X	X	X	X	X	X	X	X	X	X	X	X	X	X
X	X	X	X	X	X	X	X	X		X	X	X	X	X		X
	X		X		X	X			X	X	X	X	X	X	X	X
X	X		X		X			X		X	X	X			X	X
	X		X		X		X	X	X	X	X	X			X	X
	X		X	X	X	X		X	X	X	X	X				X
	X		X		X	X		X	X	X			X			X
			X	X	X	X			X	X	X	X	X		X	X
	X	X	X			X			X	X	X	X	X	X		X

Special Features Index

State	Activities Director	Bank	Barber Shop	Beauty Salon	Cable TV	Chapel	Coffee Shop	Crafts Program	Exercise Program
HAWAII									
Arcadia	x		x	x	x	x		x	x
IDAHO									
Sunny Ridge Manor	x		x	x	x	x		x	
ILLINOIS									
Apartment Community of Our Lady	x		x	x	x	x		x	x
Apostolic Christian Resthaven	x		x	x		x		x	
Baptist	x	x	x	x		x		x	x
Beacon Hill	x	x	x	x	x	x		x	x
Bethany Methodist Home	x	x	x	x		x	x	x	x
Clark-Lindsey Village	x		x	x	x	x		x	x
Covenant Village of Northbrook	x	x	x	x		x		x	x
DeKalb Area Retirement Center	x		x	x	x	x		x	x
Fairview Baptist Home	x	x	x	x		x	x	x	x
Friendship Manor	x		x	x	x	x		x	x
Friendship Village	x	x	x	x		x		x	x
Georgian Home	x	x		x		x	x	x	x
Holmstad	x	x	x	x	x	x		x	x
Maple Lawn Homes	x	x	x	x	x	x		x	x
Meadow Crest of the Bensenville Home Society			x	x	x			x	
Presbyterian Home	x		x	x		x	x	x	x
Proctor Home	x	x	x	x	x	x	x	x	x
Westminster Village	x	x	x	x	x			x	x
INDIANA									
Apostolic Christian (Parkview Haven)	x		x	x		x		x	x
Brethren's Home of Indiana	x		x	x	x	x	x		x
Greencroft	x		x	x	x	x		x	x
Greenwood Village South	x	x	x	x	x	x		x	x
Indiana Asbury Towers	x			x	x				x
Indiana Masonic Homes	x		x	x		x	x	x	x
Lutheran Homes	x	x	x	x	x	x	x	x	x
Marquette Manor	x	x	x	x		x		x	x

Fireplaces	Game Room	Greenhouse	Guest Accommodations	Hiking/Walking Trails	Library	Master TV Antenna	Pharmacy	Private Dining Room	Religious Services	Resident Association	Sauna/Whirlpool	Security System	Store/Gift Shop	Swimming Pool-Indoor	Swimming Pool-Outdoor	Woodwork/Metal Shop
	x		x		x	x		x	x	x		x	x			x
x	x	x	x		x			x	x	x		x	x			x
	x		x	x	x	x		x	x	x		x	x			x
				x		x		x	x			x	x			
	x		x		x	x	x	x	x	x	x	x	x			
x	x	x	x		x			x	x	x	x	x	x			x
x	x		x	x	x	x		x	x	x		x	x			
	x			x	x	x	x	x	x	x		x	x			x
x	x		x		x	x		x	x	x		x	x			x
x	x		x	x	x	x		x	x	x		x	x			x
	x		x		x	x		x	x	x		x	x			x
x	x		x	x	x	x		x	x	x			x			x
x	x		x	x	x	x		x	x	x	x	x				x
	x				x	x		x				x				
		x	x		x		x	x	x	x		x	x			x
	x				x	x	x		x			x	x			x
	x		x		x		x	x	x	x		x	x			x
x			x		x	x		x	x	x	x	x	x			
x		x		x		x	x				x	x	x	x		
x	x			x	x	x		x	x			x	x			x
	x	x	x	x	x	x	x	x	x	x	x	x	x			x
			x		x			x	x	x		x				
	x	x	x		x		x		x	x		x	x			x
x	x		x		x	x	x	x	x	x		x	x			
	x	x	x	x	x	x		x	x	x		x	x			x

Special Features Index

Fireplaces	Game Room	Greenhouse	Guest Accommodations	Hiking/Walking Trails	Library	Master TV Antenna	Pharmacy	Private Dining Room	Religious Services	Resident Association	Sauna/Whirlpool	Security System	Store/Gift Shop	Swimming Pool-Indoor	Swimming Pool-Outdoor	Woodwork/Metal Shop
	x		x		x	x			x	x		x	x			x
x	x		x	x	x	x		x	x	x		x	x			x
x	x		x	x	x	x		x	x	x			x			x
	x		x	x	x	x	x	x	x	x	x	x	x			x
x	x	x	x		x			x	x	x		x	x	x		x
	x		x	x	x			x	x			x	x			x
x	x		x	x	x	x	x	x	x	x	x	x	x			
	x		x	x	x		x	x	x	x		x	x			x
	x		x	x	x		x	x	x	x		x	x			x
	x		x		x			x	x	x	x	x	x			
	x		x		x	x		x	x	x			x			x
	x		x	x	x	x	x	x	x	x	x	x	x			x
	x	x	x	x	x	x	x	x	x	x	x	x	x			x
	x		x		x	x				x						
	x		x		x	x	x	x	x	x		x	x			x
	x		x	x	x			x	x	x	x		x			
	x		x	x	x	x			x	x		x	x			x
x		x		x	x	x		x	x	x		x	x			x
x	x		x		x	x		x	x	x	x	x				x
x	x		x	x	x	x		x	x	x	x	x	x			x
x	x		x	x	x				x	x	x					
	x		x		x	x	x		x	x		x				
	x	x	x	x	x			x	x	x	x	x	x			x
	x	x	x	x	x			x	x	x	x	x	x			
x	x		x		x	x		x	x	x		x				
	x				x			x	x	x	x	x	x			x
x					x			x	x			x	x			x
x			x		x			x	x	x						

Special Features Index

State	Activities Director	Bank	Barber Shop	Beauty Salon	Cable TV	Chapel	Coffee Shop	Crafts Program	Exercise Program
KANSAS (continued)									
Kansas City Presbyterian Manor	x	x	x	x		x	x	x	
Larksfield Place	x		x	x	x	x	x	x	
Lawrence Presbyterian Manor	x		x	x	x		x	x	
Newton Presbyterian Manor	x		x	x	x	x	x	x	
Parkside Homes	x	x	x	x	x	x	x	x	
Schowalter Villa	x		x	x	x	x		x	
Topeka Presbyterian Manor	x		x	x	x	x	x	x	
Wesley Towers	x		x	x	x	x	x	x	
Wichita Presbyterian Manor	x		x	x	x	x	x	x	
KENTUCKY									
Masonic Widows and Orphans Home	x			x		x		x	x
Westminster Terrace	x		x	x		x		x	x
LOUISIANA									
Live Oak	x		x	x	x	x	x	x	
Saint James Place	x	x	x	x	x	x	x	x	
MARYLAND									
Asbury Methodist Village	x	x	x	x		x	x	x	
Broadmead	x	x	x	x			x	x	x
Carroll Lutheran Village	x	x	x	x	x			x	x
Charlestown		x	x	x		x	x	x	x
Collington Episcopal	x	x	x	x	x	x	x	x	
Edenwald	x	x	x	x	x		x	x	
Fahrney-Keedy Memorial Home	x		x	x	x	x	x	x	
Fairhaven	x	x	x	x		x	x	x	x
Homewood	x	x	x	x	x	x	x	x	
National Lutheran Home for Aged	x	x	x	x		x	x		x
Notchcliff	x	x	x	x		x	x	x	x
Ravenwood Lutheran Village	x		x	x	x	x		x	x
Wesleyan Heritage Community	x		x	x	x	x		x	
William Hill Manor	x	x	x	x	x			x	x

Fireplaces	Game Room	Greenhouse	Guest Accommodations	Hiking/Walking Trails	Library	Master TV Antenna	Pharmacy	Private Dining Room	Religious Services	Resident Association	Sauna/Whirlpool	Security System	Store/Gift Shop	Swimming Pool-Indoor	Swimming Pool-Outdoor	Woodwork/Metal Shop
			x	x	x	x		x	x	x	x	x	x			
	x		x	x	x			x	x	x		x	x	x		x
	x		x	x	x	x		x	x	x	x		x			
x	x	x	x		x	x		x	x	x		x	x			
						x		x	x	x		x				
	x			x	x	x		x	x			x	x			x
	x	x			x	x		x	x	x		x	x			
x	x		x	x	x	x		x	x	x	x	x	x	x		x
x				x	x	x	x	x	x	x		x	x			
								x	x		x					
			x	x	x	x		x	x			x				
x	x		x	x	x			x	x	x		x	x			
			x	x	x	x		x	x	x	x	x	x	x		x
	x	x		x	x	x		x	x	x		x	x			x
x	x	x	x	x	x	x		x	x	x		x	x			x
	x		x		x	x		x	x	x		x	x			x
x	x		x	x	x	x	x		x	x		x	x			x
x	x		x	x	x		x	x	x	x	x	x	x	x		x
	x		x	x	x	x		x	x	x		x	x			x
			x	x				x	x			x				
	x		x	x	x	x	x	x	x	x		x	x			x
	x	x	x	x	x	x		x	x	x	x	x	x	x		x
			x	x	x			x				x				x
x	x		x	x	x			x	x	x		x	x			x
								x	x							
x				x				x	x			x				
x				x	x	x		x	x	x		x	x			

Special Features Index

State	Activities Director	Bank	Barber Shop	Beauty Salon	Cable TV	Chapel	Coffee Shop	Crafts Program	Exercise Program
MASSACHUSETTS									
Carleton-Willard Homes	x	x	x	x	x	x	x	x	x
Loomis House	x		x	x	x			x	x
North Hill	x	x	x	x	x			x	x
Willows at Westborough	x	x	x	x	x		x	x	x
MICHIGAN									
Friendship Village	x		x	x	x	x			
Glacier Hills		x		x	x	x		x	x
Vista Grande Villa	x		x	x	x	x		x	x
MINNESOTA									
Bethany Covenant Home	x	x	x	x		x	x	x	x
Covenant Manor and Colonial Acres	x		x	x		x	x	x	x
Thorne Crest	x		x	x	x	x		x	x
MISSOURI									
Chateau Girardeau	x		x	x		x		x	x
Friendship Village of South County	x		x	x		x		x	x
Friendship Village of West County	x		x	x		x		x	x
Good Samaritan Home	x		x	x		x		x	x
Kingswood Manor	x	x	x	x		x	x	x	x
Lenoir	x		x	x	x	x		x	x
Presbyterian Manor at Farmington	x	x	x	x	x			x	x
Village North	x		x	x				x	x
NEBRASKA									
Gateway Manor	x	x	x	x	x			x	
Northfield Villa	x		x	x	x	x	x	x	x
Skyline Manor	x			x	x	x		x	x
NEW HAMPSHIRE									
Hunt Community	x		x	x	x	x	x	x	x
NEW JERSEY									
Cadbury	x		x	x				x	x
Harrogate	x	x	x	x	x			x	x
Meadow Lakes	x	x	x	x		x	x	x	x
Medford Leas	x	x	x	x	x		x	x	x
Westmont Home	x	x	x	x		x		x	x

416

Fireplaces	Game Room	Greenhouse	Guest Accommodations	Hiking/Walking Trails	Library	Master TV Antenna	Pharmacy	Private Dining Room	Religious Services	Resident Association	Sauna/Whirlpool	Security System	Store/Gift Shop	Swimming Pool-Indoor	Swimming Pool-Outdoor	Woodwork/Metal Shop
x	x			x	x	x		x	x	x		x	x			x
	x	x	x	x	x			x	x	x		x	x			x
x	x	x	x	x	x			x		x	x	x		x		x
	x	x		x	x	x		x		x		x	x			x
	x		x		x			x	x	x						x
	x		x	x	x	x		x	x	x		x	x			x
	x		x		x		x	x	x		x	x				x
x					x	x			x	x		x	x			
x	x	x	x	x	x	x	x	x	x	x	x	x	x	x		x
	x		x		x			x	x	x	x	x	x			x
	x		x	x	x	x	x	x	x	x			x			x
	x		x	x	x	x			x	x		x				x
x	x		x	x	x	x		x	x	x		x				x
	x		x	x	x	x	x	x	x	x		x				
	x		x	x	x	x	x	x	x	x	x	x	x			x
x			x	x	x			x	x	x						
			x		x	x			x	x		x	x			
x	x		x	x	x	x		x	x	x		x	x			x
	x		x		x	x			x	x		x				
x	x		x	x	x				x	x	x					x
	x		x	x	x	x		x	x	x		x	x			x
	x		x	x	x	x		x		x		x	x			x
x	x		x	x	x			x	x	x		x	x			x
x	x		x	x	x	x			x	x	x	x	x	x		x
x	x	x	x	x	x	x	x	x	x	x		x			x	x
x	x	x	x	x	x	x	x	x	x	x		x	x	x		x
				x	x			x	x	x	x	x	x			

Special Features Index

State	Activities Director	Bank	Barber Shop	Beauty Salon	Cable TV	Chapel	Coffee Shop	Crafts Program	Exercise Program
NEW MEXICO									
Landsun Homes	x	x	x	x	x	x		x	x
La Vida Llena	x		x	x	x	x	x	x	x
NEW YORK									
Eddy Memorial			x	x	x		x		
GreerCrest	x		x	x			x	x	x
NORTH CAROLINA									
Baptist Retirement Homes	x		x	x	x	x		x	x
Carol Woods	x	x	x	x	x			x	x
Carolina Meadows	x				x			x	x
Carolina Village	x		x	x	x	x	x	x	x
Covenant Village	x		x	x	x	x		x	x
Deerfield Episcopal	x		x	x	x	x		x	x
Episcopal Home for the Ageing	x	x	x	x	x	x	x	x	x
Friends Homes	x		x	x	x			x	x
J. W. Abernethy Center	x		x	x		x	x	x	x
Maryfield Nursing Home	x			x	x			x	x
Methodist Home for the Aged	x	x	x	x	x	x	x	x	x
Moravian Home	x		x	x	x	x		x	x
Piedmont Center	x		x	x		x	x	x	x
Pines at Davidson	x	x	x	x	x	x	x	x	x
Presbyterian Home at Charlotte	x	x	x	x		x	x	x	x
Presbyterian Home at High Point	x	x	x	x			x		
Triad United Methodist Home	x	x	x	x	x	x		x	x
Twin Lakes Center	x		x	x	x	x		x	x
Wesley Pines	x	x	x	x	x	x		x	x
OHIO									
Breckenridge Village	x		x	x	x		x	x	x
Brethren Care			x	x	x	x	x		
Copeland Oaks	x	x	x	x	x	x		x	x
Dupree House East	x				x			x	
First Community Village	x	x	x	x	x	x	x	x	x

Fireplaces	Game Room	Greenhouse	Guest Accommodations	Hiking/Walking Trails	Library	Master TV Antenna	Pharmacy	Private Dining Room	Religious Services	Resident Association	Sauna/Whirlpool	Security System	Store/Gift Shop	Swimming Pool-Indoor	Swimming Pool-Outdoor	Woodwork/Metal Shop
	x		x		x		x	x	x	x	x	x				x
	x	x	x	x	x	x		x	x	x	x	x	x	x		x
			x		x			x	x	x		x	x			
x	x	x	x	x	x	x		x	x	x		x	x		x	x
			x	x	x			x	x			x				
	x	x	x	x	x		x	x		x		x	x			x
x			x	x	x	x		x		x		x				x
x	x		x	x	x		x	x	x	x		x				x
x			x	x	x			x	x	x	x	x	x			
x			x	x	x	x		x								
x			x	x	x	x	x	x	x			x				x
x	x		x	x	x			x	x	x	x	x	x			x
x	x		x	x	x	x		x	x	x		x	x			x
			x		x			x	x			x				
	x	x	x	x	x			x	x	x	x		x	x		x
	x	x	x		x	x	x		x			x	x			x
x	x	x		x	x	x		x	x	x		x	x	x		x
x	x		x	x				x	x	x	x	x	x			x
	x		x	x	x	x		x	x	x		x	x			
	x		x	x		x	x		x			x				
	x		x	x	x			x	x	x		x	x			
	x			x	x			x	x	x		x				
x		x			x	x		x	x	x		x				
	x				x	x		x	x	x	x	x				x
								x	x			x				
	x	x	x	x	x			x	x		x	x				x
	x		x	x	x	x			x			x			x	x
	x		x	x	x	x	x	x	x	x		x	x			x

Special Features Index

State	Activities Director	Bank	Barber Shop	Beauty Salon	Cable TV	Chapel	Coffee Shop	Crafts Program	Exercise Program
OHIO (continued)									
Friendship Village of Columbus	x	x	x	x	x	x		x	
Judson Village Baptist Home	x		x	x		x		x	x
Llanfair	x	x	x	x		x	x	x	x
Marjorie P. Lee Home	x		x	x	x	x		x	x
Mennonite Memorial Home	x	x	x	x		x		x	x
Mount Pleasant	x		x	x	x	x		x	x
Park Vista	x	x	x	x	x	x		x	x
Rockynol	x	x	x	x	x	x		x	x
Schroder Manor	x	x	x	x	x	x		x	x
Trinity Home	x		x	x		x		x	x
Wesley Glen	x	x	x	x		x	x	x	x
Westminster Terrace	x	x	x	x	x	x		x	x
OKLAHOMA									
Franciscan Villa	x	x	x	x	x	x	x	x	x
Spanish Cove	x	x	x	x	x	x		x	x
Westminster Village	x		x	x	x	x		x	x
OREGON									
Capital Manor		x				x		x	
Cascade Manor	x			x	x	x	x	x	x
Friendsview Manor	x	x	x	x		x		x	
Hillside Manor		x	x	x		x	x	x	x
PENNSYLVANIA									
Beaumont at Bryn Mawr	x	x	x	x	x		x	x	x
Bethany Village	x		x	x	x	x	x	x	x
Brethren Home	x	x	x	x	x	x	x	x	x
Calvary Fellowship Homes	x		x	x	x	x	x	x	x
Cathedral Village	x	x	x	x			x	x	x
Cornwall Manor	x	x	x	x	x	x	x	x	x
Crosslands		x	x	x			x	x	
Dunwoody Village	x	x	x	x	x	x	x	x	
Evangelical Manor	x	x	x	x		x	x	x	x
Fort Washington Estates	x	x	x	x			x	x	x
Foulkeways at Gwynedd		x	x	x			x	x	x
Granite Farms Estates	x	x	x	x	x		x	x	x
Green Ridge Village	x			x				x	

Fireplaces	Game Room	Greenhouse	Guest Accommodations	Hiking/Walking Trails	Library	Master TV Antenna	Pharmacy	Private Dining Room	Religious Services	Resident Association	Sauna/Whirlpool	Security System	Store/Gift Shop	Swimming Pool-Indoor	Swimming Pool-Outdoor	Woodwork/Metal Shop
x	x		x	x	x	x	x	x	x	x		x	x			x
			x		x	x			x	x		x	x			
	x		x	x	x	x	x		x	x		x	x			x
	x		x		x	x		x	x	x		x	x			
	x			x	x	x			x	x		x	x			
x	x		x	x	x			x	x	x		x	x			x
	x		x	x	x	x			x	x	x	x	x		x	
	x				x				x	x		x	x			x
x		x	x	x	x	x		x	x			x	x			
	x		x	x	x	x		x	x	x		x	x			x
	x			x	x	x		x	x	x		x				x
	x		x		x	x	x		x	x		x			x	x
x	x	x	x	x	x	x		x	x	x		x	x			
	x		x	x	x	x		x	x	x		x			x	x
			x		x			x	x	x		x	x			
	x	x	x	x	x	x		x	x	x		x	x			x
	x				x	x		x	x	x		x				x
	x		x	x	x	x			x	x						x
x	x	x	x	x	x	x	x		x	x	x	x		x		x
x	x	x	x	x	x			x	x		x	x	x	x	x	x
			x	x	x			x	x	x		x	x			x
	x	x		x			x	x	x	x	x	x	x			x
	x		x	x	x				x	x			x			x
x	x		x	x	x			x	x	x		x	x			x
x	x	x	x	x	x	x	x	x	x	x	x	x	x			x
x	x		x	x	x	x	x	x		x			x	x		x
x	x	x	x	x	x	x		x		x	x	x	x	x		x
	x			x	x		x		x	x		x	x			
	x			x	x			x	x	x		x				
x	x	x	x	x	x	x	x	x	x	x		x	x			x
	x			x	x	x		x	x	x		x	x			x
x	x	x	x	x	x	x		x		x						x

Special Features Index

State	Activities Director	Bank	Barber Shop	Beauty Salon	Cable TV	Chapel	Coffee Shop	Crafts Program	Exercise Program
PENNSYLVANIA (cont.)									
Greensburg Home of the Presbytery of Redstone	x		x	x	x	x		x	x
Gwynedd Estates	x	x	x	x			x	x	x
Heritage Towers	x			x	x			x	x
Kendal at Longwood		x	x	x			x	x	
Landis Homes	x		x	x	x	x		x	x
Lebanon Valley Brethren Home	x	x	x	x	x	x		x	x
Lima Estates	x	x	x	x		x	x	x	x
Logan Square East	x	x	x	x				x	x
Luther Crest	x	x	x	x	x	x	x	x	x
Lutheran Home	x	x	x	x	x	x		x	x
Martins Run	x	x	x	x		x		x	x
Meadowood	x	x	x	x	x		x	x	x
Menno-Haven/ Menno-Village	x		x	x	x	x	x	x	x
Messiah Village	x		x	x	x	x	x	x	x
Normandy Farms Estates	x		x	x	x	x	x	x	x
Oxford Manor-Steward Home	x		x	x	x			x	
Passavant	x	x	x	x	x	x	x	x	x
Paul's Run	x	x	x	x		x	x	x	x
Pennswood Village	x		x	x			x	x	x
Peter Becker Community	x	x	x	x		x		x	x
Philadelphia Protestant Home	x	x	x	x	x	x		x	x
Phoebe Terrace	x			x	x			x	x
Presbyterian Home at 58th Street	x	x	x	x		x	x	x	x
Quarryville Presbyterian Home	x		x	x		x		x	x
Quincy United Methodist Home	x		x	x	x	x	x	x	
Rockhill Mennonite Community	x	x	x	x	x	x		x	x
Rosemont Presbyterian Village			x	x		x		x	x
Rydal Park	x		x	x				x	

Fireplaces	Game Room	Greenhouse	Guest Accommodations	Hiking/Walking Trails	Library	Master TV Antenna	Pharmacy	Private Dining Room	Religious Services	Resident Association	Sauna/Whirlpool	Security System	Store/Gift Shop	Swimming Pool-Indoor	Swimming Pool-Outdoor	Woodwork/Metal Shop
			x	x	x	x		x	x	x	x	x				
	x		x	x	x		x	x	x	x		x	x			
		x	x		x			x	x			x				
x	x		x	x	x	x	x	x		x		x			x	x
x			x	x	x			x	x	x	x	x				x
		x			x	x		x	x	x	x	x				x
	x		x	x	x	x	x	x	x	x		x			x	x
		x	x	x	x	x	x	x		x	x	x				x
x	x				x		x	x	x	x		x				x
	x	x	x	x				x	x	x		x				x
	x				x	x		x	x	x		x			x	x
x	x	x	x	x	x	x	x	x	x	x		x				x
	x	x	x	x				x	x				x	x		x
	x	x			x		x		x	x	x		x	x		x
	x		x	x	x			x	x	x	x	x				x
x	x	x			x					x						x
	x		x	x				x	x	x	x	x				x
x	x	x	x		x	x	x	x	x	x		x				x
x	x	x	x	x	x	x	x	x	x	x	x	x	x	x		x
	x	x	x		x	x	x	x	x	x		x				x
	x	x	x		x	x	x	x	x	x		x	x	x		x
					x		x			x		x				
x	x		x	x	x			x	x	x	x	x				
		x			x	x		x	x				x			x
		x			x	x		x	x	x		x	x			x
	x	x	x	x	x	x			x	x		x	x			
x	x		x	x	x	x			x	x	x	x	x			x
	x	x		x	x	x	x	x	x	x		x	x			x

423

Special Features Index

State	Activities Director	Bank	Barber Shop	Beauty Salon	Cable TV	Chapel	Coffee Shop	Crafts Program	Exercise Program
PENNSYLVANIA (cont.)									
Saint Barnabas	x	x	x	x	x	x	x	x	x
Saint Paul Homes	x			x	x	x		x	
Sherwood Oaks		x	x	x	x	x	x	x	x
Southampton Estates	x	x	x	x			x	x	x
Springfield/All Saints'	x			x		x	x	x	x
Springhouse Estates	x	x	x	x			x	x	
Twining Village	x	x	x				x	x	
United Methodist Home	x		x	x	x	x	x	x	x
Westminster Village	x		x	x	x			x	x
Willow Valley Manor	x		x	x	x		x	x	x
Wood River Village	x	x	x	x				x	x
SOUTH CAROLINA									
Heritage Hills/Greenwood	x		x	x	x	x		x	x
Seabrook of Hilton Head	x		x	x	x			x	x
SOUTH DAKOTA									
Westhills Village	x	x	x	x	x	x	x	x	x
TENNESSEE									
Alexian Village of Tennessee	x	x	x	x		x	x	x	x
Trezevant Manor and Allen Morgan Center	x		x	x	x	x		x	x
TEXAS									
Air Force Village	x			x	x	x		x	x
Bayou Manor	x	x	x	x		x		x	x
Buckner	x		x	x		x	x	x	x
Eden Home	x		x	x		x		x	x
Good Samaritan Village	x		x	x	x	x	x	x	x
Hallmark	x			x					x
John Knox Village of the Rio Grande Valley	x		x	x	x	x	x	x	x
John Knox Village of West Texas	x	x	x	x	x	x	x	x	x
Lakewood Village	x		x	x	x	x	x	x	
Mesa Springs	x		x	x	x	x	x	x	x
Presbyterian Manor	x	x	x	x	x		x	x	x
Presbyterian Village	x		x	x		x		x	x

Fireplaces	Game Room	Greenhouse	Guest Accommodations	Hiking/Walking Trails	Library	Master TV Antenna	Pharmacy	Private Dining Room	Religious Services	Resident Association	Sauna/Whirlpool	Security System	Store/Gift Shop	Swimming Pool-Indoor	Swimming Pool-Outdoor	Woodwork/Metal Shop
x	x		x	x	x	x		x	x	x	x	x	x			x
x	x			x	x			x	x	x		x	x			
x	x	x	x	x	x	x		x	x	x	x	x	x	x		x
	x		x	x	x			x	x	x		x	x		x	
x	x		x		x	x	x	x	x	x		x	x			
	x		x	x	x			x	x	x		x	x			x
x	x		x	x	x	x		x	x	x	x	x	x	x		x
	x		x	x	x		x		x	x		x	x			x
x			x		x		x	x	x	x	x	x	x			
	x							x	x	x		x				x
x	x	x			x	x		x	x	x	x	x	x	x		x
x	x	x		x	x			x	x	x			x			
x	x		x	x	x			x	x	x		x			x	x
	x	x	x	x	x	x		x	x	x	x	x	x			x
	x		x	x	x	x	x	x	x	x	x	x			x	x
			x		x	x		x	x			x	x			
	x		x		x	x	x	x	x	x		x	x			x
x	x		x	x	x	x		x	x	x		x	x			x
				x	x			x								
				x					x	x		x				
	x		x	x	x	x		x	x	x		x	x			
x		x	x		x	x		x	x	x					x	x
	x		x	x	x	x		x	x	x	x	x	x		x	x
x	x		x		x	x	x	x	x	x	x		x	x		x
	x			x	x			x	x	x		x				
x	x		x	x	x			x	x	x		x				
x	x		x		x	x		x	x	x			x			x
x	x	x	x	x	x			x	x	x		x				

Special Features Index

State	Activities Director	Bank	Barber Shop	Beauty Salon	Cable TV	Chapel	Coffee Shop	Crafts Program	Exercise Program
TEXAS (continued)									
Rolling Meadows	x		x	x	x	x	x	x	x
Trinity Terrace	x	x	x	x	x	x	x	x	x
Trinity Towers Manor Park	x	x	x	x	x	x	x	x	x
Westminster Manor	x		x	x	x	x	x	x	x
VIRGINIA									
Brandermill Woods	x	x	x	x	x	x	x	x	x
Goodwin House	x		x	x	x	x	x	x	x
Goodwin House West	x			x	x	x		x	x
Hermitage	x		x	x		x	x	x	x
Hermitage in Northern Virginia	x	x	x	x	x	x	x	x	x
Hermitage on the Eastern Shore	x			x		x		x	x
Lakewood Manor Baptist	x	x	x	x		x		x	x
Newport News Baptist	x		x	x		x	x	x	x
Rappahannock Westminster-Canterbury	x	x	x	x	x		x	x	x
Roanoke United Methodist Home	x			x		x		x	
Sunnyside Presbyterian Home	x		x	x	x	x		x	
Virginian	x		x	x		x		x	x
Warwick Forest	x		x	x	x			x	x
Washington House	x	x	x	x	x	x	x	x	x
Westminster Canterbury House	x	x	x	x		x	x	x	x
Westminster-Canterbury of Lynchburg	x		x	x	x	x		x	x
Westminster-Canterbury in Virginia Beach	x		x	x	x	x		x	x
Westminster-Canterbury of Winchester	x		x	x	x		x	x	x
Williamsburg Landing	x	x	x	x	x	x		x	x
WASHINGTON									
Bayview Manor	x	x	x	x	x	x		x	x
Crista Senior Community	x		x	x	x	x		x	x
Exeter House	x		x	x	x	x	x	x	x

Fireplaces	Game Room	Greenhouse	Guest Accommodations	Hiking/Walking Trails	Library	Master TV Antenna	Pharmacy	Private Dining Room	Religious Services	Resident Association	Sauna/Whirlpool	Security System	Store/Gift Shop	Swimming Pool-Indoor	Swimming Pool-Outdoor	Woodwork/Metal Shop
x	x	x	x	x	x	x		x	x	x	x	x	x		x	x
	x		x		x			x	x	x	x	x	x			x
x	x		x	x	x	x		x	x	x	x	x	x			
	x		x		x			x	x	x		x	x			x
	x	x	x	x	x			x	x	x		x		x		
x	x		x	x	x	x	x	x	x	x		x	x			x
	x		x	x	x	x	x	x	x	x		x				
x	x		x		x		x	x	x	x	x	x	x			x
	x	x	x	x	x	x	x	x	x	x		x	x			x
	x		x	x	x			x	x	x	x	x	x			
	x		x	x	x	x	x		x	x		x	x			x
	x		x	x	x	x	x	x	x	x	x	x	x			x
x	x		x	x	x			x	x	x		x	x			x
		x		x	x	x			x	x		x	x			x
	x		x	x	x			x	x			x	x			
	x		x	x	x	x		x	x			x	x			
	x		x		x	x		x				x	x	x		
	x		x		x	x			x	x			x			x
	x	x	x	x	x	x	x	x	x	x		x	x			x
	x		x	x	x	x		x	x	x		x	x			x
x	x		x	x	x	x		x	x	x	x	x	x	x		x
x			x	x	x			x		x		x	x			x
x			x	x	x	x	x	x	x	x	x	x	x		x	x
x	x	x	x		x			x	x	x		x				x
x	x	x	x	x	x			x	x	x	x	x	x	x		x
	x	x	x	x	x				x	x		x				x

427

Special Features Index

State	Activities Director	Bank	Barber Shop	Beauty Salon	Cable TV	Chapel	Coffee Shop	Crafts Program	Exercise Program
WASHINGTON (*cont.*)									
Hearthstone	x		x	x	x	x		x	x
Horizon House	x		x	x	x	x		x	x
Judson Park	x		x	x	x	x	x	x	x
Norse Home	x		x	x		x		x	x
Park Shore	x	x	x	x		x		x	x
Rockwood Manor	x	x	x	x	x	x		x	x
Samuel and Jessie Kenney Presbyterian Home	x			x		x		x	x
WISCONSIN									
Alexian Village of Milwaukee	x	x	x	x	x	x	x	x	x
Attic Angel Nursing Home and Tower	x		x	x	x	x		x	x
Cedar Lake Home Campus	x		x	x	x	x	x	x	x
Evergreen Manor	x		x	x	x	x		x	x
Fairhaven	x	x	x	x	x	x		x	x
Friendship Village of Greater Milwaukee	x		x	x		x		x	
Luther Manor	x	x	x	x	x	x	x	x	x
Methodist Manor	x		x	x		x	x	x	x
Milwaukee Catholic Home	x		x	x		x		x	x
Milwaukee Protestant Home—Bradford Terrace	x			x				x	
New Glarus Home	x	x	x	x			x	x	x
Oakwood Lutheran Homes	x		x	x	x	x	x	x	x
Saint John's Home of Milwaukee	x	x	x	x		x		x	x
Tudor Oaks	x	x	x	x	x	x		x	x
Villa Clement	x	x	x	x	x	x	x	x	x

Fireplaces	Game Room	Greenhouse	Guest Accommodations	Hiking/Walking Trails	Library	Master TV Antenna	Pharmacy	Private Dining Room	Religious Services	Resident Association	Sauna/Whirlpool	Security System	Store/Gift Shop	Swimming Pool-Indoor	Swimming Pool-Outdoor	Woodwork/Metal Shop
x	x		x	x	x	x		x	x	x		x				x
	x		x		x	x		x	x	x						x
x	x	x	x	x	x			x	x	x	x	x	x			x
	x		x		x	x			x	x		x				
x	x		x		x	x		x	x	x		x				x
	x		x	x	x	x			x			x				x
x	x	x	x			x	x			x	x		x			x
	x		x			x	x	x	x	x	x	x	x	x			x
	x	x	x		x			x	x		x	x				
	x	x	x	x	x		x	x	x	x	x	x	x	x		x
x	x	x	x	x	x			x	x	x		x	x			x
	x	x	x	x	x			x	x	x						x
x	x		x		x	x		x	x	x		x	x			x
x	x	x	x		x		x	x	x	x		x	x			x
x	x	x	x		x	x	x	x	x	x		x	x			x
	x		x		x	x			x			x				
			x					x						x		
	x	x		x	x	x	x		x	x		x				x
	x			x	x			x	x	x		x	x			x
	x		x		x	x		x	x	x		x	x			
x	x	x	x	x	x	x		x	x	x	x	x	x			x
	x			x	x	x	x	x	x	x		x	x			x

Metropolitan Area Index

CONTINUING CARE RETIREMENT COMMUNITIES
LOCATED IN METROPOLITAN AREAS

Abilene, Texas
Mesa Springs

Akron, Ohio
Rockynol

Albany, New York
Eddy Memorial Geriatric Center

Albuquerque, New Mexico
La Vida Llena

Allentown, Pennsylvania
Luther Crest
Lutheran Home
Phoebe Terrace
Westminster Village

Ann Arbor, Michigan
Glacier Hills

Asheville, North Carolina
Deerfield Episcopal

Ashland, Ohio
Brethren Care

Atlanta, Georgia
Lenbrook Square

Austin, Texas
Buckner Retirement Village
Westminster Manor

Bakersfield, California
Rosewood

Baltimore, Maryland
Broadmead
Charlestown
Edenwald
Fairhaven
Notchcliff

Baton Rouge, Louisiana
Saint James Place

Birmingham, Alabama
Kirkwood by the River

Bloomington, Illinois
Westminster Village

Boston, Massachusetts
Carleton-Willard Homes
North Hill

Bradenton, Florida. See Sarasota, Florida

Bridgeport, Connecticut
Thirty Thirty Park

Burlington, North Carolina
Twin Lakes Center

Cape Coral, Florida
Gulf Coast Village

Cape Girardeau, Missouri
Chateau Girardeau

Carlsbad, New Mexico
Landsun Homes

Carmel, California. See Monterey,
    California

Cedar Rapids, Iowa
Meth-Wick Manor

Champaign, Illinois
Clark-Lindsey Village

Chapel Hill, North Carolina. See
    Raleigh, North Carolina

Charlotte, North Carolina
Covenant Village
Methodist Home for the Aged
Pines at Davidson
Presbyterian Home at Charlotte

Chattanooga, Tennessee
Alexian Village of Tennessee

Chicago, Illinois
Apostolic Christian Resthaven
Baptist Retirement Home
Beacon Hill
Bethany Methodist Home
Covenant Village of Northbrook
Fairview Baptist Home
Friendship Village
Georgian Home
Holmstad
Meadow Crest of the Bensenville
    Home Society
Pines Village (Indiana)
Presbyterian Home

Cincinnati, Ohio
Dupree House East
Judson Village Baptist Home
Llanfair
Marjorie P. Lee Home
Schroder Manor

Clearwater, Florida. See Saint
    Petersburg, Florida

Cleveland, Ohio
Breckenridge Village

Colorado Springs, Colorado
Medalion
Medalion West

Columbia, Missouri
Lenoir

Columbus, Ohio
First Community Village
Friendship Village of Columbus
Wesley Glen
Westminster Terrace

Dallas-Fort Worth, Texas
Good Samaritan Village
Lakewood Village
Presbyterian Village
Trinity Terrace

**Davenport, Iowa; Rock Island-
    Moline, Illinois**
Friendship Manor (Illinois)
Ridgecrest (Iowa)

Dayton, Ohio
Trinity Home

DeKalb, Illinois
DeKalb Area Retirement Center

Delray Beach, Florida
Abbey Delray

Denver, Colorado
Sunny Acres Villa

Des Moines, Iowa
Bishop Drumm
Calvin Manor
Heather Manor

District of Columbia
Asbury Methodist Village
    (Maryland)
Collington Episcopal (Maryland)
Goodwin House (Virginia)
Goodwin House West (Virginia)
Hermitage in Northern Virginia
    (Virginia)
National Lutheran Home for Aged
    (Maryland)
Thomas House
Virginian (Virginia)
Washington House (Virginia)

Durham, North Carolina. *See*
    Raleigh, North Carolina

Emporia, Kansas
Emporia Presbyterian Manor

Eugene, Oregon
Cascade Manor

Fayetteville, Arkansas
Butterfield Trail Village

Fort Dodge, Iowa
Friendship Haven

Fort Myers, Florida
Shell Point Village

Fort Wayne, Indiana
Lutheran Home

Forth Worth, Texas. *See* Dallas,
    Texas

Fresno, California
San Joaquin Gardens

Greensboro, North Carolina. *See*
    Winston-Salem, North Carolina

Greenwood, South Carolina
Heritage Hills/Greenwood Methodist
    Home

Hagerstown, Maryland
Fahrney-Keedy Memorial Home
Homewood
Ravenwood Lutheran Village

Hanover, Pennsylvania
Brethren Home

Harrisburg, Pennsylvania
Bethany Village
Lebanon Valley Brethren Home
Messiah Village

Hartford, Connecticut
Covenant Village and Pilgrim Manor
Duncaster

Hickory, North Carolina
J. W. Abernethy

High Point, North Carolina. *See*
    Winston-Salem, North Carolina

Honolulu, Hawaii
Arcadia

Houston, Texas
Bayou Manor
Hallmark

Hutchinson, Kansas
Wesley Towers

Indianapolis, Indiana
Greenwood Village South
Marquette Manor
Westminster Village North

Iowa City, Iowa
Oaknoll

Jackson, Michigan
Vista Grande Villa

Kalamazoo, Michigan
Friendship Village

Kansas City, Missouri/Kansas
Kansas City Presbyterian Manor
    (Kansas)
Kingswood Manor (Missouri)

Lafayette, Indiana
Westminster Village West Lafayette

Lakeland, Florida
Florida United Presbyterian Homes

Lakewood, New Jersey
Harrogate

Lancaster, Pennsylvania
Calvary Fellowship Homes
Landis Homes
Quarryville Presbyterian Home
Willow Valley Manor

Lawrence, Kansas
Lawrence Presbyterian Manor

Lebanon, Pennsylvania
Cornwall Manor

Lincoln, Nebraska
Gateway Manor

Little Rock, Arkansas
Woodland Heights

Long Beach, California
Bixby Knolls Towers

Los Angeles, California
Brethren Hillcrest Homes
Hollenbeck Home
Inland Christian Home
La Serena
Mount San Antonio Gardens
Quaker Gardens
Scripps Home
Solheim Lutheran Homes
Villa Gardens
Windsor Manor

Louisville, Kentucky
Masonic Widows and Orphans Home
Westminster Terrace
Westminster Village Kentuckiana
    (Indiana)

Lubbock, Texas
John Knox Village of West Texas

Lynchburg, Virginia
Westminster-Canterbury of
    Lynchburg

Madison, Wisconsin
Attic Angel Nursing Home and
    Tower
Oakwood Lutheran Homes

Manhattan, Kansas
Clay Center Presbyterian Manor

Memphis, Tennessee
Trezevant Manor and Allen Morgan
    Center

Meriden, Connecticut
Elim Park Baptist Home

Miami, Florida
Covenant Village
Cross Keys Village
East Ridge
Edgewater Pointe
John Knox Village of Florida
Saint Andrews North Estates
Saint Andrews South Estates

Middletown, Ohio
Mount Pleasant

Midland, Texas
Trinity Towers Manor Park

Milwaukee, Wisconsin
Alexian Village of Milwaukee
Friendship Village of Greater
    Milwaukee
Luther Manor

Methodist Manor
Milwaukee Catholic Home
Milwaukee Protestant Home—
    Bradford Terrace
Saint John's Home of Milwaukee
Tudor Oaks
Villa Clement

Minneapolis, Minnesota
Bethany Covenant Home
Covenant Manor and Colonial Acres

Mobile, Alabama
Westminster Village

Moline, Illinois. See Davenport, Iowa

Monterey-Carmel, California
Carmel Valley Manor

Nampa, Idaho
Sunny Ridge Manor

Nashua, New Hampshire
Hunt Community

New Haven, Connecticut
Masonic Home and Hospital
Whitney Center

New York, New York
Westmont Home (New Jersey)

Newport News, Virginia. See
    Norfolk, Virginia

**Norfolk-Newport News-Virginia
    Beach, Virginia**
Newport News Baptist Retirement
    Community
Warwick Forest
Westminster-Canterbury in Virginia
    Beach

Oakland, California. See San
    Francisco, California

Oklahoma City, Oklahoma
Spanish Cove

Omaha, Nebraska
Skyline Manor

Orlando, Florida
Central Park Lodge
Orlando Lutheran Towers
Village on the Green
Westminster Towers
Winter Park Towers

Oshkosh, Wisconsin
Evergreen Manor

Pensacola, Florida
Azalea Trace

Peoria, Illinois
Maple Lawn Homes
Proctor Home

Philadelphia, Pennsylvania
Beaumont at Bryn Mawr
Cadbury (New Jersey)
Cathedral Village
Crosslands
Dunwoody Village
Evangelical Manor
Fort Washington Estates
Foulkeways at Gwynedd
Granite Farms Estates
Gwynedd Estates
Heritage Towers
Kendal at Longwood
Lima Estates
Logan Square East
Martins Run
Meadowood
Medford Leas (New Jersey)
Normandy Farms Estates
Paul's Run
Pennswood Village
Philadelphia Protestant Home
Presbyterian Home at 58th Street
Rockhill Mennonite Community
Rosemont Presbyterian Village
Rydal Park
Southampton Estates
Springfield Retirement Residence/All
    Saints' Rehabilitation Hospital

Springhouse Estates
Twining Village
Wood River Village

Phoenix, Arizona
Pueblo Norte
Royal Oaks
Westminster Village

Pittsburgh, Pennsylvania
Greensburg Home of the Presbytery
  of Redstone
Passavant Retirement Center
Saint Barnabas
Sherwood Oaks
United Methodist Home

Ponca City, Oklahoma
Westminster Village

Portland, Oregon
Friendsview Manor
Hillside Manor

Poughkeepsie, New York
GreerCrest

Pueblo, Colorado
Villa Pueblo Towers

**Raleigh-Durham-Chapel Hill, North
  Carolina**
Carol Woods
Carolina Meadows

Rapid City, South Dakota
Westhills Village

Richmond, Virginia
Brandermill Woods
Hermitage
Lakewood Manor Baptist Retirement
  Community
Westminster Canterbury House

Roanoke, Virginia
Roanoke United Methodist Home

Rock Island, Illinois. *See* Davenport,
  Iowa

Saint Louis, Missouri
Apartment Community of Our Lady
  (Illinois)
Friendship Village of South County
Friendship Village of West County
Good Samaritan Home
Village North

**Saint Petersburg-Tampa-Clearwater,
  Florida**
Canterbury Tower
Mease Manor
Oak Cove
Palm Shores
Saint Mark Village

Salem, Oregon
Capital Manor

San Antonio, Texas
Air Force Village
Eden Home

San Diego, California
Mount Miguel Covenant Village
Redwood Terrace
White Sands of La Jolla

San Francisco-Oakland, California
Aldersly
Channing House
Grand Lake Gardens
Heritage
Lake Park
Los Gatos Meadows
Piedmont Gardens
Pilgrim Haven
Saint Paul's Towers
The Sequoias-San Francisco
Sunny View Lutheran Home
Webster House

Santa Barbara, California
Casa Dorinda
Samarkand of Santa Barbara
Valle Verde

Santa Rosa, California
Friends House

Sarasota-Bradenton, Florida
Asbury Towers
Bay Village of Sarasota
Bradenton Manor
Freedom Village
Lake Pointe Woods
Plymouth Harbor

Savannah, Georgia
Seabrook of Hilton Head (South
    Carolina)

Seattle-Tacoma, Washington
Bayview Manor
Crista Senior Community
Exeter House
Hearthstone
Horizon House
Judson Park
Norse Home
Park Shore
Samuel and Jessie Kenney
    Presbyterian Home

Shreveport, Louisiana
Live Oak

Spokane, Washington
Rockwood Manor

Springfield, Massachusetts
Loomis House

Tacoma, Washington. See Seattle,
    Washington

Tallahassee, Florida
Westminster Oaks

Tampa, Florida. See Saint
    Petersburg, Florida

Terre Haute, Indiana
Westminster Village Terre Haute

Topeka, Kansas
Aldersgate Village
Brewster Place
Topeka Presbyterian Manor

Tulsa, Oklahoma
Franciscan Villa

Turlock, California
Covenant Village and Pilgrim Home

Virginia Beach, Virginia. See
    Norfolk, Virginia

Wabash, Indiana
Peabody
Timbercrest—Church of the
    Brethren

Waterloo, Iowa
Friendship Village
Western Home

West Palm Beach, Florida
Waterford

Wichita, Kansas
Kansas Christian Home
Larksfield Place
Newton Presbyterian Manor
Schowalter Villa
Wichita Presbyterian Manor

Wichita Falls, Texas
Presbyterian Manor
Rolling Meadows

Wilmington, Delaware
Cokesbury Village
Methodist Country House

Winchester, Virginia
Westminster-Canterbury of
    Winchester

**Winston-Salem-Greensboro-High
    Point, North Carolina**
Baptist Retirement Homes
Friends Homes

Maryfield Nursing Home
Moravian Home
Piedmont Center
Presbyterian Home at High Point
Triad United Methodist Home

Worchester, Massachusetts
Willows at Westborough

Youngstown, Ohio
Park Vista

CONTINUING CARE RETIREMENT COMMUNITIES LOCATED IN NONMETROPOLITAN AREAS

Delaware
Methodist Manor House (Seaford)

Florida
Indian River Estates (Vero Beach)
John Knox Village of Central Florida
   (Orange City)
Moorings Park (Naples)
Palms (Sebring)
South Port Square (Port Charlotte)
Southwest Florida Retirement Center
   (Venice)

Indiana
Apostolic Christian Retirement
   Home/Parkview Haven
   (Francesville)
Brethren's Home of Indiana (Flora)
Greencroft (Goshen)
Indiana Asbury Towers (Greencastle)
Indiana Masonic Homes (Franklin)
United Methodist Memorial Home
   (Warren)
Wesley Manor (Frankfort)

Iowa
Halcyon House (Washington)
Heritage House (Atlantic)
Mayflower Homes (Grinnell)
United Presbyterian Home
   (Washington)

Kansas
Apostolic Christian Home (Sabetha)
Parkside Homes (Hillsboro)

Maryland
Carroll Lutheran Village
   (Westminster)
Wesleyan Heritage Community
   (Denton)
William Hill Manor (Easton)

Minnesota
Thorne Crest (Albert Lea)

Missouri
Presbyterian Manor at Farmington
   (Farmington)

Nebraska
Northfield Village (Gering)

New Jersey
Meadow Lakes, Hightstown

North Carolina
Carolina Village (Hendersonville)
Episcopal Home for the Aging
   (Southern Pines)
Wesley Pines (Lumberton)

Ohio
Copeland Oaks (Sebring)
Mennonite Memorial Home
   (Bluffton)

Pennsylvania
Green Ridge Village (Newville)
Menno-Haven/Menno-Village
   (Chambersburg)

Oxford Manor-Steward Home
(Oxford)
Peter Becker Community
(Harleysville)
Quincy United Methodist Home
(Quincy)
Saint Paul Homes (Greenville)

Texas
John Knox Village of the Rio Grande
Valley (Weslaco)

Virginia
Hermitage on the Eastern Shore
(Onancock)
Rappahannock Westminster-
Canterbury (Irvington)
Sunnyside Presbyterian Home
(Harrisonburg)
Williamsburg Landing
(Williamsburg)

Wisconsin
Cedar Lake Home Campus (West
Bend)
Fairhaven (Whitewater)
New Glarus Home (New Glarus)

Subject Index

About the Editors

Ann Trueblood Raper is a consultant in the field of continuing care. Since 1980 she has directed several gerontological research and publication projects for the American Association of Homes for the Aging. As a research member of the University of Pennsylvania Continuing Care Retirement Community Study in 1981–82, she collaborated on the study publication *Continuing Care Retirement Communities: An Empirical, Financial, and Legal Analysis*. She has also served as gerontological consultant to the Federal National Mortgage Association in producing Forum III, a national grass-roots symposium on the housing, finance, and lifestyle needs and preferences of moderate- and middle-income retirees.

Ms. Raper graduated from Cornell University and received her master of science in social work degree from the University of Wisconsin. Over the years she has worked closely with both residents and staff of continuing care retirement communities.

Anne Cleveland Kalicki served as publications-projects specialist for the American Association of Homes for the Aging in Washington, D.C., from 1986 to 1987. She supervised all book-length projects and edited *Confronting Alzheimer's Disease*, a collection of essays by experts specializing in care of the mentally impaired elderly. During a long career as a free-lance writer and editorial consultant, she contributed to the *Washington Post*, the *Christian Science Monitor*, *National Geographic*, the National Academy of Sciences, the National Science Foundation, and the following five Time-Life Books series: *Seafarers*, *Planet Earth*, *Epic of Flight*, *Library of Health*, and *Your Home*.

Ms. Kalicki earned a bachelor's degree at Barnard College, Columbia University, and a master of science degree from the London School of Economics. She is currently working toward an additional graduate degree in creative writing at George Mason University.

AARP Books

AARP PHARMACY SERVICE PRESCRIPTION DRUG HANDBOOK
by AARP Pharmacy Service
$13.95/ AARP member price $9.95   Order #835P

ALONE—NOT LONELY: Independent Living for Women Over Fifty
by Jane Seskin
$6.95 / AARP member price $4.95   Order #810

CAREGIVING: Helping An Aging Loved One
by Jo Horne
$13.95 / AARP member price $9.95   Order #819

CATARACTS: The Complete Guide—from Diagnosis to Recovery—
for Patients and Families
by Julius Shulman, M.D.
$7.95 / AARP member price $5.80   Order #815

THE ESSENTIAL GUIDE TO WILLS, ESTATES, TRUSTS, AND
DEATH TAXES
by Alex J. Soled
$12.95 / AARP member price $9.45   Order #805P

FITNESS FOR LIFE: Exercises for People Over 50
by Theodore Berland
$12.95 / AARP member price $9.45   Order #818

THE GADGET BOOK: Ingenious Devices for Easier Living
Edited by Dennis R. La Buda
$10.95 / AARP member price $7.95   Order #820

HOMESHARING AND OTHER LIFESTYLE OPTIONS
by Jo Horne with Leo Baldwin
$12.95/AARP member price $9.45   Order #834

HOW TO PLAN YOUR SUCCESSFUL RETIREMENT
$9.95/AARP member price $6.95   Order #836

THE INSIDE TRACT: Understanding and Preventing Digestive
Disorders
by Myron D. Goldberg, M.D., and Julie Rubin
$9.95 / AARP member price $6.95   Order #823

IT'S YOUR CHOICE: The Practical Guide to Planning a Funeral
by Thomas C. Nelson
$4.95 / AARP member price $3.00   Order #804

KEEPING OUT OF CRIME'S WAY: The Practical Guide for People
Over 50
by J. E. Persico with George Sunderland
$6.95 / AARP member price $4.95   Order #812

LIFE AFTER WORK: Planning It, Living It, Loving It
by Allan Fromme
$6.95 / AARP member price $4.95   Order #809

MEDICAL AND HEALTH GUIDE FOR PEOPLE OVER FIFTY
by Dartmouth Institute for Better Health
$14.95 / AARP member price $10.85   Order #813

THE MYTH OF SENILITY: The Truth About the Brain and Aging
by Robin Marantz Henig
$14.95 / AARP member price $10.85   Order #814

NATIONAL CONTINUING CARE DIRECTORY: Retirement
Communities with Prepaid Medical Plans
Edited by Ann Trueblood Raper
$13.95 / AARP member price $9.95   Order #807

ON THE ROAD IN AN RV
by Richard Dunlop
$8.95 / AARP member price $6.50   Order #833

THE OVER EASY FOOT CARE BOOK
by Timothy P. Shea, D.P.M., and Joan K. Smith
$6.95 / AARP member price $4.95   Order #806

PLANNING YOUR RETIREMENT HOUSING
by Michael Sumichrast, Ronald G. Shafer, and Marika Sumichrast
$8.95 / AARP member price $6.50   Order #801

POLICY WISE: The Practical Guide to Insurance Decisions for
Older Consumers
by Nancy H. Chasen
$5.95 / AARP member price $4.35   Order #803

RETIREMENT EDENS OUTSIDE THE SUNBELT
by Peter A. Dickinson
$10.95 / AARP member price $7.95   Order #829

THE SLEEP BOOK: Understanding and Preventing Sleep Problems
in People Over 50
by Ernest Hartmann, M.D.
$10.95 / AARP member price $7.95   Order #832

SUNBELT RETIREMENT
by Peter A. Dickinson
$11.95 / AARP member price $8.50   Order #822

SURVIVAL HANDBOOK FOR WIDOWS (and for relatives and
friends who want to understand)
by Ruth J. Loewinsohn
$5.95 / AARP member price $4.35   Order #808

THINK OF YOUR FUTURE: Retirement Planning Workbook
$24.95/AARP member price $18.25   Order #826

TRAVEL EASY: The Practical Guide for People Over Fifty
by Rosalind Massow
$8.95 / AARP member price $6.50   Order #811

WALKING FOR THE HEALTH OF IT: The Easy and Effective
Exercise for People Over 50
by Jeannie Ralston
$6.95 / AARP member price $4.95   Order #824

A WOMAN'S GUIDE TO GOOD HEALTH AFTER 50
by Marie Feltin, M.D.
$12.95 / AARP member price $9.45   Order #825

YOUR VITAL PAPERS LOGBOOK
$4.95 / AARP member price $2.95   Order #181

For complete information write AARP Books, 1900 East Lake
Avenue, Glenview, IL 60025 or contact your local bookstore.

Prices subject to change.